COMPLETE
SPANISH GRAMMAR
REVIEW

William C. Harvey, M.S.

BARRON'S

All inquiries should be addressed to:
Barron's Educational Series, Inc.
250 Wireless Boulevard
Hauppauge, NY 11788
www.barronseduc.com

Library of Congress Catalog Card Number 2006042847

ISBN-13: 978-0-7641-3375-6
ISBN-10: 0-7641-3375-6

Library of Congress Cataloging-in-Publication Data
Harvey, William C.
    Complete Spanish grammar review / by William C. Harvey.
        p. cm.
    ISBN-10: 0-7641-3375-6 (alk. paper)
    ISBN-13: 978-0-7641-3375-6 (alk. paper)
    1. Spanish language—Grammar. 2. Spanish language—Self-instruction.
    3. Spanish language—Grammar—Problems, exercises, etc. I. Title.

PC4112.5.H37   2006
468.2'421—dc22   2006042847

Printed in the United States of America
9 8 7 6 5 4 3 2

Contents

PART III: *Nouns, Modifiers, and Other Parts of Speech* 169

Introduction

¡Bienvenido al mundo de la gramática española!

As frightening as it may sound, there is truly no way to avoid the rules of grammar as a language student. The good news is that this book is designed for those who want to learn or review all there is to know about Spanish without being overburdened with useless dialogs, readings, and vocabulary lists.

Instead, grammar lessons are presented in an easy-to-use format and then followed by simple practice activities and review material. More important, those areas of grammar that create the most problems for learners are explained in clear terms with careful detail, and then reinforced with plenty of examples.

Complete Spanish Grammar Review presents a full overview of Spanish grammar and offers much more than a traditional language manual. Not only can readers review and gain new skills by completing the exercises, but there are a variety of reference lists and guides that will only enhance the learning process.

Moreover, all new material in this book is presented in manageable proportions, and each topic can be found quickly by looking for the following icons:

- **¿CUÁNTO SABE USTED?** (Preview questions that open each chapter)
- **TIPS** (Language details that support core lesson material)
- **EL REPASO** (Periodic review questions)
- **POR SU CUENTA** (Open-ended language activities)
- **LA PRÁCTICA** (Practice grammar exercises after each lesson)
- **CULTURE CAPSULE** (Cultural insights in Spanish with practice)

Grammatical Definitions

Before you begin, review the following definitions and/or examples:

adjective: describes noun and pronoun (la niña bonita, yo soy guapo)
adverb: describes verb, adjective, adverb (baila bien, canta profesionalmente)
affirmative, emphatic, and interrogative: e.g., Trabajan, ¡Trabajen!, ¿Trabajan?
conjugation: e.g., first (-ar), second (-er), and third (-ir)
consonants: all letters that aren't vowels (b, c, d, f, etc.)
demonstrative: e.g., éste, eso, aquella, etc.
gender: masculine and feminine (el libro, la mesa, el hombre, la mujer)
imperative mood: e.g., ¡Vaya a su casa!
indicative mood: e.g., Ella va a su casa.
irregular verb: does not follow the regular conjugation pattern (dar, saber, ir)
negation: e.g., Lo tengo—No lo tengo
noun: person, place or thing (amigo, casa, amor)
number: singular and plural (libro – libros, yo – nosotros)

past participle: most end in -ado, -ido (pintado, servido, visto)

person: first (yo, nosotros), second (tú, vosotros), third (él, ella, Ud., ellos, Uds.)

possessive: e.g., mi, su, nuestro, etc.

preposition: e.g., en, para, detrás de, etc.

present participle: ends in -ing (fumando, corriendo, durmiendo)

pronoun: takes the place of a noun (Juan entiende = Él entiende)

reflexive verbs: end in -se (bañarse, sentarse, despertarse)

regular verb: follows the regular conjugation pattern (hablar, comer, escribir)

subject, object of a sentence: e.g., Juan tiene carro; subject is Juan, object is carro

subjunctive mood: doubt, desire, emotion (Espero que vaya a su casa.)

syllable: las par-tes de ca-da pa-la-bra

verb infinitives: end in -ar, -er, -ir (manejar, beber, salir)

verb stem and ending: e.g., hablamos; stem is habl-, ending is -amos

verb tense: present, past, future, conditional, etc. (veo, vi, veré, vería, etc.)

vowels: a, e, i, o, u

Book Overview

Complete Spanish Grammar Review is divided into twenty-eight chapters, each one exploring a different realm of Spanish grammar. The chapters are organized into four main parts:

- **Part I** consists of two chapters which focus on the basics of Spanish, in order to review the fundamental skills of pronunciation, spelling, and basic sentence structures.
- **Part II** consists of ten chapters that present the forms and uses of Spanish verbs, which include every conjugation, tense, and mood.
- **Part III** consists of ten chapters covering the other parts of speech, which include the articles, nouns, adjectives, demonstratives, possessives, pronouns, adverbs, prepositions, and interrogatives. Part III also includes chapters on Negation and Word Formation.
- **Part IV** consists of six chapters which deal with the special topics of Spanish, such as the numbers, time-telling, dates, the weather, idiomatic expressions, synonyms, antonyms, cognates, conversational skills, and written communication.

At the back of the book, you will find a list of the most frequently used words in Spanish, along with useful verb charts, and answers to the language exercises. To look up any grammatical topic, simply use the index.

This book provides you, the learner, with a complete guide to learning or reviewing Spanish grammar. Although it is designed as a user-friendly guidebook, do not just skim over the material. Bear in mind that everything you read is important, and will assist in accelerating the language learning process. Before you know it, Spanish grammar will begin to make more sense, and you will be putting your words together naturally. So enjoy the experience and *¡muy buena suerte!*

PART I:
Reviewing and Practicing the Basics

1

Spanish Sounds and Spelling

¿Cuánto sabe usted?

How Much Do You Know Already?

(?)

1. Why is there an accent on the word sí?

2. Which syllable is stressed in the word tratamiento?

3. Name one triphthong in Spanish.

4. How many consonants are there in the Spanish alphabet?

5. Which of the following are capitalized in Spanish: religions, months, or languages?

Vowels
Las vocales

There are two basic kinds of sound in any language: VOWELS and CONSO-NANTS. To become a fluent speaker in Spanish, you must know the following sounds by heart. Begin by repeating the five main vowels:

a (*ah*)	like *yacht*	cha-cha-cha
e (*eh*)	like *met*	excelente
i (*ee*)	like *keep*	dividir
o (*oh*)	like *open*	loco
u (*oo*)	like *spoon*	Lulú

Remember that Spanish vowels are produced by expelling air from the mouth without blockage, and there is no "gliding" of the vowels as there is in English. Also bear in mind that Spanish sounds are usually made toward the front of the mouth instead of back.

A, e, and o are known as the strong vowels, i (or y) and u, as weak vowels. A DIPHTHONG is the blending of two vowels into a single syllable. The sound of each vowel, however, should be heard distinctly. A diphthong may be formed of a strong vowel and a weak vowel, or vice versa, or of two weak vowels, but never of two strong vowels. The usual Spanish diphthongs are:

DIPHTHONG	ENGLISH EXAMPLE	SPANISH EXAMPLE
ai *o* ay	*aisle*	el aire *(air)*
au	*house*	el aula *(classroom)*
ei *or* ey	*they*	la ley *(law)*
eu	*wayward*	Europa *(Europe)*
ia	*yard*	enviar *(to send)*
ie	*yes*	tienda *(store)*
io	*yore*	el apio *(celery)*
iu	*you*	la viuda *(widow)*
oi *or* oy	*toy*	doy *(I give)*
ua	*want*	el guante *(glove)*
ue	*way*	la muestra *(sample)*
ui *or* uy	*week*	muy *(very)*
uo	*woke*	la cuota *(dues)*

A TRIPHTHONG is a blending of three vowels into a single syllable. The most common combinations in Spanish are:

TRIPHTHONG	ENGLISH EXAMPLE	SPANISH EXAMPLE
iai	*yipe*	cambiáis *(you change)*
iei	*yea*	enviéis *(that you send)*
uai *or* uay	*wise*	Paraguay
uei *or* uey	*wait*	el buey *(ox)*

LA PRÁCTICA 1

Read this list of words aloud. Be sure to focus on each vowel sound:

el pan	la cuadra	confiáis
la pera	la abuela	enfriéis
el coco	la nieve	decíais
el tomate	la criada	continuéis
la espinaca	el afeite	Uruguay
la lechuga	la causa	actuéis
la uva	la mercancía	
la ensalada	el viudo	
el encurtido	el yeso	
el trigo	el yodo	
el batido	el suizo	
la leche	el cuarto	
la limonada		
el vino		

Consonants
Las consonantes

Consonants are produced by blocking the air partially or completely in speech. As a rule, most of these sounds are pronounced the way they are written:

SPANISH LETTER	ENGLISH SOUND
c (after an e or i)	*s* as in *Sam* (cigarro)
ch	*ch* as in *China* (chica)
d (between vowels, final)	*th* as in *that* (nada, verdad)
g (after an e or i)	*h* as in *Harry* (general)
h	silent, like the *k* in *knife* (hola)
j	*h* as in *hot* (Juan)
ll	*y* as in *yes* (llama)
ñ	*ny* as in *canyon* (niño)
q (followed by ue or ui)	*k* as in *kit* (tequila)
r (beginning, after l, n)	"rolled" *r* (Rosa, amarillo)
rr	"rolled" *r* (carro)
v	*b* as in *blue* (viva)
z	*s* as in *sun* (cerveza)

Generally, b, d, f, k, l, m, n, p, s, t and y are similar to their English equivalents: bobo, dogo, foro, kilo, loro, mono, nodo, poro, solo, topo, yo-yo. There are very few words in Spanish that begin with w or x: whiskey, xerografía.

Remember that gue is pronounced like the *gai* in *gai-ly* and gui is pronounced like the *gee* in *gee-zer* (la guerra, el guisante).

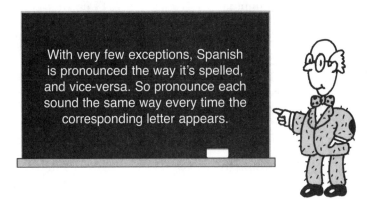

With very few exceptions, Spanish is pronounced the way it's spelled, and vice-versa. So pronounce each sound the same way every time the corresponding letter appears.

LA PRÁCTICA 2

Pronounce these common words. Remember to sound out each letter:

el amigo	el macho
el amor	la mujer
el carro	el pollo
el español	el quince
la experiencia	la plaza
el general	el zapato
la granja	el guerrero
el señor	el hombro
la reina	el amor
el hada	el queso
la bondad	el ñoño
el guiso	la victoria
la vida	el rastro

Syllabication and Stress
El silabeo y la acentuación

A SYLLABLE is a piece of a word that must contain at least one vowel. To divide Spanish words into syllables, here are some general rules:

- A single consonant (including ch, ll, and rr) is pronounced with the following break in syllables: ca-be-za, mu-cha-cho, ce-bo-lla, gue-rra.
- Combinations of two consonants between vowels are generally separated: car-ta, cin-co, tar-de.
- However, the combination is usually inseparable if the second consonant is l or r: ta-bla, li-bro, pue-blo.
- When three or more consonants are together between vowels, generally the last one joins the next vowel (unless it is l or r): ins-ti-gar, cons-tan-te, in-glés.
- Diphthongs and triphthongs form no separate syllables: i-gual, ca-yen-do, oi-go, Pa-ra-guay, con-ti-nuéis.

- When two strong vowels are together in a word, they are separated into syllables: cre-er, em-ple-an, le-o.
- There is also separation when there is an accented weak vowel before or after a strong vowel: co-mí-an, grú-a, tí-a.
- The letter y is considered a consonant when a vowel follows it, and it remains with that vowel when the word is divided: a-yu-da-mos, a-yu-na, a-yer.

The rules for STRESS or accentuation in Spanish simply state that accented (´) parts of words should always be pronounced louder and with more emphasis (olé). If there's no accent mark, the last part of the word is pronounced louder (español). For words ending in a vowel, or in n or s, the next to the last part of the word is stressed (importante). A written ACCENT MARK either denotes an exception to the rules above or a need to distinguish words that are similar in spelling but different in meaning:

> **TIP**
> Accent marks are frequently found on verb endings, question words, and demonstratives:
>
> verb endings: volvió, preparándome, tráiganos
>
> question words: ¿Qué?, ¿Cuánto?, ¿Cómo?
>
> demonstratives: ése, aquél, ésto

japonés	ends in s, so it normally should be stressed on the second to last syllable; an accent indicates that it is an exception.
dé	is the command *give*; without an accent, it is the preposition de which means *of* or *from*.

LA PRÁCTICA 3

Divide these words into syllables:

1. milla   mi-lla
2. extraño   ex-tra-ño
3. tío   tí-o
4. escribir   _____
5. construcción   _____
6. enviáis   _____
7. Uruguay   _____
8. carro   _____

9. miércoles   _____

10. pagaréis   _____

11. nuestro   _____

12. reímos   _____

13. dieciséis   _____

14. ciudad   _____

15. viene   _____

Add an accent to those words that require one. Leave the others blank:

16. soledad   *solédad*

17. averiguais   _____

18. violin   _____

19. diecisiete   _____

20. aula   _____

21. ruido   _____

22. tunel   _____

23. examen   _____

24. frances   _____

25. murcielago   _____

26. caracter   _____

27. buho   _____

28. capitulo   _____

29. dame   _____

30. vivi   _____

The Alphabet and Spelling Conventions
El abecedario y las convenciones del deletreo

Take a few moments to review the ALPHABET (el abecedario) in Spanish.

Letter	Pronunciation
a	(ah)
b	(beh)
c	(seh)
ch	(cheh)*
d	(deh)
e	(eh)
f	(eh'-feh)
g	(heh)
h	(ah'-cheh)
I	(ee)
j	(hoh'-tah)
k	(kah)
l	(eh'-leh)
ll	(eh'-yeh)*
m	(eh'-meh)
n	(eh'-neh)
ñ	(ehn'-yeh)*
o	(oh)
p	(peh)
q	(koo)
r	(eh'-reh)
rr	(eh'-rreh)
s	(eh'-seh)
t	(teh)
u	(oo)
v	(veh)
w	(veh doh'-bleh)
x	(eh'-kees)
y	(ee-gree-eh'-gah)
z	(seh'-tah)

> **TIP**
> This question is useful when you are practicing spelling words in Spanish:
>
> ¿Cómo se deletrea?
> *How do you spell it?*
> ¿Cómo se deletrea su nombre en español?
> *How do you spell your name in Spanish?*

*These letters have been removed from the official Spanish alphabet. However, people still refer to them when spelling out a word. Also remember that Spanish dialects do vary, so some texts will provide different pronunciation guides from the ones listed above.

Spanish utilizes many of the same PUNCTUATION MARKS as English (period, comma, semicolon, etc.). However, when writing exclamations or questions in Spanish, you must include an upside down mark at the beginning.

¿Cómo está?
¿Es usted estudiante de español?
¡Caramba!
¡Adiós!

There are also some differences in the use of CAPITAL LETTERS (las mayúsculas) in Spanish. These are the general rules:

- The first word of a sentence is always capitalized:

  ¿Cómo está?

- Proper names of people, places, and things are capitalized:

  Carlos es de Cuba.

- Days of the week and months of the year are **not** capitalized:

  lunes, el diez de mayo

- Religions, nationalities, and languages are **not** capitalized:

  Juan es español, católico y habla el español.

- In titles of books or works of art, only the first word is capitalized:

  Me gustó La casa de los espíritus.

- Most abbreviations are capitalized:

  E.E.U.U., Ud., Uds., Sr., Sra., Srta., Dr., Dra., etc.

POR SU CUENTA

This exercise with trabalenguas (tongue-twisters) will not only help your pronunciation skills, but you can acquire new Spanish words as well. How fast can you say these one-liners without hurting yourself?

Tres tristes tigres trillaron trigo en un trigal.
Three sad tigers threshed wheat in a wheat field.

Compre poca capa parda, porque el que poca capa parda compra
    poca capa parda paga.
*Buy only a little brown cape, for he who buys only a little brown cape pays
    only for a little brown cape.*

Ñoño Yáñez come ñame en las mañanas con el niño.
Squeamish Yáñez eats yams in the mountains with the child.

2

The Spanish Sentence

¿Cuánto sabe usted?
How Much Do You Know Already?

1. Identify the subject and predicate in this sentence:
   Mi tío Jaime, que tiene ochenta, nunca se casó.

2. What is an *imperative*?

3. What do y and o have in common?

4. Which one is introduced by a—a direct or an indirect object?

5. What introduces a relative clause?

The Sentence
La oración

A SENTENCE is an organized sequence of words that expresses a complete thought or asks a question. It is easily identified in writing because it begins with a capitalized word and ends in a period, a question mark, or an exclamation mark. Notice the three main sentence types:

Tengo un libro nuevo.	*I have a new book.*	(*affirmative*)
¿Dónde está el gato?	*Where's the cat?*	(*interrogative*)
¡Ven acá!	*Come here!*	(*imperative*)

Sentences basically consist of two parts: the SUBJECT (noun or pronoun) and its modifiers, and the PREDICATE (verb) and its modifiers. The subject usually begins a sentence, telling *who* or *what* is involved:

Mi hermano	vino con su esposa.
(My brother)	(came with his wife)
SUBJECT	PREDICATE

The predicate provides information about the subject and includes the verb. The verb expresses the action or state either perpetrated by, or connected with, the subject. In Spanish, the predicate may also precede the subject:

Comeremos nosotros más tarde.	*We will eat later.*
Está durmiendo la bebita.	*The little baby girl is sleeping.*
¿Van a jugar Uds.?	*Are you guys going to play?*

A subject generally consists of a noun, a noun phrase, or a pronoun. In Spanish, however, the English pronoun subject *it* (plural *they*) does not have an equivalent. Notice how the meaning is implied by the verb:

Es mío.	*It is mine.*
Cuesta mucho.	*It costs a lot.*
Hace frío.	*It is cold.*

A sentence can have more than one subject or predicate. The main subject and verb are often found in a MAIN CLAUSE of a sentence. The added parts are called SUBORDINATE CLAUSES:

• **Main Clause**		• **Subordinate Clause**	
María y Eva	dicen que	sus amigos	son cubanos.
(*María and Eva*)	(*say that*)	(*their friends*)	(*are Cuban*)
MAIN SUBJECT	MAIN PREDICATE	SUB. SUBJECT	SUB. PREDICATE

A sentence may be composed of one or more clauses. For example, an INDEPENDENT CLAUSE may either stand alone or be attached to another independent clause by a coordinating conjunction:

Fuimos a la clase.
We went to class.
INDEPENDENT CLAUSE

Fuimos a la clase	y	vimos una película.
We went to class	*and*	*we saw a movie.*
INDEPENDENT CLAUSE		INDEPENDENT CLAUSE

COORDINATING CONJUNCTIONS join two parts of speech or link two similar clauses. The most common conjunctions in a sentence are y (*and*), o (*or*), and pero (*but*):

Nora es alta y muy fuerte.   *Nora is tall and very strong.*
¿Prefieres sentarse aquí o allá?   *Do you prefer to sit here or there?*
Tiene carro, <u>pero</u> no maneja mucho.   *He has a car, but doesn't drive much.*

Note that the conjunction y becomes e before words beginning with i or hi, and o becomes u before words beginning with o or ho:

Leímos un artículo acerca
   de Irán <u>e</u> Iraq.
*We read an article about Iran
   and Iraq.*

Me quedaré en moteles <u>u</u>
   hoteles.
I will stay in motels or hotels.

> **TIP**
> A subordinate clause is sometimes called a dependent clause because, in order to have meaning, it depends on the information in the main clause.
>
> Si no llueve,   iremos al partido.
> *If it doesn't rain,*   *we'll go to the game.*
> DEPENDENT CLAUSE   MAIN CLAUSE

To avoid confusion with zero, the word o is written with an accent between numerical figures:

Dame 10 <u>ó</u> 11, por favor.   *Give me ten or eleven, please.*

LA PRÁCTICA 1

Choose the best way to complete these sentences in Spanish. Follow the example of the first exercise:

1. Mi hermano y yo	A. a la dueña de casa.	I
2. En un asiento cerca de mí	B. y se lastimó la pierna.	_____
3. Todas las cosas	C. abrir la lata grande.	_____
4. Han hecho muchos planes	D. está ubicada en el norte.	_____
5. El nuevo estudiante	E. parecían muy hermosas.	_____
6. Muchos niños reciben	F. dos hombres conversaban.	_____
7. Yo no conozco	G. para el próximo día.	_____
8. Miguel resbaló	H. usará el mismo uniforme.	_____
9. No pueden	I. dormimos en el mismo cuarto.	_____
10. La capital	J. juguetes de regalo.	_____

Affirmative and Negative Sentences
Las oraciones afirmativas y negativas

Sentences generally make statements, ask questions, or give commands. An AFFIRMATIVE statement expresses thoughts in a straightforward manner:

Manuel vive en Miami.	*Manuel lives in Miami.*
Va a llover mañana.	*It's going to rain tomorrow.*
Han trabajado ahí por años.	*They've worked there for years.*

The predicate of an affirmative sentence may or may not have an OBJECT. An object is frequently a noun, pronoun, or noun phrase that is affected by the verb. There are two types of objects, DIRECT and INDIRECT, which will be discussed later. In Spanish, a direct object is usually a noun, pronoun, or noun phrase that directly follows the verb and receives the action the subject performs. An indirect object may or may not follow the verb, and is basically the person or thing for whom the subject performs the action. It is generally introduced by the preposition a:

Jaime llevó	la pelota.	Jaime llamó	a	su amigo.
	DIRECT OBJECT			INDIRECT OBJECT

Whether the object of a sentence is direct or indirect often depends on the verb. Some verbs must be followed by one type of object or the other. Fortunately, most verbs in Spanish match their English equivalents when it comes to whether or not a direct or indirect object should follow:

Comimos	el pan con queso.	*We ate the bread and cheese.*
	DIRECT OBJECT	

Guillermo besó	a su novia.	*Guillermo kissed his girlfiend.*
	INDIRECT OBJECT	

Some sentences include both types of objects:

Nos	dieron	el dinero. (a nosotros)	*They gave us the money.*
INDIRECT OBJECT		DIRECT OBJECT	

Affirmative sentences in Spanish may vary in length:

Él va.   *He's going.*

Me dijo que iba a llegar a la fiesta a las ocho y media de la noche con todos los regalos, pero estaba lloviendo y su carro tenía problemas.
He told me that he was going to arrive to the party at eight-thirty P.M. with all the gifts, but it was raining and he was having car trouble.

A NEGATIVE sentence expresses the opposite message of an affirmative sentence. To form a negative statement, simply place the word no before the predicate of an affirmative statement:

Pedro me dió la respuesta.
Pedro no me dió la respuesta.

Pedro gave me the answer.
Pedro didn't give me the answer.

Estudiamos todos los días.
No estudiamos todos los días.

We study every day.
We don't study every day.

Remember that Spanish requires a double negative in some cases, which is not used in English:

No hay nadie. *There isn't anyone.*
("There is not nobody.")
No tengo nada. *I don't have anything.*
("I don't have nothing.")

LA PRÁCTICA 2

Change these affirmative statements to the negative:

1. Había allí una hermosa porcelana china.

   No había allí una hermosa porcelana china.

2. Mi primo vivía en una casa de las afueras.

   _____

3. Los médicos y las enfermeras son peruanos.

   _____

4. Se despierta temprano.

   _____

5. Al ver la policía, el muchacho se marchó.

   _____

6. Las tiendas cerrarán a las once.

_____

7. ¿Por qué estás en el jardín?

_____

8. Se abrazaron los novios.

_____

9. Toda la noche llovía.

_____

10. Cuando entramos a la oficina, sonó la alarma.

_____

_____

Interrogative and Imperative Sentences
Oraciones interrogativas e imperativas

An INTERROGATIVE sentence asks a question, and is always written in Spanish with a question mark at the end and an inverted mark at the beginning:

¿Tienes las llaves?	*Do you have the keys?*
¿Qué pasó?	*What happened?*

Most questions either elicit a *yes/no* response or ask for specific information using a *question word*. In Spanish, an affirmative statement is frequently converted into a question simply by raising one's voice slightly at the end:

Habla español.	*He speaks Spanish.*
¿Habla <u>español</u>?	*Does he speak Spanish?*

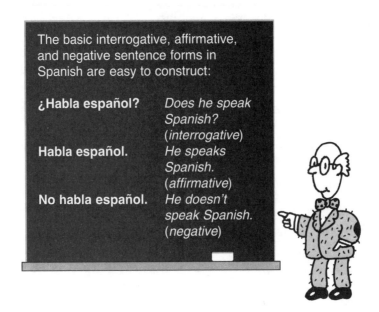

The basic interrogative, affirmative, and negative sentence forms in Spanish are easy to construct:

¿Habla español?   *Does he speak Spanish?* (interrogative)

Habla español.   *He speaks Spanish.* (affirmative)

No habla español.   *He doesn't speak Spanish.* (negative)

An IMPERATIVE *or emphatic* sentence is simply one that commands, instructs, or directs another person to do something. In Spanish, there are many different ways to express an imperative thought. To make a negative command, the sentence often changes, but still includes the word no:

Escribamos el e-mail.	*Let's write the e-mail.*
Traiga el carro.	*Bring the car.*
Vamos a la playa.	*Let's go to the beach.*
No le diga nada.	*Do not tell him anything.*
Quiero que tú salgas.	*I'd like you to leave.*
Enséñemelos.	*Show them to me.*
Favor de no hablar.	*Please do not speak.*
Hay que estudiar.	*We have to study.*

LA PRÁCTICA 3

Change each affirmative sentence to the negative and interrogative forms:

1. Baila mucho. _No baila mucho._ _¿Baila mucho?_

2. Van a bajar la ventana. _____ _____

3. Tiene una familia grande. _____ _____

4. Fumaron. _____ _____

5. Son argentinos. _____ _____

6. Se escapó. _____ _____

7. Trabaja hasta tarde. _____ _____

8. Es muy difícil. _____ _____

9. Entiendes español. _____ _____

10. Han comprado la ropa. _____ _____

Other Types of Sentences
Otros tipos de oración

Sentences either have a SIMPLE or COMPLEX structure. A simple sentence has one (main) subject and one (main) predicate that form the main clause. A complex sentence has at least one other clause (subordinate) besides the main clause:

SIMPLE
El hombre está manejando.
The man is driving.

COMPLEX
El hombre que está manejando habla inglés.
The man who is driving speaks English.

When two or more independent clauses are joined together by a coordinating conjunction, it is called a *compound sentence*:
Llegué a mi casa y comí algo y me acosté temprano.
I got home and ate something and went to bed early.

There are two main types of subordinate clauses. A RELATIVE CLAUSE is a dependent clause introduced by a relative pronoun such as que.

MAIN CLAUSE
La chica trabaja en la universidad.
The girl works at the university.

RELATIVE CLAUSE
La conocimos ayer.
We met the girl yesterday.

RELATIVE PRONOUN
que
who, that, which

COMPLEX SENTENCE
La chica que conocimos ayer trabaja en la universidad.
The girl who we met yesterday works at the university.

However, a TEMPORAL CLAUSE is a dependent clause introduced by subordinating conjunctions that tell *when* and refer to time:

Cuando
SUORDINATING CONJUNCTION

Cuando la clase termina,   vamos a la biblioteca.
TEMPORAL CLAUSE   MAIN CLAUSE

COMPLEX SENTENCE
Cuando la clase termina, vamos a la biblioteca.
When class is over, let's go to the library.

Some subordinating conjunctions may also express *where* or *why*. Again, notice how the two clauses form a complex sentence:

Donde vive ella, hay menos tráfico.
Where she lives, there is less traffic.

Porque no se siente bien, el artista no puede venir.
Because he doesn't feel well, the artist can't come.

Still another sentence type in Spanish is that heard in everyday conversation. Instead of using complete sentences that include subjects and verbs, people frequently use idiomatic expressions, short phrases, or even single words to send messages:

¿Comó estas?	*How are you?*
¡Buena suerte!	*Good luck!*
Yo también.	*Me, too!*
Nada.	*Nothing.*
¡Qué lindo!	*How pretty!*
¡Ojo!	*Be careful!*

Spanish also has a variety of interjections that are merely exclamatory outbursts expressed in conversations between native speakers. These sometimes differ from one region to the next:

¡Caramba!	*Wow!*
¡Chitón!	*Hush!*
¡Dios mío!	*My gosh!*
¡Pamplinas!	*Fiddlesticks!*
¡Socorro!	*Help!*
¡Ojalá!	*I hope so!*

This review so far has focused on Spanish sentences in the ACTIVE VOICE, where the verb expresses action performed by the subject. However, many of these examples have corresponding sentences in the PASSIVE VOICE as well, which will be discussed later. Notice how the action is shifted onto the subject in the passive voice:

→

María come el arroz.
María eats rice.

←

El arroz es comido por María.
Rice is eaten by María.

→

Ellos manejaron el carro.
They drove the car.

←

El carro fue manejado por ellos.
The car was driven by them.

LA PRÁCTICA 4

Identify the main clause in each of these sentences:

1. Juana vendía ropa hace años.   Juana vendía ropa.

2. Después de comer, el vendedor barrió la entrada.   _____

3. Hablamos con la policía que trabaja en este vecindario.   _____

4. Supuestamente, Marta y Samuel viven juntos.   _____

5. Si tuviera el dinero, me compraría una casa.   _____

6. Mientras yo estudiaba, él llamó por teléfono.   _____

7. Ella ha viajado con todas sus amigas.   _____

8. Quitó la olla del fuego cuando la sopa estaba caliente.   _____

9. Durante la clase, escuchamos música clásica.   _____

10. Vamos a repasar el capítulo antes del examen.   _____

Translate these into Spanish:

Across
1. predicate
3. punctuation
7. complex
9. accent
10. letter
11. clause
14. consonant
17. sentence
18. to spell
19. verb

Down
2. alphabet
3. to pronounce
4. noun
5. imperative
6. capital letter
8. object
12. vowel
13. word
15. subject
16. syllable

Culture Capsule 1

Greeting and Politeness
Los saludos y los gestos de cortesía

Las cortesías básicas son iguales entre los habitantes del mundo occidental. Cuando los españoles o latinoamericanos se encuentran, normalmente se dan la mano para saludar, igual que en los Estados Unidos. También se besan en la mejilla o se abrazan cuando son familiares o amigos, especialmente cuando no se han visto en mucho tiempo. Los saludos más comunes incluyen "Buenos días", "Buenas tardes" y "Buenas noches", aunque se saludan también con "Hola". La despedida básica es "Adiós", pero a veces añaden otras palabras como "Hasta luego" o "Nos vemos". Cuando a Ud. le presentan a alguien, la persona generalmente le dice "Mucho gusto" o "Encantado" y le estrecha la mano.

Una diferencia grande con el mundo anglosajón es la palabra "tú", la cual es la forma familiar para expresar *you (singular)*. Esta forma es generalmente usada entre los familiares o amigos íntimos, pero también se usa cuando los adultos conversan con los niños. Si la gente no se conoce, la palabra más formal "usted" se usa en lugar de "tú". "Usted" o su forma plural "ustedes" es una expresión de respeto que proviene de la antigua frase "vuestras mercedes".

Las demostraciones públicas de afecto entre personas de distinto sexo son más abiertas entre españoles y latinoamericanos, pero no así entre gente del mismo sexo. Aunque la liberalización en las costumbres ha sido muy grande en los últimos 20 o 30 años, la sociedad latina sigue siendo más conservadora al respecto.

PREGUNTAS

- ¿De dónde viene la palabra "usted"?

- ¿Con quién se usa la palabra "tú"?

- ¿Qué hacen los amigos cuando se encuentran en la calle?

- ¿Cuáles son algunas despedidas comunes en español?

PART II:
Reviewing and
Practicing the Verbs

3

The Simple Present Tense

¿Cuánto sabe usted?

How Much Do You Know Already?

1. How do you say *My wife is sleeping* using the present indicative?

2. What is the conjugation of the verb conocer in the present indicative?

3. How do you say *I protect and I contribute* in Spanish?

4. What are the six present indicative forms of the verb ir?

5. How do you say, *We'll speak tomorrow* using the present indicative?

Regular Verbs
Los verbos regulares

Any Spanish verb has a stem and an ending, which in the infinitive may be **-ar**, **-er**, or **-ir**. The verbs in the present tense tell us that an action takes place now or on a regular basis. To form the simple present (indicative) tense in Spanish regular verbs, the following endings are added to the stems of regular verbs:

	Hablar *(to speak)*	Comer *(to eat)*	Escribir *(to write)*
(yo)	**habl**o	**com**o	**escrib**o
(tú)	**habl**as	**com**es	**escrib**es
(él, ella, Ud.)	**habl**a	**com**e	**escrib**e
(nosotros)	**habl**amos	**com**emos	**escrib**imos
(vosotros)	**habl**áis	**com**éis	**escrib**ís
(ellos, ellas, Uds.)	**habl**an	**com**en	**escrib**en

27

¿Quién habla?	*Who's speaking?*
Comemos a las doce.	*We eat at twelve o'clock.*
No escriben mucho.	*They don't write much.*

The simple present tense, which is the most common in Spanish and English, is also called *indicative* because it is primarily used to make statements or ask questions. The present tense pattern is easy to follow for all regular -ar, -er, and -ir verbs, with the stem staying the same and the endings always following the same pattern.

> **TIP**
> Several well-known words and expressions that refer to time are used with the present tense:
>
> | | |
> |---|---|
> | Estudio… | *I study …* |
> | con frecuencia | *frequently* |
> | de vez en cuando | *once in a while* |
> | generalmente | *usually* |
> | casi nunca | *seldom* |
> | nunca | *never* |
> | siempre | *always* |
> | todos los días | *every day* |
> | todo el tiempo | *all the time* |

Regular verbs often refer to everyday actions or events. Here are some examples:

Common -AR Verbs

acabar	to finish	cocinar	to cook
acompañar	to accompany	colocar	to place
aconsejar	to advise	comprar	to buy
adivinar	to guess	contestar	to answer
agarrar	to grab	contratar	to hire
ahorrar	to save	cortar	to cut
alquilar	to rent	cruzar	to cross
amar	to love	dejar	to allow, leave
andar	to go, walk	descansar	to rest
apagar	to turn off	desear	to desire
apreciar	to appreciate	dibujar	to draw
arreglar	to arrange, fix	disfrutar	to enjoy
aumentar	to increase	doblar	to turn, bend
averiguar	to find out	durar	to last
ayudar	to help	echar	to throw
bailar	to dance	empujar	to push
bajar	to lower	enseñar	to show, teach
besar	to kiss	entrar	to enter
borrar	to erase	entregar	to turn in
brincar	to bounce	escuchar	to listen
bromear	to tease	estacionar	to park
buscar	to look for	estudiar	to study
cambiar	to change	evitar	to avoid
caminar	to walk	explicar	to explain
cantar	to sing	felicitar	to congratulate
cargar	to charge	firmar	to sign
charlar	to chat	fumar	to smoke
chocar	to crash	ganar	to earn, win

Common -AR Verbs (continued)

gastar	to spend, waste	pintar	to paint
gritar	to shout	practicar	to practice
hablar	to speak	preguntar	to ask
invitar	to invite	preparar	to prepare
jalar	to pull	presentar	to introduce, present
lavar	to wash	pronunciar	to pronounce
limpiar	to clean	quitar	to remove
llamar	to call	regresar	to return
llegar	to arrive	repasar	to review
llenar	to fill	respirar	to breathe
llevar	to carry	rezar	to pray
llorar	to cry	sacar	to take out
mandar	to send	saludar	to greet
manejar	to drive	secar	to dry
marcar	to dial, mark	terminar	to end
mirar	to look	tirar	to throw
nadar	to swim	tocar	to play a musical
necesitar	to need		instrument, touch
ordenar	to order	tomar	to drink, take
pagar	to pay	trabajar	to work
parar	to stop	tratar	to try
pasar	to happen, pass	usar	to use, wear
pegar	to hit	viajar	to travel
pelear	to fight	visitar	to visit
pescar	to fish		

Common -ER Verbs

aprender	to learn	deber	to owe, be supposed to
barrer	to sweep	leer	to read
beber	to drink	meter	to put inside
caber	to fit	prender	to turn on
comer	to eat	prometer	to promise
comprender	to comprehend	romper	to break
correr	to run	vender	to sell
creer	to believe		

Common -IR Verbs

abrir	to open	insistir	to insist
añadir	to add	ocurrir	to happen
asistir	to attend	permitir	to allow
cubrir	to cover	recibir	to receive
decidir	to decide	subir	to climb
discutir	to argue, discuss	vivir	to live
escribir	to write		

LA PRÁCTICA 1

Supply the correct form of the verb in the present tense:

1. Jaime (comer) mucho.   *Jaime come mucho.*

2. Nosotros (apagar) las luces. _____

3. ¿(fumar) usted? _____

4. Ellos no (beber) café. _____

5. Yo (comprar) la comida hoy. _____

6. ¿Dónde (vivir) tú? _____

7. El señor Lara (vender) carros. _____

8. Nosotros (recibir) mucho correo. _____

9. ¿Cuándo (viajar) ustedes? _____

10. El gato (correr) en el jardín. _____

Use the present tense as you translate:

11. *I work on Saturdays.*   *Trabajo los sábados.*

12. *We leave school at three.* _____

13. *They're studying their lessons.* _____

14. *I read the book today.* _____

15. *Do you (inf. sing.) drive that car?* _____

16. *She cleans her house every Sunday.* _____

17. *I do not attend the classes.* _____

18. *Do you (form. sing.) dance a lot?* _____

19. *The store opens at nine.* _____

20. *What do we review?* _____

Follow the example as you answer in complete sentences:

21. Ellos leen las noticias. ¿Y ella?   *Sí, ella lee las noticias, también.*

22. Yo vivo en Los Angeles. ¿Y tú? _____

23. Él vende zapatos. ¿Y Roberto? _____

24. Recibimos el mensaje. ¿Y él? _____

25. Usa el martillo. ¿Y Uds.? _____

26. Ella asiste a la escuela. ¿Y ellos? _____

27. Elena dibuja bien. ¿Y tú? _____

28. Comemos vegetales. ¿Y Paulo? _____

29. Ellas llegan temprano. ¿Y Uds.? _____

30. Yo aprendo rápido. ¿Y ella? _____

Irregular Verbs
Los verbos irregulares

There are several sets of irregular verbs that can be grouped for easy review. The following have an irregular change in the <u>first person singular</u> only. Notice the letter g:

Poner *(to put)*		
	Singular	Plural
1st person	pongo	ponemos
2nd person	pones	ponéis
3rd person	pone	ponen

Caer *(to fall)*		Hacer *(to do, make)*	
caigo	caemos	hago	hacemos
caes	caéis	haces	hacéis
cae	caen	hace	hacen

Salir *(to leave)*		Traer *(to bring)*		Valer *(to be worth)*	
salgo	salimos	traigo	traemos	valgo	valemos
sales	salís	traes	traéis	vales	valéis
sale	salen	trae	traen	vale	valen

EJEMPLOS

Las hojas caen al agua.	*The leaves fall into the water.*
¿Cuándo traes la leche?	*When are you bringing the milk?*
Ponemos todo en la mesa.	*We put everything on the table.*
Salgo a las dos de la tarde.	*I leave at two in the afternoon.*
Mi hermano no hace nada.	*My brother doesn't do anything.*

These verbs also make the g-change in the first person singular, but they have a variety of other irregular forms:

Tener *(to have)*		Venir *(to come)*	
tengo	tenemos	vengo	venimos
tienes	tenéis	vienes	venís
tiene	tienen	viene	vienen
Decir *(to say, tell)*		Oír *(to hear)*	
digo	decimos	oigo	oímos
dices	decís	oyes	oís
dice	dicen	oye	oyen

EJEMPLOS

¿Qué dice el profesor?	*What's the teacher saying?*
Tenemos una cama grande.	*We have a big bed.*
¿A qué hora vienes?	*What time are you coming?*

The following two verbs have similar conjugations and are also irregular in the first person singular only:

Saber *(to know something)*		Caber *(to fit)*	
sé	sabemos	quepo	cabemos
sabes	sabéis	cabes	cabéis
sabe	saben	cabe	caben

The verb ir is very irregular, and has similar conjugations to another irregular verb, dar:

Ir *(to go)*		Dar *(to give)*	
voy	vamos	doy	damos
vas	vais	das	dais
va	van	da	dan

The verb ver is irregular in the first person singular as well, and like ir and dar there is no accent on the vosotros form because it is only one syllable:

Ver *(to see)*	
veo	vemos
ves	veis
ve	ven

EJEMPLOS

¿Por qué no vemos una película?	*Why don't we see a movie?*
La bicicleta no cabe en el carro.	*The bike doesn't fit in the car.*
No van a la playa mucho.	*They don't go to the beach much.*
Yo sé el número.	*I know the number.*
Siempre le da dinero.	*She's always giving him money.*

In most verbs that end in a vowel plus -cer or -cir, the c changes to zc before o and a. Most verbs ending in -ecer and -ucir have the -zco ending in the yo form only:

Conducir *(to drive)*	
conduzco	conducimos
conduces	conducís
conduce	conducen

Conocer *(to know personally)*		Obedecer *(to obey)*	
conozco	conocemos	obedezco	obedecemos
conoces	conocéis	obedeces	obedecéis
conoce	conocen	obedece	obedecen

Other -er verbs conjugated in the same way include adormecer (*to go numb*), agradecer (*to be thankful*), aparecer (*to appear*), complacer (*to please*), crecer (*to grow*), desaparecer (*to disappear*), establecer (*to establish*), merecer (*to deserve*), ofrecer (*to offer*), parecer (*to seem*), permanecer (*to remain*), pertenecer (*to belong to*), lucir (*to shine*), producir (*to produce*), reducir (*to reduce*), traducir (*to translate*).

EJEMPLOS

No la conoces.	*You don't know her.*
¿Quién conduce?	*Who's driving?*
Lo traduzco para mañana.	*I'm translating it for tomorrow.*

The verb haber, *to have*, is often used as an auxiliary with past participles to form the compound tenses of verbs. These are its irregular forms:

haber (to have)	
he	hemos
has	habéis
ha	han

However, when haber is used as the main verb, the third person singular form varies slightly to become the word hay, which means *there is* or *there are*:

Hay un hombre en la sala y hay dos más en la cocina.
There is one man in the living room and there are two more in the kitchen.

LA PRÁCTICA 2

Answer these questions using the <u>first person singular</u> form:

1. ¿Quién hace la comida? Yo hago la comida.

2. ¿Quién trae el pelota? yo traigo el pelota.

3. ¿Quién va a la tienda? yo

4. ¿Quién dice la verdad? _____

5. ¿Quién obedece la ley? _____

6. ¿Quién sale temprano? _____

7. ¿Quién tiene una sonrisa? _____

8. ¿Quién sabe hablar español? _____

9. ¿Quién merece un regalo? _____

10. ¿Quién pone la música? _____

Follow the example and practice the present tense:

11. Jaime / ir / a Chicago. <u>Jaime va a Chicago.</u>

12. Yo / ver / las películas nuevas. _____

13. Sara y Daniel / decir / muchos chistes. _____

14. Nosotros / hacer / la tarea. _____

15. Tú / venir / conmigo al supermercado. _____

16. Yo / dar / una fiesta en mi casa. _____

17. Ellos / conocer / al alcalde. _____

18. Dra. Laura / conducir / un Mercedes. _____

19. Uds. no / oír / el ruído afuera. _____

20. El metro / salir / a las cinco y media. _____

Two Verbs *To Be*
Ser *y* estar

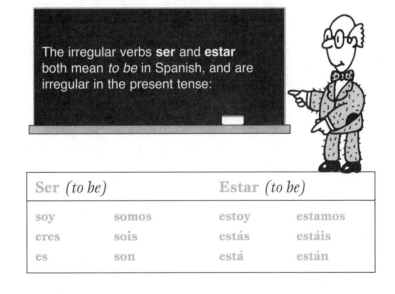

The irregular verbs **ser** and **estar** both mean *to be* in Spanish, and are irregular in the present tense:

Ser *(to be)*		Estar *(to be)*	
soy	somos	estoy	estamos
eres	sois	estás	estáis
es	son	está	están

In general, ser is used to express a natural, inherent characteristic or situation, and one that is more of a lasting or permanent nature. It is often used before adjectives that indicate qualities such as age, personality, appearance, nationality, origin, ownership, occupation, material, and religion. Ser is also used to express time and dates, and when combined with past participles, it is used to form the passive voice:

Somos estudiantes.	We're students.
Tú eres la más alta.	You're the tallest.
Él no es de Francia.	He's not from France.
Son las ocho.	It's eight o'clock.
Neruda es leído por muchos.	Neruda is read by many.

Estar, however, is generally used to express some temporary or accidental situation or condition, as well as the location or position of something or someone. It is often used before adjectives to express a brief change from a normal state. It is also used with a past participle to express the result of an action, and with present participles to express continuous action in the present progressive tense (estar + gerund):

La puerta está abierta.	The door is open.
Estoy muy enfermo.	I'm very sick.
¿Dónde están las niñas?	Where are the girls?
Toda la casa está pintada.	The entire house is painted.
No estás tomando la cerveza.	You aren't drinking the beer.

Additional Characteristics of *Ser* and *Estar*

- Ser is often combined with the preposition de to indicate possession, origin, or material from which something is made:

| Es de Antonio. | Es de China. | Es de madera. |
| *It's Antonio's.* | *It's from China.* | *It's made of wood.* |

- Forms of ser often link nouns and pronouns:

| Ellos son los dueños. | They are the owners. |
| La manzana es una fruta. | The apple is a fruit. |

- When estar is used to express location, it can be either permanent or temporary:

| San Diego está en California. | San Diego is in California. |
| Mi papá está en el baño. | My dad is in the bathroom. |

- Estar and ser differ in meaning when they refer to food:

| El pescado es malo. | Fish is bad for you. |
| El pescado está malo. | The fish tastes bad. |

- Ser and estar cannot be used interchangeably. Certain adjectives change their meaning when used with these verbs:

| Están listos. | They're ready. |
| Son listos. | They're clever. |

Mi desayuno <u>está</u> bueno.
My breakfast tastes good.
Mi hijo <u>es</u> bueno.
My son is a good boy.

¿<u>Está</u> seguro?
Are you sure?
¿<u>Es</u> seguro?
Is it safe?

Las chicas <u>están</u> aburridas.   *The girls are bored.*
Las chicas <u>son</u> aburridas.   *The girls are boring.*

El niño <u>está</u> vivo.   *The child is alive.*
El niño <u>es</u> vivo.   *The child is bright.*

Alfredo <u>es</u> pálido.   *Alfredo is light-complexioned.*
Alfredo <u>está</u> pálido.   *Alfredo looks pale.*

TIP
Both ser and estar are used in several
common expressions in Spanish:
¿De quién es?	*Whose is it?*
¿Cómo está Ud.?	*How are you?*
¿De dónde es Ud.?	*Where are you from?*
Es posible.	*It's possible.*
¿Qué hora es?	*What time is it?*
Estoy de acuerdo.	*I agree.*

LA PRÁCTICA 3

Fill in the blank with the appropriate form of either ser or estar:

1. Paulo _____ médico.   Paulo es médico.

2. El agua en la tina no_____ caliente.   _____

3. Ellas _____ las hijas de la señora.   _____

4. Nosotros _____ de Cuba.   _____

5. ¿Dónde _____ la policía?   _____

6. Yo _____ un buen estudiante.   _____

7. ¿Cómo _____ tú hoy día?   _____

8. Los hombres _____ en la cocina.   _____

9. Yo _____ listo para salir.   _____

10. ¿Qué hora _____?   _____

If it is correct, write C (Correcto), and I (Incorrecto) if it is not:

11. ¡<u>Eres</u> loco, amigo!   I

12. Me dijeron que <u>están</u> enamorados.   _____

13. No <u>está</u> recomendable tomar ese medicamento.   _____

14. <u>Es</u> un pueblo muy triste. _____

15. Las revistas <u>son</u> pasadas de moda. _____

16. <u>Somos</u> contentos con el cambio de clima. _____

17. Los niños <u>son</u> entretenidos con sus juguetes. _____

18. Yo <u>estoy</u> seguro de que se lo dije. _____

19. ¿Cuántos estudiantes <u>están</u> enfermos hoy? _____

20. Ud. <u>es</u> libre de hacer lo que quiera. _____

Stem-changing Verbs
Verbos con cambios de raíz

Stem-changing verbs that end in -ar or -er change the stressed e to ie and the stressed o to ue in the present tense:

- E → ie

	Entender *(to understand)*	Querer *(to want)*
(yo)	entiendo	quiero
(tú)	entiendes	quieres
(él, ella, Ud.)	entiende	quiere
(nosotros)	entendemos	queremos
(vosotros)	entendéis	queréis
(ellos, ellas, Uds.)	entienden	quieren

- O → ue

	Recordar *(to remember)*	Poder *(to be able to)*
(yo)	recuerdo	puedo
(tú)	recuerdas	puedes
(él, ella, Ud.)	recuerda	puede
(nosotros)	recordamos	podemos
(vosotros)	recordáis	podéis
(ellos, ellas, Uds.)	recuerdan	pueden

Other Similar Stem-changing Verbs

- **E → ie**

  apretar (*to tighten*), ascender (*to climb*), atravesar (*to cross*), calentar (*to heat*), cerrar (*to close*), comenzar (*to begin*), confesar (*to confess*), defender (*to defend*), despertar (*to wake up*), empezar (*to begin*), encender (*to ignite*), enterrar (*to bury*), gobernar (*to govern*), negar (*to deny*), pensar (*to think*), perder (*to lose*), recomendar (*to recommend*), regar (*to water*), reventar (*to burst*), sembrar (*to sow*), sentarse (*to sit*), temblar (*to tremble*), tropezar (*to trip*).

- **O → ue**

  acordarse (*to remember*), acostarse (*to lie down*), almorzar (*to have lunch*), apostar (*to bet*), aprobar (*to approve*), avergonzar (*to shame*), colgar (*to hang*), contar (*to count*), costar (*to cost*), doler (*to hurt*), demostrar (*to demonstrate*), forzar (*to force*), morder (*to bite*), mostrar (*to show*), mover (*to move*), probar (*to prove*), resolver (*to resolve*), soltar (*to loosen*), soñar (*to dream*), torcer (*to twist*), volar (*to fly*), volver (*to return*).

EJEMPLOS

¿Puedes tocar la guitarra?	*Can you play the guitar?*
La conferencia empieza más tarde.	*The meeting will begin later.*
No colgamos la ropa aquí.	*We don't hang the clothes here.*
Quiero hablar con el jefe.	*I want to speak with the boss.*
El perro no muerde.	*The dog doesn't bite.*

There are two major types of stem-changing verbs that end in -ir:

- Those that change their stressed e → ie or o → ue.

- Those that change their stressed e → i.

e → ie		o → ue	
Mentir *(to lie)*		**Dormir** *(to sleep)*	
miento	mentimos	duermo	dormimos
mientes	mentís	duermes	dormís
miente	mienten	duerme	duermen

e → i	
Servir *(to serve)*	
sirvo	servimos
sirves	servís
sirve	sirven

Other Similar Stem-changing Verbs

- e → ie

  convertir (*to transform*), digerir (*to digest*), divertirse (*to have fun*),
  herir (*to hurt*), hervir (*to boil*), preferir (*to prefer*), referirse (*to refer
  to*), sentir (*to feel*), sugerir (*to suggest*).

- o → ue

  morirse (*to die*).

- e → i

> **TIP**
> Notice how the stem-changing alterations occur in all but the nosotros and vosotros forms in the present tense.

  competir (*to compete*), corregir (*to correct*),
  despedir (*to say good-bye*), elegir (*to choose*),
  freír (*to fry*), medir (*to measure*), pedir (*to ask for*), reírse (*to laugh*),
  repetir (*to repeat*), seguir (*to follow*), sonreír (*to smile*), teñir (*to dye*),
  vestirse (*to get dressed*).

These two stem-changing verbs also have unique forms in the present tense:

Jugar *(to play)*		Oler *(to smell)*	
juego	jugamos	huelo	olemos
juegas	jugáis	hueles	oléis
juega	juegan	huele	huelen

These two verbs have only one form in the present tense due to their unique meanings:

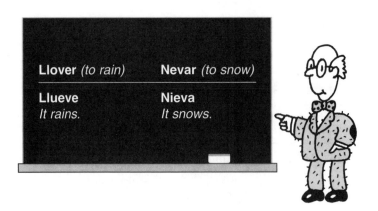

Llover *(to rain)*	Nevar *(to snow)*
Llueve	**Nieva**
It rains.	*It snows.*

> **TIP**
> Remember that reflexive verbs in Spanish include both regular and irregular forms in the present tense:
>
> | | |
> |---|---|
> | Se casan mañana. | *They're getting married tomorrow.* |
> | Él se acuerda de ella. | *He remembers her.* |
> | Yo me opongo a las drogas. | *I'm against drugs.* |

Reír (*to laugh*) and sonreír (*to smile*) have í as the stem vowel in the following forms:

Reír (*to laugh*)		Sonreír (*to smile*)	
río	reímos	sonrío	sonreímos
ríes	reís	sonríes	sonreís
ríe	ríen	sonríe	sonríen

LA PRÁCTICA 4

Write the first person singular form for each of the following verbs:

1. recomendar   <u>recomiendo</u>

2. apostar   _____

3. recordar   _____

4. sonreír   _____

5. despedir   _____

6. demostrar   _____

7. servir   _____

8. negar   _____

9. contar   _____

10. tropezar   _____

Verbs Ending in *-uir*, *-iar*, and *-uar*
Verbos con terminaciones en -uir, -iar e -uar

Verbs ending in -uir (not -guir) add y after the u in all but the nosotros and vosotros forms in the present tense:

Incluir (*to include*)	
incluyo	incluímos
incluyes	incluís
incluye	incluyen

Other similar verbs are atribuir *(to attribute)*, concluir *(to conclude)*, construir *(to construct)*, contribuir *(to contribute)*, destruir *(to destroy)*, distribuir *(to distribute)*, huir *(to flee)*, influir *(to influence)*, sustituir *(to substitute)*.

Verbs that end in -iar or -uar generally stress the i (í) or the u (ú) in all but the nosotros and vosotros forms in the present tense.

Enviar *(to send)*		Continuar *(to continue)*	
envío	enviamos	continúo	continuamos
envías	enviáis	continúas	continuáis
envía	envían	continúa	continúan

Other Similar -ar and -uar Verbs

- -i (í)

    guiar *(to guide)*, confiar *(to confide)*, espiar *(to spy)*, resfriarse *(to catch cold)*, variar *(to alter)*.

- -u (ú)

    actuar *(to act)*, descontinuar *(to discontinue)*, evacuar *(to evacuate)*, graduarse *(to graduate)*, insinuar *(to insinuate)*.

> **TIP**
> Verbs ending in -guir do not add the y after the u in the present tense (e.g., seguir: sigo, sigue, etc.). And, verbs ending in -guar do not take the accent on the u in the present tense (e.g., averiguar: averiguo, averigua, etc.).

EJEMPLOS

El precio no incluye la comida.	The price doesn't include the meal.
Ellas continúan con la lección.	They're continuing with the lesson.
Confío en nuestros líderes.	I trust in our leaders.

LA PRÁCTICA 5

If the verb is correct, put C. If it is not, put I:

1. *It includes* = incluye   <u>C</u>

2. *We distribute* = distribuímos   <u>   </u>

3. *They spy* = espían   <u>   </u>

4. *I contribute* = contribuyo   <u>   </u>

5. *He builds* = construye   <u>   </u>

6. *You continue* = continuyas   _____

7. *They act* = actuían   _____

8. *We find out* = averiguamos   _____

9. *I flee* = huyo   _____

10. *We confide* = confíamos   _____

Verbs with Spelling Changes
Verbos con cambios de deletreo

For verbs ending in **-ger** and **-gir**, the final **g** of the stem changes to **j** in the first person singular of the present tense, in order to retain the soft sound of **g**:

Recoger *(to gather, pick up)*		Dirigir *(to direct)*	
recojo	recogemos	dirijo	dirigimos
recoges	recogéis	diriges	dirigéis
recoge	recogen	dirige	dirigen

Other similar verbs include escoger (*to choose*), encoger (*to shrink*), exigir (*to demand*), fingir (*to pretend*), proteger (*to protect*).

For verbs ending in -guir, the gu changes to g before o and a in order to retain the hard sound of g:

Distinguir *(to distinguish)*	
distingo	distinguimos
distingues	distinguís
distingue	distinguen

Other similar verbs are conseguir (*to obtain*), perseguir (*to chase*), seguir (*to follow*).

TIP
Verbs like seguir, perseguir, and conseguir are conjugated like distinguir, but they include the stem change e → i (e.g., sigo, sigues, etc.).
And, verbs like torcer, contorcer, and destorcer follow the same pattern as vencer, but require the o → ue stem change (e.g., tuerzo, tuerces, etc.).

Verbs ending in -cer or -cir in the present tense change the c to z before o and a in order to remove the hard c sound:

Vencer *(to conquer)*	
ven**z**o	vencemos
vences	vencéis
vence	vencen

Other such verbs include convencer *(to convince)*, esparcir *(to spread)*, ejercer *(to exercise)*, fruncir *(to frown)*, torcer *(to twist)*.

EJEMPLOS

A veces recojo los libros.   *Sometimes I collect the books.*
Usualmente sigo la ley.   *I usually obey the law.*
Nunca convenzo a nadie.   *I never convince anyone.*

LA PRÁCTICA 6

Supply the correct present tense form of the verb:

1. Los niños siempre (destruir) las flores en el jardín.   destruyen

2. Yo (recoger) mi correo a las cinco.   _____

3. ¿Cuándo (enviar) tú el paquete?   _____

4. Nosotros (seguir) las instrucciones en el exámen.   _____

5. Yo (proteger) a mi familia.   _____

6. El vendedor no me (convencer).   _____

7. Los chicos (graduarse) en junio.   _____

8. ¿Tú (contribuir) mucho a las obras de caridad?   _____

9. Casi siempre yo (confiar) en mis amigos.   _____

10. Mi esposa y yo (escoger) la mejor fruta.   _____

Using the Present Indicative Tense

Basic Structure and Usage
Estructura y empleo básicos

The present indicative tense in Spanish may express an action that is taking place regularly or universally at the present time, or an action that is actually in progress at this moment:

Juan Carlos come mucho.
{
Juan Carlos eats a lot.

Juan Carlos is eating a lot.

To form the negative in the present tense, as with all tenses, requires the adverb no in front of the verb:

Juan Carlos <u>no</u> come mucho.　　*Juan Carlos doesn't eat much.*

To form a question, either the subject is placed after the verb, or there is a change in intonation:

¿Come mucho Juan Carlos?

¿Juan Carlos come mucho?
}
Does Juan Carlos eat a lot?

Other Uses of the Present Indicative
Otros usos del presente de indicativo

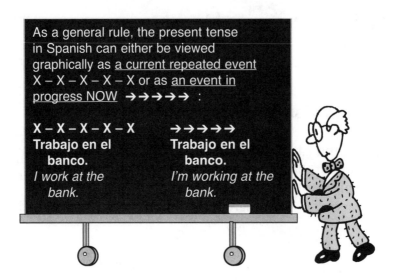

As a general rule, the present tense in Spanish can either be viewed graphically as <u>a current repeated event</u> X – X – X – X – X or as <u>an event in progress NOW</u> →→→→→ :

X – X – X – X – X	→→→→→
Trabajo en el banco.	**Trabajo en el banco.**
I work at the bank.	*I'm working at the bank.*

However, the present indicative may sometimes be used to convey an order or a request:

Me <u>hace</u> el favor de manejar despacio.   *Please drive slowly.*
¿<u>Terminamos</u> más tarde?   *Shall we finish later?*

The present indicative can also refer to a future event if there is another reference to the future in the sentence.

Ellos <u>salen</u> el sábado.   *They leave on Saturday.*

The present tense is often used after si (*if*) to refer to future time:

Si <u>viajan</u>, iré con ustedes.   *If you travel, I'll go with you guys.*

By using the following two constructions, the present indicative can be used to designate actions that began in the past and continue into the present:

Hace _____ que _____
Hace años que <u>estudio</u> inglés.   *I've been studying English for years.*
Hace semanas que no <u>veo</u> a Tomás.   *I haven't seen Tomás for weeks.*

_____ desde hace _____
No <u>fumo</u> desde hace un mes.   *I haven't smoked for a month.*
<u>Trabajo</u> aquí desde hace dos días.   *I've been working here for two days.*

The idiomatic expression acabar de, when used in the present tense, actually implies activity in the past:

<u>Acabo de</u> comer.   *I just finished eating.*
<u>Acaban de</u> salir.   *They just left.*

LA PRÁCTICA 7

Change each verb form in the present tense to match the person indicated:

1. ponemos   (yo)   _pongo_
2. viene   (nosotros)   _____
3. conocen   (yo)   _____
4. tengo   (ellos)   _____
5. oímos   (tú)   _____
6. caigo   (ella)   _____
7. venzo   (él)   _____
8. sabemos   (yo)   _____
9. podemos   (ellas)   _____
10. repiten   (nosotros)   _____
11. sigo   (tú)   _____
12. recoge   (yo)   _____
13. continúo   (ella)   _____
14. incluís   (ellos)   _____
15. se ríe   (nosotros)   _____

Translate these sentences into Spanish using only the present tense:

16. What are you looking for?   _¿Qué buscas?_____
17. I haven't seen Ana María for a month.   _____
18. I don't know him.   _____
19. They're coming tomorrow.   _____
20. It always rains a lot.   _____
21. Does she tell the truth?   _____
22. Sometimes they do the work.   _____
23. Shall we finish later?   _____
24. He wants to work tonight.   _____
25. I'm picking up the mail.   _____

CROSSWORD 2

Translate these into Spanish:

Across
- 2. to see
- 5. to pick up
- 6. to smile
- 10. to put
- 11. to chat
- 13. to remember
- 15. to leave
- 16. to follow
- 17. to have

Down
- 1. to rain
- 2. to come
- 3. to know someone
- 4. to be
- 7. to deny
- 8. to send
- 9. to fit
- 12. to lie
- 14. to argue

EL REPASO

1. Explain the difference between a dependent and an independent clause.

2. Explain how to pronounce a Spanish word that has no written accent.

3. Name the three basic kinds of sentences in Spanish.

4. Name five regular -er verbs.

5. Use the present indicative tense to refer to an action in the future.

6. Identify one Spanish verb that is only irregular in the first person singular.

7. What are two differences between the uses of ser and estar?

8. Conjugate the verb sonreír in the present indicative tense.

9. Name one stem-changing verb in Spanish.

10. What is unique about the phrase acabar de in the present tense?

4

The Past Tense

¿Cuánto sabe usted?
How Much Do You Know Already?

1. Change the verb in bold from the present indicative to the preterit:
   No lo **veo**.

2. Give two ways to translate the word **fueron**.

3. What's the difference in meaning between **él comió** and **él comía**?

4. How do you say *I used to read magazines* in Spanish?

5. Conjugate the verb **beber** in the imperfect tense.

The Preterit

Regular Verbs
Verbos regulares

   Spanish has two basic past tenses—the preterit and the imperfect. The preterit is a bit more common, because it refers to actions that were completed in past time. To form the preterit, the following endings are added to the stem of regular verbs:

	Hablar *(to speak)*	Comer *(to eat)*	Escribir *(to write)*
(yo)	hablé	comí	escribí
(tú)	hablaste	comiste	escribiste
(él, ella, Ud.)	habló	comió	escribió
(nosotros)	hablamos	comimos	escribimos
(vosotros)	hablasteis	comisteis	escribisteis
(ellos, ellas, Uds.)	hablaron	comieron	escribieron

EJEMPLOS

¿Hablaste con el médico?	*Did you speak with the doctor?*
Comimos a las ocho.	*We ate at eight o'clock.*
No escribió en el cuaderno	*He didn't write in the notebook.*

The e → ie or o → ue stem-changing verbs in the present tense do not make those changes in the preterit (i.e., entiendo → entendí, cuento → conté). However, stem-changing -ir verbs in the present tense do change from e → i or from o → u in the third person singular and plural of the preterit:

Repetir *(to repeat)*		Dormir *(to sleep)*	
repetí	repetimos	dormí	dormimos
repetiste	repetisteis	dormiste	dormisteis
repitió	repitieron	durmió	durmieron

The preterit endings are the same for both **-er** and **-ir** verbs. For **-ar** and **-ir** verbs, the first person plural is the same in the present and the preterit tense (e.g., **hablamos hoy**, **hablamos ayer**). Also, all preterit forms are stressed on the endings rather than the stems.

LA PRÁCTICA 1

Change these sentences from the present to the preterit tense:

1. Carlos toma café. _Carlos tomó café._

2. Nosotros vendemos el carro. _____

3. ¿Qué estudias? _____

4. No viven aquí. _____

5. Entiendo el ejercicio. _____

6. Conversan en español. _____

7. Ella pide comida. _____

8. No encuentro las llaves. _____

9. ¿Cuándo viajas? _____

10. El bebé duerme mucho. _____

Translate into Spanish:

11. He called me twice. _Me llamó dos veces._

12. I bought the dress yesterday. _____

13. She lived there for two years. _____

14. Our neighbor died last night. _____

15. They asked for more money. _____

16. Did you close the door? _____

17. I didn't drive yesterday. _____

18. He repeated the lesson. _____

19. We didn't visit Spain. _____

20. What did they serve? _____

Verbs with Spelling Changes
Verbos con cambios de deletreo

Many Spanish verbs appear to be irregular in the preterit simply due to their changes in spelling. Changes are made in the first person singular in order to retain the normal sounds in speech.

- (/k/)

Explicar *(to explain)*	
expliqué	explicamos
explicaste	explicasteis
explicó	explicaron

Other similar verbs are buscar *(to look for)*, sacar *(to remove)*, mascar *(to chew)*, pescar *(to fish)*, equivocarse *(to be wrong)*, secar *(to dry)*, colocar *(to place)*, acercarse *(to get near)*, embarcarse *(to board)*, indicar *(to indicate)*, marcar *(to dial)*, educar *(to educate)*.

- (/g/)

Llegar *(to arrive)*	
llegué	llegamos
llegaste	llegasteis
llegó	llegaron

Other similar verbs are agregar *(to add)*, entregar *(to turn in)*, pegar *(to hit, to stick)*, apagar *(to turn off)*, pagar *(to pay)*, jugar *(to play)*, castigar *(to punish)*, navegar *(to sail)*, cargar *(to charge)*, juzgar *(to judge)*, colgar *(to hang)*, tragar *(to swallow)*.

- (/z/)

Rezar *(to pray)*	
recé	rezamos
rezaste	rezasteis
rezó	rezaron

Other identical conjugations include abrazar *(to hug)*, alcanzar *(to reach)*, almorzar *(to have lunch)*, cruzar *(to cross)*, gozar *(to enjoy)*, organizar *(to organize)*, empezar *(to begin)*, rechazar *(to refuse)*, comenzar *(to start)*, reemplazar *(to replace)*, tropezar *(to trip)*.

EJEMPLOS

¡Caramba! ¡Me equivoqué!   *Shucks! I made a mistake!*
Colgué la ropa en el ropero.   *I hung up the clothes in the closet.*
No desayuné con mi familia.   *I didn't have breakfast with my family.*

Additional Characteristics About Verbs with Spelling Changes

- Verbs like reír (*to laugh*), freír (*to fry*), and sonreír (*to smile*) have a written accent mark on most of the forms in the preterit (i.e., reí, reíste, rió, reímos, reísteis, rieron).

- The verb ver (*to see*) is regular in the preterit, but has no written accent marks (i.e., vi, viste, vio, vimos, visteis, vieron).

- -ir verbs with stems ending in ñ drop the i in the third person in the preterit (e.g., gruñir [*to grunt*] – gruñó, gruñeron).

> **TIP**
> Do not confuse words with the first person singular -o endings in the present indicative with words that have the third person singular -ó endings in the preterit.

- Verbs ending in -guar, like averiguar (*to investigate*) change spelling in the first person singular in the preterit (averigüé, averiguaste, averiguó, averiguamos, averiguasteis, averiguaron).

LA PRÁCTICA 2

Write the first person singular form for each of these verbs:

1. secar   sequé

2. alcanzar   _____

3. colocar   _____

4. pegar   _____

5. averiguar   _____

6. freír   _____

7. ver   _____

8. gruñir   _____

9. mascar   _____

10. cruzar   _____

Verbs with Special Conjugations
Verbos con conjugaciones especiales

When the stem of an **-er** or **-ir** verb ends in **a**, **e**, **i**, or **o**, the following changes are made in the third person. Notice the written accent marks:

Creer *(to believe)*		Oír *(to hear)*	
creí	creímos	oí	oímos
creíste	creísteis	oíste	oísteis
creyó	creyeron	oyó	oyeron

Other verbs with such conjugations include **leer** *(to read)*, **caer** *(to fall)*, **poseer** *(to possess)*, **proveer** *(to provide)*.

With all verbs ending in **-uir** (except **-guir**), the pattern is somewhat similar:

Incluir *(to include)*	
incluí	incluimos
incluiste	incluisteis
incluyó	incluyeron

Other similar verbs are **obstruir** *(to block)*, **concluir** *(to conclude)*, **destruir** *(to destroy)*, **contribuir** *(to contribute)* **distribuir** *(to distribute)*, **substituir** *(to substitute)*, **construir** *(to build)*, **huir** *(to escape)*.

LA PRÁCTICA 3

¿Qué pasó ayer? Follow the model:

1. organizar la oficina (yo)   *Organicé la oficina ayer.* _____

2. tocar el piano (él) _____

3. llegar tarde (ellos) _____

4. distribuir los periódicos (tú) _____

5. construir el mueble (ella) _____

6. empezar a estudiar (yo) _____

7. leer la historia (nosotros) _____

8. ver una película (Ud.) _____

9. pagar la cuenta (ellas) _____

10. pescar en el río (Uds.) _____

_____

Irregular Verbs
Verbos irregulares

Although several Spanish verbs have an irregular stem that must be memorized, most take the same endings in the preterit:

	Tener (to have)	Estar (to be)	Andar (to go, walk)
(yo)	tuve	estuve	anduve
(tú)	tuviste	estuviste	anduviste
(él, ella, Ud.)	tuvo	estuvo	anduvo
(nosotros)	tuvimos	estuvimos	anduvimos
(vosotros)	tuvisteis	estuvisteis	anduvisteis
(ellos, ellas, Uds.)	tuvieron	estuvieron	anduvieron

	Traer (to bring)	Decir (to say, tell)	Traducir (to translate)
(yo)	traje	dije	traduje
(tú)	trajiste	dijiste	tradujiste
(él, ella, Ud.)	trajo	dijo	tradujo
(nosotros)	trajimos	dijimos	tradujimos
(vosotros)	trajisteis	dijisteis	tradujisteis
(ellos, ellas, Uds.)	trajeron	dijeron	tradujeron

	Querer (to want)	Poner (to put)	Hacer (to do, make)
(yo)	quise	puse	hice
(tú)	quisiste	pusiste	hiciste
(él, ella, Ud.)	quiso	puso	hizo
(nosotros)	quisimos	pusimos	hicimos
(vosotros)	quisisteis	pusisteis	hicisteis
(ellos, ellas, Uds.)	quisieron	pusieron	hicieron

	Saber *(to know)*	Caber *(to fit)*	Venir *(to come)*
(yo)	supe	cupe	vine
(tú)	supiste	cupiste	viniste
(él, ella, Ud.)	supo	cupo	vino
(nosotros)	supimos	cupimos	vinimos
(vosotros)	supisteis	cupisteis	vinisteis
(ellos, ellas, Uds.)	supieron	cupieron	vinieron

Ser *(to be)* and ir *(to go)* are irregular verbs also, but they have identical preterit forms. The meanings of the forms of ser and ir in the preterit are understood when placed in context. The verb dar *(to give)* is similar to the regular verb ver *(to see)*:

> **TIP**
> Notice how the third person singular of hacer in the preterit is spelled hizo, and how the third person plural form of verbs with stems ending in j, such as trajeron (traer) or dijeron (decir), do not have the -ieron ending.

	Ser	Ir	Dar
(yo)	fui	fui	di
(tú)	fuiste	fuiste	diste
(él, ella, Ud.)	fue	fue	dio
(nosotros)	fuimos	fuimos	dimos
(vosotros)	fuisteis	fuisteis	disteis
(ellos, ellas, Uds.)	fueron	fueron	dieron

EJEMPLOS

¿Supiste que se casó Eva?	*Did you know that Eva got married?*
Anoche estuvimos en su casa.	*We were at their house last night.*
Quiso tener una fiesta familiar.	*She wanted to have a family party.*
Fueron todos sus primos.	*All of her cousins went.*
Le trajeron docenas de regalos.	*They brought her dozens of gifts.*
Puse la comida en la mesa.	*I put the food on the table.*

In some cases, the preterit tense may actually alter the meaning of a verb:

conocer (to know personally)	La conocí.	*I met her.*
querer (to want)	No quise ir.	*I refused to go.*
saber (to know something)	Supe la fecha.	*I found out the date.*

LA PRÁCTICA 4

¿Qué pasó anteayer? Follow the example.

1. Ud. / ir / al cine   Anteayer usted fue al cine.

2. Nosotros / hacer / la tarea   _____

3. Ellas / andar / al supermercado   _____

4. Carlos / poner / plantas en el jardín _____

5. Tú / venir / conmigo a la escuela   _____

6. Yo no / querer / ir al trabajo   _____

7. Ella / tener / problemas con su carro _____

8. Tú y yo / traer / libros a la clase _____

9. Uds. / traducir / los ejercicios   _____

10. La directora me / dar / un chocolate _____

The Imperfect

Regular Verbs

Verbos regulares

The imperfect tense in Spanish is another common way to discuss what took place in the past. Unlike the preterit, however, which expresses completed action in past time, the imperfect tense generally expresses repeated or continuous action. These are the endings that are added to the stem of most verbs:

	Hablar *(to speak)*	Comer *(to eat)*	Escribir *(to write)*
(yo)	hablaba	comía	escribía
(tú)	hablabas	comías	escribías
(él, ella, Ud.)	hablaba	comía	escribía
(nosotros)	hablábamos	comíamos	escribíamos
(vosotros)	hablabais	comíais	escribíais
(ellos, ellas, Uds.)	hablaban	comían	escribían

Los chicos hablaban toda la noche. *The kids were talking all night.*
Comíamos pescado los viernes. *We used to eat fish on Fridays.*
¿Escribías mucho durante la clase? *Did you write a lot during class?*

LA PRÁCTICA 5

Write the first person plural form of the imperfect tense for each verb:

1. investigar   investigábamos

2. encontrar   _____

3. elegir   _____

4. agarrar   _____

5. sentir   _____

6. morder   _____

7. comenzar   _____

8. golpear   _____

9. hacer   _____

10. partir   _____

Irregular Verbs
Verbos irregulares

The only irregular verbs in the imperfect tense are ir, ser, and ver:

Ir *(to go)*		Ser *(to be)*		Ver *(to see)*	
iba	íbamos	era	éramos	veía	veíamos
ibas	ibais	eras	erais	veías	veíais
iba	iban	era	eran	veía	veían

TIP
Notice how the first and third person singular forms are the same in the imperfect tense, and are understood when put into context.

EJEMPLOS

Yo iba a la iglesia con mi tía. *I used to go to church with my aunt.*
Veíamos videos cuando llegó. *We were watching videos when he arrived.*
Eran soldados muy valientes. *They were very brave soldiers.*

> **TIP**
> The preterit form of hay (*there is, there are*) is hubo (e.g., hubo un accidente, *there was an accident*), and the imperfect form is había or habían (e.g., habían dos chicas, *there were two girls*).

LA PRÁCTICA 6

Insert the correct form of the imperfect on each line below:

1. (comer) Samuel _____ en el hotel con frecuencia.

2. (ir) A veces los estudiantes _____ a la biblioteca.

3. (jugar) Yo _____ con el perro todos los días.

4. (vivir) Ella _____ cerca de un lago en las montañas.

5. (cantar) ¿ _____ mucho cuando era más joven?

6. (dormirse) En aquella época tú _____ a las doce.

7. (ver) Nosotros siempre _____ películas con la familia.

8. (hay) En esa esquina _____ dos gasolineras.

9. (hablar) Cuando llegamos ellos _____ inglés.

10. (ser) De vez en cuando Lupe _____ muy traviesa.

Imperfect vs. Preterit: A Difference in Usage
El imperfecto comparado con el pretérito: una diferencia en el uso

Generally, a Spanish speaker views a past event in two different ways. If the speaker views the entire event as <u>a completed event</u> → |, started or finished in the past, he will use the preterit. However, if the speaker views the past as <u>an event in progress</u> → → →, as a frequently repeated act, or as a description or background activity, he will use the imperfect.

→ |	→ → →
Viajé a Miami el mes pasado.	**Frecuentemente viajaba a Miami.**
I traveled to Miami last month.	*I used to travel to Miami frequently.*

Adverbial phrases such as con frecuencia, de vez en cuando, and muchas veces often accompany the imperfect because they imply an unspecified period of time, whereas more concise terminology such as ayer, anoche, and el otro día often accompany the preterit. Moods, emotions, and thoughts are also expressed with the imperfect tense (e.g., ¿Qué pensaba ella de mí? [*What did she think of me?*]). However, the imperfect, and not the preterit, is used to tell what time it *was* in the past (Eran las tres. [*It was three o'clock.*]).

Sometimes the preterit and the imperfect are used together, either when one action interrupts another, or when there is indirect discourse; that is, to report what was said before:

Tocaban música cuando llamé.	**Él me dijo que fumabas.**
They were playing music when I called.	*He told me you used to smoke.*

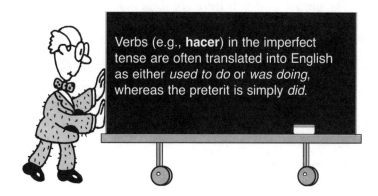

Verbs (e.g., **hacer**) in the imperfect tense are often translated into English as either *used to do* or *was doing*, whereas the preterit is simply *did*.

LA PRÁCTICA 7

Complete the translations using either the preterit or the imperfect:

1. *They ate the pie last night.*   Anoche ellos **comieron** el pastel.

2. *She used to wash dishes.*   Ella _____ los platos.

3. *We were cleaning the bathroom.*   _____ el baño.

4. *Did you wake up at six o'clock?*   ¿Te _____ a las seis?

5. *I studied all day long.*   Toda el día yo _____.

6. *You guys refused to go.*   Ustedes no _____ ir.

7. *The party lasted six hours.*   La fiesta _____ seis horas.

8. *Who was living here last year?*   ¿Quién _____ aquí el año pasado?

9. *She liked to swim in the river.*   Le _____ bañarse en el río.

10. *There was an accident on Friday.*   _____ un accidente el viernes.

Continue to translate using forms of the preterit and the imperfect:

11. *While we were practicing, he arrived with the pizza.*

   Mientras que _____ él _____ con la pizza.

12. *She played the guitar and you were singing.*

   Ella _____ la guitarra y tú _____.

13. *I went home after work and took a bath.*

   _____ a mi casa después del trabajo y me _____.

14. *He stood up and began to read.*

   Se _____ y _____ a leer.

15. *They said you were going to the store.*

   Ellos _____ que tú _____ a la tienda.

_____

POR SU CUENTA

Conteste las preguntas con respuestas completas:

1. ¿Dónde nacieron sus padres?

2. ¿Gastó mucho dinero la semana pasada?

3. ¿Estudiaba español el año pasado?

4. ¿Se lavó las manos hoy?

5. ¿Quién estaba en su casa anoche?

6. ¿A qué hora te acostó ayer?

7. ¿Qué tomó cuando tenía dolor de cabeza?

8. ¿Entendió todas las palabras en esta lección?

9. ¿Usaba la computadora cuando era más joven?

10. ¿Tuvo una fiesta para celebrar su cumpleaños?

EL REPASO

Are the following statements true or false? (No answers are given: you'll have to check what you have read.)

1. The present indicative tense can refer to future action. _____

2. The preterit tense tells what used to happen in the past. _____

3. The imperfect can refer to actions that were happening in the past. _____

4. The 1st person plural form is the same in the preterit and the present. _____

5. Endings are the same for regular -er and -ir verbs in the imperfect. _____

6. The verbs ser and ir have the same forms in the preterit tense. _____

7. Most spelling changes in the preterit occur in the 1st person singular form. _____

8. The verb imponer is conjugated the same as poner. _____

9. Hubo and hay are forms of the verb hallar. _____

10. The imperfect tense is used to tell what time it was in the past. _____

CROSSWORD 3

Translate these into Spanish:

Across
2. She came
4. I had
6. I wanted
8. They were
11. I used to travel
12. They danced
14. It was
15. We went
17. I said
18. They heard

Down
1. You did (sing. inf.)
3. You were working (sing. inf.)
5. You explained (sing. inf.)
7. We found out
9. There was
10. You ate (sing. inf.)
13. They fell
16. We gave

5

The Future and Conditional Tenses

¿Cuánto sabe usted?
How Much Do You Know Already?

1. How do you say, *I will be able to go* in Spanish?

2. Conjugate the verb hacer in the conditional tense.

3. What does Saldríamos mean in English?

4. Name two ways to say *I will learn* in Spanish.

5. What does Sería la una de la noche mean in English?

The Future Tense

Regular Verbs
Verbos regulares

The future tense expresses future time. The endings that form the future tense in Spanish are the same for all -ar, -er, and -ir verbs. These endings are simply added to the infinitive:

	Hablar *(to speak)*	Comer *(to eat)*	Escribir *(to write)*
(yo)	hablaré	comeré	escribiré
(tú)	hablarás	comerás	escribirás
(él, ella, Ud.)	hablará	comerá	escribirá
(nosotros)	hablaremos	comeremos	escribiremos
(vosotros)	hablaréis	comeréis	escribiréis
(ellos, ellas, Uds.)	hablarán	comerán	escribirán

EJEMPLOS

¿Cuándo irás a México?   When will you go to Mexico?
Le llamaré en la tarde.   I'll call him in the afternoon.
No prenderemos las luces.   We won't turn on the lights.

LA PRÁCTICA 1

Write the third person plural form in the future tense for each verb:

1. guardar   guardarán _____

2. juntarse   _____

3. mostrar   _____

4. vestirse   _____

5. barrer   _____

6. persistir   _____

7. sentarse   _____

8. perdonar   _____

9. esconder   _____

10. abandonar   _____

Irregular Verbs
Verbos irregulares

Several verbs are irregular in the future tense. The twelve examples that follow are the most common. First are those that drop the e of the infinitive ending before adding the future tense endings:

Saber *(to know)*		Caber *(to fit)*	
sabré	sabremos	cabré	cabremos
sabrás	sabréis	cabrás	cabréis
sabrá	sabrán	cabrá	cabrán

Poder *(to be able)*		Querer *(to wish, to want)*	
podré	podremos	querré	querremos
podrás	podréis	querrás	querréis
podrá	podrán	querrá	querrán

Haber *(to have, to possess)*	
habré	habremos
habrás	habréis
habrá	habrán

The following verbs replace the e or i stem of the infinitive with the letter d before adding the endings of the future tense:

Poner *(to put)*		Salir *(to leave)*	
pondré	pondremos	saldré	saldremos
pondrás	pondréis	saldrás	saldréis
pondrá	pondrán	saldrá	saldrán

Tener *(to have)*		Venir *(to come)*	
tendré	tendremos	vendré	vendremos
tendrás	tendréis	vendrás	vendréis
tendrá	tendrán	vendrá	vendrán

Valer *(to be worth)*	
valdré	valdremos
valdrás	valdréis
valdrá	valdrán

The following verbs drop the e and c of the infinitive before adding the endings of the future tense:

Decir *(to say)*		Hacer *(to make)*	
diré	diremos	haré	haremos
dirás	diréis	harás	haréis
dirá	dirán	hará	harán

EJEMPLOS

Sabrán la respuesta.	*They will know the answer.*
Lo haremos el domingo.	*We'll do it on Sunday.*
No tendré problemas con el carro.	*I won't have trouble with my car.*
¿Dónde pondrás las maletas?	*Where will you put the suitcases?*
Ella podrá hacerlo.	*She will be able to do it.*

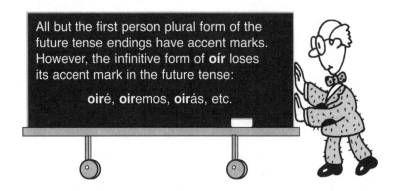

All but the first person plural form of the future tense endings have accent marks. However, the infinitive form of **oír** loses its accent mark in the future tense:

oiré, **oir**emos, **oir**ás, etc.

LA PRÁCTICA 2

Change the underlined word from the past tense to the future tense:

1. Ella <u>tenía</u> un apartamento en el centro. tendrá

2. Ellos <u>hicieron</u> todo el trabajo. _____

3. ¿Cuándo <u>viniste</u>? _____

4. Lo <u>puse</u> en la bolsa. _____

5. <u>Volvimos</u> muy tarde. _____

6. <u>Salieron</u> a las dos. _____

7. ¿Qué <u>dijo</u> su mamá? _____

8. <u>Había</u> un árbol en el jardín. _____

9. No <u>pudieron</u> vender el barco. _____

10. <u>Estábamos</u> en la biblioteca. _____

Using the Future Tense
Usos del tiempo futuro

The future tense in Spanish expresses an anticipated event, just as it does in English. Specifically, it is used to express promise, determination, or assurance regarding some future act:

<u>Visitaré</u> a mi abuela en Panamá.	*I'll visit my grandmother in Panama.*
¿Por qué no <u>irás</u> a despedirme?	*Why won't you go to say good-bye to me?*
Uds. <u>leerán</u> todas las revistas.	*You guys will read all the magazines.*

Depending on the context, the future tense may also be used in Spanish to express conjecture, probability, or inference in present time. For example, ¿Quién ganará? could mean either *Who will win?* or *I wonder who will win?*

<u>Serán</u> las siete.	*It's probably seven o'clock.*
¿Dónde <u>estará</u> mi celular?	*I wonder where my cell phone is.*
<u>Tomaremos</u> un taxi.	*We might take a taxi.*

Remember that the future tense may be replaced by the present indicative tense when there is mention of some future time in the sentence:

<u>Viene</u> el sábado.	
<u>Vendrá</u> el sábado.	*He's coming Saturday.*

The present tense can also replace the future tense when there is a request for instructions:

¿<u>Manejo</u> el carro?	*Shall I drive the car?*

Sometimes, the future tense is used in conditional sentences, when the "if-clause" has the verb in the present tense. Notice the conditional tone created by the word si (*if*):

Si ellos entran, nosotros <u>saldremos</u>.	*If they enter, we'll leave.*
<u>Pintará</u> la casa si le dan el dinero.	*He'll paint the house if they pay him.*

However, the future tense is not used to express a wish or desire. Instead, the verb querer is used:

¿Quieres ir conmigo?	*Will you go with me?*

TIP
The construction ir + a + infinitive is another way to express some future action or state of being, although it implies more immediate activity:

<u>Van a tener</u> una fiesta en su casa.	*They're going to have a party (soon).*
<u>Tendrán</u> una fiesta.	*They will have a party (sometime).*

LA PRÁCTICA 3

Change each infinitive to the future tense:

1. Natalia (poner) las flores en el jardín.   pondrá

2. Los bebitos (dormir) porque tienen sueño.   _____

3. Yo no (poder) comprar el brazalete.   _____

4. ¿Tú (tomar) todos los refrescos?   _____

5. La próxima semana Nicolás (empezar) a estudiar.   _____

6. En la fiesta (haber) un mago.   _____

7. Algún día nosotros (ser) soldados.   _____

8. Ellos (estar) en el centro commercial.   _____

9. ¿Cuánto (valer) el carro en dos años?   _____

10. Yo (hacer) la comida para mañana.   _____

Replace the underlined phrase with a future tense form:

11. <u>Voy a decir</u> una historia.   Diré

12. <u>Vamos a salir</u> temprano.   _____

13. <u>Van a tener</u> muchos clientes.   _____

14. ¿<u>Va a caber</u> en la cartera?   _____

15. <u>Vas a venir</u> en el verano.   _____

16. <u>Vamos a saber</u> más castellano.   _____

17. <u>Van a hacer</u> el almuerzo.   _____

18. <u>Va a querer</u> las joyas.   _____

19. <u>Van a poder</u> hablar contigo.   _____

20. <u>Voy a poner</u> el CD.   _____

Change these sentences to questions of probability in the future tense:

21. Probablemente llega pasado mañana.   ¿Llegará pasado mañana?

22. Probablemente hay contaminación.   _____

23. Probablemente comienza un poco tarde.   _____

24. Probablemente no comemos con ella. _____

25. Probablemente mira television ahora. _____

26. Probablemente trae algo de España. _____

27. Probablemente pasamos por su casa. _____

28. Probablemente hago el trabajo. _____

29. Probablemente sabes la dirección. _____

30. Probablemente salen con Ronaldo. _____

The Conditional Tense

Regular Verbs
Verbos regulares

The conditional tense either looks ahead to future time from the perspective of the past, or it expresses probability. Like the future tense, the endings that form the conditional in Spanish are the same for nearly all -ar, -er, and -ir verbs. These endings are added to the infinitive:

> **TIP**
> Unlike the future tense, all added endings in the conditional have accent marks, including the first person plural form.

	Hablar (to speak)	Comer (to eat)	Escribir (to write)
(yo)	hablaría	comería	escribiría
(tú)	hablarías	comerías	escribirías
(él, ella, Ud.)	hablaría	comería	escribiría
(nosotros)	hablaríamos	comeríamos	escribiríamos
(vosotros)	hablaríais	comeríais	escribiríais
(ellos, ellas, Uds.)	hablarían	comerían	escribirían

EJEMPLOS

Dijo que comeríamos en el comedor.	*She said we'd eat in the dining room.*
¿Dónde estaría Paco?	*I wonder where Paco is.*
Él sabía que comprarías los zapatos.	*He knew that you'd buy the shoes.*

LA PRÁCTICA 4

Change these present tense forms to the conditional:

1. ordeno   ordenaría _____

2. crezco   _____

3. juegan   _____

4. vamos   _____

5. ves   _____

6. tocan   _____

7. oigo   _____

8. es   _____

9. están   _____

10. aplicas   _____

Irregular Verbs
Verbos irregulares

The root forms of the conditional tense follow a pattern that is similar to that of the future tense:

Saber *(to know)*		Caber *(to fit)*	
sabría	sabríamos	cabría	cabríamos
sabrías	sabríais	cabrías	cabríais
sabría	sabrían	cabría	cabrían

Poder *(to be able)*		Querer *(to wish, to want)*	
podría	podríamos	querría	querríamos
podrías	podríais	querrías	querríais
podría	podrían	querría	querrían

Haber *(to have, to possess)*	
habría	habríamos
habrías	habríais
habría	habrían

Poner *(to put)*		Salir *(to leave)*	
pondría	pondríamos	saldría	saldríamos
pondrías	pondríais	saldrías	saldríais
pondría	pondrían	saldría	saldrían

Tener *(to have)*		Venir *(to come)*	
tendría	tendríamos	vendría	vendríamos
tendrías	tendríais	vendrías	vendríais
tendría	tendrían	vendría	vendrían

Valer *(to be worth)*	
valdría	valdríamos
valdrías	valdríais
valdría	valdrían

Decir *(to say)*		Hacer *(to do, to make)*	
diría	diríamos	haría	haríamos
dirías	diríais	harías	haríais
diría	dirían	haría	harían

EJEMPLOS

¿Adónde habría ido?	*I wonder where she had gone?*
Me prometío que lo haría.	*He promised me he'd do it.*
Dijeron que saldrías el lunes.	*They said you would leave on Monday.*

When *would* is intended to mean *used to* in a sentence, it is translated by the imperfect tense in Spanish, and not the conditional:

Cuando era niño, jugaba en
   el patio.
*When I was a child, I would play in
   the yard.*

> **TIP**
> The conditional form is often used to form more courteous expressions:
> ¿Puedes ayudarme?
> *Can you help me?*
> ¿Podrías ayudarme?
> *Could you help me?*

LA PRÁCTICA 5

Put C (Correcto) if it is correct and I (Incorrecto) if it isn't:

1. it would fit	=	cabría		C
2. it would be able to	=	podería		____
3. it would come	=	vendría		____
4. it would help	=	ayudría		____
5. it would want	=	quiería		____
6. it would move	=	movería		____
7. it would have	=	tendría		____
8. it would make	=	hacerría		____
9. it would say	=	diría		____
10. it would be worth	=	valdría		____

Using the Conditional Tense
Usos del tiempo condicional

To contrast the use of the conditional tense with the future, notice the graphic below. In essence, the conditional tense perceives the future from the past, while the future tense perceives the future from the present:

CONDITIONAL	FUTURE
→ → **X** |	| → → **X**
Sabía que me llamaría.	Te llamaré mañana.
I knew he would call me.	*I will call you tomorrow.*

As a rule, the conditional tense is used similarly in both Spanish and English. If the main verb of a sentence is in the past tense, the second verb is put into the conditional form when it denotes future action in the past:

Me prometió que traería el postre.
He promised me that he would bring the dessert.

In sentences such as these, the main verb clause generally expresses communication, belief, or knowledge:

Mis amigos dijeron que <u>irían</u> al parque.
My friends said that <u>they would go</u> to the park.

Yo creía que <u>ganaríamos</u> el juego.
I thought that <u>we would win</u> the game.

Sabía que <u>venderían</u> la máquina.
She knew that <u>they would sell</u> the machine.

Depending upon the context, however, the conditional tense may also be used in Spanish to express conjecture, probability, or inference in past time:

¿Dónde estaría David?
I wonder where David was?
Sería la una y media.
It was probably one-thirty.

In addition, the conditional tense is used with the SUBJUNCTIVE mood, which will be discussed later.

Si yo fuera usted, no le hablaría.
I wouldn't talk to him if I were you.

The construction deber de + infinitive may also express probability in past time, as well as in the future:

deber de (in the imperfect tense) + infinitive
Debían de ser las dos.   *It was probably two o'clock.*

deber de (in the present tense) + infinitive
Debo de ponerlo en el garaje.   *I might put it in the garage.*

Both the conditional and the future tenses are used after si (in if-clauses) when it implies *whether*:

No sé si vendrá.   *I don't know whether he will come.*
No me dijo si vendría.   *He did not tell me whether he would come.*

The conditional tense is used in many constructions that somehow suggest a hypothetical situation:

En ese caso, no lo haría.   *In that case, I wouldn't do it.*

> **TIP**
> The future and conditional tenses of hay (*there is/are*) are habrá (*there will be*) and habría (*there would be*), respectively. Generally, however, haber is used as an auxiliary verb:
>
> Habrá dos pájaros en la jaula.
> *There will be two birds in the cage.*
>
> Pensé que <u>habría</u> mucha gente en el estadio.
> *I thought there would be a lot of people in the stadium.*
>
> En cinco años, <u>habrán ganado</u> un partido.
> *In five years, they'll have won a game.*

LA PRÁCTICA 6

Write the correct form of the conditional tense on the line provided:

1. Me explicó que habían tres vuelos que (SALIR) a las cuatro. *saldrían*

2. Dije que ella (TENER) el dinero para ahorrar en el banco. _____

3. Leí en el periódico que los dos (CASARSE) en Nueva York. _____

4. Preguntamos si tú (PODER) abrir las ventanas. _____

5. Me escribío que él no (VOLVER) a su trabajo. _____

6. Yo en su lugar no le (DECIR) nada. _____

7. ¿Dónde (ESTAR) mis lentes de sol? _____

8. No sabíamos si Sandra (LLAMAR). _____

9. Tú no (DEBER) decir mentiras. _____

10. ¿Cuántas personas (HABER) en la clase? _____

Translate these sentences into Spanish using the conditional tense:

11. I knew that he would want to drive. *Sabía que él querría manejar.*

12. We said that we'd leave at midnight. _____

13. Would you please come to the office? _____

14. I was asking if they would work. _____

15. We would probably wash the clothes. _____

16. I wonder where Cristina was. _____

17. He promised he would sing. _____

18. They said they'd be at the movies. _____

19. In that case, I would buy the car. _____

20. It was probably six in the morning. _____

_____

POR SU CUENTA

¿Qué haría Ud. si tuviera diez millones de dólares?
(*What would you do if you had ten million dollars?*)

1. Compraría _____

2. Viajaría a _____

3. Regalaría _____

4. Ahorraría _____

5. Donaría _____

6. Apostaría _____

7. Compartiría _____

8. Invertiría _____

9. Gastaría _____

10. Construiría _____

6

The Reflexive Verbs

¿Cuánto sabe usted?
How Much Do You Know Already?

1. Change the command Cepíllate los dientes to the negative.

2. What is the difference in meaning between perder and perderse?

3. How do you say *We will get married* in Spanish?

4. What is the difference in meaning between beber and beberse?

5. Name three ways to say *to become* in Spanish.

Forming the Reflexive
Formación del verbo reflexivo

Reflexive verbs in Spanish are easy to recognize because they have the pronoun se attached to the infinitive. These verbs have *reflexive* pronouns that refer to the same person or thing as the subject, and are normally placed directly before the verb in conjugation. Notice the translation of the reflexive in the present tense:

Bañarse *(to bathe oneself)*		
(yo)	me baño	*I bathe myself*
(tú)	te bañas	*you bathe yourself* (inf. sing.)
(él, ella, Ud.)	se baña	*he bathes himself* or *she bathes herself* or *you bathe yourself* (form. sing.)
(nosotros)	nos bañamos	*we bathe ourselves*
(vosotros)	os bañáis	*you bathe yourselves* (inf. pl.)
(ellos, ellas, Uds.)	se bañan	*they bathe themselves* or *you bathe yourselves* (form. pl.)

Other such verbs are acostarse (*to lie down*), vestirse (*to get dressed*), afeitarse (*to shave*), peinarse (*to comb*), levantarse (*to stand*), sentarse (*to sit*), despertarse (*to wake up*), dormirse (*to fall asleep*), lavarse (*to wash*), lastimarse (*to hurt oneself*), cansarse (*to get tired*), arreglarse (*to get fixed up*), enfermarse (*to get sick*), maquillarse (*to put on make-up*), mojarse (*to get wet*), secarse (*to dry oneself*).

> **TIP**
> Many reflexive verbs are parts of familiar everyday expressions:
>
> | | |
> |---|---|
> | ¡Date prisa! | *Hurry up!* |
> | ¿Cómo te llamas? | *What's your name?* |
> | No me acuerdo. | *I don't remember.* |

EJEMPLOS

¿A qué hora <u>se despertó</u>?	*What time did he wake up?*
Siempre <u>me baño</u> en agua caliente.	*I always bathe in hot water.*
No <u>se acostarán</u> en la alfombra.	*They will not lie down on the rug.*

When used with affirmative commands, infinitives, or present participles in a sentence, the reflexive pronoun is often attached to the end of the verb. Reflexive pronouns change in accordance with the person(s) to which they refer:

Vís<u>te</u>te.	*Get dressed.*
Quiere vestir<u>se</u>.	*He wants to get dressed.*
Estoy vistiéndo<u>me</u>.	*I'm getting dressed.*

However, the personal pronouns of reflexive verbs generally maintain their position before verb forms in questions and negative statements:

¿<u>Te</u> lavaste las manos?	*Did you wash your hands?*
Sí, pero no <u>me</u> afeité.	*Yes, but I didn't shave.*

LA PRÁCTICA 1

¿Qué hace la gente cada mañana? Follow the model given:

1. despertarse   <u>se despiertan</u>

2. estirarse   _____

3. bañarse   _____

4. secarse   _____

5. lavarse los dientes   _____

6. afeitarse   _____

7. cepillarse _____

8. peinarse _____

9. maquillarse _____

10. vestirse _____

Using the Reflexive
Empleo del verbo reflexivo

Reflexive verbs generally correspond to intransitive verbs in English; that is, where there is no direct object. As a general rule, the reflexive in Spanish indicates some form of change or onset of an action:

Ella se cansa en la clase.	*She gets tired in class.*
Ella se sentó en la cama.	*She sat down on the bed.*
Ella se dormirá muy pronto.	*She will fall asleep very soon.*

Most reflexive verbs also have a related transitive verb that is <u>not</u> reflexive. Any transitive verb may be used reflexively if its subject performs the action upon itself:

Ella vistió a su hija.	*She dressed her daughter.*
Ella se vistió rápido.	*She got (herself) dressed quickly.*
Despertaba a todos.	*I used to wake up everyone.*
Me despertaba tarde.	*I used to wake up (myself) late.*

With some Spanish verbs, the reflexive pronouns are used as indirect objects instead of direct objects. Many of these verbs refer to clothing or parts of the human body, for example, ponerse (*to put on*), quitarse (*to take off*), lavarse (*to wash oneself*), quebrarse (*to get broken*), quemarse (*to get burned*):

Brenda se quitó el abrigo.
Brenda took off her coat.

El niño nunca se lava las manos.
The boy never washes his hands.

> **TIP**
> There are a variety of other daily activities that can be expressed with reflexive verbs:
> amarrarse los pasadores
> *to tie one's shoelaces*
> limarse las uñas
> *to file one's nails*
> pintarse los labios
> *to put lipstick on*

The reflexive may also replace a construction in the passive voice, where the "doer" of the action is not mentioned. These indefinite constructions in English are expressed by the third person reflexive in Spanish, and may be translated in a variety of ways:

¿Cómo <u>se escribe</u> la palabra?   *How does one write the word?*
¡No <u>se puede</u> decir eso!   *You can't say that!*
Aquí <u>se habla</u> español.   *Spanish is spoken here.*

LA PRÁCTICA 2

Write C (Correcto) if the sentence is correct and I (Incorrecto) if it is not:

1. Siempre se acuesta muy tarde. <u>   C   </u>

2. Siempre se hablan con el profesor. _____

3. Siempre se comen en el café. _____

4. Siempre se quita el sombrero. _____

5. Siempre se escriben por E-mail. _____

6. Siempre se bailan con su marido. _____

7. Siempre se ponen las medias blancas. _____

8. Siempre se pueden hacer el trabajo. _____

9. Siempre se sientan en el sillón. _____

10. Siempre se estudian las lecciones. _____

Reflexives as Commands
Los verbos reflexivos en el imperativo

Reflexive pronouns are attached to the ends of affirmative commands and precede them in the negative:

Siéntense aquí, estudiantes.   *Sit here, students.*
No te vayas, por favor.   *Please don't go.*

LA PRÁCTICA 3

Write each reflexive in its infinitive form:

1. Despiértate   despertarse
2. Báñate   _____
3. Levántense   _____
4. Vete   _____
5. Vístase   _____
6. Siéntense   _____
7. Lávate   _____
8. Péinese   _____
9. Arréglate   _____
10. Séquese   _____

CROSSWORD 4

Translate these into Spanish:

Across
1. to brush oneself
5. to get wet
6. to take a shower
7. to shave
8. to lie down
11. to comb oneself
15. to get sick
16. to get angry
17. to get dressed
18. to fall down
19. to be wrong

Down
2. to get lost
3. to fall asleep
4. to sit down
6. to wake up
9. to get tired
10. to leave
12. to get up
13. to get fixed up
14. to wash oneself

Reflexives with Reciprocal Meanings
Los verbos reflexivos con significados recíprocos

In some cases, reflexive verbs in their plural form may express reciprocal action. Although the phrase el uno al otro (*one to the other*) can be added for emphasis, the precise meaning of a reciprocal phrase is usually clarified by the context:

Pepe y Linda se quieren mucho.	Carlos and Linda **love each other** a lot.
Nos conocimos hace años.	**We met** years ago.
Se hablaban por horas.	They would **talk to one another** for hours.

With reference to things, reflexive verbs generally express *by itself* or *by themselves*:

Se cerraron las puertas.	*The doors closed (by themselves).*

However, when the reflexive verb relates to parts of the body or articles of clothing, the definite article follows the reflexive pronoun instead of the personal pronoun forms. As a rule, the definite article is singular, even when the subject is plural:

Nos pusimos la corbata.
We put on neck ties.
Se lavaron la cara.
They washed their faces.

> **TIP**
> Reflexive verbs often express the concept of *to get* + *past participle* or *adjective* in English:
> *We're getting tired.*
> Estamos cansándonos.
> *I would get mad.*
> Yo me enojaba.
> *They will get married.*
> Ellos se casarán.

LA PRÁCTICA 4

Fill in the blanks with the correct form of the reflexive verb. Use only the present tense:

1. Juan (quitarse) la camisa y (ponerse) una limpia.   se quita, se pone

2. ¿Tú (cepillarse) los dientes después de comer? _____

3. Los niños (lavarse) las manos con agua y jabón. _____

4. Cuando viajo en barco siempre (marearse). _____

5. Nos metemos en calles desconocidas y (perderse). _____

6. ¿Cómo (vestirse) el Sr. Martínez? _____

7. Ella no (maquillarse) porque sólo tiene nueve años. _____

8. A mí (aburrirse) la clase de historia. _____

9. Tú (emborracharse) con dos vasos de vino.   _____

10. Trabajamos todo el día y (acostarse) temprano.   _____

Translate these sentences into English:

11. Felipe se cansó rápidamente.   *__Felipe got tired quickly.__*

12. No se vende tabaco en la escuela.   _____

13. No te limes las uñas enfrente del profesor.   _____

14. Las amigas se llamaron por teléfono celular.   _____

15. Siéntense conmigo, por favor.   _____

16. Tendría que irme en seguida.   _____

17. Las hojas se caen del árbol en octubre.   _____

18. Nos ayudábamos el uno al otro.   _____

19. Quiero afeitarme en el otro baño.   _____

20. Se enviará un mensaje por correo electrónico.   _____

Reflexives with Special Forms and Meanings
Verbos reflexivos con formas y significados especiales

Most reflexive verbs in Spanish relate closely in meaning to the corresponding nonreflexive verb. The following refer to a person's emotions or feelings:

aburrir	*to bore someone*	aburrirse	*to get bored*
alegrar	*to make someone glad*	alegrarse	*to be glad*
divertir	*to amuse*	divertirse	*to be amused*
calmar	*to calm someone down*	calmarse	*to calm down*
enojar	*to make someone angry*	enojarse	*to get angry*
molestar	*to bother someone*	molestarse	*to be bothered*
sorprender	*to surprise someone*	sorprenderse	*to be surprised*

However, the meanings of some verbs are modified significantly when they are used in the reflexive form:

arreglar	*to arrange*	arreglarse	*to get ready to go out*
despedir	*to fire*	despedirse de	*to say good-bye*
dormir	*to sleep*	dormirse	*to fall asleep*
probar	*to taste, try*	probarse	*to try on*
ir	*to go*	irse	*to leave*
poner	*to put*	ponerse	*to put on*
levantar	*to lift*	levantarse	*to get up*
llamar	*to call*	llamarse	*to name oneself*

hacer	to make	hacerse	to become
parar	to stop	pararse	to stand up
perder	to lose	perderse	to get lost
marchar	to march	marcharse	to depart
volver	to return	volverse	to turn around
figurar	to depict	figurarse	to imagine
ocurrir	to happen	ocurrirse	to think of something

Several Spanish verbs have reflexive forms, but do not have reflexive meanings. The following verbs exist exclusively in the reflexive:

acordarse	to remember
arrepentirse	to repent
atreverse	to dare
desmayarse	to faint
divorciarse	to divorce
jactarse	to boast
quejarse	to complaint
rebelarse	to rebel
suicidarse	to commit suicide

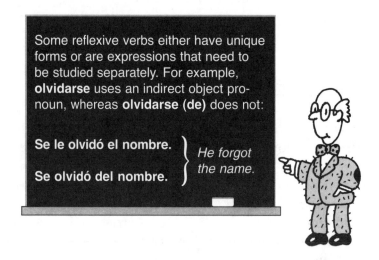

Some reflexive verbs either have unique forms or are expressions that need to be studied separately. For example, **olvidarse** uses an indirect object pronoun, whereas **olvidarse (de)** does not:

Se le olvidó el nombre.

Se olvidó del nombre.

} *He forgot the name.*

Another example is equivocarse, which means *to be wrong* only when the subject is a person. Estar equivocado and equivocarse (de) can refer to either people or things:

Te equivocas si piensas que voy a pagar la cuenta.
You are wrong if you you think I'm going to pay the bill.

¿Está equivocada la traducción?
Is the translation wrong?

Me equivoqué de calle.
I took the wrong street.

There are also reflexive verbs in Spanish that express the concept of *to become*. Hacerse is used with nouns or adjectives:

Todos <u>se hicieron</u> médicos.	*They all became doctors.*
Quiero <u>hacerme</u> famoso.	*I want to become famous.*

Ponerse and volverse also mean *to become*, but are used with adjectives. Volverse implies a more dramatic change:

<u>Nos poníamos</u> molestos con el perro.	*We used to get upset with the dog.*
La vecina <u>se volverá</u> loca.	*The neighbor will go crazy.*

The reflexives convertirse en and transformarse en both mean *to become,* but imply obvious changes from one form to another:

El negocio privado <u>se convirtió</u> en una compañía pública.
The private business became a public company.

El líquido <u>se ha transformado</u> en sólido.
The liquid has turned to solid.

Although quedarse generally means *to stay* in English, it can also express *to become*:

Me <u>quedé</u> sorprendido.	*I was (became) surprised.*
Mi abuela <u>se quedó</u> ciega.	*My grandmother went (became) blind.*

Several reflexive verbs are considered to be idiomatic expressions, and are generally used as complete phrases by themselves; for example, figurarse (*to imagine*), ponerse de acuerdo (*to come to an agreement*), darse por vencido (*to surrender*), llevarse bien (*to be on good terms*), ponerse rojo (*to blush*), venirse abajo (*to collapse*), etc. Here are a few more:

> **TIP**
> These are other ways to express *to become* in Spanish:
> Patricia llegó a ser profesora.
> *Patricia became a professor.*
> Ellos no se enriquecieron.
> *They did not become rich.*
> Yo sabía que te engordarías.
> *I knew you'd become fat.*

Darse cuenta	*(to realize)*
No me dí cuenta.	*I didn't realize.*
Hacerse daño	*(to hurt oneself)*
Me hice daño.	*I hurt myself.*
Tratarse de	*(to be about)*
¿De qué se trata?	*What's it about?*

Most reflexive verbs can be grouped into categories according to usage.

- Change of motion or position:

caerse	to fall down
detenerse	to stop
instalarse	to move in
moverse	to move
mudarse	to change residence
echarse	to lie down
inclinarse	to bend over
quedarse	to remain
pasearse	to stroll

- Reflexive verbs that include or require the preposition de:

  aprovecharse (de) *to take advantage (of)*
  enterarse de (*to find out*)
  olvidarse de (*to forget*)
  acordarse de (*to remember*)
  apoderarse de (*to seize*)
  alejarse de (*to draw away*)

- Reflexives that require the preposition a:

  acostumbrarse a (*to become accustomed to*)
  decidirse a (*to decide to do something*)
  dirigirse a (*to head for*)
  disponerse a (*to prepare oneself*)
  negarse a (*to refuse to*)

- Reflexives that need en:

  fijarse en (*to notice something*)
  empeñarse en (*to insist on doing something*)
  especializarse en (*to specialize in doing something*)

- Reflexives that require con:

  citarse con (*to arrange to meet*)
  encontrarse con (*to run into someone*)
  pelearse con (*to get into a fight with someone*)
  meterse con (*to hassle with*)

In some cases, the reflexive pronoun intensifies the affect of the action of the base verb. For example, beber (*to drink*) is exaggerated slightly when it becomes beberse (*to drink up*):

¿Te bebiste toda la limonada?
Did you drink up all the lemonade?

In the construction hacerse + definite article + adjective, the verb hacerse means *to pretend to be*:

Jaime <u>se hizo</u> el dormido.
Jaime pretended to be asleep.

The reflexive verbs encontrarse and hallarse (*to find oneself*) may sometimes be translated as though they were estar:

¿Cómo <u>se encuentra</u> Ud.?   *How are you?*
¡<u>Se hallaban</u> en medio del desierto!   *They were in the middle of the desert!*

LA PRÁCTICA 5

Look at the key word in English, and fill in the missing reflexive verb form:

1. (*cut*)   ¡Me veo horrible! Voy a _____ el pelo.   cortarme

2. (*realize*)   El problema fue que ellos no _____ cuenta.   _____

3. (*tie*)   _____ los pasadores de tu zapato, por favor.   _____

4. (*say*)   _____ que Pancho Villa admiraba el valor.   _____

5. (*be wrong*)   A veces nosotros _____ de dirección.   _____

6. (*rebel*)   Es cierto—los jóvenes _____ a esa edad.   _____

7. (*say bye*)   ¿Ya _____ de tu abuelo?   _____

8. (*leave*)   ¡No _____, chicos! Hay que comer primero.   _____

9. (*forget*)   ¡Caramba! ¡Se _____ mi libro de inglés!   _____

10. (*take advantage*) Ella quiere _____ de la situación.   _____

Identify the base verb and then translate it:

11. Ellos se mudaron. <u>mudarse</u> <u>***to change residence***</u>

12. Él se inclinaría. _____ _____

13. Tú te alabaste. _____ _____

14. Yo me engañé. _____ _____

15. Ella se mató. _____ _____

16. Nos enfriamos. _____ _____

17. Uds. se asustarán. _____ _____

18. Me quejarían. _____ _____

19. Él se cenó. _____ _____

20. Ellos se callaban. _____ _____

21. Te enfermas. _____ _____

22. Ud. se cortó. _____ _____

23. Nos reíamos. _____ _____

24. Uds. se pelearon. _____ _____

25. Ellas se abrazarán. _____ _____

Use verbs that mean to become *to form sentences in the future tense:*

26. El agua/ convertirse/ hielo <u>El agua se convertirá en hielo.</u>

27. Yo/ volverse/ loco _____

28. Ella/ ponerse/ nerviosa _____

29. Uds./ quedarse/ callados _____

30. Nosotros/ hacerse/ abogados _____

_____

POR SU CUENTA

Answer these questions about yourself in complete sentences:

1. ¿A qué hora se despierta Ud.?

2. ¿Se desayuna Ud. con su familia?

3. ¿Cuánto tiempo necesita Ud. para arreglarse?

4. ¿A Ud. le gusta ponerse ropa nueva?

5. ¿Cuándo se marchó Ud. de su casa hoy?

6. ¿Se pasea Ud. por el parque a veces?

7. ¿Con quién se confía Ud.?

8. ¿Se equivoca Ud. al hablar español?

9. ¿Se cansa mucho Ud. con sus estudios?

10. ¿Cuántas veces por semana se reúne Ud. con sus amigos?

7

The Perfect Tenses

¿Cuánto sabe usted?
How Much Do You Know Already?

1. Change the present tense form voy to the present perfect.
2. Conjugate the verb escribir in the present perfect for tú.
3. How do you say *We would have eaten later* in Spanish?
4. What's the past participle of the verb romper?
5. How do you form the past participle endings for regular verbs?

The Present Perfect Tense

The Past Participle
El participio pasado

The past participle is a verb form that, in English, usually ends in -ed. For example, *worked, arrived,* as in *I have worked, I have arrived.* For most Spanish verbs, the past participle is formed as follows:

PAST PARTICIPLE FORMATION
-ar verbs drop and change endings to -ado
llamar (to call) → llamado
-er and -ir verbs drop and change endings to -ido
aprender (*to learn*) → aprendido
permitir (*to allow*) → permitido

Even the following verbs have regular past participles, although there is an accent mark over the í in oír and reír because their verb stems end in a vowel:

ser (*to be*) → sido ir (*to go*) → ido
oír (*to hear*) → oído reír (*to laugh*) → reído

The following verbs have irregular past participles ending in -to and -cho:

-to **Endings**		
abrir (*to open*)	→	abierto
cubrir (*to cover*)	→	cubierto
poner (*to put*)	→	puesto
volver (*to return*)	→	vuelto
escribir (*to write*)	→	escrito
romper (*to break*)	→	roto
morir (*to die*)	→	muerto
ver (*to see*)	→	visto
-cho **Endings**		
decir (*to say, tell*)	→	dicho
hacer (*to do, make*)	→	hecho

The past participle is used in the formation of the perfect tenses, where it remains the same regardless of person, number, or gender:

He <u>hablado</u> con ellos muchas veces. *I have spoken to them many times.*
No habían <u>hablado</u> conmigo antes. *They had not spoken to me before.*

Although past participles form part of the perfect tenses, just as they do in English, their uses vary throughout the Spanish language:

> **TIP**
> Don't forget that verbs with the same base form as the ten irregular verbs in the previous box also have the same irregular past participles:
> descubrir (*to discover*) → descrito
> revolver (*to stir*) → revuelto
> predecir (*to predict*) → predicho

- With the passive voice:

    Ha sido comprado por
    su compañía.
    *It has been bought by your
    company.*

- With estar to indicate a condition:

    El motor está roto. *The engine is broken.*

- With ser or estar in an impersonal sense:

    No es permitido. *It is not permitted.*
    Todo está hecho. *Everything is done.*

LA PRÁCTICA 1

Fill in the correct verb infinitive and its past participle:

1. vimos   ver   visto _____

2. pondría _____ _____

3. voy _____ _____

4. tuve _____ _____

5. devuelves _____ _____

6. soy _____ _____

7. escribían _____ _____

8. hicimos _____ _____

9. estuve _____ _____

10. oigo _____ _____

Forming the Present Perfect
Formación del perfecto de indicativo

     The perfect tenses are often referred to as *compound tenses* because they consist of more than one component. In Spanish, the present perfect tense refers to completed events in relation to the present, the same as it does in English. It is formed by the present tense of haber (*to have*) plus the past participle:

		Hablar *(to speak)*	Comer *(to eat)*	Escribir *(to write)*
(yo)	he	hablado	comido	escrito
(tú)	has	hablado	comido	escrito
(él, ella, Ud.)	ha	hablado	comido	escrito
(nosotros)	hemos	hablado	comido	escrito
(vosotros)	habéis	hablado	comido	escrito
(ellos, ellas, Uds.)	han	hablado	comido	escrito

LA PRÁCTICA 2

Change these past tense verbs to the present perfect:

1. vimos   hemos visto

2. puse _____

3. tenías _____

4. pudieron _____

5. estaban _____

6. abrí _____

7. dijeron _____

8. escribiste _____

9. rompieron _____

10. vivíamos _____

Using the Present Perfect
Empleo del perfecto de indicativo

      The perfect tenses express a state or action as having been completed at the time expressed by the verb haber. The present perfect tense is often used in Spanish to report a single finished act or to ask about completed events that relate to present time.

> ¿Cuántos libros has leído?
> *How many books have you read?*
> He leído varios en español.
> *I've read several in Spanish.*

EJEMPLOS

Ya hemos comido las verduras.
¿Has encontrado la cartera?
No hemos visto el río Grande.

We've already eaten the vegetables.
Have you found the wallet?
We haven't seen the Río Grande.

> **TIP**
> To form a question in the perfect tenses, the subject pronoun follows the past participle; for example, ¿Dónde has trabajado tú? (*Where have you worked?*). In the negative, the word no precedes the forms of the verb haber (e.g., No hemos comenzado. [*We haven't begun.*]). Also, whenever object pronouns are used with the present perfect, they precede the forms of the verb haber (e.g., Ellos me lo han dicho. [*They have told me about it.*]).

LA PRÁCTICA 3

Translate these sentences into Spanish:

1. *What have they done?* ¿Qué han hecho?

2. *Have you left* (fam. sing.)? _____

3. *Has he called?* _____

4. *Where have they been?* _____

5. *What has she broken?* _____

6. *How much have we read?* _____

7. *How many have you seen* (form. pl.)? _____

8. *Why has it died?* _____

9. *Who has written?* _____

10. *What have they said?* _____

The Past Perfect Tense

Forming the Past Perfect
Formación del pluscuamperfecto de indicativo

The past perfect (or pluperfect) tense is formed by placing the imperfect tense of the verb **haber** before the past participle of the main verb. It is similar in both Spanish and English in that it expresses *had done something*:

		Hablar *(to speak)*	Comer *(to eat)*	Escribir *(to write)*
(yo)	había	hablado	comido	escrito
(tú)	habías	hablado	comido	escrito
(él, ella, Ud.)	había	hablado	comido	escrito
(nosotros)	habíamos	hablado	comido	escrito
(vosotros)	habíais	hablado	comido	escrito
(ellos, ellas, Uds.)	habían	hablado	comido	escrito

LA PRÁCTICA 4

Change these present tense verb forms to the past perfect tense:

1. come   había comido
2. devuelvo   _____
3. dicen   _____
4. escribimos   _____
5. es   _____
6. pongo   _____
7. haces   _____
8. descubren   _____
9. venimos   _____
10. veo   _____

Using the Past Perfect
Empleo del pluscuamperfecto de indicativo

The past perfect tense is used to describe a past action that took place before some other past action, and was already complete at the time of that action.

> Cuando llegamos, ellos no habían comido todavía.
> *When we arrived, they had not eaten yet.*

EJEMPLOS

> No habíamos visitado las ruinas hasta este viaje.
> *We had not visited the ruins until this trip.*

> ¿Habías terminado el proyecto cuando llegó el profesor?
> *Had you finished the project when the professor arrived?*

> Pregunté a mi padre si ya había prendido las luces.
> *I asked my father if he already had turned on the lights.*

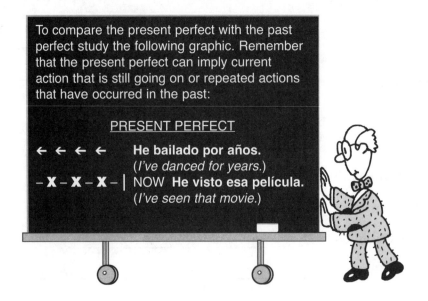

To compare the present perfect with the past perfect study the following graphic. Remember that the present perfect can imply current action that is still going on or repeated actions that have occurred in the past:

PRESENT PERFECT

← ← ← ←   **He bailado por años.**
               (*I've danced for years.*)
– **X** – **X** – **X** – | NOW **He visto esa película.**
               (*I've seen that movie.*)

TIP

Although seldom used, the preterit perfect tense in Spanish may replace the preterit indicative. All the forms of haber are in the preterit:

After they'd eaten,
they went to work.
{
   Después de que <u>hubieron comido</u>, ellos fueron al trabajo.

   Después de que <u>comieron</u>, ellos fueron al trabajo.
}

Notice how the past perfect is usually used together with a second verb in the simple past tense:

Ya habíamos salido cuando ella <u>llamó</u>.
We had already left when she called.

Carolina <u>dijo</u> que había hablado contigo.
Carolina said that she had spoken with you.

The past perfect, however, expresses action that was already completed before a specific time in the past.

PAST PERFECT

Dijo que había comido antes de la clase.
(*He said he'd eaten before class.*)
– X – X – X – |← ← ← | NOW

LA PRÁCTICA 5

Follow the pattern given as you practice the past perfect tense:

1. ¿Estudiaron? No, habían estudiado antes.

2. ¿Escribió? _____

3. ¿Estacionaron? _____

4. ¿Comió? _____

5. ¿Volvieron? _____

6. ¿Salió? _____

7. ¿Llamaron? _____

8. ¿Se despertó? _____

9. ¿Trabajaron? _____

10. ¿Se fue? _____

The Future Perfect Tense

Forming the Future Perfect
La formación del futuro perfecto

The future perfect tense refers to an event that will be completed before a specific time or before another event in the future. It is formed by placing the future tense of the verb haber before the past participle of the main verb:

		Hablar (to speak)	Comer (to eat)	Escribir (to write)
(yo)	habré	hablado	comido	escrito
(tú)	habrás	hablado	comido	escrito
(él, ella, Ud.)	habrá	hablado	comido	escrito
(nosotros)	habremos	hablado	comido	escrito
(vosotros)	habréis	hablado	comido	escrito
(ellos, ellas, Uds.)	habrán	hablado	comido	escrito

LA PRÁCTICA 6

Change these verb forms in the future tense to the future perfect:

1. tendré   <u>habré tenido</u>
2. iremos
3. contará
4. escribirán
5. verás
6. dire
7. abriremos
8. pondrán
9. podrá
10. morirá

Using the Future Perfect
Empleo del futuro perfecto

     Although seldom heard in everyday conversation, the future perfect tense is primarily used to describe an action that will take place before a specific time in the future or before some other future action. Like all perfect tenses, the action will already be completed.

> El Sr. García <u>habrá firmado</u> el contrato para las tres.
> *Mr. García will have signed the contract before three o'clock.*

> Todo lo <u>habré arreglado</u> antes de irme.
> *I will have arranged everything before leaving.*

     The future perfect tense may also be used to express probability in past time, which makes it similar in meaning to the preterit or the present perfect tense:

> ¿Qué <u>habrá ocurrido</u> con Juan? (¿Qué pasó con Juan?)
> *What (may have) happened to Juan?*

> <u>Habrá tenido</u> un accidente. (Probablemente tuvo un accidente.)
> *(Maybe) he had an accident.*

EJEMPLOS

Habré viajado a Paraguay antes de diciembre.
I will have traveled to Paraguay before December.

Habrán vendido la casa antes de mudarse.
They will have sold the house before moving.

Son las dos en Lima y mi familia se habrá acostado.
It's two o'clock in Lima, and my family probably went to bed.

- Haber + past participle forms the perfect infinitive, which is usually used as a complement to some verbs or after a preposition:

  Mi hermano es mucho más fuerte por haber tomado sus vitaminas.
  My brother is much stronger for having taken his vitamins.

- The construction deber de + perfect infinitive is used to express probability in place of the future perfect tense:

  Sandra <u>debe de haber perdido</u>
     las llaves.
  Sandra <u>habrá perdido</u>
     las llaves.
  } *Sandra must have (probably) lost the keys.*

LA PRÁCTICA 7

Change each verb in parentheses to the future perfect tense:

1. Si llegamos tarde, (irse) ella.   se habrá ido

2. No te preocupes; todo lo (comprar) nosotros. _____

3. ¿(quedarse) ellos en algún hotel? _____

4. Ricardo (volver) para el verano. _____

5. Ellos (terminar) de limpiar antes de las ocho. _____

6. Yo (graduarse) para el próximo año. _____

7. (Llegar) el correo. _____

8. Tina y yo (hacer) la tarea antes de salir. _____

9. ¿(Ganar) el premio tú? _____

10. Nosotros (poner) el árbol antes de la Navidad. _____

The Conditional Perfect Tense

Forming the Conditional Perfect
Formación del potencial compuesto

The conditional perfect tense in Spanish expresses the concept of *would have done something*. It is formed by placing the conditional tense of the verb **haber** before the past participle of the main verb:

		Hablar *(to speak)*	Comer *(to eat)*	Escribir *(to write)*
(yo)	habría	hablado	comido	escrito
(tú)	habrías	hablado	comido	escrito
(él, ella, Ud.)	habría	hablado	comido	escrito
(nosotros)	habríamos	hablado	comido	escrito
(vosotros)	habríais	hablado	comido	escrito
(ellos, ellas, Uds.)	habrían	hablado	comido	escrito

LA PRÁCTICA 8

Change these conditional verb forms to the conditional perfect:

1. pondríamos   _habríamos puesto_____

2. vendría   _____

3. romperías   _____

4. dirían   _____

5. haríamos   _____

6. verías   _____

7. abriría   _____

8. cubrirían   _____

9. podría   _____

10. escribirías   _____

Using the Conditional Perfect
Empleo del potencial compuesto

The conditional perfect tense describes events that would have happened in the past. The circumstances (or conditions) can either be stated or implied:

Me dijeron que lo <u>habrían hecho</u>.
They told me that they would have done it.

Yo <u>habría comido</u> todo el helado.
I would have eaten all the ice cream.

The conditional perfect is also used to express probability or conjecture about a completed event from the past perspective:

<u>Habría dejado</u> mensajes en mi teléfono celular.
He probably had left messages on my cell phone.

<u>Habrían bailado</u> Salsa toda la noche.
They probably had danced the Salsa all night.

The conditional perfect is often used with hypothetical situations that would have taken place in the past if certain conditions—expressed in the imperfect subjunctive—had been met:

Si yo hubiera tenido un carro, <u>habría pasado</u> mis vacaciones en la playa.
If I would have had a car, I would have spent my vacation at the beach.

> **TIP**
> The present perfect form of the word hay is ha(n) habido (*there has* or *have been*):
> Ha habido una serie de tormentas en esta región.
> *There have been a series of storms in this region.*
>
> The past perfect form of hay is había(n) habido (*there had been*):
> Antes del tornado, habían habido tormentas en esta región.
> *Before the tornado, there had been a series of storms in this region.*
>
> The future perfect form of hay is habrá(n) habido (*there will have been*):
> Habrá habido mucho tráfico antes del partido.
> *There will have been a lot of traffic before the game.*
>
> And the conditional perfect form of hay is habría(n) habido (*there would have been*):
> Habría habido música en la fiesta, pero no pude encontrar una banda.
> *There would have been music at the party, but I couldn't find a band.*

EJEMPLOS

Me dijeron que <u>habrían traído</u> la comida, pero no hubo mucho tiempo. *They told me they would have brought the food, but there wasn't much time.*

<u>Habrían sido</u> las seis cuando ellos se fueron.
It was probably six o'clock when they left.

Sé que tú no lo <u>habrías hecho</u> solo.
I know that you would not have done it alone.

Si hubiéramos tenido el dinero, lo <u>habríamos comprado</u>.
If we would have had the money, we would have bought it.

LA PRÁCTICA 9

Use the key words to form sentences in the conditional perfect tense:

1. yo/ visitar a mis amigos   Habría visitado a mis amigos.

2. Nosotros/ volver a la casa _____

3. Él/ vivir muchos años más _____

4. Tú/ hacer el trabajo _____

5. Ellos/ creer la historia _____

6. Julio y yo/ visitar el museo _____

7. Yo/ conocer a mucha gente _____

8. Ella/ jugar al golf _____

9. Los niños/ beber la leche _____

10. Tú/ poner la música _____

What were you thinking about doing today? Follow the pattern as you practice the conditional perfect tense:

Yo pensaba que para hoy... (*I was thinking that for today...*)

11. (estudiar) para el examen   habría estudiado   (*I would study*)

12. (hablar) con mi familia _____

13. (llegar) más temprano _____

14. (salir) a las ocho   _____

15. (ver) un DVD   _____

16. (tomar) una cerveza   _____

17. (comprar) la computadora   _____

18. (ponerse) el abrigo   _____

19. (leer) el capítulo dos   _____

20. (preparar) el almuerzo   _____

First name the correct tense in each sentence (present, past, future, or conditional perfect) and then translate it into English.

21. Habían dado el dinero al vendedor ayer.   ***Past perfect***

   They had given the money to the salesman before.

22. Siempre hemos sido amigos.   _____

23. No habrían comido la carne.   _____

24. Cuando comience la clase, ya habré estudiado.   _____

25. ¿Cuándo has visto a las chicas?   _____

26. Me dijeron que ella ya había abierto las ventanas.   _____

27. Habrán ido a Colorado.   _____

28. Sin ayuda médica, él habría muerto antes.   _____

29. ¿Qué habrá sido de mis amigos en California?   _____

30. Ella no había desayunado cuando salió.   _____

CROSSWORD 5

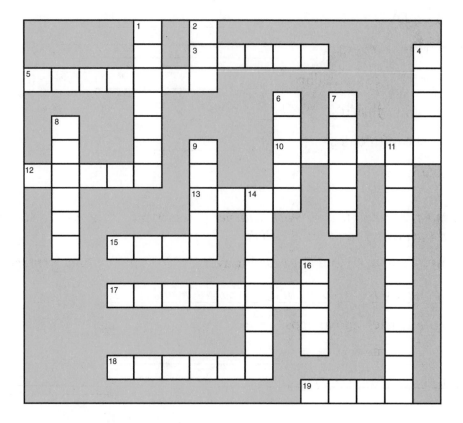

Translate these into Spanish:

Across
3. said
5. written
10. believed
12. read
13. been
15. given
17. covered
18. had
19. heard

Down
1. open
2. gone
4. fried
6. done
7. put
8. returned
9. seen
11. discovered
14. described
16. broken

8

The Progressive Tenses

The Present Participle

Forming the Present Participle
Formación del gerundio

The present participle in Spanish is much like the *-ing* verb construction in English. It is formed by dropping the ending and adding -ando to the stem of -ar verbs and -iendo to the stems of -er and -ir verbs:

INFINITIVE	PRESENT PARTICIPLE	
hablar	hablando	*speaking*
comer	comiendo	*eating*
escribir	escribiendo	*writing*

The present participles of the following verbs are irregular in Spanish, because the letter i of the participial ending must change to y when it is between two vowels:

INFINITIVE	PRESENT PARTICIPLE	
caer	cayendo	*falling*
creer	creyendo	*believing*
leer	leyendo	*reading*
oír	oyendo	*hearing*
traer	trayendo	*bringing*

Present participles of vowel-changing -ir verbs have the same stem as the third person singular of the preterit tense:

INFINITIVE	PRETERITE	PRESENT PARTICIPLE
sentir	sintió	sintiendo *(feeling)*
servir	sirvió	sirviendo *(serving)*
dormir	durmió	durmiendo *(sleeping)*
morir	murió	muriendo *(dying)*

Two completely irregular present participles that you must memorize are:

ir	➔	yendo	*going*
poder	➔	pudiendo	*being able to*

> **TIP**
> When reflexive and object pronouns follow the present participle, they are attached in writing. The gerund ending then includes an accent mark over the a or e:
> preguntándole *asking him*
> bañándonos *bathing ourselves*
> leyéndolas *reading them*

LA PRÁCTICA 1

Change these infinitives to the gerund form:

1. caer   cayendo
2. servir   _____
3. leer   _____
4. decir   _____
5. poder   _____

6. sentir   _____

7. creer   _____

8. morir   _____

9. traer   _____

10. oír   _____

11. corregir   _____

12. leer   _____

13. medir   _____

14. dormir   _____

15. repetir   _____

Using the Present Participle
Empleo del gerundio

The present participle is generally used with the verb estar to express continued action in the PROGRESSIVE TENSES:

Está llamando.	*He's calling.*
Estábamos aprendiendo.	*We were learning.*
Estaré escribiendo.	*I'll be writing.*

The present participle is sometimes used after a verb to describe the action of that verb:

Los niños salieron gritando.	*The children left screaming.*
María entró sonriendo.	*María entered smiling.*

The present participle is also used as a gerund phrase to introduce subordinate clauses that imply *by, if, because, when,* or *while*:

Caminando por el camino, encontré un billete de cinco dólares.
(While) walking along the road, I found a five-dollar bill.

EJEMPLOS

Fidel está jugando tenis con Noé.	*Fidel is playing tennis with Noe.*
El perro se fue corriendo.	*The dog took off running.*
Leyendo, se aprende mucho.	*One learns a lot (by) reading.*

The following verbs give a progressive sense or meaning to the action of the present participle:

Ir	Voy limpiando.	*I'm cleaning little by little.*
Seguir	Sigue trabajando.	*He's continuing to work.*
Andar	Andamos buscando.	*We're still looking.*

With verbs like ver, oír, mirar, and escuchar, either the infinitive or the present participle can be used:

Escuchamos <u>bailar</u> a los vecinos.

Escuchamos a los vecinos <u>bailando</u>. $\Big\}$ *We heard the neighbors dancing.*

- The present participle can never be used as an adjective or a noun, as in English:

  The man sitting in the armchair is my grandfather.
  El señor sentado en el sillón es mi abuelo.

- Nor can it be used with the verb ser:

  My favorite sport is riding bikes.
  Mi pasatiempo favorito es
    andar en bicicleta.

- In English, the present participle is used to express an action or condition after a preposition. In Spanish, the infinitive is used instead:

  After taking her medication, Julia went to bed.
  Después de tomar su medicina, Julia se acostó.

> **TIP**
> The present participle form of haber is habiendo (*having*):
> Habiendo tenido dolor de cabeza por horas, Mario se quedó en casa.
> *Having had a headache for hours, Mario stayed home.*

LA PRÁCTICA 2

Change these past participles to present participles:

1. tenido   teniendo

2. visto   _____

3. hecho   _____

4. abierto   _____

5. ido   _____

6. dicho   _____

7. leído   _____

8. dormido   _____

9. puesto   _____

10. vuelto   _____

The Progressive Tenses

Forming the Progressive Tenses
Formación de los tiempos durativos

The progressive tenses emphasize the fact that an action is in progress and, therefore, presents a more vivid picture. It is formed by placing the present, past, future, and conditional tenses of the verb estar before the present participle of the main verb:

PROGRESSIVE TENSES		
Estoy corriendo	→	*I am running*
Estaba corriendo	→	*I was running*
Estuve corriendo	→	*I was running*
Estaré corriendo	→	*I will be running*
Estaría corriendo	→	*I would be running*

In the progressive tenses, the reflexive or pronoun object may either precede the verb estar or be attached to the present participle:

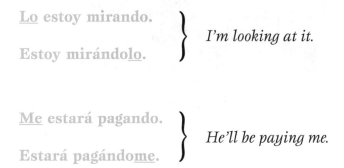

Lo estoy mirando.

Estoy mirándolo.
> *I'm looking at it.*

Me estará pagando.

Estará pagándome.
> *He'll be paying me.*

LA PRÁCTICA 3

Change each word to a progressive tense form:

1. trabajaba   estaba trabajando

2. beberé   _____

3. vimos   _____

4. pagarían   _____

5. salías   _____

6. pondrán   _____

7. tomaba   _____

8. hiciste   _____

9. dibujarán   _____

10. iríamos   _____

Using the Progressive Tenses
Empleo de los tiempos durativos

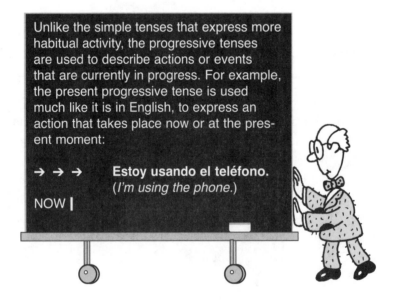

Unlike the simple tenses that express more habitual activity, the progressive tenses are used to describe actions or events that are currently in progress. For example, the present progressive tense is used much like it is in English, to express an action that takes place now or at the present moment:

→ → →   **Estoy usando el teléfono.**
           (*I'm using the phone.*)

NOW |

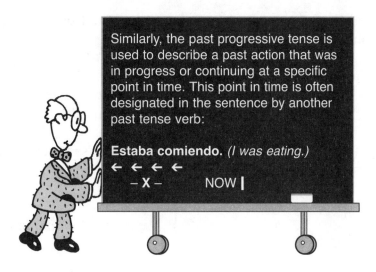

Similarly, the past progressive tense is used to describe a past action that was in progress or continuing at a specific point in time. This point in time is often designated in the sentence by another past tense verb:

Estaba comiendo. *(I was eating.)*

← ← ← ←
– X –　　　　　NOW |

Notice how it compares to the present indicative:

Ellos están cantando.	*They are singing.*	(now)
Ellos cantan.	*They sing.*	(generally)

Esteban_estaba practicando_ cuando todos _entraron_ al salón de clases.
Estéban was practicing when they all entered the classroom.

A progressive tense is also used to express an action that is temporary, or perhaps suggests a sudden change.

Estábamos cocinando.	*We were cooking.*
Está lloviendo.	*It's raining.*

EJEMPLOS

La estamos ayudando con sus estudios.
We're helping her with her studies.

Estaban jugando fútbol cuando llamaste.
They were playing soccer when you called.

Mireya estará cenando a las ocho.
Mireya will be having dinner at eight.

Unlike English, the present progressive tense is not used to express a future action in Spanish:

Salgo mañana.
Saldré mañana.   } *I'm leaving tomorrow.* ("Estoy saliendo
Voy a salir mañana.   mañana" is not used.)

The imperfect tense of a verb often expresses the same meaning as the past imperfect progressive:

<u>Nadábamos</u> en la nueva piscina.

                                      } *We were swimming in the new pool.*

<u>Estábamos nadando</u> en la nueva
    piscina.

The verb estar determines when and how the future and conditional progressives describe an action in progress:

¿<u>Estará durmiendo</u> en el sofá?
Could he be sleeping on the couch?

<u>Estaríamos jugando</u>, pero no tenemos
    una pelota.
We would be playing, but we don't have a ball.

> **TIP**
> The preterit progressive tense is used to express an action that was in progress but is now complete:
> Estuve pintando la casa hasta que empezó a llover.
> *I was painting the house until it began to rain.*

Other tenses of the verb estar may be used with a present participle to express actions at various points in time:

<u>Hemos estado usando</u> la nueva computadora en la oficina.
We have been using the new computer in the office.

<u>Habría estado fumando</u>, pero le quitamos sus cigarrillos.
He would have been smoking, but we took away his cigarettes.

LA PRÁCTICA 4

Change these simple tense sentences to the progressive:

1. Lo permitmos. _____Lo estamos permitiendo._____

2. ¿Te lavarás las manos? _____

3. Jugaban con los niños. _____

4. ¿Nieva? _____

5. Cenaré a las siete. _____

6. ¿Qué te hacían? _____

7. Oirían música. _____

8. Me miraron cuando entré. _____

9. Sacarán los boletos. _____

10. No me siento bien. _____

Translate these sentences into Spanish:

11. *He was running in the park.* _____Estaba corriendo en el parque._____

12. *I am doing the job.* _____

13. *They will be arriving at four o'clock.* _____

14. *She wouldn't be walking to school.* _____

15. *Are you bathing?* (inf. sing.) _____

16. *Who will be calling?* _____

17. *We would be taking the bus.* _____

18. *The lamp is falling!* _____

19. *What were you saying?* (form. sing.) _____

20. *I'm going to bed now.* _____

POR SU CUENTA

¿Qué estaba haciendo anoche? Reply using progressive tenses.

1. ¿Estaba comiendo?

2. ¿Estaba trabajando?

3. ¿Estaba mirando televisión?

4. ¿Estaba practicando un deporte?

5. ¿Estaba usando la computadora?

EL REPASO

Follow the instructions as you review material from each chapter:

Chapter One: Write the complete Spanish alphabet.

Chapter Two: Name three different kinds of sentences.

Chapter Three: List five irregular verbs in the present tense.

Chapter Four: How is the imperfect different from the preterit?

Chapter Five: When do you use the conditional tense?

Chapter Six: Identify and conjugate three reflexive verbs.

Chapter Seven: Use the past perfect tense in a sentence.

Chapter Eight: Explain the formation of the progressive tenses.

CROSSWORD 6

Translate these into Spanish:

Across
2. dying
4. asking for
6. playing
8. serving
9. hearing
12. opening
14. singing
15. sleeping
16. feeling
17. going
18. running

Down
1. believing
3. using
5. saying
7. asking
8. smiling
10. reading
11. repeating
13. seeing
14. falling

9

The Passive and Impersonal Constructions

¿Cuánto sabe usted?
How Much Do You Know Already?

1. Change this sentence to the passive voice: Ella escribió una carta.

2. Create a passive sentence with the phrase Se vende.

3. How do you say *The books were lost by them* in Spanish?

4. Express the sentence *It was turned off* two different ways in Spanish.

5. What does Se vive para bailar mean in English?

Forming and Using the Passive Voice
Formación y uso de la voz pasiva

     In both Spanish and English, there is the ACTIVE VOICE in which the subject does the acting, and the PASSIVE VOICE, in which the subject is acted upon by an agent or doer of the action. The passive voice in Spanish is formed with the verb ser + past participle:

ACTIVE VOICE	PASSIVE VOICE
Ellos <u>sirvieron</u> el desayuno.	El desayuno <u>será servido</u> por ellos.
They served breakfast.	*Breakfast will be served by them.*

    The passive voice focuses on the direct object of the sentence instead of the performer of the action. In a sense, the direct object becomes the subject:

El *país* <u>fue descubierto</u> por los españoles.
The country was discovered by the Spanish.

EJEMPLOS

El alcalde fue admirado por el pueblo.
The mayor was admired by the town.

Las puertas serán abiertas por la dueña.
The doors will be opened by the owner.

Mi tío ha sido ayudado por mis hermanas.
My aunt has been helped by my sisters.

In the passive construction, the past participle and the subject must agree in number and gender. The agent phrase is usually introduced by the word por:

La escena <u>fue pintada por</u> un artista famoso.
The scene was painted by a famous artist.

Los criminales <u>fueron arrestados por</u> la policía.
The criminals were arrested by the police.

In the passive voice, all tenses of the verb ser are conjugated normally. However, the verb is in the preterit when referring to past time:

Los documentos <u>son recibidos</u> por el funcionario.
The documents are received by the government official.

Los documentos fueron recibidos.
  (*were received*)
Los documentos serán recibidos.
  (*will be received*)
Los documentos han sido recibidos.
  (*have been received*)

> **TIP**
> Estar can never replace ser in a passive construction. Estar + past participle expresses a description instead of an action:
> La lámpara <u>estuvo prendida.</u>
> *The lamp was (turned) on.*
> La lámpara <u>fue prendida</u> por Eva.
> *The lamp was turned on by Eva.*

LA PRÁCTICA 1

Change these sentences from the active voice to the passive:

1. El autor escribió un nuevo libro.   El libro fue escrito por el autor.

2. Nosotros hemos cambiado el número.   _____

3. El perro atacará al gato.   _____

4. El cartero ha perdido la carta.   _____

5. Ellas preparan la comida.   _____

6. Delia ama a Raymundo.   _____

7. Todos admiran a los soldados.   _____

8. La vecina cerró las ventanas.   _____

9. Los niños tocarán los instrumentos.   _____

10. El camión recoge la basura.   _____

_____

Passive Sentences With *se*
Oraciones pasivas con se

The reflexive verb form is often used as a substitute for the passive voice when the agent is not expressed. The verb is either in the third person singular or plural:

Se vende licor en el restaurante.   *Liquor is sold at the restaurant.*
Se venden flores en el mercado.   *Flowers are sold at the market.*

Passive sentences with se can be translated in a variety of ways:

Se habla español aquí.   { *They speak Spanish here.*
Spanish is spoken here.
People speak Spanish here. }

Se sabe la razón.   { *You know the reason.*
The reason is known.
One knows the reason. }

Notice that in constructions with se, the subject generally follows the verb:

Se dieron los regalos.   *Gifts were given.*

Some reflexive verbs must add a subject to the third person singular in order to express the passive voice:

Uno se acuesta tarde en París.
One goes to bed late in Paris.

Uno se divierte mucho en las montañas.
One has a lot of fun in the mountains.

La gente (*people*) is also used with a third person singular verb to identify the indefinite subject in a passive construction:

La gente se queda para ver la película.
People stay in order to see the movie.

The third person plural of a verb sometimes expresses a passive meaning by not referring to the actual subject:

> Le <u>quitaron</u> su pasaporte.
> *His passport was taken away.*
> <u>Envían</u> los cheques por correo.
> *The checks are sent by mail.*

And in the following construction with intransitive verbs, passive sentences are only used in the third person singular:

> <u>Se entra</u> por allí.   *You enter through there.*
> <u>Se corre</u> en la arena.   *People run on the sand.*
> <u>Se vive</u> para trabajar.   *One lives to work.*

LA PRÁCTICA 2

Translate these sentences into passive constructions with se:

1. *The room will get warm.*   <u>Se calentará el cuarto.</u>

2. *Two houses were built.*   _____

3. *English is spoken here.*   _____

4. *Lunch will be served at twelve.*   _____

5. *One never knows.*   _____

6. *The book was published in Mexico.*   _____

7. *A message will be sent.*   _____

8. *You go out this way.*   _____

9. *The bill has been paid.*   _____

10. *Houses are sold everywhere.*   _____

10

The Subjunctive

¿Cuánto sabe usted?

How Much Do You Know Already?

1. Conjugate the verb pedir in the present subjunctive.

2. How do you say *If she'd study, she'd pass the test* in Spanish?

3. Conjugate the verb decir in the imperfect subjunctive.

4. How do you form the present perfect subjunctive?

5. Use the subjunctive to say *I need someone who can work nights.*

The Present Subjunctive

Regular Verbs
Verbos regulares

Unlike the verb tenses in Spanish, which indicate when an action takes place, the subjunctive mood expresses important changes in the speaker's attitude or emotion. To form the present subjunctive in regular verbs, change the vowel a of the present indicative to e in -ar verbs, and the vowels e and i to a in -er and -ir verbs:

	Hablar (to speak)	Comer (to eat)	Escribir (to write)
(yo)	hable	coma	escriba
(tú)	hables	comas	escribas
(él, ella, Ud.)	hable	coma	escriba
(nosotros)	hablemos	comamos	escribamos
(vosotros)	habléis	comáis	escribáis
(ellos, ellas, Uds.)	hablen	coman	escriban

EJEMPLOS

Dudo que <u>hablen</u> español.	*I doubt they speak Spanish.*
Esperamos que <u>coma</u> la ensalada.	*We hope she eats the salad.*
Es importante que <u>escribas</u> rápido.	*It's important you write quickly.*

Whenever the -ar, -er, or -ir verb is stem-changing in the present indicative, the present subjunctive will usually show the same changes:

(cerrar) Espero que *cierren* las puertas.	*I hope they close the doors.*
(volver) Nos encanta que *vuelvas* hoy.	*We're happy you return today.*
(mentir) Le acoseja que no *mienta*.	*He suggests that you don't lie.*
(pedir) Prefiero que se lo *pida* a él.	*I prefer that you ask him for it.*

However, although morir and dormir have the o → ue stem change, there is a u in the first person and second person plural forms (e.g., muera, mueras, muera, muramos, muráis, mueran).

In the present subjunctive, most verbs that end in -iar or -uar have an accent mark on the í or ú in all forms but the first person plural:

Vaciar *(to empty)*

vacíe, vacíes, vacíe, vaciemos, vaciéis, vacíen

Graduar *(to graduate)*

gradúe, gradúes, gradúe, graduemos, graduéis, gradúen

> **TIP**
> Notice that the first person and third person singular forms are the same for all regular verbs in the present subjunctive. Also notice that regular -er and -ir verbs have the exact same endings.

LA PRÁCTICA 1

Write the correct form of the present subjunctive on the line provided:

1. Quiero que (tú/estudiar) idiomas. ___estudies_____

2. Le aconsejo que (él/pensar) en el futuro. _____

3. Espero que (ellas/cerrar) las ventanas. _____

4. Me encanta que (Ud./vivir) cerca de aquí. _____

5. Prefiero que (ella/enviar) el paquete. _____

6. Ojalá que (Uds./quedarse) en casa. _____

7. No creo que (yo/volver) muy pronto. _____

8. Me alegra que (ellos/entender) el inglés. _____

9. Necesito que (tú/dormir) en el dormitorio. _____

10. Es necesario que (Uds./seguir) las leyes. _____

Irregular Verbs
Verbos irregulares

If the verb is irregular in the simple present tense, the present subjunctive generally shows the same irregularities. Most irregularities in the present subjunctive occur in -er and -ir verbs, and all have the same stem as that of the first person singular in the present indicative:

Conocer (conozco)
conozca, conozcas, conozca, conozcamos, conozcáis, conozcan

Conducir (conduzco)
conduzca, conduzcas, conduzca, conduzcamos, conduzcáis, conduzcan

Caber (quepo)
quepa, quepas, quepa, quepamos, quepáis, quepan

Construir (construyo)
construya, construyas, construya, construyamos, construyáis, construyan

Ver (veo)
vea, veas, vea, veamos, veáis, vean

Other irregular verbs so conjugated are parecer (*to seem*), destruir (*to destroy*), nacer (*to be born*), traducir (*to translate*), crecer (*to grow*).

The following all have g changes in the irregular verb stem. The present indicative yo form is in parentheses:

Caer (caigo)	caiga, caigas, caiga, caigamos, caigáis caigan
Decir (digo)	diga, digas, diga, digamos, digáis, digan
Hacer (hago)	haga, hagas, haga, hagamos, hagáis, hagan
Oír (oigo)	oiga, oigas, oiga, oigamos, oigáis, oigan
Poner (pongo)	ponga, pongas, ponga, pongamos, pongáis, pongan
Salir (salgo)	salga, salgas, salga, salgamos, salgáis, salgan
Tener (tengo)	tenga, tengas, tenga, tengamos, tengáis, tengan
Traer (traigo)	traiga, traigas, traiga, traigamos, traigáis, traigan
Venir (vengo)	venga, vengas, venga, vengamos, vengáis, vengan

Although their endings are regular, the stems of these verbs are irregular in the present subjunctive and therefore must be learned separately:

Haber (*to have*)	haya, hayas, haya, hayamos, hayáis, hayan
Ir (*to go*)	vaya, vayas, vaya, vayamos, vayáis, vayan
Saber (*to know*)	sepa, sepas, sepa, sepamos, sepáis, sepan
Ser (*to be*)	sea, seas, sea, seamos, seáis, sean

The verbs dar and estar are considered irregular because of the accent marks. The first and third person singular of dar have accents to differentiate them from the preposition de:

Dar	dé, des, dé, demos, deis, den
Estar	esté, estés, esté, estemos, estéis, estén

EJEMPLOS

Quiero que conozcas a mi familia.	*I want you to know my family.*
Insistimos en que nos veas.	*We insist that you see us.*
Espera que construyan la pared.	*She hopes that they build the wall.*
Le exigen que lo haga.	*They demand that he does it.*
Dudamos que tenga veinte años.	*We doubt she is twenty years old.*
Es importante que sepan la verdad.	*It's important they know the truth.*
Sugiero que sea más estudioso.	*I suggest that you be more studious.*
Prefiere que le demos todo.	*He prefers that we give it all to him.*

LA PRÁCTICA 2

Change each present tense indicative form to the subjunctive:

1. él va   _vaya_

2. Uds. parecen   _____

3. tú sales   _____

4. ella oye   _____

5. ellos están   _____

6. yo digo   _____

7. nosotros conducimos   _____

8. Ud. viene   _____

9. él cae   _____

10. alguién es   _____

Verbs with Spelling Changes
Verbos con cambios de deletreo

In the present subjunctive, -ar verbs have three basic spelling changes in the verb stem:

- G → GU

    PEGAR (*to hit, to stick*)   Esperamos que pegue a la pelota.

- C → QU

    PESCAR (*to fish*)   Me alegro que pesquen allí.

- Z → C

    EMPEZAR (*to begin*)   Quiero que empecemos a las dos.

Other verbs that undergo such spelling changes are agregar (*to add*), entregar (*to deliver*), pagar (*to pay*), pecar (*to sin*), masticar (*to chew*), sacar (*to remove*), comenzar (*to begin*), lanzar (*to throw*), rezar (*to pray*).

Note that -er and -ir verbs also have three basic spelling changes in the present subjunctive:

- G → J

    RECOGER (*to pick up*)   Es importante que recojamos la basura.

- GU → G

    SEGUIR (*to follow*)   Es necesario que siga el camino.

- C → Z

    VENCER (*to conquer*)   Quizás venzan sus problemas.

Other such verbs are encoger (*to shrink*), proteger (*to protect*), escoger (*to choose*), perseguir (*to chase*), distinguir (*to distinguish*), conseguir (*to obtain*), torcer (*to twist*), convencer (*to convince*), ejercer (*to exercise*).

Spelling changes such as C → Z do not affect irregular verbs in the present subjunctive (e.g., hacer: hago, hagas, etc.). Also, -ar verbs with stems ending in j do not change to g before the letter e (e.g., empujar: empuje, empujes, etc.).

LA PRÁCTICA 3

Fill in the blanks with the correct forms of the present subjunctive:

	Singular	Plural
1. REZAR	rece, reces, rece	recemos, recéis, recen
2. PROTEGER		
3. SACAR		
4. PERSEGUIR		
5. PAGAR		
6. CONVENCER		

	Singular	*Plural*
7. ESCOGER	_____	_____
8. MASTICAR	_____	_____
9. CONSEGUIR	_____	_____
10. EMPUJAR	_____	_____

Using the Present Subjunctive
Uso del presente de subjuntivo

Unlike the indicative mood, which is based on fact and certainty, the subjunctive is used to express an action as a mere supposition, wish, or condition. It is often referred to as the "unreal" mode, used to express those delicate shades of meaning behind one's message. The basic forms of the subjunctive include the present, the present perfect, the imperfect, and the past perfect.

The present subjunctive is used extensively in Spanish, usually in dependent noun clauses introduced by the conjunction que. These dependent clauses follow main clauses that express a variety of messages—from emotion and doubt to insistence and advice:

Yo dudo	que puedan jugar bien.	*I doubt (that) <u>they</u> can play well.*
MAIN	DEPENDENT	
CLAUSE	CLAUSE	

Notice how the two clauses refer to two different subjects. If the subject of the two verbs (that of the main clause and that of the dependent clause) are one and the same, the infinitive is generally used instead of the subjunctive:

Queremos ir.	**We** want <u>to go</u>.
Queremos que tú vayas.	**We** want <u>**you**</u> <u>to go</u>.

In Spanish, the present subjunctive is used when the speaker refers to present or future time. Perhaps the most common use of the present subjunctive is after verbs of DESIRE or COMMAND:

Preferimos que él maneje despacio.	*We prefer that he drives slowly.*
Quiero que me escribas.	*I want you to write to me.*
Manda que se vayan ahora.	*She orders that they leave now.*

Other such verbs are exigir (*to demand*), desear (*to desire*), pedir (*to ask for*), insistir (*to insist*), sugerir (*to suggest*), rogar (*to beg*), avisar (*to advise*), esperar (*to hope*), aconsejar (*to counsel*), recomendar (*to recommend*), permitir (*to allow*), decir (*to tell*), proponer (*to propose*), convencer (*to convince*), impedir (*to prevent*), advertir (*to warn*), suplicar (*to implore*), dejar (*to allow*).

The present subjunctive also follows expressions that express an EMOTION or ATTITUDE:

Me sorprende que no tenga carro.	It surprises me you don't have a car.
Tememos que él llegue tarde.	We fear that he'll arrive late.
Le gusta que compremos dulces.	He likes that we're buying candy.

Other similar verbs are alegrarse (*to be happy*), tener miedo (*to fear*), lamentarse (*to mourn*), extrañarse (*to find strange*), sentir (*to be sorry*), avergonzarse (*to be ashamed*), molestarse (*to be bothered*), enojarse (*to be angry*).

The present subjunctive also follows verbs of DOUBT, DENIAL, and REFUSAL, or verbs that are used negatively or interrogatively expressing belief or understanding:

Dudamos que lo compren.	We doubt that they'll buy it.
Ella niega que lo tenga él.	She denies that he has it.
Te prohíbe que manejes el carro.	He prohibits you from driving the car.

Other such verbs are no pensar (*to not think*), no creer (*to not believe*), no imaginarse (*to not imagine*), no estar seguro (*to not be sure*).

Remember that the subjunctive never makes a direct statement or asks a direct question, because it is usually part of a dependent noun clause; that is, one that depends on the meaning of the main clause. Notice how the verb of the main clause often causes another person or thing to act (or not act) in the dependent clause:

(Yo) prefiero	que (ella) lo haga.
MAIN NOUN CLAUSE (subject)	DEPENDENT NOUN CLAUSE (object)
(*I'd prefer*	*that she does it.*)

(Nosotros) exigimos	que (tú) no manejes.
MAIN NOUN CLAUSE (subject)	DEPENDENT NOUN CLAUSE (object)
(*We order*	*that you don't drive.*)

When used with the subjunctive, the following verbs often include an indirect object pronoun:

PEDIR: Nos pide que lleguemos temprano.	She asks us to arrive early.
PERMITIR: Te permito que me llames.	I allow you to call me.
SUGERIR: Le sugirieron que se vaya.	They suggested that he leave.

Other such verbs are sorprender (*to surprise*), mandar (*to send*), extrañar (*to miss*), gustar (*to like*), decir (*to say*), convencer (*to convince*), advertir (*to warn*), aconsejar (*to advise),* exigir (*to demand*), prohibir (*to prohibit*), rogar (*to beg*).

The verb decir may be followed by a dependent clause in either the subjunctive or the indicative, when it simply reports what someone says:

Subjunctive: Nos dice que comamos mucho.   *He tells us to eat a lot.*
Indicative: Nos dice que come mucho.   *He tells us he eats a lot.*

Several verbs in Spanish can be followed either by the subjunctive in a noun clause or by an infinitive and still keep the same meaning. Notice how the indirect object pronoun is required when the verb is used with the infinitive:

Permito que compres la motocicleta.

Te permito comprar la motocicleta.

} *I give you permission to buy the motorcycle.*

Others are sugerir (*to suggest*), molestar (*to bother*), impedir (*to prevent*), prohibir (*to prohibit*), recomendar (*to recommend*).

Dejar (*to allow*), hacer (*to do, cause*), and obligar (*to force*) are a few verbs that often take a direct object pronoun before a subjunctive clause:

Lo obligan a que trabaje.   *They force him to work.*
Las dejamos que salgan.   *We allow them to leave.*

The verbs in the main clause of a sentence in the present subjunctive may be in the present, present perfect, or future tense, or in the imperative mood:

Queremos que le <u>digan</u>.   *We want you guys to tell her.*
Han dudado que <u>puedas</u> cocinar.   *They have doubted that you can cook.*
Insistiré que no <u>maneje</u>.   *I will insist that he does not drive.*
Dígale que <u>ponga</u> la silla aquí.   *Tell him to put the chair here.*

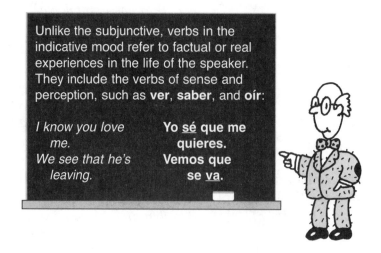

Unlike the subjunctive, verbs in the indicative mood refer to factual or real experiences in the life of the speaker. They include the verbs of sense and perception, such as **ver**, **saber**, and **oír**:

I know you love me.	**Yo <u>sé</u> que me quieres.**
We see that he's leaving.	**Vemos que se <u>va</u>.**

LA PRÁCTICA 4

Write the correct form of the present subjunctive on the line provided:

1. No creemos que el Sr. Mora (SER) de Guatemala.   _sea_

2. Ella quiere que Ud. (VENIR) a la fiesta.   _____

3. Mi mamá no permitirá que yo (IR) contigo.   _____

4. Prefiero que él (VOLVER) el sábado.   _____

5. Les ruego que ellos no lo (HACER) por mí.   _____

6. Esperamos que Joaquín (LLEGAR) a tiempo.   _____

7. Siento que tú (ESTAR) enfermo.   _____

8. No niegan que él lo (MERECER).   _____

9. Ella duda que yo (TENER) tanto dinero.   _____

10. Les pido que Uds. no (ABRIR) las ventanas.   _____

First fill in the correct present subjunctive form on the line provided, and then translate the sentence:

11. Ella no cree que él la (QUERER).   _quiera_

    She doesn't believe he loves her. _____

12. Me sorprende que tú no (ENTENDER).   _____

    _____

13. No me gusta que Uds. me (GRITAR).   _____

    _____

14. Recomiendo que ella (DORMIR) más.   _____

    _____

15. Mandamos que ellos (IRSE).   _____

    _____

16. Insisten en que nosotros (SALIR) ahora. _____

_____

17. No pienso que tú le (CONOCER). _____

_____

18. Se alegran que Ud. (PAGAR) la cuenta. _____

_____

19. ¿Desea que yo le (SERVIR) algo de comer? _____

_____

20. Nos dice que (LEER) más libros en español. _____

_____

LA PRÁCTICA 5

Each word is in the first person singular form of the present subjunctive, such as vaya, duerma, and estudie. However, all are either irregular or have some other stem or spelling change. Your task is to unscramble them.

1. enitam   mienta

2. eavlvu   _____

3. antneied   _____

4. aicag   _____

5. seacjo   _____

6. actruyons   _____

7. asequ   _____

8. aayh   _____

9. agoi   _____

10. ocnacoz   _____

11. sae   _____

12. tnaeg   _____

13. ajeroc   _____

14. pugee   _____

15. ecer   _____

16. smueqa   _____

17. apsgeir   _____

18. dpuea   _____

The Present Perfect Subjunctive
El perfecto de subjuntivo

The present perfect subjunctive is formed by combining the present subjunctive of the verb haber with the past participle.

		Hablar (to speak)	Comer (to eat)	Escribir (to write)
(yo)	haya	hablado	comido	escrito
(tú)	hayas	hablado	comido	escrito
(él, ella, Ud.)	haya	hablado	comido	escrito
(nosotros)	hayamos	hablado	comido	escrito
(vosotros)	hayáis	hablado	comido	escrito
(ellos, ellas, Uds.)	hayan	hablado	comido	escrito

The present perfect subjunctive is used in the same way that the present subjunctive is used: in a dependent clause when the main clause expresses doubt, emotion, desire, etc. The present perfect, however, indicates that the action in the dependent clause occurs <u>before</u> the action of the main clause:

TIP
The present subjunctive is also used after impersonal verbs or expressions:
Ojalá que lleguen pronto.
<u>*One can only hope*</u> *they arrive soon.*

Dudo que ellos <u>hayan llegado.</u>   *I doubt they (have) arrived.*
Esperamos que <u>hayas dormido.</u>   *We hope you (have) slept.*
No creen que <u>haya terminado.</u>   *They don't believe that he (has) finished.*

LA PRÁCTICA 6

Change these sentences from the present to the present perfect subjunctive:

1. Prefiero que no se lo diga.   Prefiero que no se lo haya dicho.

2. ¿Crees que tengas razón?   _____

3. Dudamos que llueva mucho.   _____

4. Teme que no le escriban.   _____

5. Me alegro que Ud. venga.   _____

6. Ella quiere que esperemos aquí.   _____

7. Nos sorprende que no lo sepas.   _____

8. Les pido que me llamen.   _____

9. Mandan que no lo haga.   _____

10. ¿Piensas que él sea honesto?   _____

Impersonal Expressions and the Present Subjunctive
Las expresiones impersonales y el presente de subjuntivo

Impersonal expressions in Spanish are those phrases that do not include a specific subject, such as es posible, es útil, es fantástico, etc. When these are combined with a dependent noun clause, the subjunctive is used to express a state or event that is unreal, uncertain, or not actually true:

Es posible que <u>vengan</u> mis amigos.   *It's possible my friends are coming.*
Es importante que <u>limpiemos</u> la casa.   *It's important we clean the house.*
Es dudoso que <u>regrese</u> el domingo.   *It's doubtful he'll return on Sunday.*

Impersonal expressions used with the subjunctive include those that express an emotion, opinion, or attitude:

Es malo que no tengan seguro.   *It's not good that they don't have insurance.*

Es mejor que vivamos aquí.   *It's better that we live here.*
Es una lástima que no sepas inglés.   *It's a shame that you don't know English.*

Some expressions are used with the subjunctive only when they are in the negative, implying that the action in the dependent clause is uncertain or not true:

No es cierto que   ⎫   *It isn't sure that*   ⎫
No es obvio que   ⎬ viajen.   *It isn't clear that* ⎬ *they're traveling.*
No es verdad que ⎭   *It isn't true that*   ⎭

Impersonal expressions are followed by the infinitive when the subject is not clearly identified in the dependent clause:

Es imposible montar ese caballo.
It is impossible to ride that horse.
Es imposible que yo monte ese caballo.
There's no way I'm riding that horse.

Some expressions implying doubt may be followed by either the subjunctive or the indicative in a dependent clause, depending on what the speaker is actually trying to say:

> **TIP**
> Spanish is full of expressions that work well with the subjunctive:
> más vale que (*it's better that*)
> ojalá que (*I hope that*)
> tal vez (*perhaps*)

No creo que hablan japonés.
I believe without a doubt they don't speak Japanese.
No creo que hablen japonés.
I believe, but I'm not really sure, if they speak Japanese.

Since dudar (*to doubt*) already implies uncertainty, when it is used in the negative, the verb in the dependent clause is in the indicative:

No dudo que funciona bien.   *I don't doubt it works well.*
No es dudoso que cuesta mucho.   *I don't doubt it costs a lot.*

POR SU CUENTA

Use these other impersonal expressions that are used with the subjunctive to share your feelings and opinions about any topic you desire to discuss:

Es bueno (*good*)   que vivamos en los Estados Unidos.

Es curioso (*odd*) que   _____

Es difícil (*unlikely*) que   _____

Es dudoso (*doubtful*) que   _____

Es fácil (*easy*) que   _____

Es imposible (*impossible*) que   _____

Es injusto (*wrong*) que _____

Es inútil (*useless*) que _____

Es justo (*fair*) que _____

Es necesario (*necessary*) que _____

Es peor (*worse*) que _____

Es preciso (*necessary*) que _____

Es probable (*probable*) que _____

Es raro (*strange*) que _____

Es triste (*sad*) que _____

Es útil (*useful*) que _____

LA PRÁCTICA 7

Use each impersonal expression to create a sentence in the subjunctive:

1. Los gatos corren en el jardín. (Es malo)

   Es malo que los gatos corran en el jardín. _____

2. Mis abuelos se enferman mucho. (Es triste)

   _____

3. No hace calor en el garaje. (Es raro)

   _____

4. Aprenden mucho español. (Es importante)

   _____

5. Ellos vienen al mediodía. (Es probable)

   _____

6. Puedo conducir el autobús. (No es cierto)

   _____

7. Mandamos las cartas por correo. (Es preciso)

   _____

8. Él siempre trae amigos traviesos. (Es una lástima)

_____

9. Su madre es la nueva profesora. (Es dudoso)

_____

10. Tenemos todo listo para mañana. (Ojalá)

_____

_____

The Past Subjunctive

The Imperfect Subjunctive
El imperfecto de subjuntivo

The base form of the past or imperfect subjunctive is taken from the third person plural of the preterit, which includes all stem changes and irregularities. The **-ron** ending is simply dropped and the following are added:

Trabajar **(First Form)**
(trabajaron)

(yo)	-ra	(trabajara)
(tú)	-ras	(trabajaras)
(él, ella, Ud.)	-ra	(trabajara)
(nosotros)	-ramos	(trabajáramos)
(vosotros)	-rais	(trabajarais)
(ellos, ellas, Uds.)	-ran	(trabajaran)

A second imperfect subjunctive form exists in Spanish, but it is seldom used in everyday speech. These forms are interchangeable with the previous ones:

Trabajar (Second Form) (trabajaron)		
(yo)	-se	(trabajase)
(tú)	-ses	(trabajases)
(él, ella, Ud.)	-se	(trabajase)
(nosotros)	-semos	(trabajásemos)
(vosotros)	-seis	(trabajaseis)
(ellos, ellas, Uds.)	-sen	(trabajasen)

The imperfect subjunctive is used in the same way as the present subjunctive—in dependent noun clauses following a main clause expressing anything other than a statement of fact. The verb in the main clause, however, is in the imperfect, preterit, past perfect, or conditional tense:

Pedían que lo hiciera.	They were asking him to do it.
Pidieron que lo hiciera.	They asked him to do it.
Habían pedido que lo hiciera.	They had asked him to do it.
Pedirían que lo hiciera.	They would ask him to do it.

EJEMPLOS

Queríamos que él lo hiciera.	We wanted him to do it.
Había insistido que yo manejara.	She had insisted that I drive.
Tuve miedo que no llegaran.	I was afraid they wouldn't arrive.

As was the case for the present subjunctive, the subjects in the main and dependent clauses must be different in order for the imperfect subjunctive to be used; otherwise, the infinitive follows the main clause:

> **TIP**
> Notice that the first person plural form in the imperfect subjunctive requires an accent mark, and the first and third person singular forms are the same.

Ella quería que trabajaras.	**She** wanted **you** to work.
Ella quería trabajar.	She wanted to work (herself).

When used with the imperfect subjunctive, the expression Ojalá means *I wish* instead of *I hope*:

Ojalá vinieran.	I wish they'd come.
Ojalá vengan.	I hope they come.

The imperfect subjunctive forms of the verbs querer, deber, and poder are often used to express requests or suggestions in a polite manner:

¿**Quisieran** ordenar más fruta?   *Would they like to order more fruit?*
Debiéramos ir al mercado.   *It might be best if we go to the market.*
¿**Pudieras** hacerme un favor?   *Would you please do me a favor?*

LA PRÁCTICA 8

Change these dependent noun clauses from the present subjunctive to the imperfect subjunctive:

1. que yo estudie   _que yo estudiara_

2. que él quiera   _____

3. que ustedes den   _____

4. que tú reconozcas   _____

5. que nosotros salgamos   _____

6. que ellas tengan   _____

7. que Ud. sea   _____

8. que yo haga   _____

9. que ellos piensen   _____

10. que él diga   _____

Translate these sentences using either the present subjunctive or imperfect subjunctive. Use the main verb provided:

11. *They suggested that I practice.* (SUGERIR)

    Sugirieron que practicara. _____

12. *I hope you* (form. sing.) *have good luck.* (ESPERAR)

    _____

13. *He begged me to dance with him.* (SUPLICAR)

    _____

14. *We prefer that you* (inf. sing.) *do the job.* (PREFERIR)

    _____

15. *I did not believe that they left.* (CREER)

_____

16. *They asked him to serve the food.* (PEDIR)

_____

17. *We insisted that they pay.* (INSISTIR)

_____

18. *He fears that we won't arrive on Tuesday.* (TEMER)

_____

19. *They denied that it was true.* (NEGAR)

_____

20. *She was happy that you* (form. pl.) *came.* (ALEGRARSE)

_____

_____

The Past Perfect Subjunctive
El pluscuamperfecto de subjuntivo

The past perfect subjunctive (or pluperfect subjunctive) is formed in Spanish by combining the imperfect subjunctive of the verb haber with the past participle of the main verb. This compound tense is often used in place of the imperfect subjunctive in a dependent noun clause:

		Hablar *(to speak)*	Comer *(to eat)*	Escribir *(to write)*
(yo)	hubiera	hablado	comido	escrito
(tú)	hubieras	hablado	comido	escrito
(él, ella, Ud.)	hubiera	hablado	comido	escrito
(nosotros)	hubiéramos	hablado	comido	escrito
(vosotros)	hubierais	hablado	comido	escrito
(ellos, ellas, Uds.)	hubieran	hablado	comido	escrito

Like the past perfect indicative, this tense is used to indicate an event that took place prior to something in the past. The main verb is usually expressed by the imperfect, preterit, or past subjunctive:

Se alegró que hubieras llamado. *She was happy that you had called.*
Dudaba que hubiéramos comido. *They doubted that we had eaten.*

The past perfect subjunctive is sometimes used to express a contrary-to-fact wish in the past after the expression Ojalá que:

Ojalá que lo hubieran comprado.   *I wish they had bought it.*

The past perfect subjunctive is also used in conditional sentences, which will be presented in the next section:

Me hubiera casado contigo si me hubieras preguntado.
I would have married you if you would have asked me.

A future subjunctive tense exists in Spanish, but it is primarily found in literature. It carries the same meaning as the present subjunctive:

	Hablar (to speak)	Comer (to eat)	Escribir (to write)
(yo)	hablare	comiere	escribiere
(tú)	hablares	comieres	escribieres
(él, ella, Ud.)	hablare	comiere	escribiere
(nosotros)	habláremos	comiéremos	escribiéremos
(vosotros)	hablarais	comiereis	escribiereis
(ellos, ellas, Uds.)	hablaren	comieren	escribieren

LA PRÁCTICA 9

Fill in the correct form of the verb haber:
Todos hablan de Katrina y su nuevo medicamento...

1. Espero que lo _____ tomado.   haya

2. Esperaba que lo _____ tomado.   _____

3. Me alegro que lo _____ tomado.   _____

4. Me dijo que lo _____ tomado.   _____

5. Era posible que lo _____ tomado.   _____

6. Me dicen que lo _____ tomado.   _____

7. Puede ser que lo _____ tomado.   _____

8. Yo dudaba que lo _____ tomado.   _____

9. No es cierto que lo _____ tomado.   _____

10. Yo temía que lo _____ tomado.   _____

Conditional Sentences
Oraciones condicionales

Conditional sentences are often used with the subjunctive. A conditional sentence consists of two clauses—a dependent clause beginning with *if* (si clause), and a main clause. One example would be the present tense in the si clause and the future tense in the main clause, which expresses a simple future action that may or may not occur:

Si <u>tienes</u> una fiesta, <u>llegaré</u> temprano.
If you have a party, I will arrive early.

However, if there is some unreal or contrary-to-fact situation taking place in present time, the imperfect subjunctive is used in the si clause, and the conditional tense is used in the main clause. Notice how the action is based entirely on supposition:

Si trabajaras, te pagaría.   *If you (would) work, I would pay.*

To express this same unreal or contrary-to-fact situation in past time, the past perfect subjunctive is used in the si clause, and the conditional perfect or past perfect subjunctive is used in the main clause:

Si hubieras trabajado, te habría pagado.

Si hubieras trabajado, te hubiera pagado.

} *If you would have worked, I would have paid you.*

LA PRÁCTICA 10

Write correct verb forms on the lines provided as you create conditional sentences in present and past time:

1. Iría a la playa si ella _____ nadar. (SABER)   *supiera*

2. Si me pagaran todo, yo les _____ el dinero. (PRESTAR)   _____

3. Si fuera posible, yo _____ hasta el sábado. (QUEDARSE)   _____

4. Habríamos celebrado si ellos ____ ____ . (GANAR)   _____

5. Si pones el DVD, yo lo _____ contigo. (VER)   _____

6. Si hubiéramos comenzado ayer, ya ____ ____. (ACABAR)   _____

7. Traeré los discos compactos si Marta _____. (VENIR)   _____

8. Si hubieras salido a la hora, tú no ___ ___ tarde. (LLEGAR)   _____

9. Yo le habría llamado si Ud. ____ ____ en casa. (ESTAR)   _____

10. Habría plantado flores si él _____ el tiempo. (TENER)   _____

EL REPASO

Use only the first-person singular (yo form) to complete this chart:

TENSE	Hablar	Aprender	Venir
present	hablo	aprendo	vengo
preterit	hablé		
imperfect			
future			
conditional			
pres. perfect			
past perfect			
pres. sujunctive			
imperf. subjunctive			
past perf. subjunctive			

The Subjunctive in Adverbial Clauses
El subjuntivo en las cláusulas adverbiales

An adverbial clause, like an adverb, modifies a verb in the areas of time, manner, place, and direction. It is generally introduced by an adverbial conjunction:

Comimos <u>cuando</u> llegaron.   *We ate when they arrived.*
Salta <u>como</u> un conejo.   *He jumps like a rabbit.*

The subjunctive, however, is used after certain adverbial conjunctions when they express uncertainty in the mind of the speaker or an indefinite future time. Notice how the sequence of tenses is the same for adverbial clauses as it is for noun clauses:

* para que   *so that*

   Llegaré temprano para que <u>podamos</u> ver la película.
   I'll arrive early so that we can see the movie.

- antes (de) que   *before*

   Ricardo estudiaba antes de que <u>tomaran</u> el examen.
   Ricardo was studying before they took the exam.

- en caso (de) que   *in case that*

   Voy a comprar un paraguas en caso de que <u>llueva</u>.
   I'm going to buy an umbrella in case (that) it rains.

- Other conjunctions include:

a fin de que	*in order that*
sin que	*without*
a menos que	*unless*
con tal (de) que	*provided that*

Some conjunctions in Spanish are followed by the subjunctive when the verb in the adverbial clause expresses vagueness or uncertainty, but are followed by the indicative when the action in the clause expresses certainty or fact:

La caja llegará <u>donde</u> la <u>enviemos</u>.
The box will (hopefully) get to wherever we intend to send it.

La caja llegará <u>donde</u> la <u>enviamos</u>.
They box will get to where we send it.

- Other such conjunctions are:

según	*according to*
como	*how*
a pesar de que	*in spite of*
mientras	*while*
aunque	*although*
siempre que	*provided that*
de modo/manera que	*so that*

Most time-related conjunctions that introduce an adverbial clause are followed by the subjunctive when the main clause either includes a command or refers to future time:

Llámeme <u>cuando</u> se vayan.
Call me when(ever) they leave.

Conversaremos <u>hasta que</u> termine el juego.
We'll chat until (whenever) the game is over.

- Other similar conjunctions include:

después de que	*after*
luego que	*as soon as*

In time-related adverbial clauses, however, the indicative is used when either the sentence relates to past time, or when the action in the clause is consistent or habitual:

Se quedó en su casa <u>hasta que</u> acabó la tormenta.
He stayed in his home until the storm was over.

Ordenamos ensaladas <u>cuando</u> nos juntamos.
We (usually) order salads when we get together.

The conjunctions con tal (de) que and a menos que are unique in that they are followed by the present perfect subjunctive if the verb of the dependent clause expresses an action that takes place <u>before</u> the action of the main clause:

Vamos a viajar con tal de que <u>hayas pagado</u> los boletos.
We will go on the trip provided that you have paid for the tickets.

However, these same conjunctions are followed by the present subjunctive if the action in the dependent clause takes place <u>at the same time</u> as the main clause action:

Vamos a viajar <u>con tal de que</u> <u>pagues</u> los boletos.
We will go on the trip provided that you (will) pay for the tickets.

As with noun clauses, if the subject is the same in the main and dependent clause of an adverbial sentence, then the infinitive is used:

Van a estudiar <u>antes de</u> tomar el examen final.
They're going to study before taking the final exam.

LA PRÁCTICA 11

Write the correct form of the subjunctive on the line provided.

1. Limpiaron todo antes de que (LLEGAR) mi novia.   *llegara*

2. Ella lo hace para que nosotros no (TENER) que hacerlo.   _____

3. El gato vendrá cuando la señora lo (LLAMAR).   _____

4. Van al desierto aunque (LLOVER).   _____

5. Practiquen la canción hasta que la (SABER).   _____

6. Salí sin que Uds. me (DESPEDIR).   _____

7. Trajo un sombrero en caso de que (SALIR) sol.   _____

8. Mientras tú (MENTIR), no te escucharé.   _____

9. Lo haré a menos que (SURGIR) un problema.   _____

10. Nosotros no vamos aunque los otros (IR).   _____

Translate each of the sentences in the above exercises into English:

11. ***They cleaned everything before my girlfriend arrived.*** _____

12. _____

13. _____

14. _____

15. _____

16. _____

17. _____

18. _____

19. _____

20. _____

The Subjunctive in Adjectival Clauses
El subjuntivo en cláusulas adjetivas

An adjectival clause, like an adjective, modifies a noun. In Spanish, it often consists of a relative clause introduced by the word que (a relative pronoun) followed by a verb in either the indicative or subjunctive mood:

Quiero un empleado que <u>sepa</u> usar la computadora.
I want an employee who knows how to use the computer.

The key for usage is the ANTECEDENT, or the noun being described in the main clause. If it is clearly identified and part of reality, the indicative is used; however, if it is unknown, uncertain, or nonexistent, then the subjunctive is used:

Vamos a ver la <u>película que me compraste</u>.   *(existent)*
Let's see the movie you bought me.

Vamos a ver una <u>película que me haga llorar</u>.   *(nonexistent)*
Let's see a movie that might (possibly) make me cry.

The subjunctive is also used when adjectival clauses modify negative or undetermined antecedents:

No hay <u>ningún plato</u> en el menú que le guste ordenar.
There isn't a dish on the menu that he might (possibly) like to order.

No conozco a <u>nadie</u> que haya viajado a Chile.
I don't know anyone who might (possibly) have traveled to Chile.

Besides que, relative words such as donde and quien may also be used to introduce an adjectival clause:

Buscamos un restaurante <u>donde</u> sirvan comida cubana.
We're looking for a restaurant where they serve Cuban food.

Bear in mind that the subjunctive is based on DOUBT, DESIRES, EMOTION, DENIAL, and other INDEFINITE MESSAGES from the speaker. Notice the difference between these two sentences:

Busca una casa que <u>tiene</u> garaje.
She needs a house that has a garage. (The speaker is sure that one exists)

Busca una casa que <u>tenga</u> garaje.
She needs a house that (possibly) has a garage. (The speaker is unsure)

LA PRÁCTICA 12

Finish each sentence by creating an adjectival clause in the subjunctive:

1. Mercedes busca un carro (tener cuatro puertas).

   Mercedes busca un carro que tenga cuatro puertas.

2. Ellas querían un apartamento (estar cerca del mercado).

   _____

3. Hablaré con una persona (entender inglés).

   _____

4. No conocemos a nadie (vivir en San Antonio).

   _____

5. ¿Prefieres comprar algo (no costar tanto)?

   _____

6. No había ninguna persona (saber usar la máquina).

   _____

7. Santiago quiere tomar las clases (ser más divertidas).

   _____

8. Siempre he deseado amigos (tocar un instrumento).

   _____

9. Escoge las galletas que nos (gustar).

   _____

10. Le encanta cualquier ropa (venir de Italia).

    _____

    _____

11

The Imperative

¿Cuánto sabe usted?
How Much Do You Know Already?

1. How do you say to a group of people *Don't bring anything*.

2. Give two ways to give the command *Let's study*.

3. Conjugate the verb escoger in the command for usted.

4. How do you say, *All of you, don't leave*?

5. Change póntelas to a negative command.

Formal Commands
El imperativo

Unlike the indicative and subjunctive, the imperative mood is solely used to express requests and commands. Verbs in the imperative that are directed at usted or ustedes are called FORMAL COMMANDS. Their forms are the same as the third person singular and plural forms of the present subjunctive:

Speak	Hable, Hablen	*Tell*	Diga, Digan
Eat	Coma, Coman	*Read*	Lea, Lean
Write	Escriba, Escriban	*Sleep*	Duerma, Duerman

EXAMPLES

Venga más tarde.	*Come later (you).*
¡Sirvan los refrescos!	*Serve the soft drinks (all of you)!*
Estudie la lección.	*Study the lesson (you).*

To form negative formal commands, simply place no before the affirmative form. To be more polite in Spanish, the words Ud. or Uds. are added:

Traiga la silla Ud.	*Please bring the chair.*
No traiga la silla Ud.	*Please don't bring the chair.*
Escriban las palabras Uds.	*Write the words.*
No escriban las palabras Uds.	*Please don't write the words.*

The first person plural form of the subjunctive is also considered an imperative, except for the word vamos, which replaces vayamos, for *let's go*:

Abramos las ventanas.	*Let's open the windows.*
No cerremos las puertas.	*Let's not close the doors.*
Vamos (not Vayamos) al parque.	*Let's go to the park.*

The first person plural command form does not require Ud. or Uds., because it actually implies *Let's*. Also, the vamos a + infinitive construction may replace the first person plural affirmative command form, because it can mean the same thing:

Caminemos. ⎫
 ⎬ *Let's walk*
Vamos a caminar. ⎭

Vendamos la casa. ⎫
 ⎬ *Let's sell the house.*
Vamos a vender la casa. ⎭

With affirmative command forms, object pronouns (whether direct or indirect) are attached at the end, and a written accent is usually placed over the syllable originally stressed:

Tráigalos.	*Bring them.*
Pregúntele.	*Ask him.*
Cerrémosla.	*Let's close it.*
Expliquémoslo.	*Let's explain it to them.*

However, when nos (reflexive pronoun) or se (indirect object pronoun) are added to the first-person plural command form, the final s is dropped and an accent is written over the stressed syllable:

Levantemo (s) + nos = Levantémonos	*Let's get up.*
Digamo (s) + se + lo = Digámoselo	*Let's tell it to him.*
Pongamo (s) + nos + las = Pongámonoslas	*Let's put them on.*

Remember that with negative command forms, all object pronouns are placed before the verb instead of after:

No **me** llame.	*Do not call me.*
No **nos** sentemos.	*Let's not sit down.*
No **se** vayan Uds.	*Please don't go.*

No accent mark is needed when a single object pronoun is added to a one-syllable command form:

DAR (*to give*)   Deme la llave.   *Give me the key.*

TIP
Formal commands are actually polite requests because, in essence, they are typical subjunctive constructions of wish and desire:
Venga Ud.
Would you please come?

LA PRÁCTICA 1

Translate these sentences in the imperative into English:

1. No traiga nada.   ***Don't bring anything.***

2. Piénselo. _____

3. Comprémoslas. _____

4. No fumen Uds. _____

5. Vamos a salir. _____

6. Prende la luz. _____

7. No me diga. _____

8. Callémonos. _____

9. Cante Ud. _____

10. No la firme. _____

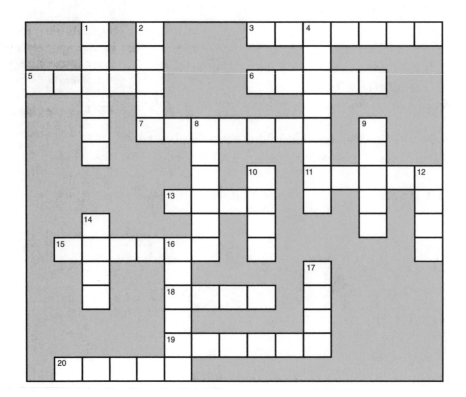

Translate these into Spanish:

Across
3. write
5. move
6. come
7. listen
11. own
13. say
15. buy
18. ask for
19. bring
20. run

Down
1. close
2. call
4. answer
8. walk
9. put
10. go
12. open
14. eat
16. repeat
17. do

Informal Commands
El imperativo informal

Informal or familiar commands in Spanish are directed at tú and vosotros, meaning that the speaker is probably addressing family, children, or friends. Tú commands are formed by dropping the final s of the second person singular of the present indicative:

Speak	hablas → Habla		*Close*	cierras → Cierra	
Run	corres → Corre		*Move*	mueves → Mueve	
Write	escribes → Escribe		*Ask for*	pides → Pide	

However, there are eight verbs which have irregular affirmative tú command forms and therefore need to be memorized:

Say	Di	(decir)	*Leave*	Sal	(salir)
Do, Make	Haz	(hacer)	*Be*	Sé	(ser)
Go	Ve	(ir)	*Have*	Ten	(tener)
Put	Pon	(poner)	*Come*	Ven	(venir)

EJEMPLOS

Ven aquí, hermanito.	*Come here, little brother.*
Cambia la música, por favor.	*Please change the music.*
Pon el libro en la mesa.	*Put the book on the table.*

The vosotros or second person plural informal command is formed by dropping the final r of the infinitive and adding d:

Look	Mirad	(mirar)
Drink	Bebed	(beber)
Serve	Servid	(servir)

With reflexive verbs, affirmative tú commands maintain their forms, whereas with vosotros the commands lose their final d when the pronoun os is attached. The verb irse (*to leave*) is the only exception (Id + os = Idos):

INFINITIVE	Tú	Vosotros
Levantarse (*to rise*)	Levántate	Levanta(d) + os = Levantaos
Dormirse (*to fall asleep*)	Duérmete	Dormi(d) + os = Dormíos
Ponerse (*to put onself*)	Ponte	Pone(d) + os = Ponéos

Negative commands in the familiar second person singular and plural require the use of these present subjunctive forms:

	AFFIRMATIVE	NEGATIVE
tú	Maneja	No manejes
vosotros	Manejad	No manejéis
tú	Come	No comas
vosotros	Comed	No comáis
tú	Di	No digas
vosotros	Decid	No digáis

Remember that with affirmative command forms, all direct, indirect, and reflexive pronouns are attached to the verb at the end. With negative command forms, all object pronouns are placed before the verb.

AFFIRMATIVE	NEGATIVE
Abridla	No la abráis
Dile	No le digas
Sírvelos	No los sirvas
Póntelas	No se las pongas
Vendédmelo	No me lo vendáis

Notice also that the affirmative informal command may be irregular, but its negative verb form is still derived from the present subjunctive:

Hazlo.   *Do it.*
No lo <u>hagas</u>.   *Don't do it.*

Idos.   *Leave.*
No <u>os vayáis</u>.   *Don't leave.*

TIP
Don't forget that ver and ir have the same affirmative tú command form:
Ve la película.
See the movie.
Ve al baño.
Go to the bathroom.

LA PRÁCTICA 2

Change these informal command phrases from the negative to the affirmative:

1. No tengas fiesta hoy.   *Ten fiesta hoy*

2. No te sientes.

3. No entres.

4. No la cierres.

5. No salgas.

6. No te pongas la gorra.

7. No contestes.

8. No le digas todo.

9. No te levantes.

10. No vayas a tu cuarto.

Indirect Commands
El imperativo indirecto

When a command is being given to one person, but is meant to be carried out by another, it is called an INDIRECT COMMAND. Indirect commands are formed by combining the word que with the present subjunctive third person singular or plural:

Que venga.	*Tell him to come.*
Que hablen.	*Let them speak.*
Que lo haga él.	*Have him do it.*

Notice how the translations of indirect commands may vary in English, and how a subject pronoun may be added at the end for emphasis. Also, unlike direct commands, the object pronouns are placed before the verb:

Que me esperen afuera.	*Have them wait for me outside.*
Que no se lo diga.	*Don't let him tell it to her.*
Que se bañen.	*Tell them to bathe.*

When indirect commands include *se* constructions with indirect object pronouns, they are often used as direct commands. Notice how the speaker is talking to *you*:

Que no <u>se les</u> pierdan las carteras.   *Don't lose your purses.*
Que no <u>se te</u> olvide el libro.   *Don't forget your book.*
Que no <u>se les</u> escapen los perritos.   *Don't let the puppies run away.*

LA PRÁCTICA 3

Use the words to create complete indirect commands:

1. ¿Los chicos? *Let them eat the meat.*   Que coman la carne.

2. ¿La lección? *Tell them to prepare it.*   _____

3. ¿Catalina? *Have her pay the bill.*   _____

4. ¿El dinero? *Don't let him give it to them.*   _____

5. ¿Tus primos? *Let them come back on Sunday.*   _____

6. ¿Los estudiantes? *Tell them not to stay there.*   _____

7. ¿El trabajo? *Let Camacho do it.*   _____

8. ¿Mis hijas? *Have them call me tomorrow.*   _____

9. ¿La Sra. Pérez? *Tell her not to wait in the car.*   _____

10. ¿La pareja? *Let them get married.*   _____

Other Command Forms
Otras formas del imperativo

The Spanish verb infinitive is often used as an imperative, particularly in its written form—on notices, in recipes, with instructions, etc.

No <u>fumar</u>.   *Do not smoke.*
<u>Enviar</u> su nombre y dirección.   *Send your name and address.*
<u>Añadir</u> sal y pimienta.   *Add salt and pepper.*

The following expressions use the infinitive to make more courteous requests in the imperative:

Haga(me) el favor de <u>salir</u> por la puerta trasera.
Please leave through the back door.

Favor de <u>firmar</u> aquí.
Please sign here.

Tengan la bondad de <u>sentarse</u> ahora mismo.
Everyone please be seated now.

¿Podrían <u>quedarse</u> en silencio, por favor?
Will you please be quiet?

Tenga la amabilidad de <u>cerrar</u> la puerta.
Please close the door.

LA PRÁCTICA 4

Turn these formal and informal commands into courteous expressions using the infinitive:

1. Tráigame el pastel.   <u>Favor de traerme el pastel.</u>

2. No suban por la escalera.   _____

3. Pon la carta en el sobre.   _____

4. Vaya a la tienda con Laura.   _____

5. No comas la fruta seca.   _____

6. Díganos la verdad.   _____

7. Hagan Uds. el trabajo.   _____

8. No escuche la radio.   _____

9. Pon los cubiertos en la mesa.   _____

10. Vengan acá.   _____

12

The Verb Infinitive

¿Cuánto sabe usted?
How Much Do You Know Already?

1. How do you say *I want to listen* in Spanish?

2. Use the construction verb + en + infinitive in a sentence.

3. What's the difference between Debe ir and Debe de ir?

4. How do you say *I saw them arrive* in Spanish?

5. Use en lugar de before an infinitive in a sentence.

The Infinitive After Conjugated Verbs
El infinitivo precedido por verbos conjugados

The infinitive is often used after conjugated verb forms in Spanish. Notice how the verb + infinitive construction does not always translate the word *to* into English:

INFINITIVE	VERB + INFINITIVE	
trabajar (*to work*)	Queremos trabajar contigo.	*We want to work with you.*
volver (*to return*)	Deben volver a la una.	*They should return at one o'clock.*
coser (*to sew*)	No sabía coser.	*I didn't know how to sew.*
hacer (*to do*)	¿Puedes hacerlo?	*Can you do it?*
tomar (*to take*)	Preferiría tomar el tren.	*He'd prefer to take the train.*

Infinitives are often used in Spanish much like they are in English—to complete or complement the main verb. Remember that the verb's tense does not affect the infinitive's meaning or form:

VERB	VERB + INFINITIVE
conseguir *(to manage to)*	Conseguimos hablar con el profesor. *We managed to talk to the professor.*

Other verbs that may be followed directly by an infinitive include:

creer	*(to believe)*	olvidar	*(to forget)*
decidir	*(to decide)*	parecer	*(to seem to)*
dejar	*(to allow, to let)*	pensar	*(to intend)*
desear	*(to want)*	permitir	*(to allow)*
escuchar	*(to listen to)*	poder	*(to be able to)*
esperar	*(to hope, to wait)*	preferir	*(to prefer)*
hacer	*(to do, to make)*	prohibir	*(to prohibit)*
intentar	*(to try to)*	prometer	*(to promise)*
lograr	*(to achieve)*	querer	*(to want)*
mandar	*(to order to)*	recordar	*(to remember)*
merecer	*(to deserve)*	saber	*(to know)*
necesitar	*(to need, to have to)*	soler	*(to be accustomed to)*
ofrecer	*(to offer)*	temer	*(to fear)*

An infinitive is also used after verbs of sense perception, such as oír, ver, sentir, mirar, and escuchar to indicate a completed event or action. Notice the difference when a gerund is used instead:

Le oí cantar.	*I heard him sing.*
Le oí <u>cantando</u>.	*I heard him (while he was) singing.*
¿Me vieron salir?	*Did you see me leave?*
¿Me vieron <u>saliendo</u>?	*Did you see me (as I was) leaving?*

Remember that an active infinitive is used in Spanish, whereas the English equivalent is passive. Verbs of this type include dejar, mandar, and hacer:

Les hicimos correr una milla.	*We made them run a mile.*
Mandé comprar los boletos.	*I ordered tickets to be purchased.*

Several verbs in Spanish require the prepositions a, de, or en before being joined with an infinitive. The following are used with a, which include verbs that express motion:

VERB	VERB + a + INFINITIVE	
bajar a (*to descend*)	Bajemos a comer.	*Let's go down(stairs) to eat.*
irse a (*to leave*)	Se fueron a jugar.	*They went out to play.*
subir a (*to go up*)	Ha subido a dormir.	*He has gone up(stairs) to sleep.*
aprender a (*to learn to*)	Aprenderé a bailar.	*I'll learn how to dance.*
comenzar a (*to begin to*)	Comenzó a llover.	*It began to rain.*
ayudar a (*to help to*)	Ayúdeme a hacerlo.	*Help me do it.*

Other such verbs are:

acercarse a	*(to approach)*	enseñar a	*(to teach, to show how)*
acostumbrarse a	*(to be accustomed to)*	invitar a	*(to invite to)*
aplicarse a	*(to apply oneself to)*	llegar a	*(to get to, to achieve)*
atreverse a	*(to dare to)*	llevar a	*(to lead to)*
cuidar a	*(to take care of)*	meterse a	*(to start to)*
decidirse a	*(to decide to)*	negarse a	*(to refuse to)*
dedicarse a	*(to devote to)*	pararse a	*(to stop to)*
disponerse a	*(to get ready to)*	ponerse a	*(to begin to)*
echarse a	*(to begin to)*	prepararse a	*(to get ready to)*
empezar a	*(to begin to)*	volver a	*(to do again)*

These verbs require a de before an infinitive:

VERB	VERB + de + INFINITIVE	
acabar de (*to have just done something*)	Acaba de sentarse.	*He has just sat down.*
dejar de (*to stop*)	Dejaron de gritar.	*They stopped yelling.*
tratar de (*to try to*)	No he tratado de entrar.	*I haven't tried to enter.*

Other such verbs include:

acordarse de	*(to remember)*	fastidiarse de	*(to be weary of)*
arrepentirse de	*(to regret)*	guardarse de	*(to keep from)*
asustarse de	*(to be afraid of)*	jactarse de	*(to boast of)*
avergonzarse de	*(to be ashamed of)*	quejarse de	*(to complain of)*
cansarse de	*(to grow tired of)*	olvidarse de	*(to forget)*
cuidar de	*(to take care of)*	presumir de	*(to boast about)*
encargarse de	*(to take charge of)*	terminar de	*(to stop)*

And these verbs take the preposition en before an infinitive:

VERB	VERB + en + INFINITIVE
consistir en *(to consist of)*	Su objetivo consiste en buscar el tesoro. *His objective consists in searching for the treasure.*
insistir en *(to insist upon)*	Insistió en pintar su carro de blanco. *He insisted in having his car painted white.*
quedar en *(to agree to)*	Han quedado en salir en la tarde. *They have agreed to leave in the afternoon.*

Other verbs using en include:

consentir en	*(to agree to)*	pensar en	*(to think of)*
dudar en	*(to hesitate over)*	persistir en	*(to persist in)*
empeñarse en	*(to insist on)*	tardar en	*(to delay in)*
fijarse en	*(to concentrate on)*	terminar en	*(to end by)*
insistir en	*(to insist on)*	vacilar en	*(to hesitate over)*

There are also a few verbs that require the preposition con before the infinitive. Here are some examples:

amenazar con *(to threaten to)* Amenazó con irse.
She threatened to leave.

contar con *(to count on)* Cuento contigo.
I'm counting on you.

soñar con *(to dream about)* Sueña con los angelitos.
Dream about little angels.

> **TIP**
> The infinitive often makes Spanish grammar easier. For example, when the subject of the main verb is the same as the one of the dependent verb, a dependent infinitive may be used:
>
> | Creo que ella tiene razón. | *I think she's right.* |
> |---|---|
> | Creo tener razón. | *I think I am right.* |
> | Geraldo dijo que eran locutores. | *Geraldo said they were announcers.* |
> | Geraldo dijo ser locutor. | *Geraldo said he was an announcer.* |

LA PRÁCTICA 1

To complete the sentence, put one of the missing words—a, de, or en—on each line below. If one is not needed, leave the line blank:

1. Le ayudaron ___a___ caminar.

2. Acaban _____ llegar.

3. Pensamos _____ hacerlo más tarde.

4. Quisiera _____ invitar a Susana.

5. Me cansé _____ manejar solo.

6. Llegará _____ ser un policía.

7. Insistían _____ no comprar un nuevo estéreo.

8. ¡Fíjate _____ tus estudios!

9. Se olvidó _____ enviarle el regalo.

10. Podemos terminar _____ pintar mañana.

The Infinitive After Prepositions
El infinitivo después de preposiciones

The infinitive is often used as an object of a preposition. In Spanish, the preposition goes first and the verb infinitive follows:

Lo hicimos <u>para</u> ayudarte.	*We did it in order to help you.*
Están cansados <u>de</u> mirar televisión.	*They're tired of watching TV.*
Comeremos <u>después de</u> jugar fútbol.	*We'll eat after playing soccer.*
La besé <u>sin</u> saber su nombre.	*I kissed her without knowing her name.*
Iría <u>a pesar de</u> no tener dinero.	*He'd go in spite of having no cash.*

Other prepositions used with infinitives are:

por medio de	*by means of*
al	*upon*
con tal de	*provided that*
por	*by*
en vez de, en lugar de	*instead of*
en caso de	*in case of*
hasta	*until*
antes de	*before*

In Spanish, the infinitive is also used after que in phrases such as algo que, poco que, mucho que, tanto que, and nada que:

Tenían <u>mucho que</u> hacer.   *They had a lot to do.*
No hay <u>nada que</u> limpiar.   *There is nothing to clean.*

However, if the sentence expresses a search, a request, or a need for something, the preposition para is generally used instead:

Buscaron algo <u>para</u> leer.   *They looked for something to read.*
Necesito tantas cosas <u>para</u> arreglarlo.   *I need so many things to fix it.*

When estar is followed by para and the infinitive, it means *to be about to*, but when estar is followed by por and the infinitive, it means *to be in favor of*:

Estoy para salir.
I'm about to leave.

Estoy por terminarlo.
I'm in favor of finishing it.

> **TIP**
> Note how in Spanish an infinitive is used after a preposition, whereas in English, a gerund (present participle) is used:
> después de viajar
> *after traveling*
> antes de comer
> *before eating*

LA PRÁCTICA 2

Put the words in order in each of the following sentences:

1. bonito/ para/ busco/ comprar/ algo   Busco algo bonito para comprar.

2. el desayuno/ listos/ comer/ estábamos/ para   _____

3. la noche/ sin/ trabajaba/ toda/ dormir   _____

4. correré/ caminar/ al parque/ en lugar de   _____

5. antes de/ te/ acostarme/ llamé   _____

6. que/ nada/ no/ decirle/ hay   _____

7. béisbol/ después de/ se bañaron/ jugar   _____

8. música/ para/ tocar/ estoy   _____

9. mucho/ tenía/ hacer/ ella/ que   _____

10. carro/ tener/ iría/ no/ a pesar de   _____

More Uses of the Infinitive
Otros usos del infinitivo

The infinitive is frequently used after impersonal expressions:

Es importante despertar temprano.	*It's important to get up early.*
Es necesario apagar las luces.	*It's necessary to turn out the lights.*
Es difícil cortar la carne.	*It's difficult to cut meat.*

Notice how the object naturally follows the transitive verb infinitive in this construction:

Es difícil <u>cortar</u> <u>la carne</u>.   *It's difficult to cut meat.*
         INFINITIVE OBJECT

However, if the object (or clause) does not follow the infinitive of a transitive verb, the construction **adjective** + de + **infinitive** is used:

<u>La carne</u> es <u>difícil de cortar</u>.   *Meat is difficult to cut.*
   OBJECT   ADJ. + DE + INFINITIVE

Infinitives are also used after an interrogative adverb or "question word" in a sentence:

¿Sabía <u>qué</u> hacer?	*Did she know what to do?*
¿Entienden <u>cómo</u> decirlo?	*Do they understand how to say it?*
¿Encontraste <u>dónde</u> mandarlas?	*Did you find out where to send them?*

The words debe (*should*) and debe de (*must*) have different meanings when they precede the infinitive:

Ella <u>debe</u> llegar a las nueve.	*She should arrive at nine.*
Ella <u>debe de</u> estar enferma.	*She must be sick.*

The phrases tener que (*to have to*) and hay que (*one must*) also precede the infinitive and have very practical uses:

Ella <u>tenía que</u> manejar rápido.
She had to drive fast.
<u>Hay que</u> evitar problemas monetarios.
One must avoid financial problems.

Sometimes infinitives are used in elliptical expressions or casual commands:

¿Ella relajarse?	*Her, relax?*
¡A estudiar!	*Off to study!*

> **TIP**
> The "perfect" infinitive is formed with the word haber + **past participle**, and it expresses an action that took place prior to the action of the main verb:
> Se fueron sin <u>haber dicho</u> nada.
> *They left without having said anything.*

LA PRÁCTICA 3

Fill in the appropriate preposition to complete each sentence:

1. (*in order to*)   Comemos _____ vivir.   para

2. (*after*)   Caminaré _____ almorzar.   _____

3. (*instead of*)   Se acostó _____ salir.   _____

4. (*of*)   Estoy cansado _____ leer.   _____

5. (*without*)   Entramos _____ pagar.   _____

6. (*before*)   Se bañaron _____ comer.   _____

7. (*upon*)   Se fue _____ oír las voces.   _____

8. (*in spite of*)   Me llama _____ vivir en Cuba.   _____

9. (*provided that*)   Iremos _____ ver al alcalde.   _____

10. (*until*)   Estaré con él _____ llegar a casa.   _____

Use infinitives as you translate these sentences into Spanish:

11. It's possible to swim in the lake.   Es posible nadar en el lago.

12. The room is easy to paint.   _____

13. We have to write these words.   _____

14. You (form. sing.) must play tennis.   _____

15. Tell (inf.) me what to do.   _____

16. They have many things to buy.   _____

17. Off to work!   _____

18. Does she know how to pronounce it?   _____

19. It's important to bring the books.   _____

20. I was looking for something to eat.   _____

Answer these questions as you review this section on Spanish verbs. Combine infinitives with prepositions in all your answers:

1. ¿Qué hace Ud. para mejorar su pronunciación en español?

2. ¿Habló Ud. español ayer?

3. ¿Escuchaba Ud. música latina con sus amigos?

4. ¿Va a tomar Ud. una clase de español el próximo año?

5. ¿Por cuánto tiempo ha estudiado Ud. el español?

6. ¿Había Ud. comprado otro libro de gramática antes de comprar éste?

7. ¿Está practicando Ud. el español en este momento?

8. ¿Anoche estaba leyendo un libro en español?

9. ¿Viajaría Ud. a España si tuviera la oportunidad?

10. ¿Por qué quiere Ud. aprender más español?

Culture Capsule 2

Religious Holidays in Latin America
Las celebraciones religiosas en Latinoamérica

La conquista española trajo consigo la influencia católica a Latinoamérica. Las fiestas religiosas más importantes son la Navidad, la Pascua de Reyes, la Cuaresma, y la Pascua de Resurrección. La celebración de la Navidad es muy similar a la estadounidense, con la gente saliendo de compras, decorando sus hogares con árboles navideños, ornamentos, y luces. Sin embargo, en Latinoamérica, el festejo de la Navidad es el día 24 en la noche (Nochebuena). En esta ocasión, las familias se juntan para conmemorar el nacimiento del niño Jesús o la encarnación de Dios, y compartir una cena suculenta, brindis y regalos. En muchos países latinoamericanos también se asiste a una misa navideña a las 12 de la noche o Misa de Gallo. La mañana comienza con un desayuno suntuoso de chocolate caliente y panetón o rosca navideña (panes dulces con frutas secas, pasas, y glaceado de azúcar). Las decoraciones de Navidad se mantienen generalmente hasta el día 6 de enero, cuando se celebra la llegada de los Reyes Magos.

La fiesta de los Reyes Magos es conocida como la Pascua de Reyes. En esta oportunidad, muchas familias y amistades se juntan en la noche del 5 de enero para celebrar el comienzo de la Epifanía o manifestación de Jesús como Dios. En algunos países latinoamericanos, los niños esperan recibir sus regalos en esta fecha. Las decoraciones típicas de esta época en muchas iglesias son de color verde, el cual simboliza crecimiento y vida. Al mismo tiempo, otros lugares en Latinoamérica celebran este día con festivales, donde se preparan y venden muchas comidas autóctonas, bajo el son de música típica y la representación de bailes folclóricos, con vestimentas tradicionales y ornamentadas.

Otra celebración importante es la Cuaresma, la cual comienza el primero de marzo y termina el día anterior a la Pascua de Resurrección. La Cuaresma son cuarenta días de reflexión y arrepentimiento en preparación a la Semana Santa. En la mayoría de las iglesias, la decoración es de color morado o azul, colores que simbolizan adoración y veneración divina.

Finalmente, otra festividad importante es la Pascua de Resurrección, donde se celebra la resurrección de Jesús tres días después de la Pascua Judía. En la mayoría de las iglesias los colores de la celebración son blanco y dorado. Una costumbre tradicional en el día de Pascua de Resurrección es la asistencia a un misa en la mañana del domingo para luego disfrutar con los familiares un almuerzo o cena, indicando el término del ayuno.

- ¿Qué sirven para el desayuno en Navidad?

- ¿Qué es la Cuaresma?

- ¿En qué fecha se celebra la Nochebuena?

- ¿Cómo celebran la fiesta de los Reyes Magos?

- ¿Cuál es una costumbre tradicional en el día de la Pascua de Resurrección?

PART III:
Nouns, Modifiers, and Other Parts of Speech

13

Nouns and Articles

¿Cuánto sabe usted?
How Much Do You Know Already?

1. What is the difference in meaning between un agua and el agua?
2. Change the sentence El lápiz es verde to the plural.
3. What is the plural for el paraguas?
4. Is dentista a masculine or feminine noun?
5. How do you say *It's the best* in Spanish?

The Nouns

Gender
El género

Nouns in Spanish are either MASCULINE (el) or FEMININE (la) in gender. The general rule is that most masculine nouns end in -o and most feminine nouns end in -a:

MASCULINE	FEMININE
el libro	la mesa
el carro	la tarjeta
el tiempo	la puerta
el perro	la libra
el juego	la computadora
el estómago	la tinta
el estudio	la cara
el punto	la mancha
el establo	la letra

Obviously, in terms of one's gender, masculine nouns refer to males, while feminine nouns refer to females:

Masculine	Feminine
el niño	la niña
el muchacho	la muchacha
el señor	la señora
el profesor	la profesora
el hombre	la mujer
el hermano	la hermana
el rey	la reina

There are, however, some nouns that end in -o that are feminine, and some nouns that end in -a that are masculine. They need to be memorized:

Masculine	Feminine
el planeta	la foto
el día	la mano
el tranvía	la radio

Notice the final -ma pattern with these masculine nouns:

Masculine	Feminine
el clima	el emblema
el problema	el dilema
el sistema	el diploma
el programa	el enigma
el idioma	el poema
el diagrama	el drama

Nouns that end in any letter besides -o or -a in Spanish generally need to be learned separately:

Masculine	Feminine
el desfile	la luz
el pie	la carne
el barril	la cárcel
el cine	la flor
el baile	la gente
el cajón	la llave
el jardín	la miel
el amor	la clase
el pan	la red
el arroz	la torre
el papel	la piel
el mes	la voz
el puente	la fuente
el ataúd	la señal

By looking at the last few letters of a noun, one can often determine its gender. For example, nouns ending in -dad, -tad, -tud, -umbre, -ión, -cia, -sis, -itis, -nza, -ie, -ez, or -eza are usually feminine:

la ver**dad** la pará**lisis**
la liber**tad** la amigdal**itis**
la vir**tud** la resper**anza**
la certid**umbre** la ser**ie**
la un**ión** la madur**ez**
la importan**cia** la trist**eza**

Similarly, nouns ending in -ambre, -or, -aje, -án, or a vowel that is stressed are usually masculine:

el **h**ambre
el tract**or**
el gar**aje**
el desv**án**
el champ**ú**

LA PRÁCTICA 1

Indicate the gender of these nouns correctly by inserting el or la:

1. _____el_____ disfraz

2. _____ mapa

3. _____ edad

4. _____ cometa

5. _____ lodo

6. _____ pasaporte

7. _____ especie

8. _____ pared

9. _____ tema

10. _____ rubí

11. _____ faringitis

12. _____ pez

13. _____ valor

14. _____ cumbre

15. _____ jarabe

LA PRÁCTICA 2

Each one of these is a common MASCULINE noun ending in the letter a; spell it correctly:

1. maoidi   _____idioma_____

2. mlica   _____

3. mntfsaaa   _____

4. bolpamre   _____

5. groaamrp   _____

6. pmaa   _____

7. ardam   _____

8. pteoa   _____

9. pnaaelt   _____

10. smtasie   _____

11. mleaid   _____

12. dirmgaaa   _____

More About Nouns and Gender
Otros aspectos de los sustantivos y sus géneros

Nouns referring to people that end in -or, -és, -ón, and -ín are generally masculine, and simply require the addition of an -a to become feminine. Notice there is no accent in the feminine form:

el director	la directora
el japonés	la japonesa
el campeón	la campeona
el bailarín	la bailarina

Some nouns that refer to people change their article but keep only one form:

el/la dentista	el/la pianista	
el/la especialista	el/la estudiante	
el/la cantante	el/la guía	
el/la demócrata	el/la líder	
el/la profesional	el/la modelo	
el/la atleta	el/la testigo	
el/la mártir	el/la joven	
el/la intérprete	el/la espía	

> **TIP**
> The letters of the alphabet are feminine: la a, la hache, la i.

However, a few nouns apply to both females and males:

la persona	el águila
el fantasma	el bebé
el amor	el personaje
el pájaro	la rata
el búho	la víctima

Remember, too, that many words change meaning with a change in gender:

el papa	pope	la papa	potato
el policía	police officer	la policía	police department
el capital	capital (money)	la capital	capital city
el mañana	tomorrow	la mañana	morning
el cura	priest	la cura	cure
el frente	front	la frente	forehead
el radio	radius	la radio	radio programming
el orden	orderliness	la orden	command

Still other nouns are altered slightly when they change from the masculine to the feminine form.

MASCULINE	FEMININE	MASCULINE	FEMININE
el poeta	la poetisa	el tigre	la tigresa
el rey	la reina	el león	la leona
el héroe	la heroína	el caballo	la yegua
el duque	la duquesa	el gallo	la gallina
el conde	la condesa	el toro	la vaca

The names for most trees are masculine, but their fruit is generally feminine:

MASCULINE TREE	FEMININE FRUIT
el palto	la palta
el olivo	la oliva
el peral	la pera
el naranjo	la naranja
el cerezo	la cereza
el manzano	la manzana
el almendro	la almendra

Masculine nouns include the names for the days of the week and the months of the year, colors and numbers, languages and foreign words, and the names for rivers, oceans, and seas:

Trabajo el lunes y él trabaja el martes.
I work on Monday and he works on Tuesday.

Enero es el mes más frío. *January is the coldest month.*
(Months are not preceded by articles, but are masculine in construction.)

El nuevo vestido no va ni con el rojo ni con el verde.
The new dress goes neither with the red nor the green one.

El tres y el siete siempre me traen mucha suerte.
Three and seven always bring me a lot of luck.

El griego y el hebreo son idiomas difíciles de aprender.
Greek and Hebrew are difficult languages to learn.

Estudiaba el **marketing**, pero trabajo en el **delivery**.
I studied marketing, but I work in delivery.

El océano Atlántico es más frío que el Pacífico.
The Atlantic Ocean is colder than the Pacific.

El río Orinoco te llevará hasta el Caribe.
The Orinoco River will take you to the Caribbean.

Compound words that are made up of a verb and a noun are also masculine:

El sacacorchos está en el lavaplatos. *(The bottle opener is in the dishwasher.)*
    VERB-NOUN   VERB-NOUN

Verb infinitives used as nouns are masculine as well:

El beber alcohol es prohibido.   *Drinking alcohol is prohibited.*

A noun that begins with a stressed a or ha is considered feminine, even though it takes the masculine article in the singular and the feminine article in the plural:

El agua está fría.   *The water is cold.*
Las aguas de Hawaii son lindas.   *The Hawaiian seas are lovely.*

The word arte is masculine in the singular and feminine in the plural:

El arte en el pasillo es magnífico.   *The art in the hallway is magnificent.*
Quisiera estudiar las artes.   *I would like to study the arts.*

LA PRÁCTICA 3

Identify the correct gender of each noun below. Write el/la if both genders apply or leave blank if no article is used:

1. ___el___   paraguas

2. _____   mayo

3. _____   turista

4. _____   persona

5. _____   Mississippi

6. _____   agente

7. _____   águila

8. _____   fantasma

9. _____   turista

10. _____   jazz

Translate the following nouns into Spanish. Some may require both el *and* la:

11. French   _el francés, la francesa_

12. apple   _____

13. victim   _____

14. Thursday   _____

15. potato   _____

16. forehead   _____

17. artist   _____

18. eighteen   _____

19. olive tree   _____

20. champion   _____

Number
El número

    "Number" refers to a noun being either SINGULAR or PLURAL. As in English, Spanish nouns form the plural by adding s or es. Those ending in a vowel add s; those ending in y or a consonant add es:

Singular	Plural
el hombre	los hombres
la cama	las camas
el cliente	los clientes
la lágrima	las lágrimas
la blusa	las blusas
el reloj	los relojes
la mujer	las mujeres
la ley	las leyes
el papel	los papeles
el azúcar	los azúcares

    Notice how nouns with an accent mark on the next to the last syllable (azúcar) in the singular do not lose the accent in the plural form (azúcares). However, nouns with a final stressed syllable generally have no accent mark in the plural:

el autobús	los autobuses
el francés	los franceses
el cartón	los cartones

Other spelling changes include those nouns ending in -z, which becomes -ces in the plural:

Compré el <u>lápiz</u> verde una <u>vez</u>.   *I bought the green pencil once.*
Compré los <u>lápices</u> rojos dos <u>veces</u>.   *I bought the red pencils twice.*

And nouns ending in -í or -ú add -es instead of -s in the plural:

Hay un dibujo de un <u>colibrí</u> en el <u>menú</u>.
There's a drawing of a hummingbird on the menu.

Hay un dibujo de los <u>colibríes</u> en los <u>menúes</u>.
There's a drawing of hummingbirds on the menus.

Some nouns remain the same in both the singular and the plural. These consist of more than one syllable and end in an unstressed vowel + s:

el análisis	los análisis
el paraguas	los paraguas
el miércoles	los miércoles
la tesis	las tesis
el lunes	los lunes

> **TIP**
> Don't forget that the masculine noun in the plural often refers to males and females combined:
> Vendrán todos mis <u>tíos</u>.
> *All my aunts and uncles will come.*
> Los <u>maestros</u> llegaron.
> *The (male and female) teachers arrived.*
> ¿Quiénes son tus <u>hermanos</u>?
> *Who are your brothers and sisters?*

Other nouns are either always or almost always used in the plural form:

las tenazas	los alrededores
los alicates	los gemelos
las cosquillas	los víveres
los modales	los anteojos
las tijeras	

Some nouns shift their stress to another syllable in the plural form (e.g., <u>régimen</u> ➔ regímenes), while nouns such as examen and origen actually add an accent mark (e.g., exámenes, orígenes).

Also remember there is no plural form for a proper name referring to a family (for example, <u>Los García van a tener una fiesta</u>); however, a plural form is used when a group of people happen to have the same name (Hay muchos Garcías en Los Angeles).

Spanish often uses the singular when the plural is used in English:

Recibieron Uds. su <u>cheque</u>.   *You all got paychecks.*
Nos quitamos el <u>abrigo</u>.   *We took off our coats.*
Se mojaron la <u>cabeza</u>.   *They got their heads wet.*

La Práctica 4

Change these isolated words to their plural form:

1. rey   <u>los reyes</u>

2. inglés   _____

3. reloj   _____

4. ganador   _____

5. trombón   _____

6. jabalí   _____

7. sábado   _____

8. cruz   _____

9. abrelatas   _____

10. té   _____

*Write **YES** if the noun has a plural form and **NO** if it does not:*

11. tráfico   **NO**

12. crisis   _____

13. algo   _____

14. deber   _____

15. razón   _____

16. hambre   _____

17. alma   _____

18. salud   _____

19. pez   _____

20. oeste   _____

The Articles

The Definite Article
El artículo definido

The definite articles in Spanish correspond to the article *the* in English. The four Spanish definite articles must agree with their nouns in both gender and number.

	MASCULINE	FEMININE
Singular	el	la
Plural	los	las

el papel y la pluma	*the paper and the pen*
los papeles y las plumas	*the papers and the pens*

Definite articles are used more frequently in Spanish than they are in English. Not only do they appear before specific persons, places, and things, but they are also used with nouns in a general or generic sense:

El cartero no vino.	*The mail carrier didn't come.*
La leche tiene muchas vitaminas.	*Milk has a lot of vitamins.*

Definite articles can be used before abstract nouns as well:

La vida es difícil.	*Life is tough.*
¿Dónde está la justicia?	*Where is justice?*

The definite article is not used, however, before those nouns that refer to an unspecified amount or only part of a complete set:

Jaime vendía zanahorias.	*Jaime used to sell carrots.*
Tu amiga necesita amor y cariño.	*Your friend needs love and care.*

Other Common Uses of the Definite Article

- Before titles of address followed by a proper name, except when the person is being spoken to directly:

La doctora Smith es la cirujana.	*Dr. Smith is the surgeon.*
¿Cuándo se casó el Sr. Prado?	*When did Mr. Prado get married?*
¿Profesor Lara, qué hora es?	*Professor Lara, what time is it?*

The definite article is dropped, however, before titles such as don, doña, Santo, San, and Santa:

¿Has leído las palabras de San Pedro?
Have you read the words of St. Peter?

- With articles of clothing and parts of the body. Notice how English uses possessive pronouns instead:

Me voy a quitar la camisa.	*I'm going to take off my shirt.*
Le duelen los brazos.	*Her arms hurt.*

- With the time of day, the days of the week, and the seasons of the year.

Tengo cita a las tres.	*I have an appointment at three.*
Trabajaban los viernes.	*They used to work on Fridays.*
El otoño es mi estación favorita.	*Fall is my favorite season.*

However, the definite article may be eliminated after the word en when it is implied that something happens every season:

Juego tenis en verano.	*I play tennis in the summer.*

Also remember that the definite article is not used with the days of the week when they follow the verb ser:

Hoy es lunes y ayer fue domingo.
Today is Monday and yesterday was Sunday.

- With the names of mountains, rivers, and oceans:

Hemos viajado por los Andes.
We have traveled through the Andes.

El río Panamá queda en Centroamérica.
The Panama River is located in Central America.

Me compraría una casa en la costa del Pacífico.
I would buy a house on the Pacific Coast.

- With the names of some countries; however, all cities, countries, and continents require the definite article when they are modified:

    El Brasil tiene música linda y alegre.
    Brazil has beautiful music.

    Estudiaron la historia de la Grecia antigua.
    They studied the history of ancient Greece.

    Los inmigrantes vendrán del África central.
    The immigrants will come from central Africa.

    Those countries that are generally preceded by a definite article include la Argentina, el Ecuador, el Perú, el Brasil, el Panamá, el Paraguay, el Uruguay, la República Dominicana, los Estados Unidos, el Canadá, la India, el Japón, and la Suiza.

- Before the names of languages, except when the name follows the word en or the verb hablar:

El inglés es difícil de aprender.	*English is difficult to learn.*
Me encanta conversar en francés.	*I love to converse in French.*
Todos hablaban italiano.	*Everyone was speaking Italian.*

- Before infinitives or adjectives that are used as nouns:

El correr es buen ejercicio.	*Running is good exercise.*
Quiere comprar el más chico.	*He wants to buy the smallest one.*

Some phrases in English require the definite article in Spanish when translated:

Let's go home.	**Vamos a la casa.**
It's two dollars per pound.	**Cuesta dos dólares la libra.**
What was on TV?	**¿Que salió en la televisión?**

Conversely, some phrases that require the definite article in English do not include it in the Spanish translation:

Se mudaron a Buenos Aires, capital de la Argentina.
*They moved to Buenos Aires, **the** capital of Argentina.*

Paramos en la gasolinera en camino.
*We stopped at the gas station on **the** way.*

¿Qué saben Uds. de Luis XIV?
*What do you know about Louis **the** Fourteenth?*

However, the definite article is almost never used after the verb **haber**. Nor is it used in compound nouns that are formed by the word **de**:

Habían moscas en la cocina.
There were flies in the kitchen.

Nora tiene <u>dolor de estómago</u>.
Nora has a stomachache.

TIP
Remember that there are only two contractions in Spanish, and they both include the definite article **el**:
de + el = del
Son plantas del desierto.
They are plants of/from the desert.
a + el = al
Fuimos al parque ayer.
We went to the park yesterday.
The only exception is when the article is part of a proper name:
¡Vamos a El Paso!   *Let's go to El Paso!*

LA PRÁCTICA 5

Translate these sentences into Spanish:

1. The office opens at seven o'clock.   La oficina abre a las siete.

2. Love is everywhere.   _____

3. It costs a dollar a foot.   _____

4. They have not worked at night.   _____

5. The man and woman are here.   _____

6. Put on your sweater, my love.   _____

7. My friend will come on Thursday.   _____

8. We went to church.   _____

9. Lima is in Peru.   _____

10. Mrs. Toledo has arrived.   _____

Fill in the blank with a definite article only if the sentence needs one:

11. Vivían en __la__ España romántica.

12. He hablado con ____ Sr. Hugo.

13. No puede decirlo en ____ inglés.

14. Tomaban ____ cerveza toda la noche.

15. ____ primavera es la estación más hermosa.

16. Venga a Quito, ____ capital del Ecuador.

17. Mañana no es ____ martes.

18. Lo escuchamos en ____ radio.

19. ____ Uruguay está en América del Sur.

20. Cruzaría ____ océano Atlántico.

21. Hay ____ niños en el jardín.

22. ____ choferes manejan los camiones.

23. Hola, ____ Dra. Roberts.

24. ____ montar caballo es divertido.

25. Hablo ____ alemán.

The Indefinite Article
El artículo indefinido

Like the definite articles, the indefinite articles must change so that they agree with their nouns in both gender and number. The indefinite articles un and una are similar to the articles *a* or *an* in English, while unos and unas mean *some* or *a few*:

	MASCULINE	FEMININE
Singular	un	una
Plural	unos	unas

un papel y una pluma	a paper and a pen
unos papeles y unas plumas	some papers and a few pens

The singular masculine form un is used before all feminine nouns that begin with a stressed a or ha. The plural form of the article, however, is in the feminine:

Vimos un águila.	We saw an eagle.
Vimos unas águilas.	We saw a couple of eagles.
Tenían un hacha.	They had a hatchet.
Tenían unas hachas.	They had some hatchets.

Other nouns following these rules are agua (*water*), ancla (*anchor*), alga (*algae*), alma (*soul*), arca (*ark*), área (*area*), arma (*weapon*), habla (*speech*), hada (*fairy*), harpa (*harp*), hambre (*hunger*), haba (*bean*).

Indefinite articles are primarily used before count nouns in a general sense, including those nouns in a series:

Una persona honesta devolvió el dinero.
An honest person returned the money.

Encontré un cuaderno, una pluma,
   y un lápiz.
I found a notebook, a pen, and a pencil.

However, the indefinite article is usually dropped after the verbs tener, llevar, buscar, comprar, sacar, and usar:

¿Compraste carne?	*Did you buy meat?*
Han tenido problemas.	*They've had problems.*
Voy a llevar impermeable.	*I'm going to wear a raincoat.*

The indefinite article is also omitted before a predicate noun that indicates nationality, profession, religion, gender, rank, or marital status. These sentences often include the verb ser:

Es pintor.	*He's a painter.*
Son griegos.	*They're Greek.*
Soy cristiana.	*I'm a Christian.*

However, when the predicate noun is modified, the indefinite article is used:

Él es un pintor de casas.	*He's a house painter.*
Son unos griegos que hablan francés.	*They're Greeks who speak French.*
Yo soy una cristiana evangélica.	*I'm an evangelical Christian.*

The definite article is also omitted in many common expressions and exclamations. These include phrases with ¡Qué...!, mil, ciento, medio, otro, sin, tal, and cierto:

¡Qué vista tan bonita!	*What a pretty view!*
Media hora	*A half hour*
¡Mil gracias!	*Many (a thousand) thanks!*
Cierto hombre	*A certain man*
¡Sin duda!	*Without a doubt!*
Otro día	*Another day*

The use or omission of an article can change the meaning of a sentence. Notice how these three sentences differ in translation:

Ella no quiere agua.	*She doesn't want (any) water.*
Ella no quiere el agua.	*She doesn't want the water (that we know about).*
Ella no quiere un agua.	*She doesn't want a (serving of) water.*

LA PRÁCTICA 6

Fill in each line with the appropriate indefinite article.

1. __un__ alma

2. _____ agua

3. _____ arpas

4. _____ medio kilo

5. _____ hacha

6. _____ cierta persona

7. _____ irlandés

8. _____ áreas

9. _____ policía

10. _____ hambre

Fill in the lines with either the definite or indefinite article if it is required. Otherwise, leave it blank:

11. ¿Dónde está __el__ arma que compraste?

12. Creo que tiene _____ problemas personales.

13. Trajo _____ agua y _____ leche?

14. Soy _____ japonés.

15. ¡Qué _____ lástima!

16. No me lavé _____ manos.

17. Me costó _____ cien dólares.

18. _____ música clásica me interesa mucho.

19. Me dijo que _____ clima había cambiado.

20. ¿Sabes tocar _____ arpa?

The Neuter Article *lo*
El artículo neutro lo

Lo is considered the neuter article in Spanish because it refers to neither the feminine nor the masculine. It is primarily used before the masculine singular form of an adjective that is being used as a noun simply to express a specific quality or abstract idea:

Lo bueno es que ellos hablan español. Lo malo es que no van a venir.
The good thing is they speak Spanish. The bad news is they're not coming.

Siempre terminan con lo más importante.
They always finish with the most important (thing).

Lo is also used before past participles:

Lo dicho fue interesante.   *What has been said was interesting.*
No entiendo lo escrito.   *I don't understand what has been written.*

The construction lo + adjective or adverb + que expresses *how* in English. Notice that the gender or number of the adjective does not matter:

Sabemos lo inteligentes que son.   *We know how smart they are.*
¿Vieron lo caro que fue?   *Did you see how expensive it was?*

Él me decía lo bien que hacías ese trabajo.
He told me how well you were doing that job.

When lo precedes de or del, it implies *the matter or business concerning*:

No hemos estudiado lo del incidente de Watergate.
We haven't studied the matter concerning Watergate.

El maestro explicará lo del examen final.
The teacher will explain the business about the final exam.

The article lo is also part of several common expressions in Spanish:

Lo contrario	*The opposite*
Lo más posible	*As much as possible*
Lo único	*The only one*
Lo mismo	*The same thing*
Lo mejor	*The best*

LA PRÁCTICA 7

Translate these phrases into Spanish using the neuter article lo:

1. It's the good, the bad, and the ugly.   Es lo bueno, lo malo, y lo feo.

2. I heard the matter concerning the doctor.   _____

3. She ran as little as possible.   _____

4. We saw how tall he is.   _____

5. They would do the same.   _____

6. What's been done is the most important.   _____

7. Have they read what is written?   _____

8. I know how necessary it is.   _____

9. We deserve the best.   _____

10. It surprises me how well he sings.   _____

Possession with *de*
La posesión con de

Possession in Spanish is expressed by de or by the construction de + article + possessor. Obviously, there is no 's as there is in English:

Tenemos el carro de Ramón.	*We have Ramón's car.*
No es la casa de Adela.	*It isn't Adela's house.*

Abra la puerta de la oficina.   *Open the office door.*
    DE + ARTICLE
    + POSSESSOR

Necesito los nombres de las chicas.   *I need the girls' names.*
    DE + ARTICLE
    + POSSESSOR

The contraction del is often used in sentences that express possession, including those where people have specific titles:

Buscaron la entrada del hospital.
They looked for the hospital entrance.

¿Dónde estará la esposa del Dr. Lara?
Where in the world is Dr. Lara's wife?

LA PRÁCTICA 8

Show possession between the following sets of words:

1. El gato/ mi hermana   el gato de mi hermana

2. Las páginas/ el libro   _____

3. El dueño/ estos zapatos   _____

4. Los libros/ Dra. Ortega   _____

5. El restaurante/ el hotel   _____

6. Las herramientas/ los obreros _____

7. Las recetas/ Silvia   _____

8. El negocio/ tu familia   _____

9. Las sonrisas/ Carla y Lidia _____

10. El trono/ rey David   _____

The Adjectives

¿Cuánto sabe usted?

How Much Do You Know Already?

1. What does Bailo tanto como tú mean?

2. Is it No necesito tanto dinero, or No necesito dinero tanto? Why?

3. What does suavísimo mean in English?

4. What are people from Berlin called in Spanish?

5. What do you call people from Costa Rica in Spanish?

Adjective Agreements
Concordancias del adjetivo

An adjective is a word that limits or describes a noun or pronoun. An adjective in Spanish must agree with the noun it modifies in gender and in number. Adjectives ending in o in the masculine change to a to form the feminine, and the plural is formed by adding an s:

Delicious		
	MASCULINE	**FEMININE**
Singular	delicioso	deliciosa
Plural	deliciosos	deliciosas

Adjectives ending in either a consonant, -e, or -ista have only one singular and one plural form:

Easy	
	MASCULINE/FEMININE
Singular	fácil
Plural	fáciles

Big	
	MASCULINE/FEMININE
Singular	grande
Plural	grandes

Socialist	
	MASCULINE/FEMININE
Singular	socialista
Plural	socialistas

Adjectives ending in the suffixes -án, -ón or -dor add an -a to form the feminine. The plurals are formed by adding -es to the masculine and -s to the feminine. Notice how the accent mark is dropped when an ending is added:

Lazy		
	MASCULINE	**FEMININE**
Singular	holgazán	holgazana
Plural	holgazanes	holgazanas

Whining		
	MASCULINE	**FEMININE**
Singular	llorón	llorona
Plural	llorones	lloronas

Hard-working		
	MASCULINE	**FEMININE**
Singular	trabajador	trabajadora
Plural	trabajadores	trabajadoras

Most adjectives of nationality or place of origin have four basic forms—two masculine (-o, -os) and two feminine (-a, -as):

Italian		
	MASCULINE	**FEMININE**
Singular	italiano	ialiana
Plural.	italianos	italianas

South American		
	MASCULINE	**FEMININE**
Singular	sudamericano	suadmericana
Plural	sudamericanos	sudamericanas

Those nationalities ending in a consonant follow the same rules as other adjectives—the **a** is added to form the feminine, **es** is added to form the masculine plural, and the accent mark is dropped when an ending is added:

French		
	MASCULINE	**FEMININE**
Singular	francés	francesa
Plural	franceses	francesas

Spanish		
	MASCULINE	**FEMININE**
Singular	español	española
Plural	españoles	españolas

However, a few nationalities and places of origin are unique and have only one singular and one plural form. These generally have the suffixes -ita, -ense, -a, -í, and -ú:

Vietnamese	
	MASCULINE/FEMININE
Singular	vietnamita
Plural	vietnamitas

Canadian	
	MASCULINE/FEMININE
Singular	canadiense
Plural	canadienses

Iraqi	
	MASCULINE/FEMININE
Singular	iraquí
Plural	iraquíes

- Countries and nationalities in Spanish

Alemania — alemán
Arabia Saudita — saudí
la Argentina — argentino
Australia — australiano
Austria — austriaco, austríaco
el Brasil — brasileño
Bélgica — belga
Bolivia — boliviano
el Canadá — canadiense
Chile — chileno
China — chino
Colombia — colombiano
Corea del Norte — norcoreano
Corea del Sur — sudcoreano
Costa Rica — costarriqueño, costarricense
Cuba — cubano
Dinamarca — danés
el Ecuador — ecuatoriano
Egipto — egipcio
El Salvador — salvadoreño
Escocia — escocés
España — español
los Estados Unidos — estadounidense, norteamericano
Finlandia — finlandés
las Filipinas — filipino
Francia — francés
Gales — galés
Gran Bretaña — británico
Grecia — griego
Guatemala — guatemalteco
Haití — haitiano
Honduras — hondureño
Hungría — húngaro
la India — indio
Inglaterra — inglés
Irak, Iraq — irakí, iraquí

Irán — Iraní
Irlanda — irlandés
Israel — israelí
Italia — italiano
el Japón — japonés
Kuwait — kuwaití
Líbano — libanés
Marruecos — marroquí
México, Méjico — mexicano, mejicano
Noruega — noruego
Nueva Zelanda — neozelandés
Nicaragua — nicaragüense
los Países Bajos — holandés
Palestina — palestino
el Panamá — panameño
el Paraguay — paraguayo
el Perú — peruano
Polonia — polaco
Portugal — portugués
Puerto Rico — puertorriqueño
la República Dominicana — dominicano
Rusia — ruso
Siria — sirio
Sudáfrica — sudafricano
Sudán — sudanés
Suecia — sueco
la Suiza — suizo
Tailandia — tailandés
Taiwan — taiwanés
Túnez — tunecino
Turquía — turco
el Uruguay — uruguayo
Venezuela — venezolano
Vietnám — vietnamita
Yemen — yemení

Remember that adjectives of nationality (los gentilicios) are not capitalized in Spanish:

- Continents

  Africa — africano
  la Antártida — antárctico
  el Ártico — ártico
  Asia — asiático
  Centroamérica — centroamericano
  Europa — europeo

- Islands

  las Antillas — antillano
  las Bahamas — bahamiano
  las Canarias — canario
  Córsica — corsicano
  Creta — cretense
  Mallorca — mallorquín
  Malta — maltés

- Cities

  Berlín — berlinense
  Bogotá — bogotano
  Buenos Aires — bonaerense, porteño
  Florence — florentino
  Lima — limeño
  Londres — londinense
  Madrid — madrileño
  Moscú — moscovita
  Nuevo York — neoyorquino
  París — parisino, parisiense
  Roma — romano

TIP
Learn those adjectives that describe topics that interest you most. Notice these spelling changes: indígena (*indigenous*), agrícola (*agricultural*), persa (*Persian*), andaluz (*Andalusian*).
These are adjectives of religion:
cristiano (*Christian*), judío (*Jewish*), islámico (*Islamic*), católico (*Catholic*), budista (*Buddhist*), hindú (*Hindu*), mormón (*Mormon*), protestante (*Protestant*).

LA PRÁCTICA 1

Read each sentence and tell what it is about. Use hay to respond:

1. La sopa está caliente.   Hay sopa caliente.

2. Las plumas son negras.   _____

3. Los niños son preguntones.   _____

4. Las amigas son cosmopólitas.   _____

5. Los ingleses están alegres.   _____

6. El aire está fresco.   _____

7. La fruta está podrida.   _____

8. Los compañeros son comunistas.   _____

9. El agua está sucia.   _____

10. Los estudiantes son canadienses.   _____

For each country below, write the feminine plural form for its nationality:

11. Alemania   alemanas

12. Grecia   _____

13. Italia   _____

14. España   _____

15. Vietnám   _____

16. el Brasil   _____

17. Portugal   _____

18. El Salvador   _____

19. China   _____

20. Puerto Rico   _____

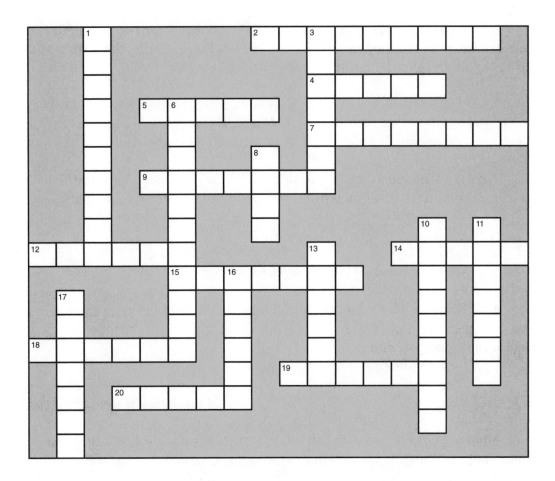

Translate these into Spanish:

Across
2. any
4. silly
5. clever
7. funny
9. third
12. several
14. happy
15. some
18. sad
19. pink
20. long

Down
1. hard-working
3. ancient
6. interesting
8. worse
10. dangerous
11. painted
13. Pole
16. Greek
17. beautiful

Adjective Position
La posición del adjetivo

Although adjectives in Spanish generally appear after the nouns they modify, there are cases where they may be placed before. For example, the adjective appears before the noun in exclamations with Qué:

¡Qué <u>linda</u> flor!	*What a lovely flower!*
¡Qué <u>brillante</u> alumno!	*What a brilliant student!*
¡Qué <u>difícil</u> problema!	*What a difficult problem!*

Adjectives of inherent nature or quality also precede the noun. Notice how these adjectives do not add new information about the nouns they modify:

el <u>frío</u> hielo	*the cold ice*
la <u>peligrosa</u> leona	*the dangerous lioness*
el <u>chistoso</u> payaso	*the funny clown*

An adjective is frequently placed before a noun when it expresses the speaker's personal opinion or judgment. These adjectives include words such as bueno, malo, mejor, and peor:

Creo que tenemos la <u>mejor</u> compañía.	*I believe we have the best company.*
Pienso que sería una <u>buena</u> idea.	*I think that it would be a good idea.*

Adjectives that express number or quantity also precede the noun in Spanish. These include words such as alguno, ninguno, poco, mucho, bastante, tanto, suficiente, todos, otro, cada, varios, mismo, and ambos:

Hemos tenido <u>bastante</u> ayuda.	*We've had plenty of help.*
Le faltan <u>dos</u> tornillos.	*It's missing two screws.*
No necesito <u>tanto</u> dinero.	*I don't need that much money.*
Tendrán que comprar <u>otra</u> cámara.	*They'll have to buy another camera.*
Hablábamos el <u>mismo</u> idioma.	*We spoke in the same language.*

Some adjectives actually differ in meaning depending on whether they precede or follow a noun. Notice how a few have shortened forms:

<u>diferentes</u> sitios	comidas <u>diferentes</u>
several places	*distinct foods*
el <u>alto</u> puesto	el árbol <u>alto</u>
the high position	*the tall tree*
la <u>pobre</u> situación	la mujer <u>pobre</u>
the pathetic situation	*the impoverished woman*
un <u>simple</u> saludo	una persona <u>simple</u>
a mere greeting	*a simple-minded person*

el <u>único</u> calcetín	la corbata <u>única</u>
the only sock	*the unique tie*
<u>viejos</u> amigos	cuchillos <u>viejos</u>
long-time friends	*old knives*
el <u>medio</u> galón	la clase <u>media</u>
the half gallon	*middle class*
<u>cierta</u> persona	promesa <u>cierta</u>
certain person	*sincere promise*
un <u>buen</u> médico	una niña <u>buena</u>
a fine doctor	*a well-behaved girl*
el <u>gran</u> actor	un martillo <u>grande</u>
a great actor	*a large hammer*

However, the adjective generally follows the noun when it is modified by an adverb:

No fue un problema <u>tan difícil</u>.	*It wasn't that difficult a problem.*
Ella tenía pelo <u>muy largo</u>.	*She had very long hair.*
Quiero una bebida <u>más dulce</u>.	*I want a sweeter drink.*

In addition, demonstrative and possessive adjectives in Spanish always precede the nouns they modify:

<u>Esas</u> respuestas son excelentes.	*Those answers are excellent.*
¿Dónde están <u>nuestros</u> periódicos?	*Where are our newspapers?*

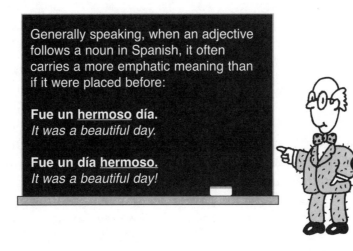

Generally speaking, when an adjective follows a noun in Spanish, it often carries a more emphatic meaning than if it were placed before:

Fue un <u>hermoso</u> día.
It was a beautiful day.

Fue un día <u>hermoso</u>.
It was a beautiful day!

LA PRÁCTICA 2

Translate these phrases from English into Spanish:

1. the only pen   la única pluma

2. bad luck

3. a very delicious pear

4. white snow

5. the green chairs

6. a certain teacher

7. the same paper

8. an impoverished man

9. the new flowers

10. What big eyes!

Adjectives in Shortened Forms
Adjetivos abreviados

Some adjectives drop their final o when placed before a masculine noun. Notice the accent mark on ningún and algún:

uno	un televisor
bueno	buen padre
malo	mal día
primero	primer hijo
tercero	tercer plato
alguno	algún libro
ninguno	ningún carro

In some cases, grande, ciento, and Santo drop their final syllable before a noun. For example, grande becomes gran before a noun when it carries the meaning of *excellence* rather than large in size:

Ella es una gran cantante.   *She's a great singer.*
Tengo pies grandes.   *I have big feet.*

Ciento becomes cien only when it is directly followed by a masculine or feminine plural noun:

> Habían <u>cien</u> mesas en la fiesta de boda.
> *There were one hundred tables at the wedding reception.*

> Mi abuelo va a cumplir <u>cien</u> años.
> *My grandfather is going to turn one hundred.*

> Me pagaron <u>ciento</u> treinta dólares.
> *They paid me one hundred thirty dollars.*

Santo (*Saint*) becomes San when it is followed by a proper noun not beginning with To... or Do...:

> San José y San Francisco
> Santa Ana y Santo Domingo

La Práctica 3

Write the shortened forms of each adjective below along with its definition in English:

1. tercero	*tercer*	***third***
2. cualquiera		
3. ciento		
4. grande		
5. primero		
6. alguno		
7. malo		
8. Santo		
9. ninguno		
10. bueno		

More Uses of the Adjective
Usos adicionales del adjetivo

An adjective that modifies two or more plural nouns of the same gender remains in the plural of that gender:

Encontramos monedas y estampillas <u>antiguas</u>.
We found antique coins and stamps.

Les mando besos y abrazos <u>amorosos</u>.
I send you loving kisses and hugs.

However, if the nouns are of different genders, the adjective is generally left in the masculine plural:

Son niños y niñas <u>europeos</u>.
They're European boys and girls.

Necesita una cuchara y un tenedor <u>limpios</u>.
He needs a clean spoon and fork.

When two adjectives modify a noun, they are generally placed after it, joined by the word y:

Ella es una estudiante <u>inteligente y disciplinada</u>.
She is an intelligent and disciplined student.

However, the two adjectives may also be joined without the y, where the adjective of greater emphasis is mentioned last:

Tenía un mueble <u>elegante francés</u>.
I had an elegant <u>French</u> piece of furniture.

Pescan en las aguas <u>azules frías</u>.
They fish in the <u>cold</u> blue waters.

Hay un hueco <u>profundo peligroso</u>.
There's a <u>dangerous</u> deep hole.

Nouns in Spanish may be used as adjectives also. A noun, however, does not have to agree in number and gender with the noun it modifies:

¿Quién es la <u>reina Madre</u>?	*Who is the Queen Mother?*
Eran <u>programas piloto</u>.	*They were pilot programs.*
Somos <u>primos hermanos</u>.	*We're first cousins.*

Past participles can also be used as adjectives, but they must agree in both gender and number with the nouns they modify. They frequently give the location or condition of people and things:

Hay dos paquetes <u>envueltos</u>.	*There are two wrapped packages.*
Mira la ropa <u>mojada</u>.	*Look at the wet clothing.*
Buscaron dulces <u>escondidos</u>.	*They looked for hidden candies.*

Past participles are frequently used as adjectives after the verbs ser and estar:

Los parlantes fueron <u>desconectados</u>.	*The speakers were disconnected.*
No estoy <u>sentado</u> en la cocina.	*I'm not sitting in the kitchen.*

Most adjectives in Spanish can also be used as nouns. They simply replace the deleted noun with the English equivalent of *the ___ one*, or *the ___ person*. Notice the use of the definite articles el, la, los, and las:

No encuentra <u>el azul</u>.	*She cannot find <u>the blue one</u>.*
Acabo de hablar con <u>la alta</u>.	*I just spoke to <u>the tall lady</u>.*
Trajo comida para <u>los pobres</u>.	*He brought food for <u>the poor people</u>.*
Tenemos que cambiar <u>las viejas</u>.	*We have to change <u>the old ones</u>.*
la Cruz <u>Roja</u>	the Red <u>Cross</u>

La Práctica 4

Translate the adjective correctly and place it after each noun or nouns:

1. *UGLY*	mesas y sillas	<u>mesas y sillas feas</u>
2. *MODERN*	apartamentos y casas	_____
3. *FAT AND SMALL*	conejos	_____
4. *WIDE*	calles y caminos	_____
5. *RED and BLUE*	el único libro	_____
6. *SWEET*	plátanos y duraznos	_____
7. *SPANISH*	vendedores y clientes	_____
8. *NEW AND PRETTY*	pantalones	_____
9. *HAPPY*	muchachas y muchachos	_____
10. *DIFFICULT*	el otro problema	_____

Combine the three key words correctly, making sure all words agree:

11. 4/ casa/ pintar   cuatro casas pintadas

12. 1/ ojo/ cerrar

13. 5/ chica/ confundir

14. 2/ juguete/ perder

15. 9/ carta/ escribir

16. 6/ plato/ preparar

17. 8/ huevo/ freír

18. 3/ cheque/ firmar

19. 7/ papa/ pelar

20. 10/ olla/ cubrir

Create sentences that replace the noun with an article and adjective:

21. Me dió un vaso sucio.   Me dió el sucio.

22. ¿Dónde están las medias negras?

23. Tráigame la piña grande.

24. Llevaron las maletas nuevas.

25. No me gusta la pintura azul.

26. ¿Has visto el drama italiano?

27. Solamente sirva el agua fría.

28. ¿Prefieres leer la novela romántica?

29. Invitamos a los estudiantes ingleses.

30. A mí me interesa la película religiosa.

Comparison of Adjectives, Adverbs, Nouns, and Verbs
Comparación de adjetivos, adverbios, sustantivos y verbos

In Spanish, the comparison of two adjectives is usually formed by placing the word **más** or **menos** before an adjective, followed by the word que:

Jorge es <u>más alto que</u> su hermano.
Jorge is taller than his brother.

Esta caja es <u>menos pesada que</u> la otra.
This box is less heavy than (not as heavy as) the other one.

Las ventanas fueron <u>más caras que</u> las puertas.
The windows were more expensive than the doors.

Los estudiantes estarán <u>menos nerviosos que</u> los profesores.
The students will be less nervous than (not as nervous as) the teachers.

The adjectives bueno and malo, however, have irregular comparative forms and do not require adverbs such as más or menos:

bueno (*good*)	→	mejor (*better*)
malo (*bad*)	→	peor (*worse*)

La sopa de pollo <u>es mejor que</u> la ensalada de atún.
The chicken soup is better than the tuna salad.

Su viaje a Europa <u>fue peor que</u> su viaje a las Bahamas.
Her trip to Europe was worse than her trip to the Bahamas.

However, the expressions más bueno and más malo are sometimes used to describe a person's moral character:

Tu primer novio fue <u>más malo que</u> el que tienes ahora.
Your first boyfriend was a worse guy than the one you have now.

The comparative forms for grande and pequeño are also irregular, but strictly refer to age:

Arturo es <u>mayor que</u> el dueño de la compañía.
Arturo is older than the owner of the company.

Creo que tu padre <u>es menor que</u> mi madre.
I believe your father is younger than my mother.

Adverbs are compared in Spanish much like adjectives:

Virginia manejaba menos <u>cuidadosamente</u> que Miguel.
Virginia used to drive less carefully than Miguel.

El pasto ha crecido más <u>rápidamente</u> que los arbustos.
The grass has grown faster than the bushes.

The comparison of equality in Spanish involves the construction tan + adjective/adverb + como.

Tus ojos son <u>tan azules como</u> el cielo.
Your eyes are as blue as the sky.

Ellos juegan <u>tan bueno como</u> Uds.
They play as well as you.

Lo hizo <u>tan fácilmente como</u> un profesional.
He did it as easily as a professional.

However, when two nouns are compared as equals, tan changes to tanto. Notice how tanto must agree with the noun it modifies:

> **TIP**
> Mejor and peor generally precede the nouns they modify, whereas mayor and menor usually follow them:
> mejor idea   *better idea*
> primo menor   *younger cousin*

Mis abuelos tuvieron <u>tantos</u> hijos
  como mis padres.
My grandparents had as many children as my parents.

When two verbs are compared as equals, tan simply changes to tanto:

La Sra. Nario cultiva flores <u>tanto</u> como su vecina.
Mrs. Nario plants flowers as much as her neighbor.

Remember that the pattern for comparing nouns or verbs is similar to the comparison of adjectives or adverbs:

ADJECTIVES: Es <u>más agudo que</u> una navaja.
               It's sharper than a razor.
ADVERBS: Pablo se mueve <u>más lentamente que</u> una tortuga.
               He moves slower than a turtle.
NOUNS: Ella tiene <u>más paciencia que</u> una Santa.
               She has more patience than a Saint.
VERBS: Ellos <u>trabajan más que</u> nosotros.
               They work more than us.

LA PRÁCTICA 5

Use either **más** *or* **menos** *to make these comparisons true:*

1. King Kong/ alto/ ratón Mickey   _más alto que_

2. El elefante/ pesado/ el ratón   _____

3. Un baile/ divertido/ un trabajo   _____

4. Las gallinas/ fuerte/ los caballos   _____

5. El dinero/ importante/ la vida   _____

6. El acero/ duro/ la madera   _____

7. Los ríos/ profundo/ los océanos   _____

8. Superhombre/ famoso/ tú   _____

9. Los conejos/ peligrosos/ los tigres   _____

10. El desierto/ seco/ la selva   _____

Replacements for *que*
Reemplazos de que

    Than is translated by **de** or **del** instead of **que** before any numeral:

Perdieron menos <u>del</u> 25 por ciento.	*They lost less than 25 percent.*
No tenía más <u>de</u> diez dólares.	*He didn't have more than ten dollars.*

    Que is also replaced by **de** before phrases which take the place of a deleted noun, such as **el que**, **la que**, **los que**, and **las que**:

Recibimos más juguetes <u>de los que</u> nos regalaste.
We received more toys than (the toys) you gave us.

Comieron menos comida <u>de la que</u> ella preparó.
They ate less food than (the food) she prepared.

    Whenever a clause suggests that there is already a standard for comparison established in a sentence, **que** is replaced by **de lo que**:

La conversación fue más larga <u>de lo que</u> pensamos.
The conversation was longer than (what) we thought.

Remember that a subject pronoun may also follow que in a comparative sentence, unless the pronoun is an object of the verb, requiring the que + a + stressed pronoun construction:

Bailo mejor que <u>tú</u>.   *I dance better than you.*
Usas el teléfono más que <u>nosotros</u>.   *You use the phone more than we do.*

Él quiere más a Cecilia <u>que a ella</u>.   *He loves Cecilia more than her.*
A ellos les gustó el baile más <u>que a él</u>. *They liked the dance more than he did.*

Nadie or nada may also follow que in a comparative sentence:

Esa actriz canta mejor <u>que nadie</u>.
That actress sings better than anyone.

Más <u>que nada,</u> quisiera recibir mi diploma.
More than anything, I would like to receive my diploma.

LA PRÁCTICA 6

Translate these sentences into Spanish:

1. *He is older than his sister.*

   Él es mayor que su hermana.

2. *She cooks more than I.*

   _____

3. *The magazines are more interesting than the newspapers.*

   _____

4. *That ball is better than the other one.*

   _____

5. *I run slower than Juan.*

   _____

6. *The situation was more difficult than what he said.*

   _____

7. *They have as many books as the library.*

_____

8. *You (sing. form.) study less than us.*

_____

9. *Sara dances better than anyone.*

_____

10. *It will take less than two hours.*

_____

11. *She is as pretty as a rose.*

_____

12. *The kitchen is worse than the bathroom.*

_____

13. *We used more pens than the ones you (sing. inf.) bought.*

_____

14. *The girls worked more carefully than the boys.*

_____

15. *My grandfather is younger than my grandmother.*

_____

Superlatives
Superlativos

The superlative in Spanish generally consists of the definite article and noun followed by the simple comparative form:

el	gato	más	grande	*the biggest cat*
DEF. ART.	NOUN	COMPARATIVE FORM		

la pregunta más complicada   *the most complicated question*
el artículo menos interesante   *the least interesting article*
los relojes más ruidosos   *the loudest clocks*

To complete a superlative sentence in Spanish, the word de is often added to a prepositional phrase.

Fue la pregunta más complicada <u>de la clase</u>.
It was the most complicated question in the class.

Leíamos el artículo menos interesante <u>de la revista</u>.
We read the least interesting article in the magazine.

Compró los perros más ruidosos <u>de la tienda</u>.
He bought the loudest dogs in the store.

The absolute superlative in Spanish consists of the suffix -ísimo, which gives the adjective a meaning that might be expressed in English by *very* or *extremely*. If the adjective ends in an unaccented vowel, the vowel is dropped before the suffix:

Este tren es lent<u>ísimo</u>.   *This train is very slow.*
Estábamos cansad<u>ísimos</u>.   *We were extremely tired.*
La piedra fue dur<u>ísima</u>.   *The rock was very hard.*
Ellas estaban ocupad<u>ísimas</u>.   *They were extremely busy.*

If the adjective ends in a consonant or accented vowel, the suffix is simply added. In terms of spelling, the z changes to c, the c changes to qu, and the g changes to gu when -ísimo is added:

difícil	→	dificilísimo
feliz	→	felicísimo
rico	→	riquísimo
largo	→	larguísimo

Technically, there are six adjectives in Spanish that do not require adverbs in the comparative and superlative forms, although some are not used in everyday speech:

POSITIVE	COMPARATIVE	SUPERLATIVE
bueno	mejor	óptimo
malo	peor	pésimo
grande	mayor	máximo
pequeño	menor	mínimo
alto	superior	supremo
bajo	inferior	ínfimo

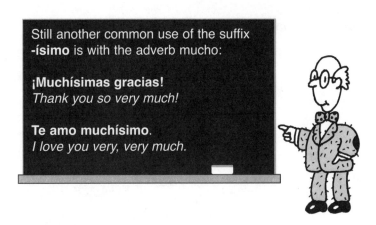

Still another common use of the suffix **-ísimo** is with the adverb mucho:

¡Muchísimas gracias!
Thank you so very much!

Te amo muchísimo.
I love you very, very much.

Although uncommon, the following absolute superlative forms are also considered irregular:

amable (*friendly*)	amabilísimo
bueno (*good*)	bonísimo
cierto (*true*)	certísimo
fiel (*faithful*)	fidelísimo
sabio (*wise*)	sapientísimo
nuevo (*new*)	novísimo
fuerte (*strong*)	fortísimo

LA PRÁCTICA 7

Change these words to the superlative form, and then translate to English:

1. cuchillo útil — el cuchillo más útil — *the most useful knife*

2. soldados valientes — _____ — _____

3. doctora capaz — _____ — _____

4. oficinas elegantes — _____ — _____

5. avenida ancha — _____ — _____

6. policías simpático — _____ — _____

7. programa terrible — _____ — _____

8. divorcio rápid — _____ — _____

9. árboles verdes — _____ — _____

10. mesera cortés — _____ — _____

Change these words to the absolute superlative form:

11. tela fina   la tela finísima

12. poema famoso   _____

13. cara pálida   _____

14. tareas fáciles   _____

15. comida rica   _____

16. falda hermosa   _____

17. perro feroz   _____

18. retratos feos   _____

19. pelo largo   _____

20. hombre feliz   _____

EL REPASO

- Name three irregular verbs in the present tense.

- Name three irregular verbs in the preterit tense.

- Name three irregular verbs in the future tense.

- Name three irregular past participles.

- Name three irregular present participles.

- Name three irregular verbs in the subjunctive mood.

- Name three irregular informal commands.

- Name three common uses of the definite article.

- Name three adjectives that have shortened forms.

- Name three nationalities found in the Far East.

15

Demonstratives and Possessives

¿Cuánto sabe usted?

How Much Do You Know Already?

1. What is the difference between este, ese, and aquel?

2. Which are the three neuter demonstrative pronouns?

3. What is the difference in meaning between ese and aquel?

4. Name the short and long possessive adjective forms for tú.

5. How do you say *These are my keys* in Spanish?

The Demonstratives

Demonstrative Adjectives
Adjetivos demostrativos

In Spanish there are three demonstrative adjectives that point out a person or an object. Each one has four different forms that must agree in number and gender with the nouns they modify. Notice how the word groups refer to three different locations:

This/These (*near the speaker*)		
	MASCULINE	**FEMININE**
Singular	este	esta
Plural	estos	estas

213

That/Those *(near the person spoken to)*		
	MASCULINE	**FEMININE**
Singular	ese	esa
Plural	esos	esas

That/Those *(away from the speaker and the person spoken to)*		
	MASCULINE	**FEMININE**
Singular	aquel	aquella
Plural	aquellos	aquellas

Demonstrative adjectives generally precede the noun. Again, notice the location words:

> ¿De quién es este lápiz? (aquí)
> *Whose pencil is this? (here)*

> ¿De quién es ese lápiz? (ahí)
> *Whose pencil is that? (there)*

> ¿De quién es aquel lápiz? (allí)
> *Whose pencil is that? (over there)*

TIP
The word ese sometimes follows a noun in a sentence to express a feeling of disgust or contempt:
¿Por qué compraste el carro ese?
Why did you buy that car?

LA PRÁCTICA 1

Rewrite each sentence with the demonstrative adjective in the plural form:

1. ¿Dónde vive este chico?   ¿Dónde viven estos chicos?

2. Esta silla está rota.   _____

3. Creo que aquel pájaro es un cuervo.   _____

4. ¿Quién compró esa galleta?   _____

5. Este avión tiene problemas.   _____

6. Subieron aquella montaña.   _____

7. Apagaré esta luz.   _____

8. ¿Cuánto cuesta ese maletín?   _____

9. Aquel disco compacto no funciona.   _____

10. Tráigame esa salchicha.   _____

Demonstrative Pronouns
Pronombres demostrativos

A demonstrative pronoun takes the place of the object or person that is being identified. They are often translated as *this one, that one, these ones,* and *those ones.* In Spanish, demonstrative pronouns have the same forms as demonstrative adjectives, but include accent marks over each stressed vowel:

This One/Those Ones *(near the speaker)*		
	MASCULINE	**FEMININE**
Singular	éste	ésta
Plural	éstos	éstas

That One/Those Ones *(near the person spoken to)*		
	MASCULINE	**FEMININE**
Singular	ése	ésa
Plural	ésos	ésas

That One/Those Ones *(away from the speaker and the person spoken to)*		
	MASCULINE	**FEMININE**
Singular	aquél	aquélla
Plural	aquéllos	aquéllas

Notice how these pronouns can stand alone, and do not precede nouns like demonstrative adjectives do:

Éste es mi libro y ése es su libro.
This (one) is my book and that (one) is his book.

Éstos son más caros que aquéllos.
These (ones) are more expensive than those (ones).

¿Prefieres ésta o aquélla?
Do you prefer this (one) or that (one)?

There are also three neuter demonstrative pronouns in Spanish—all ending in -o and without accent marks—esto, eso, and aquello. They are used in place of statements, concepts, ideas, or situations:

No entiendo esto.	*I don't understand this.*
Eso es todo.	*That's it.*
Quisiéramos hablar de aquello.	*We would like to talk about that.*

Neuter demonstratives are sometimes followed by **de** to express the English phrase *This or that matter concerning...*:

> Esto del Sr. Porras es una tragedia.
> *This matter concerning Mr. Porras is a tragedy.*

> Eso de ahorrar dinero me interesa mucho.
> *That matter concerning saving money interests me.*

LA PRÁCTICA 2

Change each English phrase to a demonstrative pronoun in Spanish:

1. Me gustó más (*this book*).   éste

2. Mire (*that tree over there*).   _____

3. (*This item*) es delicioso.   _____

4. Prefieren (*this house*) más que ésa.   _____

5. (*That over there*) fue horrible.   _____

6. ¿Y (*those papers*)?   _____

7. Deme (*that spoon over there*).   _____

8. (*That*) es muy importante.   _____

9. (*This matter*) de tu familia me amarga.   _____

10. ¿Para qué son (*these coins*)?   _____

The Possessives

Possessive Adjectives
Adjetivos posesivos

Unlike English, possessive adjectives in Spanish agree in number and gender with the nouns they modify. Notice how the **nosotros** and **vosotros** have four forms each while all the others have only two:

SHORT-FORM POSSESSIVE ADJECTIVES		
(yo)	mi/mis	*(my)*
(tú)	tu/tus	*(your: sing. inf.)*
(él, ella, Ud.)	su/sus	*(his, her, its, their, your: sing. form.)*
(nosotros)	nuestro/nuestros nuestra/nuestras	*(our)*
(vostotros)	vuestro/vuestros vuestra/vuestras	*(your: pl. inf.)*
(ellos, ellas, Uds.)	su/sus	*(their, your: pl. form.)*

EJEMPLOS

Yo perdí <u>mis</u> lentes de sol.   *I lost my sunglasses.*
<u>Nuestra</u> vecina es muy simpática.   *Our neighbor is nice.*
¿Has tomado <u>tus</u> vitaminas?   *Have you taken your vitamins?*

If a distinction is needed between *his, her, its, their,* or *your,* Spanish clarifies by using the construction de + pronoun:

¿Qué quieres, el número <u>de él</u> o <u>de ella</u>?
What do you want, his number or hers?

Long-form possessive adjectives are used to further contrast one possessor from another. Notice how the definite articles precede and the adjectives follow the nouns being modified:

LONG-FORM POSSESSIVE ADJECTIVES		
(yo)	el cuaderno mío	(*my notebook, not yours*)
	los lápices míos	(*my pencil, not theirs*)
	la pluma mía	(*my pen, not hers*)
	las tijeras mías	(*my scissors, not his*)
(tú)	tuyo/a/os/as	(*your: sing. inf.*)
(él, ella, Ud.)	suyo/a/os/as	(*his, her, its, their, your: sing. form.*)
(nosotros)	nuestro/a/os/as	(*our*)
(vostotros)	vuestro/a/os/as	(*your: pl. inf.*)
(ellos, ellas, Uds.)	suyo/a/os/as	(*their, your: pl. form.*)

EJEMPLOS

¿Dónde está el carro <u>tuyo</u>?   *Where is <u>your</u> car?*
Me prestó la tarjeta <u>suya</u>.   *He loaned me <u>his</u> card.*
Es el refrigerador <u>mío</u>.   *It's <u>my</u> refrigerator.*

The long-form possessive adjective may also be used with the indefinite article:

Fuimos a <u>una</u> clase <u>tuya</u>.   *We went to a class of yours.*

When deciding the gender and number of a possessive adjective in Spanish, simply look at the object possessed instead of the possessor:

Ella salió con <u>sus amigos</u>.   *She left with <u>her friends</u>.*

Los paquetes no tienen etiqueta. No sé si éstos son <u>de Uds.</u> o <u>de ellos</u>.
The packages don't have labels. I don't know if these are yours or theirs.

LA PRÁCTICA 3

Follow the pattern as you fill in the blanks:

	Short-form	Long-form
1. (él / camisa)	su camisa	la camisa suya
2. (tú / zapatos)		
3. (nosotras / falda)		

4. (ellas / medias) _____

5. (Ud. / suéter) _____

6. (yo / pantalones) _____

7. (Uds. / guantes) _____

8. (ellos / botas) _____

9. (ella / cinturón) _____

10. (nosotros / gorras) _____

Possessive Pronouns
Pronombres posesivos

A possessive pronoun not only expresses possession, but also takes the place of a noun. Possessive pronouns are formed by combining the definite article with the long-form possessive adjective. Note how they must agree with the item possessed:

> Tengo mis papas fritas, pero no tienes las tuyas.
> *I have my french fries, but you don't have yours.*

> Querían prestarnos su estéreo porque el mío no estaba funcionando.
> *They wanted to loan us their stereo because mine wasn't working.*

> Los boletos suyos costaron mucho más que los nuestros.
> *Your tickets cost much more than ours.*

> **TIP**
> By combining the neuter pronoun lo with the masculine singular of the long-form possessive, a neuter possessive pronoun is created.
> Lo nuestro ya está pagado.
> *Our portion is already paid.*
> ¿Qué pasó con lo suyo?
> *What happened to his part?*
> Espero que encuentren lo tuyo.
> *I hope they find your stuff.*

If the sentence uses forms of ser and expresses only possession, the definite article can be omitted entirely after the verb:

Ese perro es mío.	*That dog is mine.*
Las muñecas son nuestras.	*The dolls are ours.*
Es hermana suya.	*It's a sister of hers.*

LA PRÁCTICA 4

Replace the underlined words with a possessive pronoun:

1. Ese país es más grande que <u>nuestro país</u>.

   Ese país es más grande que el nuestro.
   _____

2. Tu computadora tiene más memoria que <u>mi computadora</u>.

   _____

3. Mi hijo es más alto que <u>su hijo</u>.

   _____

4. Ella respeta mis opiniones más que <u>las opiniones de Uds</u>.

   _____

5. Sus amigas parecen ser más fieles que <u>nuestras amigas</u>.

   _____

6. Tengo el número de él pero no tengo <u>el número de ella</u>.

   _____

7. Aquella bicicleta cuesta mucho más que <u>tu bicicleta</u>.

   _____

8. ¿Quieres ver mis formularios o <u>sus formularios</u>?

   _____

9. Mis hermanos son tan valientes como <u>tus hermanos</u>.

   _____

10. Tus gatos duermen menos que <u>mis gatos</u>.

   _____

16
Personal Pronouns

¿Cuánto sabe usted?
How Much Do You Know Already?

1. Name the subject and object pronouns for the 1st person (sing.) in Spanish.

2. How do you say *He gave them to us* in Spanish?

3. Fill in the correct indirect pronoun: No ___ dije la historia a ella.

4. What is the difference in meaning between Me gusta and Le gustan?

5. What does Se la dan de ricos mean?

The Subject Pronouns

Forming and Using Subject Pronouns
Formación y uso de los pronombres personales de sujeto

Notice how the personal subject pronouns in Spanish are different from those in English. For example, since Spanish has both a formal (usted) and an informal (tú) manner of address, there are four words that express the English pronoun *you*. The word vosotros, however, is generally used in Spain, while ustedes refers to *you*, plural, in Latin America:

SUBJECT PRONOUNS			
SINGULAR		**PLURAL**	
yo	*(I)*	nosotros/ as	*(we)*
tú	*(you: sing.inf.)*	vosotros/ as	*(you: pl. inf.)*
él	*(he)*	ellos	*(they, masc.)*
ella	*(she)*	ellas	*(they, fem.)*
usted/ Ud.	*(you: sing. form.)*	ustedes/ Uds.	*(you: pl. form.)*

EJEMPLOS

<u>Yo</u> no sé.	*I don't know.*
<u>Ella</u> me dijo.	*She told me.*
¿Cómo están <u>Uds.</u>?	*How are you (guys)?*

In Spanish, the subject pronouns are often omitted in normal conversation, because the context and verb endings indicate both the person and the number of whoever is involved:

(<u>Yo</u>) Le pregunté a Marcos pero (<u>él</u>) no me contestó.
I asked Marcos, but he didn't answer me.

(<u>Uds.</u>) Vengan mañana a las seis e (<u>nosotros</u>) iremos juntos.
You guys come tomorrow at six and we'll go together.

However, subject pronouns may be added for emphasis or to make the meaning clear:

Soy <u>yo</u>.	*It is I.*
<u>Tú</u> lo hiciste.	*You did it.*
Ella le invitó a <u>él</u>.	*She invited him.*

Notice how él, ella, ellos, and ellas may sometimes refer to things as well as people. Here they are used as objects of a preposition:

Traje mi computadora, pero no tengo los cables para <u>ella</u>.
I brought my computer, but I don't have the cables for it.

Recibí mil lápices por correo, y no sé que hacer con <u>ellos</u>.
I received 1000 pencils by mail, and I don't know what to do with them.

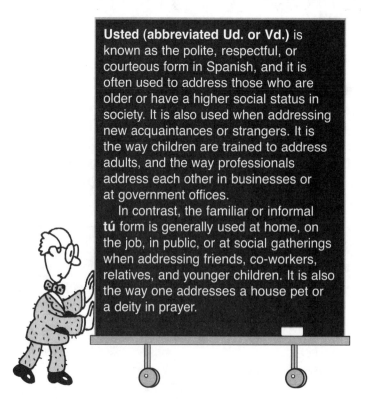

Usted (abbreviated Ud. or Vd.) is known as the polite, respectful, or courteous form in Spanish, and it is often used to address those who are older or have a higher social status in society. It is also used when addressing new acquaintances or strangers. It is the way children are trained to address adults, and the way professionals address each other in businesses or at government offices.

In contrast, the familiar or informal **tú** form is generally used at home, on the job, in public, or at social gatherings when addressing friends, co-workers, relatives, and younger children. It is also the way one addresses a house pet or a deity in prayer.

LA PRÁCTICA 1

Replace the underlined words with the correct subject pronoun:

1. <u>Toda la clase y yo</u> corríamos.   Nosotros _____

2. <u>Sandra</u> se fue.   _____

3. <u>Ud. y Alejandro</u> no pueden entrar.   _____

4. <u>Mis amigas</u> comen mucho.   _____

5. <u>San Paulo</u> lo dijo.   _____

6. <u>El presidente y yo</u> conversamos.   _____

7. <u>Los muchachos</u> en el cine gritaban.   _____

8. ¿Es española <u>Chila</u>?   _____

9. <u>Usted y yo</u> hemos tomado café.   _____

10. <u>Los soldados</u> se perdieron.   _____

Fill in the missing subject pronouns in this chart, along with the English translations of each phrase:

11. Soy   yo   (*I am*)

12. Eres   _____   ( )

13. Es   _____   ( ) _____ ( ) _____ ( )

14. Somos   _____   / _____ ( )

15. Sois   _____   / _____ ( )

16. Son   _____   ( ) _____ ( ) _____ ( )

The Prepositional Pronouns

Forming and Using Prepositional Pronouns
Formación y uso del complemento con preposición en pronombres personales

Spanish personal pronouns generally have the same form when used as objects of a preposition as when used as subjects of a sentence. The only difference is that **mí** and **ti** replace **yo** and **tú** after most prepositions.

El dinero es para . . . *(The money is for . . .)*			
SINGULAR		**PLURAL**	
mí	*(me)*	nosotros/as	*(us)*
ti	*(you: sing.inf.)*	vosotros/as	*(you: pl. inf.)*
él	*(him)*	ellos	*(them, masc.)*
ella	*(her)*	ellas	*(them, fem.)*
usted/ Ud.	*(you: sing. form.)*	ustedes/Uds.	*(you: pl. form.)*

EJEMPLOS

No te vayas sin <u>mí</u>.	*Don't leave without me.*
Se sentó detrás de <u>ti</u>.	*She sat behind you.*
Hablaría con <u>él</u>.	*I would speak with him.*
Llegaron antes de <u>ellas</u>.	*They arrived before them.*
Vivía lejos de <u>nosotros</u>.	*He used to live far from us.*

When **mí** and **ti** are used as objects of the preposition **con**, they are joined together to form a single word:

con + mí = conmigo   ¿Quieres sentarte conmigo?
Do you want to sit with me?

con + ti = contigo   No podemos jugar contigo.
We cannot play with you.

Although it is not as common, the word **consigo** is used when the subject of the verb is the same as the object of **con**. It means *with himself, with herself, with itself, with yourself,* or *with themselves*:

Ella se la llevó <u>consigo</u>.
She took it along with her(self).

Los niños están contentos <u>consigo</u> mismos.
The children are happy with themselves.

In place of prepositional pronouns, however, the subject pronouns are used after the prepositions según (*according to*), salvo, menos, or excepto (*except*), entre (*between*), and como (*like*):

Mi hijo habla <u>como yo</u>.	*My son talks like me.*
Todos se fueron <u>menos tú</u>.	*Everyone left except you.*
No había nada <u>entre tú y yo</u>.	*There was nothing between you and me.*

In fact, yo and tú replace mí and tí with any preposition whenever they follow the word y (*and*):

Preparamos comida para Nelo <u>y tú</u>.	*We prepared food for Nelo and you.*
Trabajarán sin él, ella <u>y yo</u>.	*You'll work without him, her, and me.*

LA PRÁCTICA 2

Translate the underlined English words into Spanish:

1. Las cápsulas en la botella son para <u>her</u>.　　ella

2. Su oficina está cerca de <u>me</u>.　　_____

3. Viven delante de <u>us</u>.　　_____

4. Compré el paquete y lo traje <u>with me</u>.　　_____

5. Según <u>you: sing. inform.</u>, estoy equivocado.　　_____

6. Hicimos el trabajo sin <u>him</u>.　　_____

7. No iré <u>with you: sing. inf.</u>　　_____

8. Todos lo vieron excepto <u>me</u>.　　_____

9. Estaba escrito por <u>you: pl. form</u>.　　_____

10. Había argumento entre ella y <u>me</u>.　　_____

Using Direct Objects and the Personal *a*

Uso de la preposición a *en complementos directos*

A direct object noun in Spanish and English receives the action of the verb directly. In other words, the direct object is acted upon by the subject of a sentence:

Juan	vendió	su carro.	*Juan sold his car.*
SUBJECT	VERB	DIRECT OBJECT	

Generally speaking, if the direct object is an object, it simply follows the verb:

No vimos el desfile.	*We didn't see the parade.*
¿Pagaste la cuenta?	*Did you pay the bill?*
Han comido las galletas.	*They have eaten the cookies.*

If, however, the direct object noun refers to a specific person or group, then the noun is preceded by the personal preposition a. Note that it has no English translation:

Estamos buscando <u>a</u> tu hermano.	*We're looking for your brother.*
La Sra. Jones enseña <u>a</u> los estudiantes.	*Mrs. Jones teaches the students.*
La chica le ayudaba <u>a</u> su amiga.	*The girl was helping her friend.*

The personal a precedes any noun or pronoun that refers to people:

nadie	No buscamos a nadie.
(no one)	*We're not looking for anyone. (We're looking for no one.)*
alguien	Esperaba a alguien en frente del mercado.
(someone)	*He was waiting for someone in front of the market.*
todos	¿Escuchaste a todos los estudiantes?
(all)	*Did you hear all the students?*

The personal a is used with most proper nouns, which include the names of places or personalized things:

Visité a Margarita.	*I visited Margarita.*
Escuchamos al Dr. Córdova.	*We listened to Dr. Córdova.*
No conozco a Brasil.	*I am not familiar with Brazil.*

The personal a is also used with prepositional pronouns in sentences that include object pronouns that refer to people:

Lo mandó <u>a</u> la pescadería.	*She sent him to the fish store.*
Le dijo <u>a</u> ella.	*He told her.*

However, when the direct object noun refers to people in a general sense, the personal a is not used:

Necesitamos más jugadores.
We need more players.

Buscan un buen jardinero.
They're looking for a good gardener.

Ese tren lleva mucha gente.
That train carries a lot of people.

As a rule, the personal a is not used after the verb tener:

La señora que vive en la esquina <u>tiene</u> cinco hijos.
The lady who lives on the corner has five kids.

Las nuevas compañías <u>tienen</u> empleados excelentes.
The new companies have excellent employees.

LA PRÁCTICA 3

Translate these sentences into Spanish:

1. *I help my friends.*   Ayudo a mis amigos.

2. *She's looking for the cat.* _____

3. *We called the doctor.*   _____

4. *How many cousins do you have?* _____

5. *I cannot see anything.*   _____

6. *I do not know anyone.*   _____

7. *They bought Mr. Romo's house.* _____

8. *She plays with a lot of children.* _____

9. *We didn't see Rogelio.*   _____

10. *Is he looking for someone?* _____

Translate these sentences into English:

11. ¿A quién enseña Ud.?   ***Who do you teach?***

12. Escuchamos a los dos. _____

13. Martín salía con cualquiera. _____

14. ¿Encontraste al otro? _____

15. Quiero conocer al gordo. _____

16. No invitamos a ningún maestro. _____

17. ¿A cuántos llevarán en el carro? _____

18. Abracé a la misma. _____

19. Visitaremos a la primera. _____

20. ¿A cuál cliente llamo? _____

The Object Pronouns

Forming and Using Direct Object Pronouns
*Formación y empleo del complemento sin preposición
en pronombres personales*

Personal pronouns have the following forms when they are used as direct objects of the verb. These direct object pronouns cannot be used independently:

DIRECT OBJECT PRONOUNS			
SINGULAR			**PLURAL**
yo	me	nosotros	nos
tú	te	vosotros	os
él	lo	ellos	los
ella	la	ellas	las
Ud.	lo/la	Uds.	los/las

The primary purpose of any object pronoun is to avoid the repetition of nouns in a sentence. Therefore, direct object pronouns are often used to replace direct object nouns. Like all direct objects, they receive the action of the verb. Observe how they always precede the conjugated verb form:

¿Has visto a <u>Mario</u>?	
No, no <u>lo</u> veo.	*I don't see him.*
¿Quién llamó a <u>Sandra</u>?	
Nosotras <u>la</u> hemos llamado.	*We have called her.*
Nadie compró <u>las sillas</u>.	
Tito <u>las</u> habría comprado.	*He would have bought them.*

Notice how direct object pronouns follow the verb in English:

¿<u>Me</u> invitaste?	*Did you invite <u>me</u>?*
<u>Te</u> conocí el año pasado.	*I met <u>you</u> last year.*
No <u>nos</u> llevará.	*He's not taking <u>us</u>.*

In Latin America, the direct object pronouns lo, la, los, and las generally refer to both people and things, and can be translated as *you, it, him, he,* and *them.* In Spain, however, when referring to people, le is often used instead of lo:

LATIN AMERICA
<u>Lo</u> buscábamos.
SPAIN   } *We were looking for him.*
<u>Le</u> buscábamos.

Direct object pronouns can either precede the verb estar or be attached to the present participle in the progressive tenses. Notice the accent mark on the vowel before the new -ndo ending:

<u>Las</u> estamos leyendo.
      } *We are reading them.*
Estamos leyéndo<u>las</u>.

Similarly, the direct object pronoun may either precede the verb or be attached to the infinitive in the verb + infinitive construction:

<u>Me</u> quieren preguntar algo.
      } *They want to ask me something.*
Quieren preguntar<u>me</u> algo.

Direct object pronouns are also attached to the end of affirmative commands in Spanish. Notice the accent mark on the stressed vowel in the longer command forms:

Pon<u>la</u> aquí.	*Put it here.*
Míre<u>me</u>.	*Look at me.*
Tráiga<u>lo</u>.	*Bring it.*
Prénda<u>las</u>.	*Turn them on.*

When a command is in the negative, the direct object pronoun goes before the verb form.

No lo llame Ud.
Do not call him.

No las coma todavía.
Don't eat them yet.

If ambiguity exists when the direct object pronouns lo, la, los, or las are used, the prepositional pronouns are added to clarify what is going on:

La encontré en la casa.	*(Who or what did I find?)*
La encontré <u>a ella</u>.	*I found her.*
Los dejará enfrente del colegio.	*(What or who will he leave there?)*
Los dejará <u>a Uds</u>.	*He will leave you guys there.*

Sometimes a direct object noun may precede the verb instead of follow it. In that case, the direct object pronoun must be included in the sentence. For example, here is another way to say Llevo a mi mamá (*I'm taking my mom*):

A	mi mamá	la	llevo.
	DIRECT OBJECT	D.O. PRONOUN	VERB

Direct object pronouns must also be used when forms of the pronoun todo are the direct objects of a sentence:

Lo	comieron	todo.	*They ate all of it.*
D.O. PRONOUN	VERB	DIRECT OBJECT	

LA PRÁCTICA 4

Change the underlined noun to a direct object pronoun and place it correctly in a new sentence. Some may be written two ways:

1. Tengo <u>el mapa</u>.   Lo tengo. _____

2. No puedo ver <u>a Uds</u>.   _____

3. Está estudiando <u>la lección</u>. _____

4. Alberto compró <u>un paraguas</u>. _____

5. ¿Enviaste <u>las cartas</u>? _____

6. Visitamos a <u>mis abuelos</u>. _____

7. Tiraron <u>piedras</u>. _____

8. Buscaban a <u>Cecilia</u>. _____

9. ¿Has visto <u>las fotos</u>? _____

10. No encontramos <u>problemas</u>. _____

Change these negative commands to the affirmative:

11. No lo traiga.   Tráigalo. _____

12. No me enseñe. _____

13. No los toque. _____

14. No la apague. _____

15. No nos inviten. _____

Form sentences by changing the words in parentheses to direct object pronouns:

Reconocí ...

16. (a Angela)   La reconocí. _____

17. (a ti) _____

18. (a Rosa y Eva) _____

19. (a él) _____

20. (los perritos) _____

Follow the example by placing the direct object <u>before</u> the verb:

21. Vendió su casa.   Su casa la vendió. _____

22. He invitado a Lidia. _____

23. Necesitarán los cuadernos. _____

24. Vimos a tus compañeros. _____

25. No trae su uniforme. _____

Forming and Using Indirect Object Pronouns

Formación y empleo de pronombres de complemento indirecto

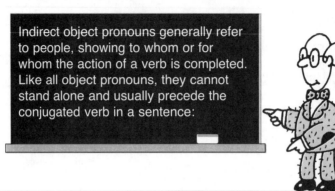

Indirect object pronouns generally refer to people, showing to whom or for whom the action of a verb is completed. Like all object pronouns, they cannot stand alone and usually precede the conjugated verb in a sentence:

INDIRECT OBJECT PRONOUNS			
SINGULAR			**PLURAL**
yo	me	nosotros	nos
tú	te	vosotros	os
él, ella, Ud.	le	ellos, ellas, Uds.	les

An indirect object receives the action of the verb indirectly. Therefore, an indirect object pronoun either receives action through the direct object or is affected in some other way by the verb:

Te mandaremos la información.	*We'll send you the information.*
Me dijo la verdad.	*He told me the truth.*
Le han quitado su licencia.	*They've taken away his license.*

Remember that indirect object pronouns have the same position in a sentence as direct object pronouns. Note how the English translations may vary:

- Present participles

  Estoy pidiéndo**te** una cita.

  Te estoy pidiendo una cita.

  } *I am asking you for an appointment.*

- Verb + infinitive

  Vamos a entregar**le** la tarea.

  Le vamos a entregar la tarea.

  } *We're going to turn in the homework to her.*

- Affirmative commands

  Enséñe**me** la evidencia.   *Show me the evidence.*

In Spanish, an indirect object is joined to the verb by a. Remember that a sentence with an indirect object noun usually includes the indirect object pronoun le or les. For example, *He gave the food to his neighbor:*

Le	dio	la comida	a	su vecino.
INDIRECT OBJECT PRONOUN	VERB	DIRECT OBJECT		INDIRECT OBJECT

The a + prepositional pronoun construction is added in Spanish to clarify, contrast, or emphasize the direct object pronoun. It is generally placed at the beginning of the sentence:

A ellos siempre les compra zapatos nuevos.
She always buys them new shoes.

A Ud., ¿cuándo le robaron el televisor?
When did they steal the TV from you?

A nosotros no nos ha dicho nada.
He has not told us anything.

Several verbs in Spanish are used regularly with an indirect object pronoun. In the sentence, a thing (the direct object) is usually given to or taken from a person (the indirect object pronoun):

mandar *(to send)*
mandarle algo a alguien   *to send something to someone*
Le mandaron la bicicleta (a él).   *They sent him the bike.*

robar *(to steal)*
robarle algo a alguien   *to steal something from someone*
Me ha robado el saco (a mí).   *She's stolen my coat from me.*

exigir *(to demand)*
exigirle algo a alguien   *to demand something of someone*
Te exijo una respuesta (a ti).   *I demand a response from you.*

Other such constructions include:

comprarle algo a alguien	*to buy something from someone*
contarle algo a alguien	*to relate something to someone*
darle algo a alguien	*to give something to someone*
decirle algo a alguien	*to tell something to someone*
devolverle algo a alguien	*to return something to someone*
esconderle algo a alguien	*to hide something from someone*
enseñarle algo a alguien	*to show something to someone*
escribirle algo a alguien	*to write something to someone*
entregarle algo a alguien	*to hand over something to someone*
enviarle algo a alguien	*to send something to someone*

explicarle algo a alguien	*to explain something to someone*
ganarle algo a alguien	*to win something from someone*
mostrarle algo a alguien	*to show something to someone*
ocultarle algo a alguien	*to hide something from someone*
ofrecerle algo a alguien	*to offer something to someone*
quitarle algo a alguien	*to take something away from someone*
regalarle algo a alguien	*to give a gift to someone*
sacarle algo a alguien	*to get something out of someone*
solicitarle algo a alguien	*to request something of someone*
traerle algo a alguien	*to bring something to someone*

Some Spanish verbs take an indirect object in Spanish, but a direct object in English:

preguntarle a alguien   (*to ask someone*)

A mí   me   preguntaron.   *They asked   me.*
     INDIRECT   DIRECT
      OBJECT   OBJECT

Other examples are:

pedirle algo a alguien	*to ask someone for something*
preguntarle alguien	*to ask someone*
recordarle a alguien	*to remind someone*

LA PRÁCTICA 5

Fill in the blanks with the appropriate indirect object pronoun, and then translate each sentence into English:

1. A ella debes dar___ la dirección.   le _____

   You should give her the address. _____

2. ¿Qué ___ pidieron a Uds.?   _____

   _____

3. A mí ___ mostraba todo el dinero.   _____

   _____

4. ___ solicité trabajo al dueño.   _____

   _____

5. A los dos ___ ha regalado libros de música. _____

_____

6. ¿A ti ___ dijo el secreto? _____

_____

7. Escríba ___ una carta a tus primos. _____

_____

8. A nosotros ___ estaba hablando en español. _____

_____

9. ¿Por qué a mí ___ quitaste el sombrero? _____

_____

10. ___ han mandado algo a Juanita. _____

_____

Use the pronoun phrase in parentheses to rewrite each sentence below:

11. Ella me daba muchas flores.   (a ellos)   Ella les daba muchas flores.

12. ¿Nos manda los datos?   (a mí)   _____

13. Ellos os quitaban la pelota.   (a él)   _____

14. Le dijo todos los números.   (a ti)   _____

15. Está enseñándoles arte.   (a Ud.)   _____

16. Tráigame la fruta fresca.   (a nosotros)   _____

17. Le mostraron el apartamento.   (a ellas)   _____

18. Nos contaba mentiras.   (a Uds.)   _____

19. Quiere regalarte diamantes.   (a nosotros)   _____

20. ¿Te devolvió el martillo?   (a ella)   _____

Gustar and Other Uses of the Indirect Object
Gustar y otros usos del complemento indirecto

Some unique verbs, like gustar, almost always take an indirect object pronoun. Observe how these verbs have only two forms that must agree with the subject. There is no matching construction in English:

Gustar *(to like)*			
SINGULAR		**PLURAL**	
me gusta	*I like it*	nos gusta	*we like it*
me gustan	*I like them*	nos gustan	*we like them*
te gusta	*you like it*	os gusta	*you like it*
te gustan	*you like them*	os gustan	*you like them*
le gusta	*he, she likes it* *you like it*	les gusta	*they like it* *you like it*
le gustan	*he, she likes them* *you like them*	les gustan	*they like them* *you like them*

Other verbs that take an indirect object pronoun are:

bastarle a alguien	*to be sufficient*
encantarle a alguien	*to love something*
entusiasmarle a alguien	*to be excited about something*
faltarle a alguien	*to be missing something*
fascinarle a alguien	*to be fascinated*
hacerle falta a alguien	*to need something*
importarle a alguien	*to care about something*
interesarle a alguien	*to be interested in something*
quedarle a alguien	*to have something left*
sobrarle a alguien	*to have more than enough of something*
tocarle a alguien	*to be someone's turn*

EJEMPLOS

Te toca a ti.	*It's your turn.*
Nos falta una llave.	*We're missing a key.*
A mí me encanta la comida rusa.	*I love Russian food.*
¿Les gustan los postres?	*Do they like desserts?*
A ella no le interesa el amor.	*She's not interested in love.*

When these verbs include an infinitive as the subject, only the third person singular form is used:

A ellos les <u>gusta</u> *bailar* Salsa.	*They like to dance Salsa.*
Le <u>falta</u> *limpiar* el baño.	*He still needs to clean the bathroom.*
Nos <u>encanta</u> *viajar* por tren.	*We love to travel by train.*

The exact translation of verbs like **gustar** may help in understanding their unique forms and usage. It is basically English in reverse, since the direct object is the subject:

Me	**gusta**	**la hamburguesa.**
to me	*it is pleasing*	*the hamburger*

(*I like the hamburger.*)

Le	**gustan**	**las papas fritas.**
to him	*they are pleasing*	*the french fries*

(*He likes the fries.*)

Again, the a + stressed pronoun construction can be added to these sentences in order to clarify, contrast, or emphasize the indirect object pronoun:

A mí me gusta el verde, pero a él le gusta el azul y a ella
   le gusta el rojo.
I like the green one, but he likes the blue one and she likes the red one.

Indirect object pronouns are also used with some verbs to communicate special messages. For example, sometimes they are added to unusual se constructions that express mishaps or unplanned events:

caérsele a alguien	*to drop*
Se *me* cayó el vaso.	*I dropped the glass.*

acabársele a alguien	*to run out of*
Se *le* acaba el dinero.	*He's running out of money.*

perdérsele a alguien	*to lose*
Se *nos* perdió la cámara.	*We lost the camera.*

With other verbs, when referring to articles of clothing or parts of the body, the indirect object functions much like a possessive in English:

Su madre le quitó el impermeable.
His mother helped him remove his raincoat.

Te lavarán el pelo en la peluquería.
They will wash your hair at the hairdresser's.

In most cases, the indirect object in Spanish simply identifies the one who receives the positive or negative results in the sentence:

Nos han preparado un almuerzo delicioso.
They have prepared us a delicious lunch.

Mi hermanito me rompió la cometa.
My little brother broke my kite.

Sometimes an indirect object pronoun is part of an informal expression. It is often used with the verb ser:

Nos es importante ganar el juego.   *It's important for us to win the game.*
Me fue fácil hacer los ejercicios.   *It was easy for me to do the exercises.*

LA PRÁCTICA 6

Translate these sentences into English:

1. A ella le falta un cuaderno.   <u>**She's missing a notebook.**</u>

2. ¿A quién le toca?   _____

3. Nos quedan veinte minutos.   _____

4. ¿Te sobra mucho trabajo?   _____

5. A ellos les encanta Nueva York.   _____

6. A Ud. le conviene manejar.   _____

7. Me interesa ver la película.   _____

8. ¿No te importa el resultado?   _____

9. Nos entusiasma la conversación.   _____

10. A él le gusta patinar sólo.   _____

Double Object Pronouns and Other Special Forms

Pronombres de complemento doble y otras formas especiales

When a verb in Spanish has two pronoun objects, the indirect object precedes the direct object:

Ella	me	las	mandó.	*She sent them to me.*
	I.O. PRONOUN	D.O. PRONOUN	VERB	

Ellos	te	lo	explicarán.	*They'll explain it to you.*
	I.O. PRONOUN	D.O. PRONOUN	VERB	

However, if the two pronouns are in the third person—where the indirect object pronoun le or les precedes the direct object pronoun lo, la, los, or las—then the indirect object changes to the word se. Se is used to prevent the repetition of the "l" sound:

Él se (le) lo dijo.	*He told it to her.*
Ella se (les) la prestó.	*She loaned it to them.*

These double object pronouns cannot be split within the sentence:

DOUBLE OBJECT PRONOUNS			
I.O. PRONOUN	**D.O. PRONOUN**	**DOUBLE OBJECT PRONOUN**	
le or les	+ lo	= se lo	(Se lo prestó)
le or les	+ los	= se los	(Se los prestó)
le or les	+ la	= se la	(Se la prestó)
le or las	+ las	= se las	(Se las prestó)

Having several meanings, se can obviously create confusion in a sentence if the context is unclear. To clarify, the a + prepositional pronoun construction is usually added:

Se los mostraba a él.	*She was showing them to him.*
No se la traigo a ellas.	*I don't bring it to them.*
¿Se lo regalaron a Ud.?	*Did they give it to you as a gift?*

Certain object pronouns in Spanish have other uses as well. For example, the pronoun lo may replace any adjective, noun, or complete clause in a sentence. It is often used to simply shorten one's response:

Me preguntaban si los chicos
eran estudiosos, y les decía
que lo son.

*They asked me if the boys were studious
and I told them that they are.*

> **TIP**
> The main difference between direct and indirect object pronouns is that a direct object pronoun is any person or thing that receives the action of the verb directly (e.g., Yo lo compré—*I bought it*) whereas the indirect object pronoun is generally a person who receives something indirectly from the subject of a sentence (e.g., Yo le compré el libro—*I bought him the book*).

Ya no son vendedores, pero <u>lo</u> fueron el año pasado.
They are no longer salesmen, but they were last year.

Also remember that the object pronouns la and las are parts of common idiomatic expressions:

Tienen que vér<u>se</u>l<u>as con</u> el juez. *You'll have to explain it to the judge.*
Ella se <u>la da de</u> famosa. *She always brags about being famous.*
Tu papá <u>me la</u> tiene jurada. *Your dad has it in for me.*

LA PRÁCTICA 7

Rewrite each sentence to include a double object pronoun:

1. Le quiere prestar la escoba a su tía. Quiere prestársela.

2. Estoy explicando el juego a los niños. _____

3. Él te vendía los helados. _____

4. Les di el dinero a ellos. _____

5. René le trajo papel. _____

6. Está mandando los muebles a nosotros. _____

7. Les llevé las revistas a Uds. _____

8. Ya le bajaron las maletas. _____

9. Siempre les hacía el desayuno. _____

10. Ella te ha devuelto las joyas. _____

Change these affirmative commands to the negative:

11. Préstemelos. No me los preste.

12. Muéstrenosla. _____

13. Entrégueselo. _____

14. Tráigasela. _____

15. Cómpremelos. _____

17

Relative Pronouns

¿Cuánto sabe usted?
How Much Do You Know Already?

1. How do you say *2000 was the year I got married* in Spanish?

2. What relative pronoun is only used after the prepositions **de**, **a**, **con**, and **en**?

3. When would you use the relative pronoun **el que** instead of **que**?

4. Name the two neuter relative pronouns.

5. Combine these into one sentence: **Ana es la maestra. Ana habla alemán.**

Using the Relative Pronoun *que*
Empleo del pronombre relativo que

A relative pronoun is used to combine two sentences that refer to the same noun. There are several common forms in Spanish:

RELATIVE PRONOUNS			
SINGULAR FORMS		**PLURAL FORMS**	
MASCULINE	**FEMININE**	**MASCULINE**	**FEMININE**
que	que	que	que
quien	quien	quienes	quienes
el que	la que	los que	las que
el cual	la cual	los cuales	las cuales
cuyo	cuya	cuyos	cuyas
cuanto	cuanta	cuantos	cuantas

Specifically, a relative pronoun refers back to the noun modified by the relative clause (the antecedent), and it connects the relative clause to the main clause. In a sentence, it immediately follows its antecedent:

1. **El muchacho llegó.**   *The boy arrived.*
2. **El muchacho es mi vecino.**   *The boy is my neighbor.*

241

El muchacho   <u>que</u>   llegó   es mi vecino.
ANTECEDENT   RELATIVE   VERB   RELATIVE
          PRONOUN   CLAUSE

The boy who arrived is my neighbor.

The relative pronoun functions as a noun, and is used much more in Spanish than it is in English. The pronoun que can be either the subject or the object of a verb or preposition in a sentence; however, it is not affected by gender or number. It is often translated as *who, whom, which* or *that*:

El hombre <u>que</u> respeto es el Sr. Torres.
The man (whom) I respect is Mr. Torres.

Tráigame los tornillos <u>que</u> están en el garaje.
Bring me the screws (that) are in the garage.

Que is also used as the subject or direct object of the relative clause when the antecedents include algo, nada, alguien, or nadie:

No hay <u>nada que</u> quiera comprar ahora.
There is nothing (that) I want to buy now.

¿Conoces a <u>alguien que</u> hable alemán?
Do you know anyone (who) speaks German?

LA PRÁCTICA 1

Use the relative pronoun que to combine each pair of sentences below:

1. Me gusta el postre. El postre es muy dulce.

   Me gusta el postre que es muy dulce.

2. Acabo de leer el libro. Me regalaste el libro.

   _____

3. La señora vivía en la esquina. La señora se murió.

   _____

4. La niña es mi hija. Ud. vio la niña.

   _____

5. Ella es la cajera. Ella trabaja conmigo.

_____

6. Uso los guantes. Ellos me compraron los guantes.

_____

7. Esta es la clase de español. Necesito la clase.

_____

8. Llame a los estudiantes. Los estudiantes estudian mucho.

_____

9. Tengo algo. Quiero decirte algo.

_____

10. Las botellas están en el piso. Las botellas están vacías.

_____

_____

Using the Relative Pronoun *quien*
Empleo del pronombre relativo quien

The relative pronoun quien or quienes refers only to people and is often used to indicate the antecedent more clearly than que. It is also used after a preposition, and it agrees in number with the noun. Notice how a quien and a quienes replace que when it is the direct object of the verb in the clause:

La persona <u>a quien</u> viste es amiga mía.
The person you saw is my friend.

Esos alumnos <u>a quienes</u> dieron un
premio son de mi escuela.
Those students who were given a prize are from my school.

> **TIP**
> The relative pronoun quien is usually translated to mean *who, whom,* or *the one who.* Notice how the relative pronouns do not have accent marks like the question words:
> Hablamos con el Sr. Goya, quien regresó de su viaje a África.
> *We spoke with Mr. Goya who returned from his trip to Africa.*
> ¿Quién es el dueño del castillo?
> *Who is the owner of the castle?*

Sometimes quien and quienes are used in place of que to introduce a nonrestrictive clause, which is a clause set apart by commas that is not needed to complete the sentence. Notice how these relative pronouns serve as the subject of the clause:

Le regaló el perfume a Pepita, <u>quien</u> es la nueva secretaria.
He gave the perfume as a gift to Pepita, who is the new secretary.

Siempre salgo con mis amigos, <u>quienes</u> me invitan a las fiestas.
I always go out with my friends, who invite me to the parties.

LA PRÁCTICA 2

Combine these pairs of sentences using a quien *or* a quienes:

1. Ya salieron los niños. Los encontraste en el parque ayer.

   Ya salieron los niños a quienes encontraste en el parque ayer.

2. El chofer llegó temprano. Lo llamamos a las ocho.

   _____

3. Ella es mi sobrina. La vi en el banco con su novio.

   _____

4. Las maestras se han ido. Las queremos mucho.

   _____

5. La chica siempre está enferma. La conocí el año pasado.

   _____

Combine these pairs of sentences using quien *or* quienes:

6. La doctora trabaja en el hospital. Ella abrió una clínica.

   La doctora, quien abrió una clínica, trabaja en el hospital.

7. Alfredo es un estudiante excelente. Él no vino hoy.

   _____

8. Algunos jugadores practican aquí. Ellos son atletas profesionales.

   _____

9. La Sra. Arenas ha sido la directora. Ella escribe libros de gramática.

   _____

10. Mis hermanas no quieren mudarse. Ellas viven conmigo.

   _____

Using the Relative Pronouns *el que* and *el cual*

Empleo de los pronombres relativos el que *y* el cual

El que, **los que**, **la que**, **las que**, **el cual**, **los cuales**, **la cual**, and **las cuales** may be used in place of que or a quien when the relative pronoun is the object of the verb and the antecedent is a person. Notice the personal a:

> El gerente, <u>al que</u> he llamado, se llama Federico.
> *The manager (whom) I have called is named Federico.*

> Las enfermeras, <u>a las que</u> hemos conocido, vendrán mañana.
> *The nurses (whom) we have met will come tomorrow.*

When there is confusion as to who or what the antecedent is, the relative pronouns el que and el cual are often used in the non-restrictive clause. They can function as either the subject or the object of the verb:

> El piso de la cocina, <u>el cual</u> no me gusta, necesita reparación.
> *The floor in the kitchen, the one (floor) that I don't like, needs repair.*

> El piso de la cocina, <u>la cual</u> no me gusta, necesita reparación.
> *The floor in the kitchen, the one (kitchen) that I don't like, needs repair.*

> El hijo de mi amiga, <u>la que</u> habla español, está estudiando medicina.
> *My friend's son, the one (female friend) who speaks Spanish, is studying medicine.*

> El hijo de mi amiga, <u>el que</u> habla español, está estudiando medicina.
> *My friend's son, the one (son) who speaks Spanish, is studying medicine.*

Spanish also has neuter relative pronouns. Lo que and lo cual appear in non-restrictive clauses that refer to a preceding concept or clause:

> Alma practica su fe todos los días, <u>lo que</u> respeto mucho de ella.
> *Alma practices her faith every day, (which) I respect her a great deal for.*

> Donamos toda la ropa usada, <u>lo cual</u> yo espero que Uds. hagan también.
> *We donated all of the used clothing, (which) I hope you guys do as well.*

When used in a sentence without an antecedent, lo que generally means *what*:

No entiendo <u>lo que</u> dice.	*I don't understand what he's saying.*
<u>Lo que</u> me gustó fue la comida.	*What I liked was the food.*

La Práctica 3

Insert lo que, el que, los que, la que, or las que into each sentence below:

1. El ingeniero inglés, _____ trabaja en Chicago, irá a Japón.   *el que* _____

2. No hablamos con Javier, _____ sorprendió a todos. _____

3. La alarma sonó, _____ asustó a los niños. _____

4. La estudiante, _____ está en frente de la clase, es mi prima. _____

5. Le han invitado a la boda, _____ le agradó mucho. _____

6. Esos hombres, _____ se visten elegantes, son los mozos. _____

7. Todas tus amigas, _____ bailan bien, fueron a la fiesta. _____

8. Nos regalaron boletos para el cine, _____ nos gustó. _____

9. El profesor, _____ siempre llega temprano, se enfermó. _____

10. La secretaria, _____ tiene los ojos azules, vive cerca de mí. _____

Using the Relative Pronoun *cuyo*
Empleo del pronombre relativo cuyo

    The relative pronoun cuyo (*whose*) and all its forms function like possessive adjectives. However, they modify and agree with the nouns that immediately follow them, instead of their antecedents. Notice how they refer to both people and things:

Conversaba con la víctima <u>cuya</u> motocicleta fue chocada.
I was speaking with the victim whose motorcycle got hit.

Tiene dos hijos <u>cuyos</u> ojos son muy grandes y azules.
She has two sons whose eyes are very big and blue.

Escuchamos a la señora <u>cuyo</u> marido es el pastor de la iglesia.
We listened to the woman whose husband is the church pastor.

Es el vecino <u>cuyas</u> hijas estudian en El Salvador.
It's the neighbor whose daughters study in El Salvador.

LA PRÁCTICA 4

Insert cuyo, cuyos, cuya, or cuyas on the lines below:

1. Ella es la dueña __cuyo__ apartamento está debajo de nosotros.

2. Quisiéramos ver el artista _____ pinturas están en exhibición.

3. No he encontrado la persona _____ perro mordió al cartero.

4. Hablé con el profesor _____ estudiantes no pasaron el examen final.

5. Acaba de llamar a la señora _____ bebito llora toda la noche.

6. Este es el pueblo _____ edificios son tan antiguos.

7. Hablaremos con los clientes _____ cuentas no están pagadas.

8. Presénteme al chico _____ hermana tiene el pelo largo.

9. Ellos son los autores _____ novelas son tan famosas.

10. Se casó con la señorita _____ padre es el alcalde.

Using Relative Pronouns After Prepositions
Empleo de pronombres relativos después de preposiciones

When the antecedent is a person, quien, el que, el cual, and all their forms may be used after prepositions:

El muchacho **con quien** salió ya tiene una novia.
The boy (whom) she went out with already has a girlfriend.

El hombre **al que** se parece Martín es mi abuelo.
The man (who) Martin looks like is my grandfather.

However, el que, el cual, and all their forms may also be used after prepositions referring to things:

La libertad **por la que** estamos luchando es preciosa.
The liberty for (that) which we are fighting is precious.

El parque **detrás del cual** vivimos está lleno de rosas.
The park behind (that) where we live is full of roses.

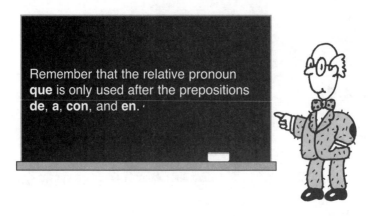

Remember that the relative pronoun **que** is only used after the prepositions **de**, **a**, **con**, and **en**.

For some reason, after more compound prepositions, el cual and all its forms are used more often than el que and its forms:

Cruzaban las montañas <u>encima de las cuales</u> había mucha nieve.
They crossed the mountains on top of which there was a lot of snow.

Nos quedamos en el hotel <u>al lado del cual</u> están reparando la calle.
We stayed in the hotel next to which they are repairing the street.

The relative pronoun que is used after the prepositions de, con, en, and a. With que, the antecedent is a thing and not a person:

No he visto la película <u>de que</u> me hablaste.
I have not seen the film (that) you talked to me about.

Está bien <u>con que</u> me dejes en la esquina.
It's fine (that) you leave me on the corner.

Ésta es la reunión <u>a que</u> acudiremos.
This is the meeting (that) we will attend to.

En que is sometimes used in Spanish to express a general location. However, it may also follow an expression of time:

¿Conoces la universidad <u>en que</u> estudiamos?
Are you familiar with the university (that) we go to?

2001 fue el año <u>en que</u> todo cambió.
2001 was the year when (that) everything changed.

Han pasado dos semanas <u>en que</u> no has jugado vólibol.
It has been two weeks since (that) you haven't played volleyball.

The relative pronoun en el que and all its forms may be used as relative pronouns to express *where* or the concept of *within*:

Me encanta el campo <u>en el que</u> estoy trabajando.
I love the field that I'm working in.

Buscaron las casas <u>en las que</u> hubo inundación.
They looked for houses where there was flooding.

Although the relative pronoun donde (*where*) is frequently used immediately after an antecedent, it may also be used after a preposition to refer to a place. Notice how it has no accent mark:

Entramos a la cueva <u>donde</u> estaban los murciélagos.
We entered the cave where the bats were.

Les gustan los cafés <u>donde</u> sirven comida orgánica.
They like cafés where they serve organic food.

Ésta es la puerta <u>por donde</u> entró el presidente.
This is the door through which the president entered.

Fuimos a la fiesta <u>a donde</u> fueron María y Juan.
We went to the party to which María and Juan went.

LA PRÁCTICA 5

Translate these sentences into English:

1. Este es el sitio donde prefiero comer comida china.

   This is the place where I prefer to eat Chinese food.

2. La mujer con quien trabajo es rusa.

   _____

3. El sillón en que me senté estaba roto.

   _____

4. La compañía para la cual trabajas es chilena.

   _____

5. Conocí al hombre al lado de quien vives.

   _____

6. No conozco la persona con la que se va a casar Alicia.

   _____

7. La señora con la cual llegaste es mi prima.

   _____

8. La escuela a la que voy es nueva.

   _____

9. Esta es la ventana por donde se escapó el perro.

_____

10. Dame la caja en la que guardo mis joyas.

_____

Translate each sentence into Spanish using the relative pronouns provided:

11. *The clients who I work for are very rich.*   (los que)

   Los clientes para los que trabajo son muy ricos. _____

12. *I don't like the world he lives in.*   (que)

_____

13. *I went to his house, behind which I saw the big tree.*   (la cual)

_____

14. *We met the students whom she spoke with.*   (los quienes)

_____

15. *They sold the pen that Washington wrote letters with.*   (que)

_____
_____

POR SU CUENTA

Create your own sentences using the following relative pronouns:

1. que   _____

2. la cual   _____

3. quienes   _____

4. cuyo   _____

5. el que   _____

6. cuantos   _____

7. lo cual   _____

8. las que   _____

9. cuyas   _____

10. quien   _____

18

Adverbs

¿Cuánto sabe usted?

How Much Do You Know Already?

1. Turn the adjective rápido into the Spanish for *rapidly*.

2. What do adverbs of manner do?

3. In general, how are most adverbs formed in Spanish?

4. What is the difference in usage between ya and todavía?

5. Name three Spanish adverbs that do not end in -mente.

Forming and Using Adverbs
Formación y empleo de adverbios

An adverb in a sentence indicates manner, quantity, time, place, or cause, and answers questions such as *how, when*, *where*, and *how much*. In English, many adverbs are formed by adding *-ly* to the adjectives. In Spanish, they are formed by adding -mente to the feminine form of the adjective:

Adjective (fem. form)		Adverb	
correcta	*correct*	correctamente	*correctly*
lenta	*slow*	lentamente	*slowly*
clara	*clear*	claramente	*clearly*
distinta	*distinct*	distintamente	*distinctly*
intensa	*intense*	intensamente	*intensely*
cuidadosa	*careful*	cuidadosamente	*carefully*

To those adjectives with no specific feminine form, the suffix -mente is added to the word in the singular:

Adjective (fem. form)		Adverb	
final	*final*	finalmente	*finally*
feliz	*happy*	felizmente	*happily*
probable	*probable*	probablemente	*probably*

251

If the adjective has an accent mark, it is retained in the adverbial form:

- **Adjective (fem. form)** **Adverb**

rápida	*quick*	rápidamente	*quickly*
fácil	*easy*	fácilmente	*easily*
cómoda	*comfortable*	cómodamente	*comfortably*

EJEMPLOS

Hicimos el trabajo <u>rápidamente</u>.
We did the job quickly.

Nos han tratado <u>amablemente</u>.
They've treated us kindly.

Tengo que analizarlo <u>lógicamente</u>.
I have to analyze it logically.

Some adverbs have irregular forms that do not include a suffix:

- **Adjective**

La máquina es <u>buena</u>. *The machine is good.*

- **Adverb**

Está funcionando <u>bien</u>. *It's working well.*

- **Adjective**

Tiene <u>mala</u> pronunciación. *He has poor pronunciation.*

- **Adverb**

La pronuncia <u>mal</u>. *He pronounces it poorly.*

Still other adverbs can be identical to their matching forms as adjectives:

- **Adjective**

Es una <u>mejor</u> idea. *It's a better idea.*

- **Adverb**

Cocina <u>mejor</u>. *He cooks better.*

- **Adjective**

Tengo una foto <u>peor</u>. *I have a worse photo.*

- **Adverb**

Bailaron <u>peor</u>. *They danced worse.*

Most adverbs of place, time, and quantity have no suffix either. Notice the pattern in these adverbs of quantity—they have the same form as the masculine singular of the adjective:

No necesito <u>tanto</u> amor.   *I don't need so much love.*
Te quiero <u>tanto</u>.   *I love you so much.*

Usamos <u>mucho</u> papel.   *We use a lot of paper.*
Escribimos <u>mucho</u>.   *We write a lot.*

Ganaba <u>poco</u> dinero.   *He was earning little money.*
Ahora hace muy <u>poco</u>.   *Now he does very little.*

TIP
Some adjectives are actually used as adverbs in everyday speech. They can be practiced in pairs:
rápido o despacio   *quickly* or *slowly*
bajo o alto   *softly* or *loudly*
diferente o igual   *differently* or *the same*
Corrió <u>rápido</u>.   *She ran fast.*
Pensamos <u>igual</u>.   *We think alike.*
Hablaban <u>alto</u>.   *They were speaking loudly.*

LA PRÁCTICA 1

Change these adjectives to their adverbial form:

1. verbal   verbalmente

2. inteligente   _____

3. justo   _____

4. tanto   _____

5. histórico   _____

6. natural   _____

7. cierto   _____

8. simple   _____

9. bueno   _____

10. peor   _____

11. sucesivo   _____

12. científico   _____

13. verdadero   _____

14. triste   _____

15. útil   _____

16. abierto   _____

17. desafortunado   _____

18. alegre   _____

19. profundo   _____

20. demasiado   _____

Using Adverbs of Manner
Empleo de adverbios de modo

Adverbs of manner tell *how* something is done and usually end in -mente. Remember that adverbs of manner are generally placed directly after the verb and never split the verb's compound forms:

Hay que hablar <u>francamente</u>.	*One must speak frankly.*
Han vivido <u>peligrosamente</u>.	*They've lived dangerously.*
Estamos descansando <u>tranquilamente</u>.	*We're resting peacefully.*

In some cases, direct objects can be placed between the main verb and the adverb of manner. Note the differences in translation:

<u>Habían examinado</u> al paciente <u>físicamente</u>.
They've physically examined the patient.

<u>Estaban renovando</u> la oficina <u>completamente</u>.
They were completely renovating the office.

Adverbs that modify other adverbs (or adjectives) are placed before the words they modify. Note how these intensifiers or adverbs of quantity may also have the suffix -mente:

Se siente <u>completamente</u> satisfecho.	*He feels completely satisfied.*
Explíquelo <u>más</u> claramente.	*Explain it more clearly.*
Estuvimos <u>totalmente</u> perdidos.	*We were totally lost.*
Los movieron <u>muy</u> lentamente.	*They moved them very slowly.*
Voy a decirlo <u>menos</u> firmemente.	*I'm going to say it less firmly.*

When two or more adverbs of manner (ending in -mente) modify the same word, the suffix is added to the last adverb only. All the others remain in their singular form:

> **La nueva lavadora puede lavar la ropa rápida y <u>fácilmente</u>.**
> *The new washing machine can wash clothes quickly and easily.*

> **Los soldados están luchando valiente y <u>profesionalmente</u>.**
> *The soldiers are fighting bravely and professionally.*

Sometimes the preposition con combines with a corresponding noun to replace an adverbial expression of manner:

> **Lo hacía alegremente.** = **Lo hacía <u>con</u> alegría.**
> *She did it happily.*   *She did it with happiness.*

> **Me lo dijo claramente.** = **Me lo dijo <u>con</u> claridad.**
> *He told it to me clearly.*   *He told it to me with clarity.*

However, several Spanish adverbs ending in -mente are not considered adverbs of manner:

probablemente	(*adverb of doubt*)
simplemente	(*adverb of quantity*)
primeramente	(*adverb of order*)
posteriormente	(*adverb of time*)

> **TIP**
> Adverbs of quantity are very common, and include words such as más, menos, demasiado, bastante, muy, casi, mucho, poco, **and** tanto.

LA PRÁCTICA 2

Use the words provided to create sentences in the simple present tense. Change each adjective to an adverb of manner.

1. Ella/ bailar/ elegante   *Ella baila elegantemente.*

2. Ellos/ mover/ tímidos   _____

3. Yo/ pronunciar/ distinto   _____

4. Ud./ traducir/ cuidadoso   _____

5. Nosotros/ no viajar/ tranquilos   _____

6. Tú/ trabajar/ diplomático   _____

7. Él/ venir/ rápido   _____

8. Los tigres/ atacar/ violentos   _____

9. Uds./ salir/ tristes   _____

10. Ellas/ dormir/ tranquilas   _____

Translate each sentence into English:

11. No hiciste nada bien.   ***You didn't do anything well.***

12. Cambió el programa sistemáticamente.   _____

13. Limpiaba su cuarto completamente.   _____

14. Me habló muy firmemente.   _____

15. Llorábamos desesperadamente.   _____

Using Adverbs of Time
Empleo de adverbios de tiempo

In Spanish, adverbs of time are found just about anywhere in a sentence. They answer the question *When?*:

<u>Siempre</u> voy al parque.	*I always go to the park.*
<u>Ahora</u> son las dos.	*It's two o'clock now.*
Comió <u>durante</u> la fiesta.	*He ate during the party.*
Bailaba <u>mientras</u> conversabas.	*I danced while you talked.*
Fuimos <u>anteayer</u>.	*We went the day before yesterday.*
Estudiarán <u>luego</u>.	*They'll study later.*

Other adverbs of time are:

hoy	*today*	temprano	*early*
ayer	*yesterday*	pronto	*soon*
mañana	*tomorrow*	a menudo	*often*
antes	*before*	anoche	*last night*
recién	*recently*	anteriormente	*formerly*
después	*after*	apenas	*scarcely*
mientras	*while*	casi nunca	*seldom*
durante	*during*	aún	*yet*
entonces	*then*	todavía	*still*
tarde	*late*	ya	*already*

The adverb recién means *recently* or *newly* and is often used before past participles:

los <u>recién</u> casados	*the newlyweds*
el <u>recién</u> nacido	*the newborn*
el perro <u>recién</u> bañado	*the recently bathed dog*

The adverb ya means *already*, *now*, or *right away*, and it is often confused
with todavía or aún in usage. Ya no means *no longer*:

Ya lo hice.	*I already did it.*
¡Ya nos vamos!	*We're leaving right now!*
Ya no toca el piano.	*He no longer plays the piano.*

Aún no he comido.	*I haven't eaten yet.*
Todavía está saliendo con ella.	*He's still going out with her.*
No saben todavía.	*They don't know yet.*

LA PRÁCTICA 3

Translate these sentences into Spanish:

1. *He doesn't have the boat anymore.*   Ya no tiene el bote.

2. *She always explains the answers.*   _____

3. *I'll be back right away.*   _____

4. *We seldom eat fish.*   _____

5. *They ate there last night.*   _____

6. *I've driven to Las Vegas before.*   _____

7. *Are they out already?*   _____

8. *Our neighbors are newlyweds.*   _____

9. *Where is she going after school?*   _____

10. *They already did it.*   _____

Using Adverbs of Location
Empleo de adverbios de lugar

There are several common adverbs of location or place in Spanish that answer the question *Where?* They are easily learned by grouping them as pairs of opposites:

arriba	*up*	abajo	*down*
en frente	*in front*	detrás	*behind*
cerca	*near*	lejos	*far*
encima	*above*	debajo	*under*
adentro	*inside*	afuera	*outside*
a la derecha	*to the right*	a la izquierda	*to the left*
por algún lado	*somewhere*	por ningún lado	*nowhere*

The adverbs *here* and *there* have different meanings in Spanish:

aquí or **acá** → *here*

ahí → → → → *there, near the person addressed*

allí → → → → → *there, away from the speaker and person addressed*

allá → → → → → → *way over there*

Adverbs of place frequently combine with prepositions and other adverbs to create complete adverbial phrases:

hasta aquí	*up to here*
desde allí	*from there*
hacia allá	*towards (over) there*
para acá	*this way (here)*
por allá	*around there*

TIP
Many adverbial expressions of time and place consist of two or more words:

otro día	*another day*
mucho antes	*a long time before*
años atrás	*years back*
al fondo	*at the bottom*
a lo largo de	*along*
al lado de	*beside*

LA PRÁCTICA 4

Write the opposite of each adverb or adverbial expression below:

1. delante   detrás _____

2. lejos _____

3. para allá _____

4. encima _____

5. adentro _____

6. a la izquierda _____

7. arriba _____

8. por ningún sitio _____

9. atrás _____

10. en lo alto _____

CROSSWORD 9

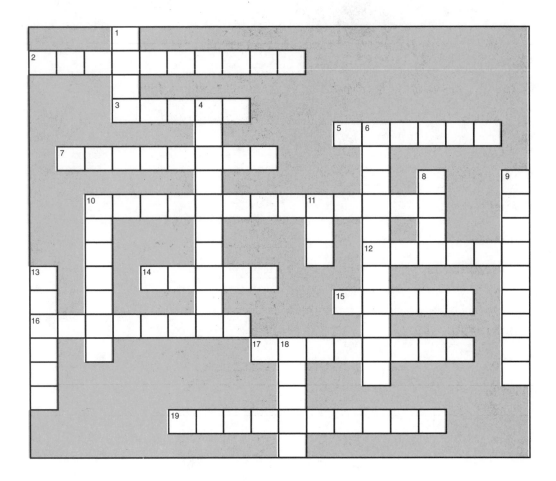

Translate these into Spanish:

Across
- 2. happily
- 3. never
- 5. outside
- 7. early
- 10. probably
- 12. up
- 14. so much
- 15. near
- 16. then
- 17. while
- 19. slowly

Down
- 1. well
- 4. clearly
- 6. frankly
- 8. worse
- 9. too much
- 10. small amount
- 11. poorly
- 13. scarcely
- 18. the same

19

Prepositions

¿Cuánto sabe usted?
How Much Do You Know Already?

1. How do you say *I went to the bank to take out money* in Spanish?

2. What do the prepositions salvo, excepto, and menos mean in English?

3. Translate para and por into English, and explain their main difference.

4. How do you say *She's living with me* in Spanish.

5. What does Salieron a pie mean in English?

Using the Preposition *de*
Empleo de la preposición de

A preposition shows the relation of a noun or pronoun to another word or part of the sentence. For example, the preposition de is used to relate one word to another in a variety of ways:

- **Characteristics**

Mario es el hombre <u>de</u> pelo largo.	*Mario is the long-haired man.*
Vivían en la casa <u>de</u> dos pisos.	*They lived in the two-story house.*

- **Possession**

Se puso el vestido <u>de</u> su mamá.	*She put on her mom's dress.*
¿Cuál es la capital <u>de</u> California?	*What's the capital of California?*

- **Origin**

Somos <u>de</u> México.	*We're from Mexico.*
Trajeron piedras <u>del</u> desierto.	*They brought rocks from the desert.*

261

- **Composition**

La ha comprado un collar <u>de</u> plata.	*He's bought her a silver necklace.*
¿Te gusta mi corbata <u>de</u> seda?	*Do you like my silk necktie?*

- **Content**

Quisiera dos vasos <u>de</u> leche.	*I would like two glasses of milk.*
Traiga la caja <u>de</u> libros.	*Bring the box of books.*

- **Time**

Celebramos el cuatro <u>de</u> julio.	*We celebrate the Fourth of July.*
Llegaron a las ocho <u>de</u> la mañana.	*They arrived at 8:00 A.M.*

- **Cause**

Se enfermó <u>de</u> cansancio.	*She got sick from being so tired.*
Sufríamos <u>de</u> sed.	*We were suffering from thirst.*

- **Manner**

Trabajaba <u>de</u> bombero.	*He worked as a firefighter.*
Lo hacía <u>de</u> buena fe.	*She was doing it out of good faith.*

- **Movement**

Están saliendo <u>de</u> la casa.	*They are leaving the house.*
Lo movimos <u>de</u> allí.	*We moved it from over there.*

Although de usually means *of* or *from* in English, it can be translated into other words as well:

- **With**

Lo llenamos <u>de</u> agua.	*We filled it with water.*
Estaba cubierto <u>de</u> barro.	*He was covered with mud.*

- **About**

¿<u>De</u> qué hablas?	*What are you talking about?*
No sabemos nada <u>de</u> él.	*We don't know anything about him.*

- **In**

¿Por qué estás vestida <u>de</u> negro?	*Why are you dressed in black?*
Ella está <u>de</u> luto.	*She's in mourning.*

De is used to form several common phrases and idiomatic expressions in Spanish:

Son menores **de** edad.	*They are minors.*
Fue un hombre **de** estatura alta.	*He was a tall man.*
Se puso **de** rodillas.	*He got on his knees.*
Es una milla **de** largo.	*It's a mile long.*
El flojo **de** su marido no me ayudó.	*Her lazy husband didn't help me.*

The preposition **de** is also used to form simple noun phrases:

TIP
De and **a** contract with **el** to form **del** and **al**:
Es el primero **del** mes.
It's the first of the month.
Vamos **al** teatro.
Let's go to the theater.

Han pintado el cuarto **de** baño.
They've painted the bathroom.

¿Dónde está la máquina **de** coser?
Where's the sewing machine?

Me encanta la clase **de** español.
I love Spanish class.

De is frequently used with both verbs and adverbs:

Acabo **de** llamar.	*I just called.*
Se acuerda **de** ti.	*She remembers you.*
Estoy afuera **del** edificio.	*I'm outside the building.*
Mire debajo **de** la cama.	*Look under the bed.*

LA PRÁCTICA 1

Translate these sentences into English:

1. Busco los aretes de oro. ***I'm looking for the gold earrings.***

2. Temblaron de susto. _____

3. Quiero usar el abrigo de ella. _____

4. Me muero de hambre. _____

5. ¿De dónde eran? _____

6. Tráigame la botella de vino. _____

7. Regreso del banco. _____

8. No salen de noche. _____

9. Es una chica de dinero. _____

10. El cuarto fue pintado de rojo. _____

_____

Using the Preposition *a*
Empleo de la preposición a

The preposition *a* also has several uses in Spanish. For example, it is frequently used as a personal *a* before direct objects that refer to people or personified things, including indefinite pronouns:

Invitaron a Juan.	*They invited Juan.*
Veo a mi gato.	*I see my cat.*
No escucho a nadie.	*I don't hear anyone.*

It also clarifies, emphasizes, or labels an indirect object pronoun:

Le dije a él.	*I told him.*
¿Les escribiste a tus padres?	*Did you write to your parents?*
Se lo regaló a Humberto.	*They gave it to Humberto as a gift.*

The preposition *a* frequently indicates motion towards somewhere:

Vamos a la playa.	*Let's go to the beach.*
Llegué a mi casa muy tarde.	*I arrived home very late.*

It may also link a verb of motion to an infinitive:

Anda a comer.	*Go eat.*
Se fueron a bailar.	*They left to go dancing.*

The preposition *a* is sometimes used to tell *how* something is done:

Preparé la comida a la italiana.	*I prepared the food Italian style.*
Salieron a pie.	*They left on foot.*

A is also used in sentences expressing a price, rate, or pace:

¿A cuánto se venden los tomates?	*What's the price of the tomatoes?*
Manejaban a cien millas por hora.	*They were driving 100 miles per hour.*
Tengo clases tres veces a la semana.	*I have classes three times a week.*

Although it generally means *to* in English, in certain expressions involving time and location, a is used to mean *at*, *upon*, or *on*.

Tenías cita a las dos.	*You had an appointment at two.*
A mi salida se puso a llorar.	*Upon my departure, she began to cry.*
El hotel está a la derecha.	*The hotel is on the right.*

Al in the construction al + infinitive carries the prepositional meaning of *upon*:

Al llegar, se fue a la cocina.	*Upon arriving, he went to the kitchen.*
Al entrar, escuchamos la música.	*Upon entering, we heard the music.*

A may also express distance or the period of time after which something took place in the past:

La tienda está a dos cuadras.
The store is two blocks away.

Se jubiló a los veinte años de trabajar en la compañía.
She retired after working in the company for twenty years.

Numerous everyday words, phrases, and expressions in Spanish include the preposition a:

a veces	*sometimes*
a sus órdenes	*at your service*
paso a paso	*step by step*
montar a caballo	*horseback riding*
a ver	*let's see*
hecho a mano	*handmade*
a la vez	*at the same time*
a menudo	*often*
a tiempo	*on time*

> **TIP**
> The construction ir + a is used to indicate future action:
> La voy a mandar las flores.
> *I'm going to send her the flowers.*

LA PRÁCTICA 2

Rewrite each sentence, inserting the preposition a only where it's needed:

1. Conozco _____ el Sr. Goya.   Conozco al Sr. Goya.

2. _____ él le gusta _____ bailar.   _____

3. Es la una y _____ media.   _____

4. La pareja montó _____ caballo.   _____

5. ¿ _____ qué hora llegaste _____ tu casa?   _____

6. Le dió el agua _____ ella.   _____

7. No han salido _____ todavía.   _____

8. Te volvió _____ llamar.   _____

9. No subimos _____ el tren.   _____

10. ¿ _____ cuánto cuesta _____ la bicicleta?   _____

POR SU CUENTA

Answer these questions as you practice the prepositions de and a:

1. ¿Vive Ud. en un edificio de muchos pisos?

2. ¿De dónde es su mejor amigo?

3. ¿Manda Ud. correo electrónico a su familia?

4. ¿Cuántas veces por semana sale Ud. a comer afuera?

5. ¿De qué color es el libro que lee?

6. ¿A qué hora se acuesta Ud.?

7. ¿Compra Ud. botellas de agua purificada?

8. ¿Adónde va Ud. para relajarse?

9. ¿Es Ud. menor de edad?

10. ¿Siempre llega Ud. a tiempo?

Using the Preposition *con*
Empleo de la preposición con

The preposition *con* generally means *with* in English and expresses accompaniment:

Trabajaron <u>con</u> mis amigos.	*They worked with my friends.*
No quiere sentarse <u>con</u>migo.	*He doesn't want to sit with me.*
Ordenamos más frijoles <u>con</u> arroz.	*Let's order more beans with rice.*

However, *con* can also mean *with* to indicate possession, description, or relationship:

¿Conoces a la señora <u>con</u> los gatos?	*Do you know the lady with the cats?*
Llame al chico <u>con</u> el pelo largo.	*Call the boy with the long hair.*
He hablado <u>con</u> su yerno.	*I've spoken with his son-in-law.*

Con may also be used with objects such as tools to indicate how a task is completed:

Estoy cortando la madera <u>con</u> el serrucho.
I'm cutting the wood with the saw.

Lo pintó <u>con</u> la tinta negra.
I painted it with black ink.

Con frequently indicates the manner in which something is done. Note how *con* is followed by a noun in these adverbial expressions:

Lo hicimos <u>con</u> amor y cariño.	*We did it with love and care.*
Empuje <u>con</u> mucha fuerza.	*Push with a lot of strength.*
Los dos salían <u>con</u> frecuencia.	*The two dated frequently.*

The preposition *con* may also be used to express *in spite of*:

<u>Con</u> toda la familia que tiene, se mudó a una casa más pequeña.
In spite of all the family he has, he moved to a smaller home.

Con appears with several common verbs and expressions in Spanish:

Se quedó <u>con</u> su libro.
She kept her book.

Te pagaré <u>con</u> tal que trabajes.
I'll pay you provided that you pay me.

Siempre sueña <u>con</u> dinero.
He always dreams about money.

LA PRÁCTICA 3

Translate these sentences into English:

1. ¿Podría hablar contigo? *Can I speak with you?*

2. Él lo secó con una toalla. _____

3. Paulo se casará con su novia. _____

4. Vamos a celebrar con alegría. _____

5. Ella se quedó con la casa blanca. _____

6. Yo trabajaba con este martillo. _____

7. Con todos sus problemas, él sigue estudiando. _____

8. ¿Quién es la niña con los ojos grandes? _____

9. Se encontraron con sus amigos. _____

10. Ellas contestaron con timidez. _____

Using the Preposition *en*
Empleo de la preposición en

The preposition en usually means *in*, *into*, *on*, *upon*, or *at*, and indicates location:

Mi cuaderno está <u>en</u> la cocina.	*My notebook is in the kitchen.*
Ponga el lápiz <u>en</u> el escritorio.	*Put the pencil on the desk.*
Se quedaron <u>en</u> su casa.	*They stayed at home.*

It is also used to express a period of time:

No puedo hacerlo <u>en</u> este momento.	*I can't do it at this moment.*
Viajaremos <u>en</u> el verano.	*We will travel in the summer.*
Terminó la clase <u>en</u> un año.	*She finished the class in a year.*

The preposition en frequently expresses *how* or the means by which an action takes place:

Viajamos <u>en</u> metro o <u>en</u> autobús.
We travel by subway or by bus.

Se parecen mucho <u>en</u> el hablar y <u>en</u> el caminar.
They're a lot alike in their speech and in their walk.

En can also be used to label a price or a percentage:

Quiere venderlo en cinco dólares.
He wants to sell it for five dollars.

El valor ha bajado en un veinte por ciento.
The value has dropped by twenty percent.

Several verb infinitives are used regularly with the word en:

¿Te fijaste en ella?	*Did you notice her?*
El agua se convierte en hielo.	*The water turned to ice.*
Siempre pienso en Uds.	*I'm always thinking of you guys.*

Several common expressions in Spanish include the word en:

en cambio	*on the other hand*
en serio	*seriously*
en cuanto	*as soon as*
en realidad	*in reality*
en seguida	*right away*

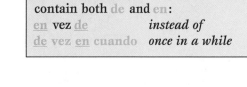

> **TIP**
> A few expressions in Spanish contain both de and en:
> en vez de   *instead of*
> de vez en cuando *once in a while*

LA PRÁCTICA 4

Translate these sentences into Spanish using the preposition en:

1. *We'll leave in ten minutes.*   Salimos en diez minutos.

2. *I went by car and by plane.*   _____

3. *The food's in the refrigerator.*   _____

4. *The price went up by 10 percent.*   _____

5. *They cleaned the house in a day.*   _____

6. *Did you notice him?*   _____

7. *In reality, he has no idea.*   _____

8. *She insists on driving.*   _____

9. *They slept on the floor.*   _____

10. *Their speech is similar.*   _____

Using *para* and *por*
Empleo de para *y* por

The difference in meaning between the prepositions por and para is determined by their usage. Although both may be translated as *for*, por generally focuses back on a cause, while para looks forward to a result.

PARA is often translated as *in order to* or *bound for* and is used in the following ways:

- **Destination**

Ya salieron para Francia.	*They already left for France.*
El paquete es para Ud.	*The package is for you.*
Tomé un taxi para el centro.	*I took a taxi downtown.*

- **Use**

Dame un vaso para el agua.	*Give me a water glass.*
No encuentra la llave para el garaje.	*She can't find the key to the garage.*
La medicina es para ayudarte.	*The medicine is to help you.*

- **Purpose**

Compró la madera para cortar.	*He bought the wood to cut.*
Están aquí para reparar la tubería.	*They're here to fix the plumbing.*
Estudia para abogado.	*She's studying to be a lawyer.*

- **Future time**

Tengo una cita para el martes.	*I have an appointment for Tuesday.*
Son veinte para las cinco.	*It's twenty until five.*
La lección para mañana es difícil.	*Tomorrow's lesson is difficult.*

- **Idiomatic expressions**

No sirve para nada.	*It's not worth anything.*
Comamos aquí para variar.	*Let's eat here for a change.*
Es pequeño para su edad.	*He's small for his age.*
El amor no dura para siempre.	*Love doesn't last forever.*
No es para tanto.	*It's not that bad.*

The preposition *para* may also be used to express one's personal opinion:

Para mí, los impuestos son muy altos.
In my opinion, the taxes are very high.

Para Hugo, este restaurante sirve el mejor bistec.
In Hugo's opinion, this restaurant serves the best steak.

Sometimes it is used to set a standard for comparing people or things with the norm:

Para ser extranjera habla el idioma muy bien.
For being a foreigner, she speaks the language very well.

Para ser hotel de pueblo chico, tiene todo lo que uno necesita.
For a small-town hotel, it has everything one needs.

POR can mean a variety of things in English and has several important uses:

- **Means or method**

Viajaron **por** tren.	*They traveled by train.*
Me manda los cheques **por** correo.	*He sends me the checks by mail.*

- **Substitution or exchange**

Ella jugará **por** la chica herida.	*She'll play in place of the injured girl.*
¿Cuánto pagaste **por** el anillo?	*How much did you pay for the ring?*

- **Reason for cause**

Se enfermó **por** el frío.	*She got sick because of the cold.*
Te quiero **por** tu linda sonrisa.	*I love you for your beautiful smile.*

- **Near, along, around, or through**

Corrían **por** el parque.	*They used to run through the park.*
Hay muchos hoteles **por** aquí.	*There are lots of hotels around here.*

- **Period of time**

He trabajado en la tienda por años. | I've worked at the store for years.

Regrese mañana por la tarde. | Come back tomorrow afternoon.

When por precedes an adverb of location, it often implies some form of motion:

El ratón corrió... | The mouse ran...
por dentro | inside
por afuera | outside
por acá | around here
por allá | around there
por encima de | over the top of
por debajo de | right under

Por is also used to express a unit of measure or number:

El precio subió cuatro por ciento. | The price went up four percent.
Cuatro por cinco son veinte. | Four times five is twenty.
Manejaban sesenta millas por hora. | They drove sixty miles an hour.

Por often expresses *on whose account* or *for whose sake* an action is completed:

Por ella, gastaba todo el dinero que tenía.
For her sake, he spent all the money he had.

No lo hagas por mí.
Don't do it on my account.

The preposition por can also mean *by* when it denotes an agent in the passive voice:

La historia fue escrita por Cervantes.
The story was written by Cervantes.

Será pintado por el obrero alto.
It'll be painted by the tall worker.

When por is preceded by estar + infinitive, it indicates that an action is *about to* happen:

Cuando ellos llegaron, él estaba por comer.
He was about to eat when they arrived.

Estoy por prender el televisor.
I'm about to turn on the TV.

Por frequently appears in common idioms:

Lo tomó por tonto.
She took him for a fool.

Hazlo de una vez por todas.
Do it once and for all.

Pasé el examen por un pelo.
I barely passed the exam.

Él trabajaba por cuatro.
He worked like a slave.

Regreso en un dos por tres.
I'll be back in a jiffy.

Quiero verlo por escrito.
I want to see it in writing.

Por is also found in several everyday expressions in Spanish:

por favor	*please*	por lo común	*usually*
por eso	*therefore*	por lo demás	*furthermore*
por ejemplo	*for example*	por lo visto	*apparently*
por lo menos	*at least*	por poco	*almost*
por si acaso	*just in case*	por aquel entonces	*at that time*
por supuesto	*of course*		
por casualidad	*by chance*	por lo pronto	*for the time being*
por ahora	*for now*	por mi parte	*as far as I'm concerned*
por cierto	*certainly*		
por fin	*finally*	por su cuenta	*on one's own*
por un lado	*on the one hand*	por desgracia	*unfortunately*
por otro lado	*on the other hand*	por primera vez	*for the first time*
por lo general	*generally*	por motivo de	*on account of*

LA PRÁCTICA 5

Fill in the blanks with either para or por. The English translation is provided:

1. <u>Para</u> estudiante tan inteligente, no fue una pregunta muy difícil.

For such an intelligent student, it wasn't a very difficult question.

2. Son producidos _____ máquinas.   *They're produced by machines.*

3. Vino _____ ayudarnos.   *She came to help us.*

4. ¿_____ qué es el martillo?   *What's the hammer for?*

5. Todo lo hizo _____ su madre.   *Everything he did was for his mother.*

6. Trabajan _____ la misma señora.   *They work for the same lady.*

7. No puedes salir _____ esa puerta.   *You can't leave through that door.*

8. Dejaremos todo _____ mañana.   *Let's leave everything for tomorrow.*

9. Se venden _____ libra.   *They're sold by the pound.*

10. _____ ser un bebito, es muy fuerte.   *For a baby, he's very strong.*

11. Ha vivido aquí _____ dos días.   *He's lived here for two days.*

12. _____ ella, es muy caro.   *For her, it is very expensive.*

13. Pagaré cien _____ el boleto.   *I'll pay a hundred for the ticket.*

14. ¿_____ dónde van Uds.?   *Where are you guys going?*

15. Fue un honor _____ mí.   *It was an honor for me.*

Fill in the blanks with either para or por:

16. Lo escuchamos _____ la radio.   <u>por</u>

17. Lo hizo _____ él y _____ él.   _____

18. Vengo _____ decirte que has ganado el premio.   _____

19. ¡_____ Dios!, ten cuidado con los vasos.   _____

20. _____ lo general, suele fumar puros.   _____

21. No necesito maletas _____ este viaje.   _____

22. Los muebles son _____ Uds.   _____

23. _____ tu culpa llegamos tarde.   _____

24. Brindamos _____ la feliz pareja.   _____

25. Ella estaba paseando _____ la ciudad.   _____

Using Other Prepositions
Empleo de otras preposiciones

The prepositions menos, excepto, and salvo all mean *except* in English:

Todos bailaron <u>menos</u> Yolanda.
Everyone danced except Yolanda.

Iremos todos <u>excepto</u> el payaso de Saúl.
We'll all go except goofy Saúl.

Amo a toda la familia <u>salvo</u> a la tía Eva.
I love the entire family, except for Aunt Eva.

Hasta can either mean *until* or *even* depending on the context:

Esperaremos <u>hasta</u> medianoche.   *We will wait until midnight.*
<u>Hasta</u> el maestro llegó tarde.   *Even the teacher arrived late.*

The preposition sobre has several different meanings in English:

Siempre discuten <u>sobre</u> política.   *They always argue about politics.*
Ella va a llegar <u>sobre</u> las ocho.   *She'll arrive approximately at eight.*
Las nubes pasan <u>sobre</u> el valle.   *The clouds pass over the valley.*
La camisa estaba <u>sobre</u> la mesa.   *The shirt was on top of the table.*

Desde means *from* or *since*, and is more specific than *de*:

Se ve todo <u>desde</u> mi cabaña en las montañas.
You can see everything from my cabin in the mountains.

<u>Desde</u> 1967 hemos vivido aquí.
We've lived here since 1967.

Sin means *without*, but has several meanings when followed by an infinitive:

El hombre estaba <u>sin</u> afeitar.   *The man was unshaven.*
Volaron <u>sin</u> parar.   *They flew nonstop.*
Me he quedado <u>sin</u> dormir.   *I haven't slept a wink.*
Pasaste el examen <u>sin</u> estudiar.   *You passed the test without studying.*

Hacia means *toward*, and is often followed by an adverb:

Marcharon <u>hacia</u> la fortaleza.   *They marched toward the fort.*
Siento resentimiento <u>hacia</u> él.   *I feel resentment toward him.*

Miramos <u>hacia</u> arriba.   *We looked upward.*
Lo empujaban <u>hacia</u> atrás.   *They were pushing him backward.*

The preposition tras means *after* and usually appears in set expressions:

Me dió una manzana tras otra.
He gave me one apple after another.

Año tras año decoramos el árbol.
We decorate the tree year after year.

Tras haber comido tanto, se enfermó.
After having eaten so much, he got sick.

Ante (*before*) and bajo (*under*) are often used figuratively in Spanish:

Se porta muy bien ante su maestro.
He behaves very well before his teacher.

Habían más problemas bajo esa forma de gobierno.
There were more problems under that form of government.

Contra means *against*, but the compound preposition en contra de expresses disagreement with another belief, policy, or point of view:

Pelearon contra el otro equipo.	*They fought against the other team.*
Déjalo contra la pared.	*Leave it against the wall.*
¿Estás en contra de la idea?	*Are you against the idea?*
Han hablado en contra de la guerra.	*They've spoken against the war.*

A few prepositions are popular time expressions:

antes de	*before*
después de	*after*
durante	*during*

A variety of single and compound prepositions indicate physical location in Spanish. Notice that many include the words a or de:

entre	*between*
junto a	*next to*
al lado de	*beside*
a lo largo de	*along*
alrededor de	*around*
(en) frente a	*across from, facing*
a través de	*through*

> **TIP**
> When using prepositions, sometimes there is more than one way to express the same idea:
> mediante, por medio de
> *by means of*
> acerca de, respecto a
> *concerning* or *about*

Some prepositions can be practiced as word pairs with opposite meanings:

delante de	*in front of*
detrás de	*behind*
dentro de	*inside of*
(a)fuera de	*outside of*
cerca de	*near, about*
lejos de	*far from*
encima de	*upon, on top of*
debajo de	*under*

Spanish is full of prepositions that are considered complete idioms or expressions all by themselves:

a pesar de	*in spite of*	<u>A pesar de</u> todo, viajan mañana.
según	*according to*	<u>Según</u> Marcos, ganamos el juego.
a causa de	*because of*	<u>A causa del</u> frío, no pude salir.

LA PRÁCTICA 6

Select the best preposition from the right column to fill in the blanks on the left:

1. Yo te vi <u>desde</u> la ventana.   hacia

2. Se quedó _____ conocimiento en la cama.   hasta

3. Hacía veinte grados _____ cero.   ante

4. _____ todo, hay que respetar a la gente mayor.   desde

5. _____ Noé, la profesora es muy simpática.   durante

6. Me dijo que Victoria se durmió _____ la ópera.   sobre

7. _____ mi padre lloraba cuando se casaron.   menos

8. Se puso la bufanda _____ la cabeza.   según

9. Tenía que caminar _____ adelante.   bajo

10. Todos hablaban en español _____ Sandra.   sin

Fill in the blank with the correct preposition. The first letter is provided.

11. Lo haremos s_____ lo ha dicho.   según

12. Llegará s_____ las cinco.   _____

13. Hay jardín e_____ el apartamento.   _____

14. Ella no hablaba a_____ de su enfermedad.   _____

15. Caminaron h_____ abajo.   _____

16. Lucharemos c_____ la corrupción.   _____

17. Confesó todo a_____ el juez.   _____

18. Le dijo todo e_____ la verdad.   _____

19. Día t_____ día no comía nada.   _____

20. Estoy en c_____ de tu decisión.   _____

EL REPASO

Take one word or phrase from each column below and create sentences as you review. Notice the example:

Juan trabajó en el hospital ayer.

1.	2.	3.	4.
Yo	ser	profesor	ahorita
Juan	estudiar	en el hospital	siempre
Ustedes	hablar	bien	mañana
Ana y Luisa	necesitar	frío	ayer
Nosotros	trabajar	en el mercado	antes
La señorita	aprender	doctor	
Tú	vivir	en Chicago	
	escribir	ensalada	
	tener	inglés	
	leer	sed	
	beber	trabajo	
	comer	veinte años	
	de México		
	cerveza		
	español		
	el periódico		
	dinero		
	en la casa		

20

Interrogatives

Using Information Questions
Empleo de frases interrogativas

An interrogative word generally begins a sentence that asks for information. Notice how these common interrogative words all have the written accents:

¿Cuál(es)?	*Which one(s)?*
¿Cuándo?	*When?*
¿Cuánto/a?	*How much?*
¿Cuántos/as?	*How many?*
¿Cómo?	*How?*
¿Dónde?	*Where?*
¿Adónde?	*To where?*
¿De dónde?	*From where?*
¿Qué?	*What?*
¿Por qué?	*Why?*
¿Para qué?	*For what purpose?*
¿Quién(es)?	*Who?*
¿De quién(es)?	*Whose?*

EJEMPLOS

¿Qué has comido?	*What have you eaten?*
¿De dónde son los turistas?	*Where are the tourists from?*
¿Cuánto me va a costar?	*How much will it cost me?*
¿Quién fue el primero?	*Who was first?*
¿Para qué son los uniformes?	*What are the uniforms for?*
¿Cuándo llegaron?	*When did they arrive?*

Interrogative or question words are used differently in Spanish than they are in English, and their translations are not always exact. For example, ¿Cuál? is used instead of ¿Qué? in questions that identify, pinpoint, or specify information, particularly after the verb ser:

¿Cuál es la capital de Montana?
What's the capital of Montana?

¿Cuáles son los días de la semana en español?
What are the days of the week in Spanish?

¿Cuál fue la diferencia entre los dos libros?
What was the difference between the two books?

Whenever ¿Qué? is followed by ser, it asks for a definition:

¿Qué es el totalitarismo?	*What is totalitarianism?*
¿Qué son los tranvías?	*What are streetcars?*

¿Qué? generally replaces ¿Cuál? or ¿Cuáles? before a noun:

¿Qué libros van a leer?	*What books are they going to read?*
¿Qué película compró Ud.?	*What movie did you buy?*
¿Qué animal te gusta más?	*What's your favorite animal?*

In sentences asking for specific figures or measurements, *How?* is not always translated directly into Spanish as ¿Cómo? because ¿Cómo? cannot be followed by an adverb or adjective:

How long before Christmas?	¿Cuánto tiempo falta para la Navidad?
How cold would Mars be?	¿Cuán frío será Marte?
How tall is he?	¿Cuánto mide él?
How fast can she walk?	¿Con qué rapidez camina?
How heavy was the purse?	¿Cuánto pesaba la cartera?
How wide is the entrance?	¿Qué ancho tiene la entrada?

¿Cómo? is also used to mean *How's that?* in everyday conversation:

—Nos casamos ayer.	*We got married yesterday.*
—¿Cómo?	*How's that?*

Interrogative words that either include or add a preposition seldom translate directly into English. Notice how prepositions in Spanish precede interrogative words in a sentence:

¿De quién es ese lápiz?   *Whose pencil is that?*
¿Con qué vamos a pintar?   *What are we going to paint with?*
¿Para cuántas personas son?   *For how many people are they?*

¿Adónde?, ¿Para dónde?, and ¿Hacia dónde? also include prepositions, and are frequently used with verbs of motion. Notice how they all imply *To where?* in English:

¿Hacia dónde están volando?
Where are they flying to?

¿Para dónde caminaron?
Where did they walk to?

¿Adónde vas?
Where are you going to?

> **TIP**
> The word *How* has several other translations in Spanish:
> *How come?*   ¿Por qué?
> *How do you do?*   Mucho gusto.
> *How pretty!*   ¡Qué bonito!

LA PRÁCTICA 1

Read each response and write in the most appropriate interrogative word:

1. A mi casa.   _¿Adónde?_

2. Su primer nombre es Juan. _____

3. Está en la mesa. _____

4. Tengo cuarenta. _____

5. Porque trabajaba anoche. _____

6. Son las cinco y media. _____

7. Cuesta treinta dólares. _____

8. A las tres de la tarde. _____

9. Ella es mi madrastra. _____

10. Estoy bien, gracias. _____

Fill in the blanks with the most appropriate question word from the right column:

11. ¿ <u>Cuáles</u> son tus mejores cursos?   Cuáles

12. ¿ _____ es su fecha de nacimiento?   Cuánto

13. ¿ _____ es el dueño de ese carro?   Qué

14. ¿ _____ hijos tiene Ud.?   Cómo

15. ¿ _____ fueron los chicos ayer?   Quién

16. ¿ De _____ nacionalidad son Uds.?   Dónde

17. ¿ _____ te sientes?   Adónde

18. ¿ _____ tiempo falta para la boda?   Cuál

19. ¿ _____ tiene que regresar a su casa?   Cuántos

20. ¿ _____ está ubicado el teatro?   Cuándo

POR SU CUENTA

Create your own interview questions by finishing the sentences below:

1. ¿Adónde   va Ud. de vacaciones? _____

2. ¿Quién es   _____ ?

3. ¿Cuántos años   _____ ?

4. ¿Por qué tiene Ud.   _____ ?

5. ¿Cuál es su   _____ ?

6. ¿Dónde   _____ ?

7. ¿Qué   _____ ?

8. ¿Cómo   _____ ?

9. ¿Cuándo   _____ ?

10. ¿Cuánto cuesta   _____ ?

Using "Yes/No" Question Forms
Empleo de formas de respuesta simple

When forming a basic *yes/no* question in Spanish, the word order can be changed to meet the needs of the speaker. As a rule, questions are often identical to statements, except that the intonation shifts from falling to rising at the end of the sentence:

Tito bailaba anoche.	¿Tito bailaba <u>anoche</u>?
Tito danced last night.	*Did Tito dance last night?*

However, the subject can also follow the verb if the speaker so desires:

¿Bailaba Tito anoche?	*Did Tito dance last night?*

And, to stress the subject in the sentence, the subject can be placed at the end:

¿Bailaba anoche Tito?	*Did <u>Tito</u> dance last night?*

EJEMPLOS

¿La señorita come en el café?
¿En el café come la señorita?   } *Does the young lady eat at the café?*
¿Come la señorita en el café?

¿Trabajamos mañana tú y yo?
¿Tú y yo trabajamos mañana?   } *Do you and I work tomorrow?*
¿Trabajamos tú y yo mañana?

To form a question with sentences consisting of the subject + ser or estar + adjective construction, generally place the subject at the end.

Tus amigos	son	agradables.	*Your friends are nice.*
SUBJECT	SER	ADJECTIVE	

¿Son agradables tus amigos?	*Are your friends nice?*

La directora	estaba	enferma.	*The principal was sick.*
SUBJECT	ESTAR	ADJECTIVE	

¿Estaba enferma la directora?	*Was the principal sick?*

For *yes/no* questions consisting of only a subject and a verb, the message also differs based on the word order. Note the difference in emphasis:

¿Antonia se durmió?	*Did Antonia <u>fall asleep</u>?*
¿Se durmió Antonia?	*Did <u>Antonia</u> fall asleep?*

LA PRÁCTICA 2

Convert these affirmative statements to two different question forms:

1. Perla está trabajando los martes.   ¿Está trabajando los martes Perla?

     ¿Perla está trabajando los martes?

2. Se venden periódicos allí. _____

   _____

3. Anoche Jesús salió con Olivia. _____

   _____

4. Ellos se van a mudar en julio. _____

   _____

5. La computadora tenía problemas. _____

   _____

6. Paco trabajaba en el banco. _____

   _____

7. Ella siempre se queda en casa. _____

   _____

8. A Mari le gustá comer pollo. _____

   _____

9. Mi hijo perdió la pelota. _____

   _____

10. El Sr. Ortiz se va mañana. _____

   _____

Using Indirect Questions
Empleo de preguntas indirectas

Any question that is incorporated into a sentence as a dependent clause is considered an indirect question. When this happens, the tense of the original question usually changes. Observe how each interrogative word keeps its accent mark:

Direct Question		Indirect Question
¿Por qué salen Uds.?	→	Me preguntó por qué salían Uds.
PRESENT TENSE		IMPERFECT TENSE
¿Qué comerá ella?	→	Me preguntó qué comería ella.
FUTURE TENSE		CONDITIONAL TENSE
¿Cuándo llegaron?	→	Me preguntó cuándo llegaron.
PRETERIT TENSE		PRETERIT TENSE
		or
		Me preguntó cuándo habían llegado.
		PLUPERFECT TENSE

The verb preguntar is in the preterit tense because questions are usually asked at a specific point in past time. However, if preguntar is in the present or future tense, then the tenses of both the direct and indirect questions remain the same:

Profesor:	Diego, ¿a qué hora te acuestas?
	Diego, at what time do you go to bed?
Diego:	Siempre me *pregunta* a qué hora me acuesto.
	He always asks me at what time I go to bed.

Look what happens to an information question with direct quotes—the second part of the sentence is separated by question marks. Also notice how the indirect question becomes a subordinate clause:

DIRECT
| Me preguntó—¿Qué hora es? | *He asked me, "What time is it?"* |

INDIRECT
| Me preguntó qué hora era. | *He asked me what time it was.* |

DIRECT
| Te pregunté—¿Dónde trabajará él? | *I asked you, "Where will he work?"* |

INDIRECT
| Te pregunté dónde trabajaría él. | *I asked you where he would work.* |

Unlike *information* questions, direct *yes/no* questions in Spanish are converted to indirect ones by adding the word si:

DIRECT
¿Compraste la comida?
Did you buy the food?

INDIRECT
Me preguntó si habías comprado la comida.
He asked me if you had bought the food.

DIRECT
¿Sabes la respuesta, José?
Do you know the answer, José?

INDIRECT
Le preguntó a José si sabía la respuesta.
She asked José if he knows the answer.

LA PRÁCTICA 3

Change these direct questions to indirect questions:

1. Me preguntó—¿Dónde vive Astrid?

   Me preguntó dónde vivía Astrid.

2. Le preguntó—¿Fumas, Valeria?

   _____

3. Te pregunté—¿Dónde lo comprarán?

   _____

4. Nos preguntan—¿Cómo se deletrean las palabras?

   _____

5. Te preguntaron—¿Cuántos años tiene la profesora?

   _____

6. Le pregunté—¿Entiendes alemán?

   _____

7. Me preguntó—¿Cuándo trabajaron ellos?

_____

8. Les pregunté—¿Qué pasó ayer?

_____

9. Me preguntarán—¿Por qué siempre llega tarde Eva?

_____

10. Te pregunté—¿Quién será el alcalde?

_____

_____

21

Negation

¿Cuánto sabe usted?

How Much Do You Know Already?

1. How do you say *He doesn't read anything* in Spanish?

2. Turn this into a negative sentence: Hemos terminado.

3. What does Ya no juego fútbol mean in English?

4. How do you say *Better late than never* in Spanish?

5. Use a double negative to say that you didn't see anything in the box.

Using Words that Express Negation
Empleo de palabras que expresan negación

Spanish has a variety of negative words and expressions that can function alone or as part of everyday expressions:

casi nunca	*hardly ever*	ninguno	*none*
de ningún modo	*by no means*	no	*no, not*
de ninguna manera	*in no way*	nunca	*never*
jamás	*never, ever*	por ningún lado	*no place*
nada	*nothing*	por ninguna parte	*nowhere*
nadie	*no one*	tampoco	*not either*
ni ... ni	*neither ... nor*	ya no	*no longer*
ni siquiera	*not even*	sin	*without*

EJEMPLOS

Ella ya no trabaja aquí.	*She no longer works here.*
Nunca he escuchado esa canción.	*I've never heard that song.*
No saldremos tampoco.	*We won't leave either.*
Él no tenía ni comida ni bebida.	*He had neither food nor drink.*
Nadie estaba en el garaje.	*No one was in the garage.*

Negative words are also parts of common Spanish idioms:

Digo que no.	*I say no.*
Él no me conoce nada.	*He doesn't know me from Adam.*
No se me da nada.	*It's no concern of mine.*
Ni hablar; ni modo.	*Nothing doing.*
Jamás de los jamases.	*Absolutely never, ever.*
Se quedó en nada.	*It turned out to be nothing.*
Es un cuento de nunca acabar.	*It's a never-ending story.*
No hay de qué.	*You're welcome.*
Por nada; de nada.	*It was nothing.*
No lo/la puedo ver ni en pintura.	*I can't stand him/her.*
Ella vino sin querer.	*She came unwillingly.*
Nada de eso.	*Nothing of the kind.*
Más vale tarde que nunca.	*Better late than never.*
No por nada lo hicimos.	*We had good reason to do it.*
No tiene nada que ver con eso.	*It has nothing to do with it.*
No tengo ni idea.	*I haven't a clue.*
Ella lo hizo como si nada.	*She did it as if it were nothing.*
No sirve para nada.	*It's totally useless.*
Conversaron nada más.	*They talked and nothing else.*

The adjective ninguno (*none*) has a shortened form before singular masculine nouns, and is only in the plural when the singular noun it modifies is also in the plural:

Ningún centavo.	*Not a penny.*
Ningunas tijeras.	*No scissors.*
Ningunos anteojos.	*Not a single pair of glasses.*
Ninguna flor.	*Not one flower.*

Spanish frequently uses a double negative, so the word no must precede the verb when a negative word or phrase follows it:

No hice *nada* ayer.	*I didn't do anything yesterday.*
No ha viajado *por ninguna parte*.	*She hasn't traveled anywhere.*
No corrimos *tampoco*.	*We did not run either.*

No is not used, however, if a negative word or phrase precedes the verb:

<u>Nunca</u> trabajo el domingo.	*I don't work on Sundays.*
<u>Ninguna</u> puerta estaba abierta.	*Not one door was open.*
Marta <u>ya no</u> habla español.	*Marta no longer speaks Spanish.*

The negative word **ni** is often repeated in a series, and can function alone to mean *not even*:

La pobre mujer no tiene <u>ni</u> casa, <u>ni</u> familia, <u>ni</u> trabajo y <u>ni</u> siquiera comida.
The poor woman has no home, no family, no job, and (even) no food.

<u>Ni</u> yo sabía eso.	*Not even I knew that.*

The verb can either be singular or plural when the **ni ... ni** construction is the subject of a sentence:

<u>Ni</u> Carlos <u>ni</u> Francisco tiene pasaporte.
Neither Carlos nor Francisco has a passport.

<u>Ni</u> el enfermero <u>ni</u> la doctora vinieron hoy.
Neither the nurse nor the doctor came today.

Sometimes, two or more negative words can be used together in a sentence. Notice the differences in translation:

<u>Nunca jamás</u> iremos allí.	*We will never, ever go there (again).*
<u>Ninguna</u> salía con <u>nadie</u>.	*Neither one went out with anyone.*
<u>Nunca</u> dicen <u>nada tampoco</u>.	*They never say anything either.*

Negative words can also be used as short answer forms to questions in conversation:

—¿Qué tienes?	*What's the matter with you?*
—<u>Nada</u>.	*Nothing.*

—¿Vienen Uds. con nosotros?	*Are you guys coming with us?*
—Yo, <u>no</u>. Él, sí.	*I'm not. He is.*

—No me gustan las arañas. ¿Y tú?	*I don't like spiders. And you?*
—A mí <u>tampoco</u>.	*I don't either.*

The conjunction **sino** must be used instead of **pero** after a negative clause:

- **Affirmative**
  Hablo inglés <u>pero</u> no hablo español.
  I speak English but I don't speak Spanish.

- **Negative**
  No hablo español, <u>sino</u> inglés.
  I don't speak Spanish, but English.

Nada and para nada can function as adverbs that modify verbs and adjectives in a sentence, whereas the negative phrase nada de is used before nouns:

No hicimos <u>nada</u> importante.	*We didn't do anything important.*
No entiendo italiano <u>para nada</u>.	*I don't understand a word of Italian.*
No quiso comprar <u>nada de</u> ropa.	*She refused to buy any clothing.*

In Spanish, constructions with antes de, sin, or que in comparatives also include negative words:

<u>Antes de</u> invitar a *nadie*, habla con tu madre.
Before inviting anyone, talk to your mother.

Nos dieron un examen <u>sin</u> decirnos *nada*.
They gave us a test without saying anything.

Se ha ganado más dinero allí <u>que</u> en *ningún* otro sitio.
More money has been earned there than in any other place.

When nadie or ninguno are direct objects in a sentence that refers to people, the personal a is used:

No traje <u>a nadie</u>.	*I didn't bring anyone.*
No invitaremos <u>a ninguno</u> de ellos.	*We won't invite any of them.*

LA PRÁCTICA 1

From the right column, select and write the opposite of each word or expression on the left column:

1. todavía   <u>ya no</u>   tampoco

2. algo   de ningún modo

3. por algún lado   nunca

4. o   ya no

5. también   ninguno

6. de algún modo   nadie

7. siempre   por ningún lado

8. alguien   ni

9. sí   nada

10. alguno   no

Translate the following sentences into English:

11. No tiene ningún interés en hacerlo.   ***He has no interest in doing it.***

12. Ella no quiere la chaqueta tampoco.

13. Jamás lo haré.

14. ¿Y si ni ella ni él llegan?

15. No vimos a nadie.

16. El gato no está por ningún lado.

17. No me dijeron nada.

18. Ellas ya no juegan como antes.

19. No comí ni un chocolate.

20. De ningún modo te dejaré salir.

21. No baila él, sino ella.

22. Nadie explica nada nunca.

23. A nosotros tampoco.

24. No practica para nada.

25. Ninguno de ellos me llamó. _____

26. El reloj no sirve para nada. _____

27. No tienes ni idea. _____

28. Comimos nada más. _____

29. No tomo nada de licor. _____

30. El argumento se quedó en nada. _____

Using Indefinite Words
Empleo de palabras indefinidas

Indefinite words include pronouns such as alguien, algunos, and algo. Another pronoun, cualquiera (*anybody, either one*), may refer to either people or things:

Cualquiera podría bailar el twist.	*Anyone can dance the twist.*
Ud. puede comer cualquiera de los dos.	*You may eat either (any) one.*
Podríamos usar cualquiera.	*We could use either one.*

However, the indefinite word cualquier is used only as an adjective:

Cualquier libro tiene valor.	*Any book is valuable.*
Le serviría cualquier regalo.	*Any gift would serve him fine.*
Llegarán en cualquier momento.	*They'll arrive at any moment.*

Algún and todo are also considered indefinite adjectives. Notice that todo is generally followed by a definite article and noun:

Han vendido todos los boletos.	*They've sold all the tickets.*
Algún día tendré un jardín de flores.	*Some day I'll have a flower garden.*
Toda la clase salió a las tres.	*The whole class left at three.*

Sometimes todo directly precedes a singular noun:

A todo americano le gusta el deporte.	*Every American likes sports.*
Toda fruta me da alergia.	*Any fruit gives me allergies.*
Vendía toda clase de carne.	*He sold each and every kind of meat.*
Toda Italia celebró la victoria.	*All of Italy celebrated the victory.*
Hemos caminado por todo París.	*We've walked throughout Paris.*

Todo can also be used as a pronoun:

Todo es lindo cerca de la playa.
Everything is pretty near the beach.

Todos dicen que los precios han
subido.
Everyone says that the prices have risen.

In some cases, indefinite words in English are translated as negative words in
Spanish. For example, notice how these indefinite constructions that express doubt
contain words with no negative meanings:

Dudamos que *ningún* empleado salga de vacaciones.
We doubt that any employee will go on vacation.

Es imposible ver a *nadie* desde aquí.
It's impossible to see anyone from here.

Era inútil decirle *nada* cuando lloraba.
It was useless to tell her anything when she was crying.

Spanish has several idiomatic expressions that include indefinite words:

¿Te pasa algo?	*Is anything the matter?*
Se cree algo tremendo.	*He thinks he's someone special.*
Por algo será.	*There must be a reason.*
No tengo interés alguno.	*I'm not interested at all.*
Algo es algo.	*Something is better than nothing.*
Todo el mundo viene.	*Everyone is coming.*
Ella es una cualquiera.	*She's a nobody.*
Es lo de siempre.	*It's the same old story.*
Algo así.	*Something like that.*

The subjunctive mood also sends a message that is indefinite, unclear, or full
of doubt:

Ayúdame con lo que puedas.	*Help me with whatever you can.*
Ellos regresan cuando quieran.	*They return whenever they want.*
Trabajaré donde me paguen mejor.	*I'll work wherever they pay me best.*

LA PRÁCTICA 2

Use indefinite words as you translate these sentences into Spanish:

1. *We saw some people dancing at the party.*

   Vimos algunos bailando en la fiesta.

2. *Anyone could do that.*

   _____

3. *All of Toledo is beautiful.*

   _____

4. *There must be a reason why she didn't come.*

   _____

5. *Someone called me last night.*

   _____

6. *I could live here forever.*

   _____

7. *They have every kind of medicine.*

   _____

8. *She wants to kiss someone.*

   _____

9. *Somehow we will finish the homework.*

   _____

10. *It's the same old story.*

   _____

CROSSWORD 10

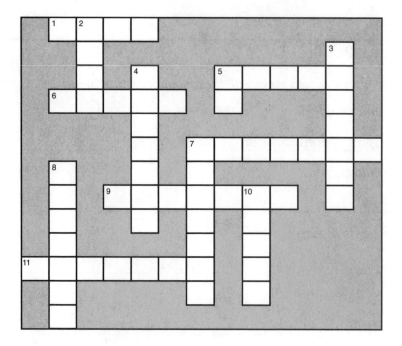

Translate these into Spanish:

Across
1. nothing
5. never
6. everyone
7. some
9. none
11. always

Down
2. something
3. neither
4. still
5. nor
7. someone
8. also
10. no one

22

Word Formations

¿Cuánto sabe usted?
How Much Do You Know Already? (?)

1. What's an autorzuelo?
2. How do you change a cup into a tiny cup in Spanish?
3. Turn the adjective triste into a verb form.
4. What noun is derived from the verb gastar?
5. What verb is derived from the noun vaso?

Diminutives and Augmentatives

Forming Diminutives
Formación de diminutivos

There are two important groups of words in Spanish that are created by adding a suffix to a noun—the diminutives and the augmentatives. The diminutive suffix -ito implies endearment or a decrease in size, though it may also be used sarcastically. Note how the ending denotes both gender and number:

el libro (*book*) → el librito (*small book*)
la mesa (*table*) → la mesita (*small table*)

mi hermano (*brother*) → mi hermanito (*my dear, little, and/or younger brother*)
mi hermana (*sister*) → mi hermanita (*my dear, little, and/or younger sister*)

mis hermanitos (*my dear/little/younger brothers or sisters*)

Some words change in spelling when the suffix is added. These include any proper names:

- g → gu   amigo → amiguito   Miguel → Miguelito
  (*friend* → *dear friend*)

- c → qu   hueco → huequito   Paco → Paquito
  (*hole* → *little hole*)

- z → c   lápiz → lapicito   Luz → Lucita
  (*pencil* → *little pencil*)

If the noun ends in -n, -r, or has more than one syllable and ends in -e, then the suffix -cito/-cita is added instead of -ito/-ita:

la sartén (*pan*)	→	la sartencita (*small pan*)
el borrador (*eraser*)	→	el borradorcito (*small eraser*)
el dulce (*sweet*)	→	el dulcecito (*small sweet*)

The suffix -ecito/-ecita is also added to two-syllable nouns ending in -o or -a that have ie or ue in the first syllable. Notice how the -o or -a is dropped first:

las piernas (*legs*)	→	las piernecitas (*short* or *thin legs*)
la pierna (*leg*)	→	la piernecita (*little leg*)
la tienda (*store*)	→	la tiendecita (*little store*)

The suffixes -zuelo/-zuela and -illo/-illa are considered other diminutive endings in Spanish, but they generally express disgust or sarcasm:

la falda (*skirt*)	→	la faldilla (*cheap skirt*)
el actor (*actor*)	→	el actorzuelo (*lousy actor*)
la casa (*house*)	→	la casilla (*insignificant house*)

Sometimes, Spanish uses the diminutive form with adjectives and adverbs:

solo (*alone*)	→	solito (*all alone*)
chica (*small*)	→	chiquita (*very small*)
verde (*green*)	→	verdecito (*greenish*)
poco (*small amount*)	→	poquito (*very small amount*)
cerca (*close*)	→	cerquita (*very close*)
ahora (*now*)	→	ahorita (*right now*)

> **TIP**
> A few diminutive forms are actually separate words in Spanish:
> | el bolso (*handbag*) | → | el bolsillo (*pocket*) |
> | la mano (*hand*) | → | la manecilla (*clock hand*) |
> | la cabra (*goat*) | → | la cabrilla (*kind of fish*) |

LA PRÁCTICA 1

Use diminutives as you translate these English phrases into Spanish:

1. very soon   prontito

2. poor little thing   _____

3. pocket   _____

4. granny   _____

5. tiny garden   _____

6. sweet Carlos   _____

7. dear owner   _____

8. small body   _____

9. a little early   _____

10. frail little doctor   _____

11. puppy   _____

12. small party   _____

13. tiny voice   _____

14. reddish   _____

15. small light   _____

Forming Augmentatives
Formación de aumentativos

      Most nouns form augmentations in Spanish by adding -ón or -ona. These suffixes normally imply an increase in size, but may also be used in sarcasm:

la jarra (*jar*)	→	el jarrón (*big jar*)
la maleta (*suitcase*)	→	el maletón (*giant suitcase*)
la mujer (*woman*)	→	la mujerona (*large woman*)
la soltera (*single woman*)	→	la solterona (*old maid*)
la nariz (*nose*)	→	el narizón (*big-nosed*)
el grito (*shout*)	→	el gritón (*loud-mouth*)

In fact, -ón and -ona are often added to the stems of verbs to form adjectives. Notice how most of these words describe a person in a negative way:

llorar (*to cry*) → llorón (*one who cries too much*)
Nanita es muy <u>llorona</u>. (*Nanita is a big crybaby.*)

quejarse (*to complain*) → quejón (*one who complains a lot*)
Ellos son <u>quejones</u>. (*They are big complainers.*)

preguntar (*to ask*) → preguntón (*one who asks too many questions*)
Tú eras <u>preguntona</u>. (*You were too inquisitive.*)

By adding the augmentative suffix -ote or -ota to a noun, one implies a stronger, more negative meaning to the concept of increased size:

los ojos (*eyes*) → los ojotes (*giant, ugly eyes*)
la camisa (*shirt*) → la camisota (*huge, repulsive shirt*)

The suffix -ucho or -ucha also suggests some form of ugliness in Spanish, but without the size:

carro (*car*) → carrucho (*old, beat-up car*)
casa (*house*) → casucha (*shabby, run-down house*)

TIP
Several words ending in the same letters as the augmentative suffixes have unique meanings and do not necessarily indicate ugliness or an increase in size:

el ratón	*mouse*	el islote	*islet*
el guapote	*handsome man*	el callejón	*alley*
el sillón	*armchair*		

LA PRÁCTICA 2

First identify the original nouns, adjectives, or adverbs within these augmentatives, and then translate them into English:

1. orejona   oreja   ***big-eared female***

2. zapatote   _____   _____

3. preguntón   _____   _____

4. malazo   _____   _____

5. cuartucho   _____   _____

6. contestón   _____   _____

7. grandote   _____   _____

8. tarjetota   _____   _____

9. flacucho   _____   _____

10. gordaza   _____   _____

Other Word Formations

Forming Nouns from Verbs
Formación de sustantivos basados en verbos

Several nouns are derived from the past participle of the verb. Notice how the -ar endings change to -ada, while the -er and -ir endings change to -ido:

oír (*to hear*)	→	el oído (*ear*)
comer (*to eat*)	→	la comida (*food*)
entrar (*to enter*)	→	la entrada (*entrance*)
subir (*to climb*)	→	la subida (*climb*)
llegar (*to arrive*)	→	la llegada (*arrival*)
salir (*to leave*)	→	la salida (*exit*)
mirar (*to look*)	→	la mirada (*look*)

Some nouns are derived from -ar verbs that change their endings to -o or -a. Notice that a few nouns include the irregular stem changes:

trabajar (*to work*)	→	el trabajo (*job*)
esperar (*to wait*)	→	la espera (*waiting*)
gastar (*to spend*)	→	el gasto (*expense*)
ayudar (*to help*)	→	la ayuda (*help*)
dudar (*to doubt*)	→	la duda (*doubt*)
charlar (*to chat*)	→	la charla (*chat*)
caminar (*to walk*)	→	el camino (*road*)
besar (*to kiss*)	→	el beso (*kiss*)
cocinar (*to cook*)	→	la cocina (*kitchen*)

Other nouns actually change to forms of their irregular base verbs:

volar (*to fly*)	→	el vuelo (*flight*)
comenzar (*to begin*)	→	el comienzo (*beginning*)
decir (*to say*)	→	el dicho (*saying*)
volver (*to return*)	→	la vuelta (*return*)
caer (*to fall*)	→	la caída (*fall*)

Several nouns ending in -ción are derived from -ar verbs. Remember that words ending in *-tion* in English generally end in -ción in Spanish:

investigation	investigar	→	investigación
operation	operar	→	operación
separation	separar	→	separación
complication	complicar	→	complicación
preparation	preparar	→	preparación

Spanish nouns ending in -amiento are derived from -ar verbs, and verbs ending in -imiento are derived from -er and -ir verbs:

aflojar (*to loosen*)	→	aflojamiento (*slackening*)
conocer (*to know*)	→	conocimiento (*knowledge*)
agotar (*to exhaust*)	→	agotamiento (*exhaustion*)

Similarly, nouns ending in -ancia are derived from -ar verbs, while nouns ending in -encia are derived from -er and -ir verbs. Note the similarities between the English and Spanish noun forms:

tolerance	tolerar	→	tolerancia
appearance	aparecer	→	apariencia
preference	preferir	→	preferencia
importance	importar	→	importancia
vigilance	vigilar	→	vigilancia

> **TIP**
> Many nouns in Spanish do not fit a normal pattern, and must be memorized separately:
> | | |
> |---|---|
> | el transporte | *transportation* |
> | el aviso | *announcement* |
> | la asistencia | *attendance* |

LA PRÁCTICA 3

Create a noun from the verbs provided. Use the English translation:

1. amar   *loved one*   el amo
2. alinear   *alignment*   _____
3. contar   *bill*   _____
4. rezar   *prayer*   _____
5. anular   *annulment*   _____
6. coincidir   *coincidence*   _____
7. crecer   *growth*   _____
8. competir   *competition*   _____
9. asistir   *attendance*   _____
10. abrazar   *hug*   _____

Give the noun form of each verb and then translate it into English:

11. pagar   el pago   *payment*
12. cargar   _____   _____
13. abrazar   _____   _____
14. aumentar   _____   _____
15. entregar   _____   _____
16. tragar   _____   _____
17. practicar   _____   _____
18. regresar   _____   _____
19. espantar   _____   _____
20. fracasar   _____   _____

More Ways to Form Nouns
Otros modos de formar sustantivos

In Spanish, nouns are often formed by simply adding suffixes to other nouns. For example, by adding -astro or -astra to the names for one's relatives, the members of a step-family are created:

hijo (*son*)	→	hijastro (*stepson*)
madre (*mother*)	→	madrastra (*stepmother*)
hermano (*brother*)	→	hermanastro (*stepbrother*)

To associate a person with a specific noun, many words simply drop their final vowel and add the suffix -ero or -era:

el viaje (*trip*)	→	el viajero (*traveler*)
el mensaje (*message*)	→	la mensajera (*messenger*)
la marina (*navy*)	→	el marinero (*sailor*)
el chocolate (*chocolate*)	→	el chocolatero (*one who loves chocolate*)
el reloj (*clock*)	→	el relojero (*clockmaker*)

Words ending in -ero and -era often refer to occupations or professions in Spanish. By replacing the suffix with -ería, one can identify his or her respective place of employment:

carpintero (*carpenter*)	→	carpintería (*woodshop*)
panadero (*baker*)	→	panadería (*bakery*)
joyero (*jeweler*)	→	joyería (*jewelry store*)

The suffix -ero or -era also indicates a container for the item designated by the noun:

la leche (*milk*)	→	la lechera (*milk pitcher*)
la sal (*salt*)	→	el salero (*salt shaker*)
la flor (*flower*)	→	el florero (*flower vase*)

When added to a noun, the suffixes -ada and -azo often indicate a hit or strike by the object designated by the noun:

la pata (*paw*)	→	la patada (*kick*)
el serrucho (*saw*)	→	la serruchada (*cut with a saw*)
el puñal (*dagger*)	→	la puñalada (*stab*)
la cabeza (*head*)	→	el cabezazo (*head butt*)
la flecha (*arrow*)	→	el flechazo (*blow by an arrow*)
la bala (*bullet*)	→	el balazo (*gun shot*)

The suffix -ada or -ado also indicates the full amount that the object designated by the noun is able to hold:

la boca (*mouth*)	→	el bocado (*mouthful*)
el camión (*truck*)	→	la camionada (*truckful*)
el puño (*fist*)	→	el puñado (*fistful*)
la cuchara (*spoon*)	→	la cucharada (*spoonful*)

Although it is not heard often, the suffix -ada can be used to describe the regular actions of the person designated by the noun:

el muchacho (*kid*)	→	la muchachada (*kid's prank*)
el tonto (*silly person*)	→	la tontada (*action of a silly person*)
el bufón (*clown*)	→	la bufonada (*clownish behavior*)

Spanish has several other suffixes that are used to create nouns with special meanings:

-al	la manzana (*apple*)	→	el manzanal (*apple tree*)
	la pera (*pear*)	→	el peral (*pear tree*)
-anza	enseñar (*to teach*)	→	la enseñanza (*teaching*)
	matar (*to kill*)	→	la matanza (*killing*)
-dura	morder (*to bite*)	→	la mordedura (*bite*)
	picar (*to sting*)	→	la picadura (*sting*)
-eza	natural (*natural*)	→	la naturaleza (*nature*)
	bello (*beautiful*)	→	la belleza (*beauty*)
-ense	Canadá (*Canada*)	→	canadiense (Canadien)
	Costa Rica (*Costa Rica*)	→	costarricense (Costa Rican)

LA PRÁCTICA 4

Fill in the blanks with new nouns formed from the words in bold:

1. Al _____ le gusta el pastel.

2. El té está en la _____.

3. Le dió una _____ con el cuchillo.

4. El _____ trabaja en una cárcel.

5. Te dí un _____ con el codo.

6. No hay sal en el _____.

7. El payaso hizo una _____.

8. Me tiró la piedra y me cayó una _____ en la cabeza.

9. El _____ trabajará en la cocina.

10. La sopa está en la _____.

11. Tiró una _____ con la pala.

12. El libro está en el _____.

13. La _____ no tenía ese mueble.

14. Me dió una _____ con la palma.

15. Él es mi padre y él es mi _____.

Forming Verbs from Nouns and Adjectives
Formación de verbos basados en sustantivos y adjetivos

Several verbs in Spanish can be formed by adding a suffix or prefix to a noun or adjective. The following nouns are transformed into verbs by adding an -ar ending and the prefix en-:

el ladrillo (*brick*)	→	enladrillar (*to pave with bricks*)
el vaso (*glass container*)	→	envasar (*to bottle*)
la máscara (*mask*)	→	enmascarar (*to mask*)
el yeso (*plaster*)	→	enyesar (*to plaster*)
la harina (*flour*)	→	enharinar (*to flour*)

Other verbs are created simply by adding the suffix -ear to a noun:

la gota (*drop*)	→	gotear (*to drip*)
el paso (*step*)	→	pasear (*to stroll*)
el golpe (*punch*)	→	golpear (*to punch*)

The following adjectives are transformed into verbs by adding an -ar ending and the prefix a-:

barato (*inexpensive*)	→	abaratar (*to lower the price*)
llano (*flat*)	→	allanar (*to flatten*)
blando (*soft*)	→	ablandar (*to soften*)
flojo (*loose*)	→	aflojar (*to loosen*)
largo (*long*)	→	alargar (*to lengthen*)

Other adjectives are transformed into verbs simply by adding -ecer to their stems:

húmedo (*moist*)	→	humedecer (*to moisten*)
oscuro (*dark*)	→	oscurecer (*to darken*)
lánguido (*listless*)	→	languidecer (*to languish*)

By adding the prefix en- and the suffix -ecer to some adjectives, still more verbs can be created:

duro (*hard*)	→	en	dur	ecer	(*to harden*)
triste (*sad*)	→	en	trist	ecer	(*to sadden*)
negro (*black*)	→	en	negr	ecer	(*to blacken*)

The prefix em- replaces en- when the adjective begins with b or p:

pobre (*poor*)	→	em	pobr	ecer	(*to impoverish*)
bello (*beautiful*)	→	em	bell	ecer	(*to make beautiful*)

Most suffixes and prefixes in Spanish combine or build upon one another to create new words:

la frente (*front*) → enfrentar (*to confront*) → el enfrentamiento (*confrontation*)

la riqueza (*richness*) → enriquecer (*to enrich*) → enriquecido (*enriched*)

el sordo (*deaf person*) → ensordecer (*to deafen*) → ensordecedor (*deafening*)

Bear in mind that Spanish has a variety of prefixes that change the meanings of words when they are attached:

des (*not*)	desafortunadamente (*unfortunately*)
entre (*between*)	entrecruzar (*to interweave*)
ante (*before*)	anteayer (*the day before yesterday*)

LA PRÁCTICA 5

Change the following nouns and adjectives to their verb forms:

1. la tecla (*key*)   teclear   (*to type*)

2. duro (*hard*)   (*to harden*)

3. rojo (*red*)   (*to redden*)

4. la batalla (*battle*)   (*to battle*)

5. el papel (*paper*)   (*to wrap in paper*)

6. el gancho (*hook*)   (*to hook up*)

7. dulce (*sweet*)   (*to sweeten*)

8. la capucha (*hood*)   (*to put on a hood*)

9. grande (*large*)   (*to enlarge*)

10. el párpado (*eyelid*)   (*to blink*)

EL REPASO

Identify the following parts of speech, and then use them in a sentence:

1. interesante   ***adjective***   La película fue interesante.

2. para

3. nunca

4. verde

5. ellos

6. el pasajero

7. cuyo

8. aquellos

9. ti

10. cubana

Culture Capsule 3

Latin American Cuisine
La cocina latinoamericana

¿Qué es la comida latina? Es una mezcla de culturas, con la influencia de las gentes indígenas combinada con el toque de España, Portugal, Italia y otros países europeos. Hasta la influencia africana se deja degustar en algunos platos latinos. Es decir, la comida latinoamericana es única, colorida, especial, y sobre todo muy sabrosa.

La historia de América del Sur le da a sus comidas diversos condimentos, influencias étnicas y métodos de preparación. Por siglos, los indígenas del continente habían preparado estofados y asados cocidos lentamente a fuego abierto. Pero al llegar los europeos éstos trajeron sus artes culinarias propias, incluyendo una variedad de salsas deliciosas como el sofrito, uno de los condimentos básicos de América del Sur, que consiste de una mezcla de especias y vegetales que le da a la comida un sabor suave y suculento.

Además de ser una de las comidas latinas más conocidas en Norteamérica, los platos mexicanos también son muy picantes. Los mexicanos usan cientos de chiles diferentes para sazonar y la comida varía según la región geográfica, dependiendo de los ingredientes disponibles. Por esa razón, ciertas comidas de una región podrían tener el mismo nombre en otra, pero con condimento y sabor muy distintos. Por ejemplo, en el norte de México los tamales son preparados con el hollejo del maíz, mientras que en el sur los preparan con la hoja del plátano. Sin embargo, por todo el país las comidas y condimentos básicos son la tortilla, el arroz, los frijoles, el comino, el ajo, y chiles muy picantes.

Las comidas de América Central son parecidas a las comidas de México y América del Sur, mezclando la influencia de España con su cultura indígena. Las frutas tropicales y el maní distinguen esta región geográfica, aunque también guisan con el chile picante. En las zonas interiores de Centroamérica se encuentra más frijoles y nueces, generalmente preparados con la carne de algún animal pequeño. Las zonas de la costa tienen varios pescados y mariscos que se preparan en estofados, a la parrilla, o se sirven crudos o encurtidos como el ceviche.

PREGUNTAS

1. ¿Qué trajeron los europeos?

2. ¿Cuáles son algunas comidas típicas de Centroamérica?

3. ¿Qué tipo de comidas preparaban las gentes indígenas?

4. ¿Qué es el sofrito?

5. ¿Qué país es conocido por su comida picante?

PART IV:
Special Topics

23

The Numbers

¿Cuánto sabe usted?

How Much Do You Know Already?

1. How do you say the number *156,001* in Spanish?

2. What does noveno piso mean in English?

3. How much is un cuarto más una mitad?

4. Change the cardinal number diez to an ordinal number.

5. How many libras are there in one kilo?

Cardinal Numbers
Números cardinales

The cardinal numbers are generally used for counting or expressing quantity. From one to twenty, only the number dieciséis has a written accent:

0 cero	11 once
1 uno	12 doce
2 dos	13 trece
3 tres	14 catorce
4 cuatro	15 quince
5 cinco	16 dieciséis
6 seis	17 diecisiete
7 siete	18 dieciocho
8 ocho	19 diecinueve
9 nueve	20 veinte
10 diez	

Twenty-one to twenty-nine are usually written as one word:

21 veintiuno	22 veintidós
23 veintitrés	24 veinticuatro
25 veinticinco	26 veintiséis
27 veintisiete	28 veintiocho
29 veintinueve	

The numbers 30 to 90 end in -nta whereas 200 to 900 end in -ientos:

30 treinta	200 doscientos
40 cuarenta	300 trescientos
50 cincuenta	400 cuatrocientos
60 sesenta	500 quinientos
70 setenta	600 seiscientos
80 ochenta	700 setecientos
90 noventa	800 ochocientos
100 cien	900 novecientos
1.000 mil	
1.000.000 un millón	

Note that cien becomes ciento before another number:

101 ciento uno, 102 ciento dos ... etc.
127 ciento veintisiete
145 ciento cuarenta y cinco
1,108 mil novecientos ciento ocho
2,000,103 dos millones ciento tres

Numbers from 21 to 29, as well as those from 16 to 19, can also be written as three separate words:

veinte y uno, veinte y dos, veinte y tres, etc.
diez y seis, diez y siete, diez y ocho, etc.

Numbers ending in uno are used in counting, and must agree in gender with the nouns they modify.

No hay ochenta papeles sino ochenta y uno.
There aren't eighty papers, but eighty-one.

Compré dos plátanos y una pera.
I bought two bananas and one pear.

Necesitamos veintiuna sillas.
We need twenty-one chairs.

Uno shortens to un before masculine nouns, and una shortens to un before nouns beginning with a stressed a:

Un dólar	*One dollar*
Treinta y un libros	*Thirty-one books*
Un hada madrina	*One fairy godmother*

Notice the accent mark on the word veintiún:

Tiene veintiún años.	*She's twenty-one.*

The hundreds must also agree in gender with the nouns they modify, even if they are separated by other numbers. Numbers agree in Spanish across the word mil as well:

542 women	quinientas cuarenta y dos mujeres
398 men	trescientos noventa y ocho hombres
760,000 people	setecientas sesenta mil personas

A period is used to separate numbers when writing thousands, millions, and so on. In Spanish, a comma is used as a decimal point:

300.000	trescientos mil
1.000.000	un millón
5.854.201	cinco millones ochocientos cincuenta y cuatro mil doscientos uno
$6,25	seis dólares veinticinco centavos

Un billón is actually a trillion in English. Mil millones is a billion.

Millón is followed by de before a noun unless another number appears between millón and the following noun:

Cinco millones de estrellas.	Five million stars.
Un millón de flores.	A million flowers.
Dos millones quinientos mil habitantes.	2,500,000 inhabitants.

Don't forget that **un** and **una** are also indefinite articles in Spanish:

Comió <u>una</u> hamburguesa y <u>un</u> perro caliente.
He ate a hamburger and a hot dog.

LA PRÁCTICA 1

Write these numbers and numerical phrases out in Spanish:

1. 671 girls   <u>seiscientas setenta y una niñas</u>

2. 8 million children _____

3. $8.50   _____

4. A trillion   _____

5. 150 homes   _____

6. 51 hats   _____

7. One problem   _____

8. 99, 100, and 101   _____

9. 11,110   _____

10. 21 eagles   _____

Ordinal Numbers
Números ordinales

Ordinal numbers are used to indicate order or rank in a series. The most common ordinal numbers are *first* through *tenth*:

1st	primero
2nd	segundo
3rd	tercero
4th	cuarto
5th	quinto
6th	sexto
7th	séptimo
8th	octavo
9th	noveno
10th	décimo

As adjectives, ordinal numbers in Spanish generally appear before the noun, and must agree with the nouns they modify in gender and number. Notice how primero and tercero have shortened forms when they precede a noun in the masculine singular form:

el <u>primer</u> asiento	*the first seat*
la primera semana	*the first week*
los primeros niños	*the first children*

el segundo piso	the second floor
la segunda calle	the second street
el <u>tercer</u> día	the third day
la tercera vez	the third time

Ordinal numbers beyond 10th require memorization for 11th and 12th, but after that a pattern is established:

11th	undécimo
12th	duodécimo
13th	décimotercero
14th	décimocuarto … etc.

Nevertheless, most Spanish speakers use cardinal numbers after the noun:

Celebraron el año dieciséis de su aniversario.
They celebrated their sixteenth anniversary.

Leeremos el capítulo veinte.
We'll read the twentieth chapter.

Two other ways to use ordinals in Spanish is after the names of kings and queens and when referring to a specific century. Be aware, however, that after décimo, the cardinal numbers are used instead:

Enrique <u>octavo</u>	*Henry the Eighth*
el siglo <u>séptimo</u>	*The seventh century*
Alfonso <u>trece</u>	*Alfonso the Thirteenth*
el siglo <u>veinte</u>	*The twentieth century*

> **TIP**
> Both ordinal and cardinal numbers can be used as nouns in Spanish:
>
> Soy el séptimo.
> *I'm the seventh one.*
> Una es suficiente.
> *One is enough.*
> No vimos los primeros.
> *We didn't see the first ones.*
> Faltan cinco.
> *Five are missing.*

LA PRÁCTICA 2

Answer these questions in complete sentences using ordinal numbers:

1. ¿Cuál es el primer mes del año?   El primer mes del año es enero.

2. ¿Cual es la sexta palabra en esta oración?   _____

3. ¿Qué capítulo esta leyendo Ud. ahora?   _____

4. ¿Cuál es el tercer día de la semana?   _____

5. ¿Quién era el rey de España antes de Alfonso XIII?   _____

6. ¿En qué siglo estamos? _____

7. ¿Quién era el rey de Francia antes del
   Luis XIV? _____

8. ¿Cuál presidente de los E.E.U.U. fue
   George Washington? _____

9. ¿Cuál es el capítulo que sigue al primer
   capítulo? _____

10. ¿Qué fila precede a la novena fila? _____

Mathematical Expressions
Expresiones matemáticas

Fractions are given in Spanish as in English, using a cardinal number for the numerator and an ordinal number for the denominator. The only exceptions are ½ (un medio) and ⅓ (un tercio):

¼ un cuarto
⅜ tres octavos
⅔ dos tercios

Beyond one-tenth, the cardinal number adds the suffix -avo(s) to form the smaller fractions. Exceptions include one-hundredth (un centésimo) and one-thousandth (un milésimo):

one-thirteenth	un treceavo
four-nineteenths	cuatro diecinueveavos
three-twentieths	tres veinteavos
two-hundredths	dos centésimos

Mixed numbers have y between the whole number and the fraction. When nouns are added, they usually follow the cardinal number:

5⅔	cinco y dos tercios
7¼ pounds	siete libras y un cuarto
3½ apples	tres manzanas y media

When referring to percentages in Spanish, a singular masculine article is generally placed before the number. *Percent* is por ciento:

El veinticinco por ciento de la ciudad no tenía electricidad.
Twenty-five percent of the city did not have electrical power.

Recibimos el diez por ciento de descuento.
We received the twenty percent discount.

Mathematical expressions include several groups of vocabulary:

- **Measurements**

el centímetro	*centimeter* (0.39 in.)
el metro	*meter* (3.38 ft.)
el kilómetro	*kilometer* (0.621 mi.)
el litro	*liter* (1.75 pints)
el gramo	*gram* (0.0352 oz.)
el kilo(gramo)	*kilogram* (2.20 lbs.)
la tonelada	*ton*
la libra	*pound*
el grado	*degree*
la milla	*mile*
la onza	*ounce*
la pulgada	*inch*
el pie	*foot*
la yarda	*yard*
la docena	*dozen*

- **Mathematical operations**

sumar	*to add*
restar	*to subtract*
multiplicar	*to multiply*
dividir	*to divide*
porcentaje	*percentage*
la fracción	*fraction*
más	*plus*
menos	*minus*
por	*times*
dividido entre	*divided by*
es igual a	*equals*

> **TIP**
> Many mathematical words in Spanish are spelled the same in English:
>
> diagonal, horizontal, vertical, perpendicular, rectangular

- **Geometry**

el alto	*height*
el largo	*length*
la distancia	*distance*
el ancho	*width*
la altura	*height*
la profundidad	*depth*
el peso	*weight*
el volumen	*volume*
la línea	*line*
el cuadrado	*square*
el triángulo	*triangle*

| el círculo | circle |
| el punto | point |

- **Numerical words and phrases**

un par	a pair
doble	double
una vez	once
dos veces	twice
sólo uno	only one
ambos	both
varios	several
ninguno	none

LA PRÁCTICA 3

Write these mathematical expressions in complete Spanish sentences:

1. 13 + 12 = 25   Trece más doce son veinticinco.

2. ½ − ¼ = ¼

3. Three and a third pounds

4. 10 percent of the population

5. 500 ÷ 25 = 20

6. One fifteenth of everything

7. 12 × 10 = 120

8. The length, width, and height

9. I have to add the percentages

10. 6 × 5 ÷ 3 + 6 − 10 ÷ 6 = 1

Now answer these mathematical questions in Spanish:

11. ¿Cuántas onzas hay en dos libras?   Hay treinta y dos onzas.

12. ¿Cuántos gramos hay en un kilo?

13. ¿Cuánto es cien por diez?

14. ¿Cuántos huevos hay en dos docenas?

15. ¿Cuánto es mil dividido entre mil?

24

Time, Calendar, and the Weather

¿Cuánto sabe usted?
How Much Do You Know Already?

1. How do you say *January 1, 1999* in Spanish?

2. Is the 12-hour or the 24-hour clock used more often in Latin America?

3. Say *8:45* two different ways in Spanish.

4. How do you say *Your clock is fast* in Spanish?

5. What does Está helado y hace viento mean in English?

Hours
Horas

In Spanish, you may ask for the time in either the singular or the plural, usually with a form of the verb ser. However, the response is in the singular when referring to the one o'clock hour. Notice that the hour (la hora) is given in the feminine form with a definite article, and that the word *o'clock* is usually translated en punto:

¿Qué hora es?

¿Qué horas son? } *What time is it?*

Son las dos.   *It's two o'clock.*
Son las diez.   *It's 10:00.*
Es la una.   *It's one o'clock.*

The cardinal numbers are used when giving the hour in Spanish, and the equivalents of A.M., P.M., *noon*, and *midnight* are as follows:

12:00 A.M. (*midnight*)	Es <u>medianoche</u> / Son las doce de la noche.
9:00 A.M.	Son las nueve <u>de la mañana</u>.
12:00 P.M. (*noon*)	Es <u>mediodía</u> / Son las doce del día.
6:00 P.M.	Son las seis <u>de la tarde</u>.
10:00 P.M.	Son las diez <u>de la noche</u>.

In Spanish, the preposition a is used to express *at* what time an event takes place:

¿A qué hora?	At what time?
A las cinco.	At five o'clock.
A la una de la tarde.	At one in the afternoon.
Al mediodía.	At noon.

Other common expressions related to the hour include:

No llegue tarde.	Don't get there late.
Llegamos con anticipación.	We're early.
Favor de llegar a tiempo.	Please arrive on time.
Siento mucho llegar tarde.	I'm so sorry I'm late.
Sea puntual.	Be punctual.
Trabajan hasta tarde.	They work late.
Me acuesto temprano.	I go to bed early.
Tu reloj está adelantado.	Your clock is fast.
Tu reloj es lento.	Your watch is slow.
Estamos retrasados.	We're running late.
A las tres en punto.	At three o'clock sharp.
A eso de las siete.	At around seven o'clock.

These time expressions often replace giving the exact hour:

Al amanecer	At sunrise
A la puesta del sol	At sunset
A la madrugada	At dawn

The word *time* may be translated in a variety of ways in Spanish:

At what time? **¿A qué hora?**
There isn't much time. **No hay mucho tiempo.**
One more time. **Una vez más.**

La Práctica 1

Write out each of the following in Spanish, using complete sentences:

1. *It's two in the morning.* Son las dos de la mañana.

2. *At 1:00 P.M.*

3. *At around eleven.*

4. *9:00 A.M.*

5. *It's midnight.*

6. *At ten o'clock.*

7. *It's eight at night.*

8. *It's 4:00 P.M.*

9. *At noon.*

10. *Your clock is slow.*

Minutes
Minutos

To give the time in Spanish, simply say the hour, followed by the word y (*and*), and the minutes:

Son las tres y cuarenta.	*It's 3:40.*
A las diez y treinta y cinco.	*At 10:35.*
Es la una y veinte.	*It's 1:20.*
A las doce y cincuenta de la tarde.	*At 12:50 P.M.*

The expressions un cuarto (*a quarter*) and media (*half*) can be used to express a *quarter hour* and a *half hour*:

un cuarto para las tres	*a quarter till three*
nueve y media	*half past nine*

As the next hour approaches, there are two other ways to express the time besides giving the hour followed by the minutes. The word menos means *minus* or *less*, while the verb faltar means *to lack*:

It's 8:40 {
Son las ocho y cuarenta. (*It's eight-forty.*)
Son las nueve menos veinte. (*It's nine less twenty.*)
Faltan veinte para las nueve. (*It lacks twenty before nine.*)

At 1: 55	A la una y cincuenta y cinco.	(At one fifty-five.)
	A las dos menos cinco.	(At two minus five.)
	Faltan cinco para las dos.	(It lacks five before two.)

In Spain and Spanish America, the 24-hour clock is used much more often than the 12-hour clock. The expressions for A.M. or P.M. are seldom used, and the minutes are simply stated after the hour. Notice how the word horas is used at the end of some expressions:

A la una.	At 1:00 A.M.
A las tres horas.	At 3:00 A.M.
A las seis y quince.	At 6:15 A.M.
A las ocho y treinta.	At 8:30 A.M.
A las doce horas.	At noon.
A las quince cuarenta y cinco.	At 3:45 P.M.
A las diecinueve horas.	At 7:00 P.M.
A las veinticuatro horas.	At midnight.

LA PRÁCTICA 2

Match the correct time with each phrase below:

1. Doce menos cinco.	11:55	2:45
2. Las dieciséis horas.	_____	7:08
3. Cuatro y cuarto.	_____	5:12
4. Veinte para las ocho.	_____	3:45
5. Siete y ocho.	_____	4:30
6. Un cuarto para las cuatro.	_____	4:15
7. La una y catorce.	_____	11:55
8. Las quince menos quince.	_____	1:14
9. Las cuatro y media.	_____	4:00
10. Cinco y doce.	_____	7:40

Days, Months, and Dates
Días, meses y fechas

In Spanish, the days of the week and months of the year are not capitalized:

Los días de la semana	
lunes	*Monday*
martes	*Tuesday*
miércoles	*Wednesday*
jueves	*Thursday*
viernes	*Friday*
sábado	*Saturday*
domingo	*Sunday*

The phrase *on Monday* is actually el lunes in Spanish. The phrase *on Mondays*, which implies a repeated activity, is los lunes:

Tengo cita con el médico el jueves.
I have a doctor's appointment on Thursday.

Jugamos tenis en el parque los sábados.
We play tennis at the park on Saturdays.

Los meses del año	
enero	*January*
febrero	*February*
marzo	*March*
abril	*April*
mayo	*May*
junio	*June*
julio	*July*
agosto	*August*
septiembre	*September*
octubre	*October*
noviembre	*November*
diciembre	*December*

The preposition en (*in, on, at*) is not used when referring to the days of the week, but it is used with the months:

Salgo el viernes.	*I leave on Friday.*
Nos visitaron en abril.	*They visited us in April.*

However, the definite article el precedes the date in Spanish. Dates consist of the construction el + number + de + month. If necessary, the year may be added with de:

Celebro el cuatro de julio.	I celebrate the Fourth of July.
Nació el veintiocho de octubre.	He was born on October 28th.
Se casaron el diez de mayo de dos mil.	They married on May 10, 2000.

Ordinal numbers are used to express the date, except for *the first*, which is el primero:

> **TIP**
> In Spanish-speaking countries, the day is given before the month in its abbreviated form:
> November 16th, 2006   16-11-06
> August 1st, 1989   1-8-89

Fue al dentista el dos, el ocho, y el quince.
She went to the dentist on the second, the eighth, and the fifteenth.

Las clases comienzan el primero de febrero.
Classes begin on February 1st.

The most common request for the date is ¿Qué fecha es hoy? (*What's today's date?*). These are other important expressions related to the calendar:

¿Qué día es hoy?	What day is it today?
Lunes doce.	It's Monday the twelfth.
¿A cuántos estamos hoy?	What's the date today?
Estamos a doce de junio.	It's the twelfth of June.

• **Time expressions**

cada mes	each month
todos los días	every day
por semana	per week
un día de por medio	every other day
el fin de semana	weekend
el próximo mes	next month
la semana pasada	last week
hace un año	a year ago
pasado mañana	the day after tomorrow
anteayer	the day before yesterday
para hoy	for today
desde ayer	since yesterday
hasta mañana	until tomorrow
a mediados del mes	in the middle of the month
a principios de la semana	at the beginning of the week
al final del año	at the end of the year

When giving the year in informal conversation, often only the last two digits are mentioned. It may also be read as one large number:

Me gradué en el ochenta y dos.

Me gradué en mil novecientos ochenta y dos.

} *I graduated in 1982.*

LA PRÁCTICA 3

Look at the word in parentheses and answer the question in Spanish:

1. ¿Cuándo comenzaron las clases? (*May*)   <u>Comenzaron en mayo.</u>

2. ¿Cuándo sales a bailar? (*Fridays*)   _____

3. ¿Cuándo comes pollo? (*Saturdays*)   _____

4. ¿Cuándo viajas? (*June first*)   _____

5. ¿Cuándo estudias inglés? (*the weekend*)   _____

6. ¿Cuándo hablas con tu mamá? (*Sundays*)   _____

7. ¿Cuándo naciste? (*1/1/72*)   _____

8. ¿Cuándo te casaste? (*Dec. 5, 2002*)   _____

9. ¿Cuándo tienes vacaciones? (*August*)   _____

10. ¿Cuándo trabajas? (*next week*)   _____

Write out these abbreviated dates in Spanish:

11. 11/2/04   <u>el once de febrero, dos mil cuatro</u>

12. 1/12/75   _____

13. 9/7/00   _____

14. 25/10/66   _____

15. 31/1/07   _____

Seasons and Weather
Las estaciones y el tiempo

The seasons in Spanish are called **las estaciones**, and are often used with the preposition **en**. Notice that the article is often dropped in conversation:

Las estaciones	
la primavera	*spring*
el verano	*summer*
el otoño	*fall*
el invierno	*winter*

EJEMPLOS

No teníamos clases en el verano.	*We didn't have classes in the summer.*
Iré a las montañas en otoño.	*I'll go to the mountains in the fall.*
Han ido al Miami en invierno.	*They've been to Miami in the winter.*

When referring to the seasons, one usually comments on the weather. In Spanish, either the question **¿Qué tiempo hace?** or **¿Cómo está el clima?** can be used to ask *How's the weather?* The following are common expressions related to the weather:

El clima está maravilloso.	*The weather is beautiful.*
El clima está feo.	*The weather is bad.*
Hace buen tiempo.	*It's nice weather.*
Hace frío.	*It's cold.*
Hace calor.	*It's hot.*
Está templado.	*It's warm.*
Está fresco.	*It's cool.*
Está despejado.	*It's clear.*
Está...	*It's...*
soleado	*sunny*
ventoso	*windy*
nublado	*cloudy*
brumoso	*foggy*
helado	*icy*
húmedo	*humid*
lloviznando	*drizzling*
lloviendo	*raining*
nevando	*snowing*
granizando	*hailing*

LA PRÁCTICA 4

Translate these sentences into English:

1. Hace mucho frío en abril. *It's very cold in April.*

2. Hubieron muchos truenos durante la tormenta. _____

3. Anoche estaba lloviendo y granizando. _____

4. En el verano hace calor y mucho sol. _____

5. No me gustan el frío y el viento. _____

6. Hacía buen tiempo en la primavera. _____

7. Estará lloviznando todo el día. _____

8. El otoño es mi estación favorita. _____

9. Está nublado pero no está ventoso. _____

10. El mal clima comenzó con los relámpagos. _____

POR SU CUENTA

Answer in full sentences:

1. ¿En qué mes hace mucho frío? _____

2. ¿Cuándo hace mucho viento? _____

3. ¿Qué tipo de tormentas hay? _____

4. ¿Llueve mucho? _____

5. ¿Hace mucho calor en el verano? _____

6. ¿Hay mucha niebla? _____

7. ¿En qué mes está soleado y despejado? _____

8. ¿Está nublado hoy? _____

9. ¿Hay mucha nieve y hielo en el invierno? _____

10. ¿Cuál es su estación favorita? ¿Por qué? _____

EL REPASO

Identify the verb tenses and the parts of speech in each of the following readings. Then, translate each one into English:

Raúl López trabaja mucho en su hogar; siempre limpia la casa, lava la ropa, y cocina la comida. Raúl vive con su hermano Marcos. Marcos no trabaja. Come todo el día, bebe cerveza y mira televisión. Los dos hermanos son muy diferentes.

Cada lunes, Carla se despierta a las seis, se baña, se peina y se viste rápido. Carla es enfermera en un hopital grande. Tiene que llegar muy temprano para ayudarle al doctor. Carla no duerme mucho porque estudia medicina en la universidad.

Mañana voy a Miami. Visitaré a mis primos en el centro. Vamos a salir en la noche a comer y a bailar en los restaurantes latinos. Estaré con ellos por dos semanas. ¡Será fantástico!

La semana pasada, fuí a las montañas con mi familia. Nos divertimos mucho. Dormí bajo las estrellas y ví muchos animales. Mi hermano pescó y mis hermanas jugaron con nuestro perro. Comimos muy bien. Me gustó mi viaje a las montañas y quiero volver el próximo año.

Cuando tenía veinte años, Rosa trabajaba en una tienda. Vendía juguetes a los niños. Era una tienda pequeña y siempre venían muchos jóvenes para ver los nuevos juegos, las muñecas y las pelotas. Rosa abría la puerta a las nueve y la cerraba a las seis.

Cada sábado, había una fiesta en la tienda con globos, música y una exhibición de juguetes nuevos. Rosa era una vendedora excelente porque amaba a los niños.

He tenido una buena vida. Mi esposa y yo hemos vivido los últimos cincuenta años en la misma casa, y ahora tenemos una familia grande aquí en Colorado. Nuestros hijos y nietos nos han ayudado mucho. Nos han lavado la ropa, nos han traído comida y nos han visitado todos los domingos. Creo que he tenido una vida larga porque hemos recibido mucho amor de la familia.

Espero que mi amiga venga mañana. Me alegra que estemos de vacaciones, pero temo que no vaya a llegar temprano. Si ella tuviera un auto nuevo, yo no estaría preocupada. Yo insistía en que tomara el autobús, pero ella quería usar su propio auto. Lo probable es que no tenga ningún problema y que todo salga bien.

25

Conversation Techniques

Basic Conversation
Conversación básica

There are some aspects of communication that are purely colloquial. The following are a few of the many conversational formulas used daily in Spanish-speaking countries. They are appropriate for almost any social situation:

Hi.	Hola.
Good morning.	Buenas días.
Good afternoon.	Buenas tardes.
Good evening, good night.	Buenas noches.
How are you?	¿Cómo está?
How's it going?	¡Qué tal!
Fine, thanks.	Bien, gracias.
Not bad.	Más o menos.
Very well.	Muy bien.
What's happening?	¿Qué pasa?
What's the matter?	¿Qué pasó?
Nothing much!	¡Sin novedad!
And you?	¿Y usted?
Good-bye.	Adiós.
See you later.	Hasta luego.

Buenos días is used until about noon, **Buenas tardes** is used from about noon until dark, and **Buenas noches** is used to express both *Good evening* and *Good night*. **Hola** can be used to greet others at any time of day.

When approached by waiters, sales clerks, or anyone else in a service industry, you will probably hear the line, **¿En qué puedo servirle?** (*How may I help you?*). When meeting, running into, or socializing with others, these expressions are the most common:

What's your name?	¿Cómo se llama Ud.?
My name is…	Me llamo…
I want to introduce you to…	Quiero presentarle a…
Nice to meet you.	Mucho gusto.
Same to you.	Igualmente.
Where are you from?	¿De dónde es Ud.?
I'm from…	Soy de…
Please.	Por favor.
Thank you very much.	Muchas gracias.
You're welcome.	De nada.
Excuse me.	Con permiso.
Pardon me.	Perdón.
May I come in?	¿Se puede entrar?
Go ahead.	Pase.
Come in.	Adelante.

People often call out to one another in nothing more than short, friendly expressions. Notice how some one-liners do not directly translate into English:

- **Farewell Exchanges**

Give my regards to…	Me saluda a…
Go with God!	¡Vaya con Dios!
God bless you!	¡Dios le bendiga!
Good luck!	¡Buena suerte!
Have a nice day!	¡Qué le vaya bien!
Have a nice trip!	¡Buen viaje!
Get well!	¡Qué se mejore!
Have a good time!	¡Qué disfrute!

- **Good Tidings**

Welcome!	¡Bienvenido!
Congratulations!	¡Felicitaciones!
Happy anniversary!	¡Feliz aniversario!
Happy birthday!	¡Feliz cumpleaños!
Merry Christmas!	¡Feliz Navidad!
Happy New Year!	¡Próspero año nuevo!

• On the Phone

Hello!	¡Aló! or ¡Diga! or ¡Bueno!
This is _____ .	Este es _____ .
Who's calling?	¿Quién llama?
Please don't hang up.	No cuelgue, por favor.
Please wait a moment.	Espere un momento, por favor.
Could I speak with _____ ?	¿Puedo hablar con _____ ?
He/she is not home.	No está en casa.
When will he/she return?	¿Cuándo regresa?
May I leave a message?	¿Puedo dejar un mensaje?
Could I take a message?	¿Puedo tomar un mensaje?
I'll call back later.	Llamaré más tarde.
Please call me at _____ .	Favor de llamarme al número _____ .
It's the wrong number.	Es el número equivocado.
What number are you calling?	¿Qué número está marcando?

• For Clarification

Do you understand?	¿Entiende usted?
I don't know.	No sé.
I don't understand.	No entiendo.
More slowly.	Más despacio.
Thanks for your patience.	Gracias por su paciencia.
What does it mean?	¿Qué significa?
How do you say it?	¿Cómo se dice?
How do you spell it?	¿Cómo se deletrea?
Letter by letter.	Letra por letra.
Number by number.	Número por número.
Word for word.	Palabra por palabra.

These are considered transitional phrases that allow speakers to converse in Spanish more fluidly:

Above all…	Sobre todo…
According to…	Según…
Although…	Aunque…
At first…	Al principio…
At last…	Por fin…
At least…	Por lo menos…
Besides…	Además…
By the way…	A propósito…
For example…	Por ejemplo…
However…	Sin embargo…
In general…	En general…

> **TIP**
> Every language has synonyms, or words that carry the same meaning. They are particularly necessary when conversations become more complex:
>
> | | |
> |---|---|
> | *Nice to meet you.* | Mucho gusto. |
> | | Encantado. |
> | | A sus órdenes. |
> | *Thanks a lot.* | Muchas gracias. |
> | | Mil gracias. |
> | | Muy amable. |
> | *You're welcome.* | Por nada. |
> | | De nada. |
> | | No hay de qué. |

In other words...	Es decir...
In spite of...	A pesar de...
On the contrary...	Al contrario...
So...	Así que...
Still...	Aún...
In my opinion...	En mi opinión ...
Then...	Entonces...
Therefore...	Por eso...
Without a doubt...	Sin duda...
Yet...	Todavía...

LA PRÁCTICA 1

Translate these common expressions into Spanish:

1. See you later!   ¡Hasta luego!

2. Happy birthday!

3. Thanks a lot!

4. Good evening!

5. Good luck!

6. Merry Christmas!

7. Have a nice trip!

8. Welcome!

9. Get well!

10. Happy New Year!

POR SU CUENTA

Now explain the situations when these common expressions are normally used:

1. Buenos días, ¿Cómo esta Ud.?

2. ¿En qué puedo ayudarle?

3. ¡Hasta luego!

4. Muchas gracias. _____

5. ¿Aló? ¿Quién llama? _____

6. Mucho gusto. _____

7. ¿Qué pasa? _____

8. ¿Se puede entrar? _____

9. ¡Con su permiso! _____

10. ¡Qué tal! _____

Expressing Feelings and Opinions
Expresión de sentimientos y opiniones

Expressing how one feels about something is another important communication technique. Here are some useful expressions to help you do so:

I'm sorry!	¡Lo siento!
All the better!	¡Tanto mejor!
Good idea!	¡Buena idea!
I agree!	¡De acuerdo!
I hope so!	¡Ojalá!
I see!	¡Ya veo!
It doesn't matter!	¡No importa!
I'm so glad!	¡Me alegro!
Maybe!	¡Quizas!
No problem!	¡No hay problema!
No wonder!	¡Con razón!
Of course!	¡Por supuesto!
That's not true!	¡No es cierto!
Really?	¿De veras?
That depends!	¡Depende!
It can't be!	¡No puede ser!
That's OK!	¡Está bien!
I think so!	¡Creo que sí!
Why not!	¡Cómo no!
You're kidding!	¡No me diga!

This construction with Qué... is frequently used to express one's feelings:

¡Qué triste!	*How sad!*
¡Qué lástima!	*What a shame!*
¡Qué increíble!	*That's incredible!*
¡Qué chiste!	*What a joke!*
¡Que raro!	*How strange!*

Even though **tener** literally means *to have*, sometimes it's used instead of the verb **estar** to express a personal feeling or emotion:

(I am) afraid	(tengo) miedo
(we are) at fault	(tenemos) la culpa
(they are) doubtful	(tienen) dudas
(he is) right	(tiene) razón
(you are) lucky	(tienes) suerte
(you guys are) careful	(tengan) cuidado
(I am) sad	(tengo) pena

LA PRÁCTICA 2

Translate these expressions into English:

1. No puede ser.   _____It can't be._____

2. Tengo pena.   _____

3. ¿De veras?   _____

4. No importa.   _____

5. Lo siento.   _____

6. ¡Qué lástima!   _____

7. Creo que sí.   _____

8. Con razón.   _____

9. Por supuesto.   _____

10. Cómo no.   _____

Personal Subjects
Temas personales

Learn how to provide others with your personal information. Notice this simple formula with ¿Cuál es su...?:

What's your...?	¿Cuál es su...?
full name	nombre completo
residence	domicilio
address	dirección
phone number	número de teléfono
date of birth	fecha de nacimiento
place of birth	lugar de nacimiento
social security number	número de seguro social
marital status	estado civil
nationality	nacionalidad
first language	idioma original

It's not uncommon for someone in Spain or Latin America to have two last names. Here's the order:

First name	María
PRIMER NOMBRE	
Father's last name	García
APELLIDO PATERNO	
Mother's last name	Sánchez
APELLIDO MATERNO	
Full name	María García Sánchez
NOMBRE COMPELTO	

However, not all Hispanic people have two first names, and there is no middle name in many countries as we know it. Also, when a woman marries, she may keep her father's last name and follow it by her husband's, or she may drop her father's last name and substitute it with her husband's, or she may retain her father's and mother's last name and add (or not) her husband's: all of the above will depend on personal preferences and customs.

Here is more vocabulary that is needed to share your personal information either in everyday conversations or on documents and forms:

apartment	el apartamento
street	la calle
city	la ciudad
county	el condado
country	el país
home phone	el teléfono de la casa
cell phone	el teléfono celular
e-mail	el correo electrónico
single	soltero /a
married	casado /a
divorced	divorciado /a
race	la raza
religion	la religión
sex	el sexo

POR SU CUENTA

Review by answering these questions aloud:

1. ¿Cuál es su nombre completo?

2. ¿Cuál es su estado civil?

3. ¿Cómo se llama su mejor amigo?

4. ¿Cuántos años tiene Ud.?

5. ¿Cuál es la dirección de su correo electrónico?

6. ¿Tiene Ud. trabajo?

7. ¿Cuál es su nacionalidad?

8. ¿Dónde vive su familia?

9. ¿Cuál es su fecha de nacimiento?

10. ¿Cuántos idiomas habla Ud.?

26

Synonyms, Antonyms, and Cognates

¿Cuánto sabe usted?

How Much Do You Know Already?

1. Name two ways to express *to choose* in Spanish.

2. How would your translate embarazada, librería, and revolver?

3. What do both comenzar and empezar mean in English?

4. How do English words ending in *-ous* usually end in Spanish?

5. What is the antonym of rechazar?

Synonyms
Los sinónimos

SYNONYMS are words or expressions that have the same or approximate meaning. ANTONYMS are words or expressions that have opposite or contrastive meanings.

Synonyms allow a person to say the same thing in a different way, thus increasing communicative competence. Bear in mind, however, that no two words or expressions have precisely the same meaning in every situation. Here is a list of common synonyms in Spanish:

- **Basic Synonyms**

acordarse de, recordar	*to remember*
alimento, comida	*nourishment, food*
alumno, estudiante	*student*
andar, caminar	*to walk*
anillo, sortija	*ring (jewelry)*
antiguo, viejo	*ancient, old*

339

así que, tan pronto como	*as soon as*
asustar, espantar	*to frighten, to scare*
aún, todavía	*still, yet*
ayuda, socorro	*aid, help*
barco, buque	*boat, ship*
bastante, suficiente	*enough, sufficient*
batalla, combate	*battle, combat*
bonita, linda	*pretty, lovely*
breve, corto	*brief, short*
camarero, mozo	*waiter*
campesino, granjero	*farmer*
cara, rostro	*face*
chicos, niños	*children*
cocinar, cocer, guisar	*to cook*
comenzar, empezar	*to commence, to begin*
comprender, entender	*to comprehend, to understand*
conducir, manejar	*to drive*
conquistar, vencer	*to conquer, to vanquish*
contento, feliz, alegre	*content, happy*
contestar, responder	*to answer, to respond*
continuar, seguir	*to continue*
cruzar, atravesar	*to cross*
cuarto, habitación, pieza	*room*
cura, sacerdote	*priest*
delgado, flaco	*thin, slim*
desear, querer	*to desire, to want*
diablo, demonio	*devil, demon*
diversión, pasatiempo	*diversion, pastime*
elevar, levantar	*to elevate, to raise*
enviar, mandar	*to send*
error, falta	*error, fault, mistake*
escoger, elegir	*to choose, to select*
esposo, marido	*spouse, husband*
exhausto, cansado	*exhausted, tired*
grave, serio	*grave, serious*
hallar, encontrar	*to find, to encounter*
hermosa, bella	*beautiful*
hombre, señor	*man*
idioma, lengua	*language, tongue*
irse, salir, marcharse	*to go away, to leave*
lentamente, despacio	*slowly*
luchar, pelear	*to fight, to struggle*
lugar, sitio	*place, site*
maestro, profesor	*teacher, professor*
medias, calcetines	*socks*
miedo, temor	*fear, dread*

morir, fallecer	*to die, to expire*
mostrar, enseñar	*to show, to teach*
mujer, señora	*woman*
nunca, jamás	*never*
obrero, trabajador	*worker*
obtener, conseguir	*to obtain, to get*
odiar, aborrecer	*to hate, to abhor*
país, nación	*country, nation*
pájaro, ave	*bird*
parar, detener	*to stop*
pasear, caminar	*to take a walk*
pena, dolor	*pain, grief*
perezoso, flojo	*lazy*
poner, colocar	*to put, to place*
regresar, volver	*to return*
rezar, orar	*to pray*
rogar, suplicar	*to beg, to implore*
romper, quebrar	*to break*
similar, semejante, parecido	*similar, alike*
sorprender, asombrar	*to surprise*
tal vez, acaso, quizás	*maybe, perhaps*
tirar, lanzar	*to throw, to pitch*
trabajo, obra	*work*
ya que, puesto que	*since, inasmuch as*

It is always best to check up on the meaning of a word before putting it to use as a synonym. For example conocer (*to know someone*) is not the same as saber (*to know something*), even though both may be listed as synonyms. The same holds true for words like pero and sino, which both mean *but* in English, but are used quite differently:

Quiero comer, <u>pero</u> no tengo tiempo.
I want to eat, but I don't have the time.

No fuimos a la tienda ayer, <u>sino</u> hoy.
We didn't go to the store yesterday, but today.

La Práctica 1

List synonyms for the following common words:

1. andar   caminar _____

2. mujer _____

3. enviar _____

4. linda _____

5. conseguir _____

6. obrero _____

7. jamás _____

8. feliz _____

9. continuar _____

10. despacio _____

Replace the underlined word with a synonym:

11. <u>Salieron</u> a las siete.   Se fueron _____

12. Estaban <u>orando</u> en la mesa. _____

13. Es un caso muy <u>grave</u>. _____

14. ¿A qué hora <u>empieza</u> la clase? _____

15. Tenían <u>los rostros</u> sonrientes. _____

16. ¿Cuál <u>idioma</u> te gusta más? _____

17. Encontramos una zona llena de <u>aves</u>. _____

18. Era un hombre <u>flojo</u>. _____

19. ¡<u>Lanza</u> la pelota! _____

20. Mi papá no <u>ha vuelto</u> todavía. _____

Antonyms
Los antónimos

Antonyms are words that express opposite or contrastive meanings. Again, however, not all words on this list are exact opposites:

- ## Basic Antonyms

aceptar, *to accept*	rechazar, *to refuse*
alegre, *happy*	triste, *sad*
algo, *something*	nada, *nothing*
alguien, *someone*	nadie, *nobody*
amar, *to love*	odiar, *to hate*
amigo(a), *friend*	enemigo(a), *enemy*
antes, *before*	después, *after*
antiguo, *ancient*	moderno, *modern*
aquí, *here*	allí, *there*
arriba, *above*	abajo, *below*
ausente, *absent*	presente, *present*
bajo, *low/ short*	alto, *high/ tall*
bien, *well*	mal, *badly*
bueno, *good*	malo, *bad*
caliente, *hot*	frío, *cold*
cerca de, *near*	lejos de, *far*
cerrar, *to close*	abrir, *to open*
comprar, *to buy*	vender, *to sell*
con, *with*	sin, *without*
corto, *short* (in length)	largo, *long*
dar, *to give*	recibir, *to receive*
delante de, *in front of*	detrás de, *in back of*
empezar, *to begin*	terminar, *to finish*
entrada, *entrance*	salida, *exit*
fácil, *easy*	difícil, *difficult*
grande, *big*	pequeño, *small*
ir, *to go*	venir, *to come*
joven, *young*	viejo, *old*
levantarse, *to get up*	sentarse, *to sit down*
limpio, *clean*	sucio, *dirty*
más, *more*	menos, *less*
mucho, *much*	poco, *little*
perder, *to lose*	hallar, *to find*
pregunta, *question*	respuesta, *answer*
primero, *first*	último, *last*
rico, *rich*	pobre, *poor*
ruido, *noise*	silencio, *silence*
siempre, *always*	nunca, *never*
subir, *to go up*	bajar, *to go down*

LA PRÁCTICA 2

Select the right antonym and write it on the line provided:

1. aceptar   salir, rechazar, adelantar <u>rechazar</u>

2. corto   ancho, bajo, largo   <u>   </u>

3. ruido   silencio, bonito, fino   <u>   </u>

4. venir   dar, ir, llegar   <u>   </u>

5. algo   alguien, todos, nada   <u>   </u>

6. odiar   amar, besar, disfrutar   <u>   </u>

7. entrada   bebida, salida, caliente   <u>   </u>

8. antiguo   difícil, viejo, moderno   <u>   </u>

9. ausente   presente, listo, enfermo   <u>   </u>

10. hallar   encontrar, perder, olvidar <u>   </u>

Find a common antonym for these other words:

11. recibir   <u>dar   </u>

12. llorar   <u>   </u>

13. el oeste   <u>   </u>

14. juntar   <u>   </u>

15. ganar   <u>   </u>

16. la guerra   <u>   </u>

17. lleno   <u>   </u>

18. encender   <u>   </u>

19. olvidar   <u>   </u>

20. la noche   <u>   </u>

CROSSWORD 11

Find the opposites:

Across
3. sucio
5. abrir
7. ruido
10. dar
13. rico
15. nunca
16. entrada
17. amar
18. arriba

Down
1. viejo
2. malo
4. perder
6. nadie
8. venir
9. bajar
11. pregunta
12. triste
14. mucho

Cognates
Palabras análogas

Another excellent way to learn and remember vocabulary is to recognize cognates, or Spanish words that look very similar to English words because they are related in origin:

el bate	*bat*	el desastre	*disaster*
la palma	*palm*	la cápsula	*capsule*
el busto	*bust*	el espíritu	*spirit*

Fortunately for the English-speaker, there are hundreds of Spanish words that are easy to translate simply by looking at their endings. Notice the spelling changes in the following groups:

• **Spanish**	• **English**
<u>-ico</u> romántico	<u>-ic</u> *romantic*
<u>-ente</u> diferente	<u>-ent</u> *different*
<u>-ción</u> construcción	<u>-tion</u> *construction*
<u>-oso</u> delicioso	<u>-ous</u> *delicious*
<u>-dad</u> electricidad	<u>-ty</u> *electricity*
<u>-rio</u> necesario	<u>-ry</u> *necessary*
<u>-ista</u> artista	<u>-ist</u> *artist*

Many Spanish verb infinitives also resemble their English equivalent. Notice the patterns in the following cognates:

to absorb	absorber
to control	controlar
to plant	plantar
to refer	referir
to visit	visitar

- Verbs ending in *-ate* in English generally end in **-ar** in Spanish:

concentrate	concentrar
manipulate	manipular
investigate	investigar

- Verbs ending in *-fy* in English generally end in **-ficar** in Spanish.

verify	verificar
certify	certificar
clarify	clarificar

- Verbs ending in *-ize* or *-yze* in English generally end in **-izar** in Spanish.

analyze	analizar
authorize	autorizar
dramatize	dramatizar

Countless Spanish words are spelled exactly the same in English. They have the same meanings also, but are obviously pronounced differently:

general	**nuclear**
diabetes	**noble**
doctor	**alfalfa**
similar	**vulgar**
exterior	**pelvis**

False Cognates
Palabras de analogía engañosa

There are several false cognates in Spanish, too. These words fool students because they look like cognate words, but have very different meanings in English:

• Spanish	• English
actual	*present, of the present time*
asistir a	*to attend, to be present at*
atender	*to take care of*
el campo	*countryside*
el cargo	*duty, post, responsibility*
la carta	*letter (to mail, post)*
el collar	*necklace*
el compromiso	*promise*
constiparse	*to catch cold*
contestar	*to answer*
el delito	*crime*
la desgracia	*misfortune*
el desmayo	*fainting*
educado	*well-mannered*
embarazada	*pregnant*
el éxito	*success, outcome*
el labrador	*farmer*
largo	*long*
la lectura	*reading*
la librería	*bookstore*
molestar	*bother*
el pariente	*relative*
realizar	*to achieve*
recordar	*to remember*
revolver	*to stir, turn over*
sensible	*sensitive*
soportar	*to bear*
el suceso	*event, happening*
la tormenta	*storm*
la trampa	*trap, snare, trick*
el vaso	*drinking glass*

LA PRÁCTICA 3

Write the English translation as quickly as you can:

1. recordar   *to remember*
2. contestar
3. barrer
4. introducir
5. desmayarse
6. presentar
7. investigar
8. atender
9. adorar
10. embarazar

Underline the word with the closest meaning to each word below:

11. general   a. absolute   b. <u>general</u>   c. leader
12. vencer   a. to conquer   b. to surrender   c. to arrive
13. collar   a. collar   b. to gather   c. necklace
14. delito   a. removal   b. crime   c. cancellation
15. hallar   a. to lose   b. hallway   c. to find
16. trampa   a. vagabond   b. thief   c. trick
17. éxito   a. success   b. exit   c. departure
18. asistir   a. to join   b. to help   c. to attend
19. actual   a. actual   b. current   c. eventful
20. vulgar   a. primitive   b. criminal   c. vulgar

27

Idiomatic Expressions, Proverbs, and Sayings

> ### ¿Cuánto sabe usted?
> ## How Much Do You Know Already?
>
>
>
> 1. What does tener buena estrella mean?
>
> 2. Finish this saying, El que madruga, _____.
>
> 3. How do you say *to blush* in Spanish?
>
> 4. What would Ser de poca monta be?
>
> 5. What's the saying in Spanish that means, *All that glitters is not gold*.

Idioms
Modismos

Some of the most interesting words and expressions in Spanish are considered idiomatic, because they cannot be understood by analyzing their literal meanings. For example, Tengo frío appears to mean *I have cold*, a bizarre statement in English. However, it is a very common idiom in Latin America and Spain: *I'm cold!*

- **Idiomatic Expressions**
  The following is a categorized selection of idiomatic expressions in Spanish that begin with a basic verb:

  ABRIR
abrir el día	*to dawn*
abrir la mano	*to accept bribes*
abrir el ojo	*to be alert*
abrir los ojos a uno	*to enlighten*

350

ACABAR

acabar de	to have just
acabarse uno	to grow feeble, weary
Es cosa de nunca acabar.	It is an endless affair.

ANDAR

a más andar	at full speed
a mejor andar	at best
andar a derechas	to act honestly
andar a golpes	to come to blows
andar de boca en boca	to be the talk of the town
andar en cueros	to go stark naked
andar listo	to be diligent
andar por decir	to be determined to say
andar por hacer	to be determined to do
andar de boca en boca	to be generally known
andarse por las ramas	to beat around the bush

CABER

caber en suerte	to get lucky
caberle a uno	to be fitting to someone
no caber de gozo	to be overjoyed
no caber en sí	to be full of one's own merits
no caber en sí	to be overjoyed, or furious

CAER

caer a plomo	to fall flat
caer de espaldas	to fall backward
caer de rodillas	to fall on one's knees
caer en cama	to become sick
caer en gracia	to please someone
caer en la cuenta	to see the point
caerse de sueño	to be falling asleep
dejarse caer	to drop oneself
caerse el alma a los pies	to be down in the dumps

DAR

dar a luz	to give birth
dar asco	to disgust
dar calabazas	to jilt
dar carta blanca a uno	to give someone carte blanche
dar con	to run into
dar contra alguna cosa	to hit against something
dar cuerda a	to wind
dar de comer o beber	to feed or give a drink to
dar de gritos	to shout

Idiomatic Expressions, Proverbs, and Sayings **351**

dar de sí	*to stretch*
dar diente con diente	*to shiver with cold*
dar el golpe de gracia	*to finish someone off*
dar el pésame	*to express condolence*
dar en el blanco	*to hit the mark*
dar entre ceja y ceja	*to tell it like it is*
dar fiado	*to give credit*
dar filo	*to sharpen an instrument*
dar la enhorabuena	*to congratulate*
dar guerra	*to make trouble*
dar la hora	*to strike the hour*
dar la lata	*to make a nuisance of oneself*
dar la vuelta	*to turn back*
dar las gracias	*to thank*
dar licencia	*to give leave*
dar miedo	*to frighten*
dar por sentado	*to take for granted*
dar prestado	*to lend*
dar que hacer	*to give trouble*
dar que reír	*to make one laugh*
dar que sentir	*to hurt one's feelings*
dar rienda suelta a	*to give free rein to*
dar un paseo	*to take a walk*
dar un abrazo	*to embrace*
dar un grito	*to shout*
dar un recado	*to leave a message*
dar voces	*to scream*
dar vueltas a algo	*to think something over*
darse a	*to give oneself to*
darse cuenta de	*to realize*
darse la mano	*to shake hands*
darse maña	*to contrive*
darse por sentido	*to show resentment*
darse por vencido	*to give up*
darse prisa	*to hurry*
dar gato por liebre	*to take someone in*
No se me da nada.	*It gives me no concern.*

DECIR

decir la verdad	*to tell the truth*
decir para sí	*to talk to oneself*
decir por decir	*to talk for the sake of talking*
es decir	*that is to say*
oír decir	*to hear it said*
por mejor decir	*more properly speaking*
decirle cuatro verdades	*to tell someone a thing or two*
no decir ni pío	*not to say a word*

DEJAR

dejar de (+ infinitive)	to stop (doing something)
dejar plantado	to stand somebody up
no dejar piedra por (sin) mover	to leave no stone unturned

DORMIR

dormir a pierna suelta	to sleep like a log
dormir la mona	to sleep off a hangover
dormirse sobre sus laureles	to rest on one's laurels

ECHAR

echar a perder	to ruin, spoil
echar chispas	to be furious, get angry
echar de menos	to miss
echar flores	to flatter, sweet-talk
echar la culpa	to blame
echarse a	to start to
echárselas de	to boast of being

ESTAR

estar a punto de	to be on the verge of
estar a sus anchas	to be comfortable
estar alerta	to be on the watch
estar bien con	to be on good terms with
estar calado hasta los huesos	to be soaked to the skin
estar como el pez en el agua	to be right at home
estar con el alma en un hilo	to be in suspense
estar con el pie en el aire	to be unsettled
estar de acuerdo	to agree
estar de buen humor	to be in a good mood
estar de mal humor	to be in a bad mood
estar de más	to be in excess
estar de pie	to stand
estar de por medio	to mediate
estar de prisa	to be in haste
estar de vuelta	to be back
estar en condiciones	to be in good shape
estar en la luna	to have one's head in the clouds
estar en las nubes	to be daydreaming
estar en que	to be of the opinion that
estar en su pellejo	to be in his/her shoes
estar fuera de sí	to be beside oneself
estar hecho una sopa	to get soaked
estar mal con	to have bad relations with someone
estar mal	to be in bad shape
estar para	to be about to do something
estar por	to be inclined to do something
estar sin blanca	to be flat broke
estarse quieto	to stand still

HABER

Hay que...	*It is necessary that...*
No hay de qué.	*You are welcome.*
No hay más que pedir.	*It leaves nothing to be desired.*

HACER

Hace muchos años...	*Many years ago...*
Hace buen **o** mal tiempo.	*It's good or bad weather.*
Hace calor **o** frío.	*It's warm or cold.*
Hace viento.	*It's windy.*
hacer caso	*to pay attention*
hacer buenas migas	*to hit it off with someone*
hacer de las suyas	*to be up to one's old tricks*
hacer un papel	*to play a role*
hacer juego	*to match*
hacer la vista gorda	*to pretend not to notice*
hacer las paces	*to make peace*
hacer época	*to attract public attention*
hacer pedazos	*to break to pieces*
hacer su agosto	*to make a killing*
hacer un viaje	*to take a trip*
hacerse médico	*to become a doctor*
hacerse daño	*to hurt oneself*
hacerse tarde	*to become late*
hacérsele agua la boca	*to make one's mouth water*
hacer chacota	*to ridicule*
hacer daño	*to harm*
hacer de	*to act as*
hacer el papel	*to act the part*
hacer frente	*to face*
hacer juego	*to be well matched*
hacer pedazos	*to tear to pieces*
hacer pensar	*to give cause to suspect*
hacer pucheros	*to pout*
hacer saber	*to acquaint*
hacer su agosto	*to make good use of one's time*
hacer un pedido	*to place an order*
hacer un viaje	*to take a trip*
hacer una visita	*to pay a visit*
hacerse	*to become*

IR

ir a medias	*to go halves*
ir a pie	*to walk*
ir agua arriba	*to walk upstream*
ir tras la corriente	*to go downstream*
irse a pique	*to flounder, fall*
ir al grano	*to go straight to the point*
ir de juerga	*to be out on a spree*
ir sobre ruedas	*to run smoothly*

LLEVAR

llevar a cabo	*to carry out*
llevar la contraria	*to contradict*
llevarse como perro y gato	*to be always squabbling*
llevarse un chasco	*to be disappointed*
llevar puesto	*to have on, to be wearing*
llevar en peso	*to carry in the air*
llevar consigo	*to carry along with*
llevar a cuestas	*to carry on one's shoulder, back*
llevarse bien, **o** mal	*to be on good, or bad terms*
llevar el compás	*to beat time in music*

METER

meter la pata	*to put one's foot in one's mouth*
meterse donde no le llaman	*to meddle, to snoop around*
meterse en la boca de lobo	*to enter the lion's den*
meterse en un callejón sin salida	*to get into a jam*

PONER

poner en ridículo	*to make somebody look ridiculous*
poner las cartas sobre la mesa	*to put one's cards on the table*
poner los puntos sobre las íes	*to dot the i's and cross the t's*
poner a alguien por las nubes	*to heap praise on someone*
ponérsele a uno la carne de gallina	*to get goose pimples*
ponérsele los cabellos de punta	*to be terrified*
poner al sol	*to expose to the sun*
poner atención	*to pay attention*
poner de vuelta y media	*to humiliate a person*
poner en libertad	*to free*
poner en limpio	*to copy*
poner en obra	*to put into action*
poner en tierra	*to put ashore*
poner huevos	*to lay eggs*
poner la mesa	*to set the table*
poner por escrito	*to put in writing*
poner toda su fuerza	*to act with all one's might*
ponerse a	*to set about, to start*
ponerse en camino	*to set forth*
ponerse colorado	*to blush*

QUEDAR

quedarse boquiabierto	*to be left with your mouth open*
quedarse con	*to keep*
quedarse con el día y la noche	*to be left penniless*
quedar de una pieza	*to be dumbfounded*
quedar en	*to agree on*

QUERER

querer a	*to love*
querer decir	*to mean*
sin querer	*unwillingly*

SABER

hacer saber	*to communicate*
saber a	*to taste of*
No se sabe.	*It is not known.*

SALIR

salir bien	*to succeed*
salir con un domingo siete	*to say something irrational*
salir de alguno	*to get rid of a person*
salirse de sus casillas	*to lose one's temper*
salir del paso	*to get out of a difficulty*
salirse con las suyas	*to have one's way*
Sale el sol.	*The sun rises.*

SER

ser cómplice de	*to have a hand in*
ser de edad	*to be of age*
ser del caso	*to be fitting*
ser del parecer	*to be of the opinion*
ser uno de tantos	*to be one of the crowd*
ser de poca monta	*to be of little value*
ser el colmo	*to be the limit*
ser la flor y nata	*to be the cream of the crop*
ser de otro cantar	*to be a horse of a different color*
ser pan comido	*to be as easy as pie*
ser para chuparse los dedos	*to taste delicious*
ser todo oídos	*to be all ears*
ser un cero a la izquierda	*to be of no value*
ser una lata	*to be annoying*
ser una perla	*to be a jewel*
ser uña y carne	*to be as close as can be*
no ser cosa del otro jueves	*to be nothing out of the ordinary*
Sea lo que fuere.	*Be that as it may.*

TENER

no tener arreglo	*not be able to be helped*
no tener hiel	*to be meek and gentle*

no tener ni un pelo de tonto	*to be nobody's fool*
no tener pelos en la lengua	*to be very outspoken*
no tener pies ni cabeza	*to have no rhyme or reason*
no tener razón	*to be wrong*
tener ángel	*to be charming*
tener buena estrella	*to be lucky*
tener calor **o** frío	*to be warm or cold*
tener celos de uno	*to be jealous of someone*
tener corazón de piedra	*to be cold-hearted*
tener cuidado	*to be careful*
tener en cuenta	*to keep in mind*
tener éxito	*to be successful*
tener fama	*to have the reputation*
tener ganas	*to desire*
tener hambre	*to be hungry*
tener la culpa de	*to be at fault*
tener la razón	*to be in the right*
tener líos	*to have difficulties*
tener los huesos molidos	*to be exhausted*
tener los nervios de punta	*to have one's nerves on edge*
tener lugar	*to take place*
tener madera para	*to be cut out for*
tener mala cara	*to look bad*
tener malas pulgas	*to be short-tempered*
tener miedo de	*to be afraid of*
tener mundo	*to be sophisticated*
tener ojos de lince	*to have eyes like a hawk*
tener pájaros en la cabeza	*to have bats in the belfry*
tener palabra	*to keep one's word*
tener presente	*to bear in mind*
tener prisa	*to be in a hurry*
tener que hacer	*to have to do something*
tener que ver con	*to have to do with*
tener sed	*to be thirsty*
tener sueño	*to be sleepy*
tener suerte	*to be lucky*
tener un disgusto	*to have a falling out*
tener vergüenza	*to be ashamed of*
tenerse en pie	*to stand*

TOMAR

tomar algo a bien/a mal	*to take something well/badly*
tomar a broma	*to take a joke*
tomar a pecho	*to take to heart*
tomar en serio	*to take seriously*
tomar la palabra	*to take the floor*
tomar partido por	*to side with*
tomar la delantera	*to get ahead of*
tomarle el pelo	*to pull someone's leg*
tomárselo con calma	*to take it easy*

VALER

valer más algo que nada	*to be better than nothing*
valer más tarde que nunca	*to be better late than never*
valer la pena de	*to be worthwhile*
valer un ojo de la cara	*to be worth a fortune*
Más vale.	*It is better.*

VER

no tener nada que ver con eso	*to have nothing to do with it*
ver a hurtadillas	*to look over one's shoulders*
ver con muchos ojos	*to observe very carefully*
ver el cielo abierto	*to see a great opportunity*
verse las caras	*to see each other face to face*
A mi ver...	*In my opinion...*
A ver...	*Let us see...*
Es de ver que...	*It is worth noticing that...*
Ya se ve.	*It is evident.*

VENIR

venir de molde	*to fit like a glove*
venir lo que viniere	*to come what may*
venir al caso	*to come to the point*
venir a menos	*to decline*
venir a las manos	*to come to blows*
venir a pelo	*to come just at the right time*
venir de perilla	*to come at the nick of time*
venirse abajo	*to fall, collapse*
venirse al suelo	*to fall to the ground*
venirse el cielo abajo	*to rain heavily*
venir de perlas	*to be just the thing, just right*

• More Expressions

buscar tres pies al gato	*to split hairs*
consultar con la almohada	*to sleep on it*
dorar la píldora	*to sugarcoat something*
faltarle a uno un tornillo	*to have a screw loose*
hablar hasta por los codos	*to talk incessantly*
llamar al pan, pan y al vino, vino	*to call a spade a spade*
no importar un bledo/un comino	*to not give a damn about*
pasar las de Caín	*to go through hell*
pedir peras al olmo	*to expect the impossible*
no pegar ojo en toda la noche	*to not sleep a wink all night*
quemarse las pestañas	*to burn the midnight oil*
dejar en claro	*to make clear*
saltar a la vista	*to be obvious*
mandar a freír espárragos	*to go jump in a lake*

matar dos pájaros de un tiro	*to kill two birds with one stone*
tocar en lo vivo	*to hurt deeply*
a pedir de boca	*perfectly, smoothly*
contra viento y marea	*against all odds*
de buenas a primeras	*right off the bat*
de mal en peor	*from bad to wose*
de segunda mano	*secondhand*
el qué dirán	*what people say*
oír campanas y no saber donde	*to hear without understanding*
oír, ver y callar	*to mind your own business*
verlo todo color de rosa	*to see life through rose-colored glasses*
verlo todo color negro	*to be pessimistic*
volver a las andadas	*to go back to one's old ways*
volver en sí	*to regain consciousness*
Como Ud. quiera.	*As you will.*
Dios mediante.	*God willing.*
¿Cómo fué eso?	*How did that happen?*
Había una vez.	*Once upon a time.*
Mañana será otro día.	*Tomorrow's another day.*
Toca madera.	*Knock on wood.*
Todo el santo día.	*The whole darn day.*
Trato hecho.	*It's a deal.*

La Práctica 1

Fill in the missing words in these popular idioms, and then translate them into English:

1. Matar dos _pájaros_ de un tiro.   <u>**Kill two birds with one stone.**</u>

2. Hablé hasta por los _____.   _____

3. Mandar a freír _____.   _____

4. No tener pelos en la _____.   _____

5. Nuestro negocio iba sobre _____.   _____

6. Meterse en un _____ sin salida.   _____

7. Poner los puntos sobre las _____.   _____

8. Hacer de tripas _____.   _____

9. Estar con el _____ en el aire.   _____

10. Dar entre ceja y _____.   _____

Write down V (Verdadero) if the translation is correct or F (Falso) if it isn't:

11.	estar de prisa	to be in a hurry	V
12.	dar gato por liebre	to give freedom	___
13.	hacer chacota	to go to work	___
14.	poner en limpio	to clean thoroughly	___
15.	llevar un chasco	to bring a friend	___
16.	ir de juerga	to leave upset	___
17.	salirse con las suyas	to lose one's temper	___
18.	ser de poca monta	to be broke	___
19.	tener líos	to have difficulties	___
20.	venir de molde	to come from wealth	___

What do these common Spanish idioms mean in English?

21. Me salí de mis casillas. _____

22. No dije ni pío. _____

23. Me puse colorado. _____

24. No me di cuenta. _____

25. Me quedé boquiabierto. _____

POR SU CUENTA

List a few of your favorite idiomatic expressions in Spanish that begin with the following words:

1. estar: _____

2. poner (se): _____

3. dar (se): _____

4. tener: _____

5. hacer (se): _____

Proverbs and Sayings
Proverbios y dichos

Sayings and proverbs, meaningful words to the wise, are part of Spanish culture. Read through the following, and memorize those that suit you best.

Río que suena, piedras trae.
There's truth to the rumor.

Dime con quién andas, y te diré quién eres.
Tell me who you hang around with, and I'll tell you who you are.

Haces mal, espera otro tal.
Sow the wind and reap the whirlwind.

Ojos que le vieron ir, no verán venir.
An opportunity lost never returns.

Ojos que no ven, corazón que no siente.
Out of sight, out of mind.

Buena vida, arrugas trae.
Those who live comfortably live long.

A quien le venga el guante que se lo plante.
If the shoe fits, wear it.

Como viene, se va.
Easy come, easy go.

No hay mal que por bien no venga.
There is no evil that may not be turned to good.

Antes que te cases, mira lo que haces.
Look before you leap.

A lo hecho, pecho.
It's no use crying over spilled milk.

Querer es poder.
Where there is a will there is a way.

En boca cerrada no entran moscas.
Flies do not enter a closed mouth.

Ver es creer.
Seeing is believing.

No todo lo que brilla es oro.
All that glitters is not gold.

Más vale pájaro en mano que cien volando.
A bird in hand is worth two in the bush.

No dejes para mañana lo que puedes hacer hoy.
Don't leave for tomorrow what you can do today.

Dios los crea y ellos se juntan.
Birds of a feather flock together.

A quién madruga, Dios lo ayuda.
The early bird catches the worm.

Donde una puerta se cierra, otra se abre.
Whenever a door closes, another opens.

Donde no hay amor, no hay dolor.
Where there is no love, there is no pain.

Más valen cuatro ojos que dos.
Two heads are better than one.

Entre la espada y la pared.
Between the devil and the deep blue sea.

Hay gato encerrado.
There's something fishy.

No hay moros en la costa.
The coast is clear.

Poderoso caballero es don Dinero.
Money talks.

A dónde fueres, haz lo que vieres.
When in Rome, do as the Romans do.

A caballo regalado no se le mira el diente.
Don't look a gift horse in the mouth.

28

Written Communication

¿Cuánto sabe usted?
How Much Do You Know Already?

1. Correct the punctuation in this sentence: Ven acá Lupita!

2. Name three ways a comma is used in Spanish grammar.

3. How do you say *past progressive* in Spanish?

4. Where would the word estimado likely appear in a business letter?

5. What is @ called in a Spanish e-mail address?

Punctuation
La puntuación

      Punctuation refers to the written marks and symbols that are used to separate words into sentences, clauses, and phrases in order to give special meaning to a language in print. For example, there are three written marks that indicate that a sentence is completed. Unlike English, however, the question and exclamation also require inverted marks at the front:

period (el punto)	Estoy trabajando.
question mark (el signo interrogativo)	¿Trabajas mucho?
exclamation mark (el signo exclamativo)	¡Siempre trabajo!

- The *comma* (la coma) has several uses in Spanish.

  1. The comma separates words, phrases, or clauses that interrupt a sentence:

  > La profesora, me dijeron los estudiantes, es del Paraguay.
  > The teacher, the students told me, is from Paraguay.

2. Commas also precede and follow the name of a person who is being addressed in a sentence:

> Es importante, Nora, que te vayas.
> *It's important, Nora, that you leave.*

3. A comma is used to separate three or more words (or phrases) in a series. However, there is no comma after the last conjunction:

> Compró dos manzanas, cinco plátanos, tres peras y una sandía.
> *She bought two apples, five bananas, three pears, and a watermelon.*

4. A comma is also used after a long subordinate clause:

> Para poder llegar a tiempo con toda la familia, salió temprano.
> *In order to be able to arrive on time with the whole family, he left early.*

5. A comma is needed before and after transition words such as además, sin embargo, es decir, por ejemplo, etc.:

> Me dijo, sin embargo, que todo está bien.
> *He told me, however, that all is well.*

> Por ejemplo, hace frío en el diciembre.
> *For example, it's cold in December.*

6. A comma is also used before the conjunctions pero or mas:

> Necesitamos el dinero, pero no vamos a venderlo.
> *We need the money, but we aren't going to sell it.*

7. A comma is required after sí or no in sentences that answer a question:

> Sí, yo fui con ella.   *Yes, I went with her.*
> No, no tengo la menor idea.   *No, I don't have any idea.*

- The *semi-colon* (el punto y coma) has two primary uses in Spanish:

1. It is used to indicate a pause that is longer than one that is indicated by a comma:

> No puede entrar al edificio hoy; mañana sí podrá.
> *You can't enter the building today; tomorrow you can.*

2. A semi-colon is also used when two long sentences are joined by a conjunction or a transitional phrase:

> Le dijo al dueño que todavía tiene problemas con el apartamento; por ejemplo, el espejo en el baño está roto y el piso de la cocina tiene manchas negras.
>
> *He told the owner that he still has problems with the apartment; for example, the mirror in the bathroom is broken and the floor in the kitchen has black stains.*

- The *colon* (los dos puntos) indicates a long pause in a sentence, and serves to clarify or complete what was written earlier. It also has two main uses in a sentence:

  1. It introduces a list of words or a series of phrases:

  > Saqué todo de la billetera: el dinero, la licencia, las tarjetas de crédito, las fotos y algunas tarjetas de negocio.
  >
  > *I took everything out of my wallet: money, license, credit cards, photos, and some business cards.*

  2. It also introduces a direct quote:

  > La ley es my clara: una multa de cincuenta dólares.
  >
  > *The law is clear: a fifty-dollar fine.*

- The *apostrophe* is not used in Spanish, and *quotation marks* (las comillas) are primarily used to indicate the words of a direct quote. The *dash* (–) is generally used in dialogue instead of quotation marks, to denote the change of speaker:

  > Carlota me dijo–¡Ándate!–y yo me fui.
  >
  > *Carlota told me, "Go outside!" and I left.*

LA PRÁCTICA 1

Correct the punctuation in the following sentences:

1. La vecina me explicaba tu madre ya no tiene marido

   La vecina, me explicaba tu madre, ya no tiene marido.

2. No no vamos al desierto hoy

   _____

3. Favor de traer el tenedor el plato y el vaso

_____

4. El capitán me dijo en voz baja Siéntate y cállate y yo me senté.

_____

5. Es decir hay tanto sufrimiento en el mundo

_____

6. Cuándo va a llover

_____

7. Es cierto lo que dices sin embargo todos no están de acuerdo

_____

8. No sé Emilio qué vas a hacer con tu vida

_____

9. Nos dio una lista las medias los zapatos los pantalones y la camisa

_____

10. Sí ya hemos comido

_____

_____

Letter Writing
La correspondencia

Another important aspect of written communication is letter writing. Whether mail-delivered or by e-mail, there are two basic kinds of letters; *formal* (used when applying for a job, when writing to someone in authority, etc.) and *informal* (used when writing to family, friends, etc.). The main parts of a typical letter written in Spain or Latin America are shown below. Notice how the form for any letter is generally the same as in English letter writing:

Sender's date in the upper right
Addressee information in the upper left
Closing in the lower right

The address number follows the street name, and regional codes will vary depending on the country.

Supermercados Garza
Avenida Colón, 675
Lima 18
Perú

Estimados señores:

Hemos recibido su carta del 10 de junio, 2006, pidiendo una lista de nuestros precios.

Adjunto les enviamos nuestra nueva lista.

Esperando sus gratas órdenes, saluda atte. a Uds.,

VENTAS NACIONALES, S.A.
Diego Alba Pérez
Gerente

The salutation in business is generally the same: "Estimado(s)...:". However, in more formal settings, salutations such as "Muy señor nuestro:" or "Muy señora mía:" may be used. The closing, "Muy atentamente," (or "Saluda atte. a Ud(s).") is the most common. The phrase "A quien le corresponda:" literally means "To Whom It May Concern:".

An informal letter looks the same as the model shown, but usually includes the salutation "Querido(s)...," and a personal closing that ranges from "Con mucho cariño," to "Saludos a todos,".

LA PRÁCTICA 2

Try to guess what these Spanish words and phrases would mean in English. They are used regularly in written correspondence:

1. Cordialmente,   ___*Cordially,*___

2. Respetable señora: _____

3. Afectuosamente, _____

4. Distinguido señor, _____

5. Saluda atte. a Ud., _____

6. Recibe un abrazo de tu amigo, _____

7. Respetuosamente, _____

8. Con afecto y admiración se despide, _____

9. Gracias por su atención, _____

10. Con mi mayor respeto y consideración, _____

E-Mails
El correo electrónico

The parts of an e-mail are named as follows:

Tina	@	winner	.	provider	.	pe
NOMBRE DEL USARIO	ARROBA	NOMBRE DE DOMINIO	PUNTO	EL PROVEEDOR DE ACCESO AL INTERNET	PUNTO	EL PAÍS
(user name)	*(at)*	*(domain name)*	*(dot)*	*(provider)*	*(dot)*	*(country)*

Notice that *.com, .edu, .org,* etc. are not normal closings to an e-mail in other countries. The country such as .fr (France), .es (Spain), and .pe (Peru) each have their own abbreviation.

In Spanish, computer vocabulary is often the same as in English (el CD-ROM, el DVD, el (sometimes la) internet, etc.). However, these other words might be useful, too:

application	la aplicación
attachment	el adjunto
browser	el navegador
cable	el cable
to click	pulsar
computer	la computadora (Spain: el ordenador)
computer file	el fichero
to connect	conectar
connection	la conección
data base	la base de datos
to delete	eliminar
disc	el disco
to download	descargar
drive	la disquetera
e-mail	el correo electrónico
to file	archivar
to find	encontrar
folder	el directorio
to forward	reenviar
hard drive	el disco duro
home page	la página inicial
keyboard	el teclado
laptop	la computadora portátil
mailbox	el buzón
menu	el menú
message	el mensaje
monitor	el monitor
mouse	el ratón
password	la contaseña
to print	imprimir
program	el programa
to receive	recibir
to reply	responder

to save	ahorrar
to search	buscar
search engine	el buscador
to select	escoger
to send	enviar
server	el servidor
screen	la pantalla
trash	la basura
website	el sitio web

LA PRÁCTICA 3

Translate these words and symbols related to e-mail into Spanish:

1. @   arroba _____

2. password _____

3. user name _____

4. to click _____

5. e-mail _____

6. " . " _____

7. website _____

8. message _____

9. provider _____

10. to delete _____

POR SU CUENTA

Go online in Spanish and find out what these other words mean:

1. la charla _____

2. la marcapáginas _____

3. el apodo _____

4. navegar _____

5. la portada _____

6. la buzonfía _____

7. inalámbrica _____

8. la mensajería instantánea _____

9. estar en línea _____

10. enlazar _____

CROSSWORD 12

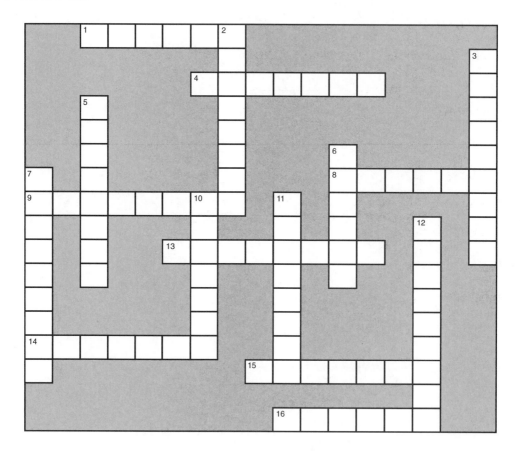

Translate these into Spanish:

Across
1. to search
4. to receive
8. to click
9. to delete
13. to connect
14. to choose
15. to turn on
16. to send

Down
2. to forward
3. to download
5. to print
6. to turn off
7. to reply
10. to save
11. to file
12. to find

EL REPASO

Review everything in this book by answering one question about information presented in each chapter. Try not to ask for help:

CH 1:   Say the Spanish alphabet.

CH 2:   Say a sentence in Spanish and identify the subject.

CH 3:   Say three sentences in Spanish using the present tense.

CH 4:   Say one sentence using the preterit and one using the imperfect.

CH 5:   Say one sentence in the future tense and one in the conditional.

CH 6:   Name three reflexive verbs in Spanish.

CH 7:   Say four sentences using the present and past perfect tenses.

CH 8:   Say four sentences using the present and past progressive.

CH 9:   Say two sentences using the passive voice in Spanish.

CH 10: Say four sentences using the present and past subjunctive.

CH 11: Give two formal and two informal commands in Spanish.

CH 12: Use the **verb + de + infinitive** construction in a sentence.

CH 13: Explain the difference between a definite and indefinite article.

CH 14: Name ten Spanish nationalities (in Spanish).

CH 15: Name three demonstrative and three possessive adjectives.

CH 16: Explain the basic uses of direct and indirect object pronouns.

CH 17: Name five relative pronouns in Spanish.

CH 18: Explain how most adverbs are formed in Spanish.

CH 19: Name six common prepositions in Spanish.

CH 20: Name six common interrogative words in Spanish.

CH 21: Name five words that express negation in Spanish.

CH 22: Name one diminutive and one augmentative ending.

CH 23: Count from one to ten using ordinal numbers in Spanish.

CH 24: Make five different comments about the weather in Spanish.

CH 25: Spend two full minutes talking about yourself in Spanish.

CH 26: Name five synonyms and five antonyms in Spanish.

CH 27: Name three idioms and one proverb in Spanish.

CH 28: Name three ways a comma is used in a Spanish sentence.

Culture Capsule 4

The Geography of Latin America
La geografía de Latinoamérica

América Latina comprende todo el territorio localizado al sur de los Estados Unidos. Los países principales incluyen México en la América del Norte; Costa Rica, Cuba, El Salvador, Guatemala, Honduras, Nicaragua, Panamá, Puerto Rico, y República Dominicana en la América Central y el mar Caribe; y Argentina, Bolivia, Brasil, Chile, Colombia, Ecuador, Paraguay, Perú, Uruguay y Venezuela en la América del Sur.

Estos países fueron antiguas colonias de países europeos, por lo general España y Portugal. Aunque muestran similitudes culturales, los países latinoamericanos observan también diferencias lingüísticas, étnicas, sociales y políticas. Se calcula que la población actual de América Latina cuenta con alrededor de 500 millones de habitantes, y se estima que para el año 2025 aumentará en 200 millones, lo que significa un crecimiento de 40%.

Geográficamente, los países latinoamericanos son muy diferentes. Por ejemplo, el país mexicano tiene regiones muy altas, incluyendo la Ciudad de México a casi 7.500 pies sobre el nivel del mar, mientras que Nicaragua es mayormente un territorio plano. En América del Sur también se encuentran regiones tan distintas como la cordillera de los Andes, las pampas Argentinas y la selva Amazónica. Estas diferencias geográficas también crean cambios climáticos. Por ejemplo, muchos países tienen zonas tropicales calurosas y húmedas, zonas desérticas secas y otras nevadas y altas. Naturalmente, semejante diversidad geográfica ejerce una tremenda influencia en el desarrollo económico y social de cada país.

PREGUNTAS

1. ¿En qué parte de Latinoamérica se encuentra la selva Amazónica?

2. ¿Qué fenómeno geográfico caracteriza a Latinoamérica?

3. ¿Cuál será la población de América Latina en 2025?

4. ¿Cuál es el país más pequeño en América del Sur?

5. ¿Por qué se ve la influencia europea en la arquitectura mexicana?

APPENDICES

Verb Charts

REGULAR VERBS						

INDICATIVE					**SUBJUNCTIVE**	
Present	**Imperfect**	**Preterit**	**Future**	**Conditional**	**Present**	**Imperfect**

Infin. hablar, *to speak; Pres. Part.,* hablando; *Past Part.,* hablado;
Imperative, habla, hablad

Present	Imperfect	Preterit	Future	Conditional	Present	Imperfect
hablo	hablaba	hablé	hablaré	hablaría	hable	hablara
hablas	hablabas	hablaste	hablarás	hablarías	hables	hablaras
habla	hablaba	habló	hablará	hablaría	hable	hablara
hablamos	hablábamos	hablamos	hablaremos	hablaríamos	hablemos	habláramos
habláis	hablabais	hablasteis	hablaréis	hablaríais	habléis	hablarais
hablan	hablaban	hablaron	hablarán	hablarían	hablen	hablaran

Infin., comer, *to eat; Pres. Part.,* comiendo; *Past Part.,* comido;
Imperative, come, comed

Present	Imperfect	Preterit	Future	Conditional	Present	Imperfect
como	comía	comí	comeré	comería	coma	comiera
comes	comías	comiste	comerás	comerías	comas	comieras
come	comía	comió	comerá	comerías	coma	comiera
comemos	comíamos	comimos	comeremos	comeríamos	comamos	comiéramos
coméis	comíais	comisteis	comeréis	comeríais	comáis	comierais
comen	comían	comieron	comerán	comerían	coman	comieran

Infin., escribir, *to write; Pres. Part.,* escribiendo; *Past Part.,* escrito;
Imperative, escribe, escribed

Present	Imperfect	Preterit	Future	Conditional	Present	Imperfect
escribo	escribía	escribí	escribiré	escribiría	escriba	escribiera
escribes	escribías	escribiste	escribirás	escribirías	escribas	escribieras
escribe	escribía	escribió	escribirá	escribiría	escriba	escribiera
escribimos	escribíamos	escribimos	escribiremos	escribiríamos	escriba-mos	escribiéra-mos
escribéis	escribíais	escribisteis	escribiréis	escribiríais	escribáis	escribierais
escriben	escribían	escribieron	escribirán	escribirían	escriban	escribieran

IRREGULAR VERBS

INDICATIVE					SUBJUNCTIVE	
Present	**Imperfect**	**Preterit**	**Future**	**Conditional**	**Present**	**Imperfect**

Infin., caber, *to fit; Pres. Part.,* cabiendo; *Past Part.,* cabido; *Imperative,* cabe, cabed

quepo	cabía	cupe	cabré	cabría	quepa	cupiera
cabes	cabías	cupiste	cabrás	cabrías	quepas	cupieras
cabe	cabía	cupo	cabrá	cabría	quepa	cupiera
cabemos	cabíamos	cupimos	cabremos	cabríamos	quepamos	cupiéramos
cabéis	cabíais	cupisteis	cabréis	cabríais	quepáis	cupierais
caben	cabían	cupieron	cabrán	cabrían	quepan	cupieran

Infin., caer, *to fall; Pres. Part.,* cayendo; *Past Part.,* caído; *Imperative,* cae, caed

caigo	caía	caí	caeré	caería	caiga	cayera
caes	caías	caíste	caerás	caerías	caigas	cayeras
cae	caía	cayó	caerá	caería	caigas	cayera
caemos	caíamos	caímos	caeremos	caeríamos	caigamos	cayéramos
caéis	caíais	caísteis	caeréis	caeríais	caigáis	cayerais
caen	caían	cayeron	caerán	caerían	caigan	cayeran

Infin., dar, *to give; Pres. Part.,* dando; *Past Part.,* dado; *Imperative,* da, dad

doy	daba	di	daré	daría	dé	diera
das	dabas	diste	darás	darías	des	dieras
da	daba	dio	dará	daría	dé	diera
damos	dábamos	dimos	daremos	daríamos	demos	diéramos
dais	dabais	disteis	daréis	daríais	deis	dierais
dan	daban	dieron	darán	darían	den	dieran

Infin., decir, *to say, to tell; Pres. Part.,* diciendo; *Past part.,* dicho; *Imperative,* di, decid

digo	decía	dije	diré	diría	diga	dijera
dices	decías	dijiste	dirás	dirías	digas	dijeras
dice	decía	dijo	dirá	diría	diga	dijera
decimos	decíamos	dijimos	diremos	diríamos	digamos	dijéramos
decís	decíais	dijisteis	diréis	diríais	digáis	dijerais
dicen	decían	dijeron	dirán	dirían	digan	dijeran

Infin., estar, *to be; Pres. Part.,* estando; *Past Part.,* estado; *Imperative,* está, estad

estoy	estaba	estuve	estaré	estaría	esté	estuviera
estás	estabas	estuviste	estarás	estarías	estés	estuvieras
está	estaba	estuvo	estará	estaría	esté	estuviera
estamos	estábamos	estuvimos	estaremos	estaríamos	estemos	estuviéramos
estáis	estabais	estuvisteis	estaréis	estaríais	estéis	estuvierais
están	estaban	estuvieron	estarán	estarían	estén	estuvieran

IRREGULAR VERBS

INDICATIVE					SUBJUNCTIVE	
Present	**Imperfect**	**Preterit**	**Future**	**Conditional**	**Present**	**Imperfect**

Infin., haber, *to have; Pres. Part.,* habiendo; *Past Part.,* habido; *Imperative (none)*

he	había	hube	habré	habría	haya	hubiera
has	habías	hubiste	habrás	habrías	hayas	hubieras
ha	había	hubo	habrá	habría	haya	hubiera
hemos	habíamos	hubimos	habremos	habríamos	hayamos	hubiéramos
habéis	habíais	hubisteis	habréis	habrâis	hayáis	hubierais
han	habían	hubieron	habrán	habrían	hayan	hubieran

Infin., hacer, *to do, to make; Pres. Part.,* haciendo; *Past Part.,* hecho;
Imperative, haz, haced

hago	hacía	hice	haré	haría	haga	hiciera
haces	hacías	hiciste	harás	harías	hagas	hicieras
hace	hacía	hizo	hará	haría	haga	hiciera
hacemos	hacíamos	hicimos	haremos	haríamos	hagamos	hiciéramos
hacéis	hacíais	hicisteis	haréis	haríais	hagáis	hicierais
hacen	hacían	hicieron	harán	harían	hagan	hicieran

Infin., ir, *to go; Pres. Part.,* yendo; *Past Part.,* ido; *Imperative,* ve, id

voy	iba	fui	iré	iría	vaya	fuera
vas	ibas	fuiste	irás	irías	vayas	fueras
va	iba	fue	irá	iría	vaya	fuera
vamos	íbmos	fuimos	iremos	iríamos	vayamos	fuéramos
vais	ibais	fuisteis	iréis	iríais	vayáis	fuerais
van	iban	fueron	irán	irían	vayan	fueran

Infin. oír, *to hear; Pres. Part.,* oyendo; *Past Part.,* oído; *Imperative,* oye, oíd

oigo	oía	oí	oiré	oiría	oiga	oyera
oyes	oías	oíste	oirás	oiríais	oigas	oyeras
oye	oía	oyó	oirá	oiría	oiga	oyera
oímos	oíamos	oímos	oiremos	oiríamos	oigamos	oyéramos
oís	oíais	oísteis	oiréis	oiríais	oigáis	oyerais
oyen	oían	oyeron	oirán	oirían	oigan	oyeran

Infin., poder, *to be able; Pres. Part.,* pudiendo; *Past Part.,* podido; *Imperative (none)*

puedo	podía	pude	podré	podría	pueda	pudiera
puedes	podías	pudiste	podrás	podrías	puedas	pudieras
puede	podía	pudo	podrá	podría	pueda	pudiera
podemos	podíamos	pudimos	podremos	podríamos	podamos	pudiéramos
podéis	podíais	pudisteis	podréis	podríais	podáis	pudierais
pueden	podían	pudieron	podrán	podrían	puedan	pudieran

IRREGULAR VERBS

	INDICATIVE				SUBJUNCTIVE	
Present	Imperfect	Preterit	Future	Conditional	Present	Imperfect

Infin., poner, *to put, to place; Pres. Part.,* poniendo; *Past Part.,* puesto;
Imperative, pon, poned

pongo	ponía	puse	pondré	pondría	ponga	pusiera
pones	ponías	pusiste	pondrás	pondrías	pongas	pusieras
pone	ponía	puso	pondrá	pondría	ponga	pusiera
ponemos	poníamos	pusimos	pondremos	pondríamos	pongamos	pusiéramos
ponéis	poníais	pusisteis	pondréis	pondríais	pongáis	pusierais
ponen	ponían	pusieron	pondrán	pondrían	pongan	pusieran

Infin., querer, *to wish, to like; Pres. Part.,* queriendo; *Past Part.,* querido;
Imperative, quiere, quered

quiero	quería	quise	querré	querría	quiera	quisiera
quieres	querías	quisiste	querrás	querrías	quieras	quisieras
quiere	quería	quiso	querrá	querría	quiera	quisiera
queremos	queríamos	quisimos	querremos	querríamos	queramos	quisiéramos
queréis	queríais	quisisteis	querréis	querríais	queráis	quisierais
quieren	querían	quisieron	querrán	querrían	quieran	quisieran

Infin., saber, *to know; Pres. Part.,* sabiendo; *Past Part.,* sabido; *Imperative,* sabe, sabed

sé	sabía	supe	sabré	sabría	sepa	supiera
sabes	sabías	supiste	sabrás	sabrías	sepas	supieras
sabe	sabía	supo	sabrá	sabría	sepa	supiera
sabemos	sabíamos	supimos	sabremos	sabríamos	sepamos	supiéramos
sabéis	sabíais	supisteis	sabréis	sabríais	sepáis	supierais
saben	sabían	supieron	sabrán	sabrían	sepan	supieran

Infin., salir, *to leave; Pres. Part.,* saliendo; *Past Part.,* salido; *Imperative,* sal, salid

salgo	salía	salí	saldré	saldría	salga	saliera
sales	salías	saliste	saldrás	saldrías	salgas	salieras
sale	salía	salío	saldrá	saldría	salga	saliera
salimos	salíamos	salimos	saldremos	saldríamos	salgamos	saliéramos
salís	salíais	salisteis	saldréis	saldríais	salgáis	salierais
salen	salían	salieron	saldrán	saldrían	salgan	salieran

Infin., ser, *to be; Pres. Part.,* siendo; *Past Part.,* sido; *Imperative,* sé, sed

soy	era	fui	seré	sería	sea	fuera
eres	eras	fuiste	serás	serías	seas	fueras
es	era	fue	será	sería	sea	fuera
somo	éramos	fuimos	seremos	seríamos	seamos	fuéramos
sois	erais	fuisteis	seréis	seríais	seáis	fuerais
son	eran	fueron	serán	serían	sean	fueran

IRREGULAR VERBS

	INDICATIVE				SUBJUNCTIVE	
Present	**Imperfect**	**Preterit**	**Future**	**Conditional**	**Present**	**Imperfect**

Infin., **tener**, *to have, Pres. Part.,* **teniendo**; *Past Part.,* **tenido**; *Imperative,* **ten**, **tened**

tengo	tenía	tuve	tendré	tendría	tenga	tuviera
tienes	tenías	tuviste	tendrás	tendrías	tengas	tuvieras
tiene	tenía	tuvo	tendrá	tendría	tenga	tuviera
tenemos	teníamos	tuvimos	tendremos	tendríamos	tengamos	tuviéramos
tenéis	teníais	tuvisteis	tendréis	tendríais	tengáis	tuvierais
tienen	tenían	tuvieron	tendrán	tendrían	tengan	tuvieran

Infin., **traer**, *to bring; Pres. Part.,* **trayendo**; *Past Part.,* **traído**; *Imperative,* **trae**, **traed**

traigo	traía	traje	traeré	traería	traiga	trajera
traes	traías	trajiste	traerás	traerías	traigas	trajeras
trae	traía	trajo	traerá	traería	traiga	trajera
traemos	traíamos	trajimos	traeremos	traeríamos	traigamos	trajéramos
traéis	traíais	trajisteis	traeréis	traeríais	traigáis	trajerais
traen	traían	trajeron	traerán	traerían	traigan	trajeran

Infin., **valer**, *to be worth; Pres. Part.,* **valiendo**; *Past Part.,* **valido**; *Imperative,* **val**, **valed**

valgo	valía	valí	valdré	valdría	valga	valiera
vales	valías	valiste	valdrás	valdrías	valgas	valieras
vale	valía	valió	valdrá	valdría	valga	valiera
valemos	valíamos	valimos	valdremos	valdríamos	valgamos	valiéramos
valéis	valíais	valisteis	valdréis	valdríais	valgáis	valierais
valen	valían	valieron	valdrán	valdrían	valgan	valieran

Infin., **venir**, *to come; Pres. Part.,* **viniendo**; *Past Part.,* **venido**; *Imperative,* **ven**, **venid**

vengo	venía	vine	vendré	vendría	venga	viniera
vienes	venías	viniste	vendrás	vendrías	vengas	vinieras
viene	venía	vino	vendrá	vendría	venga	viniera
venimos	veníamos	vinimos	vendremos	vendríamos	vengamos	viniéramos
venís	veníais	vinisteis	vendréis	vendríais	vengáis	vinierais
vienen	venían	vinieron	vendrán	vendrían	vengan	vinieran

Infin., **ver**, *to see; Pres. Part.,* **viendo**; *Past Part.,* **visto**; *Imperative,* **ve**, **ved**

veo	veía	vi	veré	vería	vea	viera
ves	veías	viste	verás	verías	veas	vieras
ve	veía	vió	verá	vería	vea	viera
vemos	veíamos	vimos	veremos	veríamos	veamos	viéramos
veis	veíais	visteis	veréis	veríais	veáis	vierais
ven	veían	vieron	verán	verían	vean	vieran

Common Words in Spanish

A

a	un *or* una
a little bit	poquito, -a
a lot	mucho, -a
above	encima
address	la dirección
after	después
all	todo, -a, -os, -as
almost	casi
always	siempre
American	americano
an	un *or* una
and	y
angry	enojado, -a
animal	el animal
another	otro, -a
apartment	el apartamento
apple	la manzana
April	abril
arm	el brazo
armchair	el sillón
art	el arte
aspirin	la aspirina
at	en
attic	el desván
August	agosto
aunt	la tía

B

baby	el/la bebé
back	la espalda
bad	malo
bag	la bolsa
ball	la pelota
banana	el plátano
bank	el banco
baseball	el béisbol

basement	el sótano
basketball	el baloncesto
bathroom	el baño
bathtub	la tina
beach	la playa
beans	los frijoles
bed	la cama
bedroom	el dormitorio
bee	la abeja
before	antes
behind	detrás
belt	el cinturón
benches	los bancos
bicycle	la bicicleta
big	grande
bird	el pájaro
black	negro, -a, -os, -as
blackboard	el pizarrón
blanket	la frazada
blouse	la blusa
blue	azul
boat	el bote
body	el cuerpo
book	el libro
bookshelf	el librero
boots	las botas
bottle	la botella
bowl	el plato hondo
boy	el niño
bracelet	el brazalete
brave	valiente
bread	el pan
breakfast	el desayuno
bridge	el puente
broom	la escoba
brother	el hermano
brown	café
bucket	el balde

building	el edificio
bus	el autobús
bush	el arbusto
but	pero
butter	la mantequilla

C

cabinet	el gabinete
cake	la torta
calendar	el calendario
camera	la cámara
candle	la vela
candy	los dulces
cap	la gorra
car	el carro, el auto
carpet	la alfombra
carrot	la zanahoria
cat	el gato, la gata
ceiling	el techo
celery	el apio
chair	la silla
chalk	la tiza
chapter	el capítulo
cheap	barato, -a, -os, -as
cheese	el queso
chest	el pecho
chicken	el pollo
children	los niños
chimney	la chimenea
chocolate	el chocolate
church	la iglesia
city	la ciudad
class	la clase
classroom	el salón de clase
clean	limpio, -a, -os, -as
clock	el reloj
closed	cerrado, -a, -os, -as
closet	el ropero
clothes	la ropa
cloud	la nube
coffee	el café
coin	la moneda
cold (flu)	el resfriado
cold (temperature)	el frío
color	el color
comb	el peine
computer	la computadora, el ordenador
cook	el cocinero

cookies	las galletas
corn	el maíz
corner	la esquina
couch	el sofá
cough	la tos
country	el país
cousin	el primo
cow	la vaca
crazy	loco, -a, -os, -as
cup	la taza
curtains	las cortinas

D

dancing	el baile
dangerous	peligroso
dark	oscuro, -a, -os, -as
daughter	la hija
day	el día
December	diciembre
deer	el venado
dentist	el/la dentista
desert	el desierto
desk	el escritorio
dessert	el postre
different	diferente
dining room	el comedor
dinner	la cena
dirt	la tierra
dirty	sucio, -a, -os, -as
dishes	los trastes
doctor	el doctor, -a
dog	el perro
dollar	el dólar
door	la puerta
down	abajo
drawing	el dibujo
dress	el vestido
dresser	el tocador
drinks	las bebidas
dry	seco, -a, -os, -as
dryer	la secadora
duck	el pato

E

each	cada
ear	la oreja, el oído
early	temprano
earrings	los aretes

easy	fácil
eggs	los huevos
eight	ocho
eighteen	dieciocho
eighty	ochenta
elevator	el ascensor
eleven	once
empty	vacío, -a, -os, -as
end	el fín
engine	el motor
English	el inglés, -a, -os, -as
enough	bastante
envelope	el sobre
eraser	el borrador
everybody	todos
excellent	excelente
excited	emocionado
expensive	caro, -a, -os, -as
eye	el ojo

F

face	la cara
factory	la fábrica
fall (season)	el otoño
family	la familia
fantastic	fantástico, -a, -os, -as
far	lejos
farm	la finca, la granja
fat	gordo, -a, -os, -as
father	el padre
fast	rápido, -a, -os, -as
faucet	el grifo
favorite	favorito, -a, -os, -as
February	febrero
fence	la cerca
fever	la fiebre
few	pocos, -as,
fifteen	quince
fifty	cincuenta
fine	bien
firefighter	el/la bombero
first	primero
fish	el pescado
five	cinco
flag	la bandera
floor	el piso
flower	la flor
fly	la mosca
food	la comida

foot	el pie
for	para, por
forest	el bosque
fork	el tenedor
forty	cuarenta
four	cuatro
fourteen	catorce
french fries	las papas fritas
Friday	viernes
friend	el amigo, la amiga
from	de
fruit	la fruta
frying pan	el sartén
full	lleno, -a, -os, -as
fun	la diversión
funny	chistoso, -as, -os, -as
furniture	los muebles

G

game	el juego, el partido
garage	el garaje
garden	el jardín
gas station	la gasolinera
gate	el portón
girl	la niña
glass	el vaso
glove	el guante
God	Dios
good	bueno, -a, -os, -as
good-bye	adiós
grandfather	el abuelo
grandmother	la abuela
grape	la uva
grass	el pasto
gray	gris
green	verde
guitar	la guitarra
gum	el chicle

H

hair	el pelo
hairbrush	el cepillo
haircut	el corte de pelo
hallway	el pasillo
ham	el jamón
hambuger	la hamburguesa
hammer	el martillo
hand	la mano

handkerchief	el pañuelo	**L**	
handsome	guapo, -a, -os, -as	ladder	la escalera
happy	feliz	lady (Mrs.)	Señora (Sra.)
hard (difficult)	difícil	lake	el lago
he	él	lamp	la lámpara
head	la cabeza	language	el lenguaje, la lengua
headache	el dolor de cabeza	last	último, -a, -os, -as
heart	el corazón	late	tarde
helicopter	el helicóptero	later	luego
her	su (de ella)	lazy	perezoso, -a, -os, -as
here	aquí, acá	left	izquierda
highway	la carretera	leg	la pierna
hill	el cerro	less	menos
his	su (de él)	lettuce	la lechuga
homework	la tarea	library	la biblioteca
honey	la miel	lights	las luces
horse	el caballo	little	chico, -a, -os, -as
hose	la manguera	living room	la sala
hospital	el hospital	long	largo, -a, -os, -as
hot	caliente	love	el amor
hotel	el hotel	lunch	el almuerzo
hour	la hora		
house	la casa		
hug	el abrazo	**M**	
husband	el esposo	magazine	la revista
		mail carrier	el cartero
		mail	el correo
I		mailbox	el buzón
I	yo	man	el hombre
ice cream	el helado	many	muchos, -as
ice	el hielo	map	el mapa
important	importante	March	marzo
in front	enfrente	May	mayo
in	en	meat	la carne
inside	adentro, dentro	mechanic	el/la mecánico
		medicine	la medicina
		milk	la leche
J		minute	el minuto
jacket	la chaqueta	mirror	el espejo
January	enero	Mister (Mr.)	Señor (Sr.)
joke	el chiste	Miss (Ms.)	Señorita (Srta.)
juice	el jugo	Monday	lunes
July	julio	money	el dinero
June	junio	month	el mes
		moon	la luna
		mop	el trapeador
K		more	más
key	la llave	morning	la mañana
kiss	el beso	mother	la madre
kitchen	la cocina	motorcycle	la motocicleta
knife	el cuchillo		

mountain	la montaña	or	o
mouse	el ratón, la ratona	orange (color)	anaranjado, -a, -os, -as
mouth	la boca		
movies	el cine	orange (fruit)	la naranja
mud	el lodo	our	nuestro, -a, -os, -as
music	la música	outside	afuera
my	mi	overcoat	el abrigo

N

nail	el clavo
name	el nombre
napkin	la servilleta
near	cerca
necessary	necesario
neck	el cuello
necklace	el collar
neighbor	el vecino, la vecina
never	nunca
new	nuevo, -a, -os, -as
newspaper	el periódico
nice	simpatico, -a, -os, -as
night	la noche
nine	nueve
nineteen	diecinueve
ninety	noventa
no one	nadie
none	ninguno, -a, -os, -as
nose	la nariz
not	no
nothing	nada
November	noviembre
now	ahora
number	el número
nurse	el enfermero, la enfermera

O

October	octubre
of	de
office	la oficina
old	viejo, -a, -os, -as
on	en
one hundred	cien
one thousand	mil
one	uno
onion	la cebolla
only	solamente
open	abierto, -a, -os, -as

P

page	la página
paint	la pintura
pajamas	el piyama
pants	los pantalones
paper	el papel
parents	los padres
park	el parque
party	la fiesta
pen	el lapicero
pencil	el lápiz
people	la gente
pepper	la pimienta
person	la persona
pet	el animal doméstico
phone number	el número de teléfono
photo	la foto
pie	el pastel
pig	el puerco
pillow	la almohada
pilot	el/la piloto
pink	rosado, -a, -os, -as
place	el lugar
plane	el avión
plant	la planta
plate	el plato
please	por favor
pliers	las pinzas
police officer	el policía, la agente de policía
police	la policía
pool	la piscina
poor	pobre
possible	posible
post office	la oficina de correos
pot	la olla
potato	la papa
present	el regalo
pretty	bonito, -a, -os, -as
proud	orgulloso, -a, -os, -as

purple	morado, -a, -os, -as	sheet	la sábana
purse	la cartera	shirt	la camisa
puzzle	el rompecabezas	shoes	los zapatos
		short	bajo, -a, -os, -as
		shorts	los pantalones cortos
R		shoulder	el hombro
radio	el radio	shovel	la pala
rain	la lluvia	shower	la ducha
raincoat	el impermeable	side	el lado
rake	el rastrillo	sidewalk	la banqueta
reading	la lectura	sign	el letrero
red	rojo, -a, -os, -as	sink	el lavabo
refrigerator	el refrigerador	sister	la hermana
restaurant	el restaurante	six	seis
restroom	el servicio	sixteen	dieciséis
rice	el arroz	sixty	sesenta
rich	rico, -a, -os, -as	size	el tamaño
right	derecho	skirt	la falda
ring	el anillo	slippers	las pantuflas
river	el río	slow	lento, -a, -os, -as
road	el camino	smart	inteligente, -s
rock	la piedra	smile	la sonrisa
room	el cuarto, la pieza	snake	la culebra
		snow	la nieve
		soap	el jabón
S		soccer	el fútbol
sad	triste	socks	los calcetines
salad	la ensalada	soda	el refresco
salesperson	el vendedor, la	soldier	el/la soldado
	vendedora	some	algunos, -as
salt	la sal	someone	alguien
same	mismo, -a, -os, -as	something	algo
Saturday	sábado	sometimes	a veces
saucer	el platillo	son	el hijo
saw	el serrucho	song	la canción
scarf	la bufanda	soon	pronto
school	la escuela	soup	la sopa
science	la ciencia	space	el espacio
scissors	las tijeras	Spanish	el español
screwdriver	el atornillador	special	especial
sea	el mar	spider	la araña
second	segundo, -a, -os, -as	sponge	la esponja
secretary	el secretario, la	spoon	la cuchara
	secretaria	sports	los deportes
September	septiembre	spring	la primavera
seven	siete	stairs	las escaleras
seventeen	diecisiete	star	la estrella
seventy	setenta	state	el estado
she	ella	steak	el bistec
sheep	la oveja		

stereo	el estéreo	to	a
stomach	el estómago	today	hoy
stomachache	el dolor de estómago	together	juntos, -as
store	la tienda	toilet	el excusado
story	el cuento	tomato	el tomate
stove	la estufa	tomorrow	mañana
strawberry	la fresa	tool	la herramienta
street	la calle	toothbrush	el cepillo de dientes
strong	fuerte, -s	toothpaste	la pasta de dientes
student	el/la estudiante	towel	la toalla
subway	el metro	town	el pueblo
sugar	el azúcar	toy	el juguete
suit	el traje	traffic light	el semáforo
Sunday	domingo	train	el tren
supermarket	el supermercado	trash can	el bote de basura
sweater	el suéter	tree	el árbol
sweet	dulce	truck	el camión
		t-shirt	la camiseta
		Tuesday	martes
T		turkey	el pavo
table	la mesa	twelve	doce
tall	alto, -a, -os, -as	twenty	veinte
tea	el té	two	dos
teacher	el maestro, la maestra		
team	el equipo	**U**	
teeth	los dientes	ugly	feo, -a, -os, -as
telephone	el teléfono	under	abajo
television	el televisor	underwear	la ropa interior
ten	diez	United States	los Estados Unidos
thanks	gracias	up	arriba
that	eso, -a, aquel, -la		
the	el, la, los, las	**V**	
their	su (de ellos)	vacation	las vacaciones
then	entonces	vacuum cleaner	la aspiradora
there	allí, ahí, allá	vegetables	los vegetales, las verduras
these	estos, estas		
thin	delgado, -a, -os, -as	very	muy
thing	la cosa	vitamin	la vitamina
third	tercero		
thirteen	trece		
thirty	treinta	**W**	
this	esto, -a	waiter	el mesero, la mesera
those	esos, -as	wall	la pared
throat	la garganta	wallet	la billetera
three	tres	washer	la lavadora
Thursday	jueves	watch	el reloj
tie	la corbata	water	el agua
time	el tiempo	we	nosotros
tired	cansado, -o, -os, -as	weak	débil, -es

weather	el clima	**Y**	
Wednesday	miércoles	yard	el patio
week	la semana	year	el año
white	blanco, -a, -os, -as	yellow	amarillo, -a, -os, -as
wife	la esposa	yes	sí
window	la ventana	yesterday	ayer
winter	el invierno	you (formal)	usted, ustedes
with	con	you (informal)	tú, vosotros
without	sin	young	joven
woman	la mujer	your	tu, su, vuestro,
word	la palabra		vuestra
work	el trabajo		
worker	el trabajador, la		
	trabajadora	**Z**	
world	el mundo	zero	cero

Common Expressions in Spanish

And you? — ¿Y tú?, ¿Y usted?

At night — De noche

At__o'clock — A las ___.

Congratulations! — ¡Felicitaciones!

Do you have __? — ¿Tiene(s) ___?

Do you know __? — ¿Sabe(s) ___?

Do you like __? — ¿Te (le) gusta(n) ___?

Do you need help? — ¿Necesita(s) ayuda?

Do you understand? — ¿Entiende(s)?

Do you want __? — ¿Quiere(s) ___?

Excuse me. — Con permiso.

Good afternoon. — Buenas tardes.

Good luck! — ¡Buena suerte!

Good morning. — Buenos días.

Good night. — Buenas noches.

Happy Birthday! — ¡Feliz cumpleaños!

Hi! — ¡Hola!

How are you? — ¿Cómo está(s)?

How many? — ¿Cuántos?, ¿Cuántas?

How much? — ¿Cuánto?

How old are you? — ¿Cuántos años tiene(s)?

How pretty! — ¡Qué bonito!

How's that? — ¿Cómo?

How's the weather? — ¿Qué tiempo hace?

I don't know. — No sé.

I don't remember. — No recuerdo.

I don't understand. — No entiendo.

I need the __. — Necesito ___.

I want the __. — Quiero ___.

I'm hungry. — Tengo hambre.

I'm sick. — Estoy enfermo, -a.

I'm sorry. — Lo siento.

I'm thirsty. — Tengo sed.

It's __ o'clock. — Son las ___.

It's cold. — Hace frío.

It's hot. — Hace calor.

It's raining. — Está lloviendo.

It's snowing. — Está nevando.

It's sunny. — Hace sol.

Let's go to the __. — Vamos a ___.

Me, too. — Yo, también.

Merry Christmas! — ¡Feliz Navidad!

My name is __. — Me llamo ___.

Not much. — Sin novedad.

See you later. — Hasta luego.

Speak more slowly. — Habla (Hable) más despacio.

Sure. — Claro.

Thanks a lot. — Muchas gracias.

There is/are __. — Hay ___.

Very well. — Muy bien.

Welcome! — ¡Bienvenido(s)!

What time is it? — ¿Qué hora es?

What? — ¿Qué?

What's going on? — ¿Qué pasa?

What's the date? — ¿Cuál es la fecha?

What's the matter? — ¿Qué te (le) pasa?

What's your name? — ¿Cómo (se) te llama(s)?

When? — ¿Cuándo?

Where do you live? — ¿Dónde vive(s)?

Where is __? — ¿Dónde está ___?

Where? — ¿Dónde?

Which? — ¿Cuál?

Who? — ¿Quién?

Why? — ¿Por qué?

You're welcome. — De nada.

Common Verbs in Spanish

A

absorb, to	absorber
accept, to	aceptar
acquire, to	adquirir
add, to	agregar, añadir
adhere, to	adherir
adjust, to	ajustar
advance, to	avanzar
advise, to	advertir
affirm, to	afirmar
agree, to	convenir
alienate, to	alienar
allow, to	dejar
alter, to	alterar
analyze, to	analizar
anger, to	enojar
annul, to	anular
answer, to	contestar
appear, to	aparecer
appreciate, to	apreciar
arrange, to	arreglar
arrest, to	arrestar
arrive, to	llegar
ascend, to	ascender
ask for, to	pedir
ask, to	preguntar
assist, to	asistir
attack, to	atacar
attend, to	atender
attract, to	atraer
authorize, to	autorizar

B

balance, to	equilibrar
be able to, to	poder
be born, to	nacer
be, to	estar, ser
be missing, to	faltar
be worth, to	valer
bear, to	aguantar
beat, to	batir
beg, to	suplicar
begin, to	comenzar, empezar
believe, to	creer
belong, to	pertenecer
bend, to	doblar
bet, to	apostar
bite, to	morder
bleed, to	sangrar
block, to	impedir
blow, to	soplar
boil, to	hervir
break, to	quebrar, romper
breathe, to	respirar
bring, to	traer
build, to	construir
burst, to	estallar
buy, to	comprar

C

call, to	llamar
calm, to	calmar
caress, to	acariciar
carry, to	llevar
catch, to	atrapar
cause, to	causar
change, to	cambiar
charge, to	cargar
chat, to	platicar
choose, to	escoger
circulate, to	circular
clean, to	limpiar
climb, to	subir
close, to	cerrar

collect, to	coleccionar	direct, to	dirigir
come, to	venir	discover, to	descubrir
communicate, to	comunicar	discuss, to	discutir
compensate, to	compensar	dissolve, to	disolver
compete, to	competir	distinguish, to	distinguir
concede, to	conceder	distract, to	distraer
conceive, to	concebir	distribute, to	distribuir
concentrate, to	concentrar	divide, to	dividir
conclude, to	concluir	do, to	hacer
confuse, to	confundir	draw, to	dibujar
consent, to	consentir	dream, to	soñar
conserve, to	conservar	drink, to	beber, tomar
consider, to	considerar	drive, to	manejar
consist, to	consistir	dry, to	secar
consult, to	consultar		
contain, to	contener		
contract, to	contraer	**E**	
contribute, to	contribuir	earn, to	ganar
control, to	controlar	eat, to	comer
converse, to	conversar	eliminate, to	eliminar
convert, to	convertir	empty, to	vaciar
convince, to	convencer	end, to	acabar, terminar
cook, to	cocinar	enter, to	entrar
correct, to	corregir	entertain, to	entretener
cost, to	costar	escape, to	huir
count, to	contar	evacuate, to	evacuar
cover, to	cubrir, tapar	evaluate, to	evaluar
crash, to	chocar	examine, to	examinar
cross, to	cruzar, atravesar	exchange, to	cambiar
cry, to	llorar	exist, to	existir
cure, to	curar	explain, to	explicar
cut, to	cortar	explore, to	explorar

D		**F**	
dance, to	bailar	facilitate, to	facilitar
decide, to	decidir	fall, to	caer
declare, to	declarar	fear, to	temer
dedicate, to	dedicar	feed, to	alimentar
defend, to	defender	feel, to	sentir
deliver, to	entregar	fight, to	pelear
deny, to	negar	fill, to	llenar
depend, to	depender	find, to	encontrar
describe, to	describir	find out, to	averiguar
desire, to	desear	fish, to	pescar
destroy, to	destruir	fit, to	caber
detain, to	detener	fix, to	componer
die, to	morir	flee, to	huir
dig, to	excavar	fly, to	volar
diminish, to	disminuir	follow, to	seguir

forget, to	olvidar	**J**	
forgive, to	perdonar	judge, to	juzgar
form, to	formar	jump, to	saltar
freeze, to	congelar		
frighten, to	espantar		
function, to	funcionar	**K**	
		keep, to	guardar
G		kick, to	patear
get down, to	bajar	kiss, to	besar
get near, to	acercar	know	
get, to	obtener	(someone), to	conocer
give, to	dar	know (something),	
go, to	ir	to	saber
go out, to	salir		
grind, to	moler	**L**	
grow, to	crecer	lay, to	colocar
		lead, to	guiar
		learn, to	aprender
H		leave, to	salir
hang, to	colgar	lend, to	prestar
happen, to	suceder	let, to	permitir
hate, to	odiar	lie, to	mentir
have, to	haber, tener	lift, to	levantar
hear, to	oír	light, to	encender
help, to	ayudar	like, to	gustar
hide, to	esconder	listen, to	escuchar
hire, to	contratar	live, to	vivir
hit, to	pegar	look, to	mirar
hold, to	detener	loosen, to	soltar
hug, to	abrazar	lose, to	perder
hunt, to	cazar	love, to	amar
hurt, to	doler		
		M	
		maintain, to	mantener
I		make, to	hacer
imagine, to	imaginar	mark, to	marcar
include, to	incluir	mean, to	significar
indicate, to	indicar	measure, to	medir
inform, to	informar	meet, to	encontrar
inhibit, to	inhibir	melt, to	derretir
injure, to	herir	move, to	mover
insert, to	meter		
insist, to	insistir	**N**	
install, to	instalar		
interpret, to	interpretar	need, to	necesitar
invest, to	invertir	note, to	notar
investigate, to	investigar	notify, to	notificar
involve, to	envolver		

O

obey, to	obedecer
oblige, to	obligar
observe, to	observar
obstruct, to	obstruir
obtain, to	obtener
occur, to	ocurrir
offend, to	ofender
offer, to	ofrecer
omit, to	omitir
open, to	abrir
operate, to	operar
oppose, to	oponer
order, to	ordenar
owe, to	deber

P

park, to	estacionar
pay, to	pagar
perceive, to	percibir
permit, to	permitir
persist, to	persistir
pick up, to	recoger
plant, to	plantar
play, to	jugar
plug in, to	enchufar
polish, to	bruñir, pulir
practice, to	practicar
pray, to	rezar
prefer, to	preferir
prepare, to	preparar
present, to	presentar
prevent, to	prevenir
proceed, to	proceder
produce, to	producir
progress, to	progresar
prohibit, to	prohibir
promise, to	prometer
pronounce, to	pronunciar
propose, to	proponer
protect, to	proteger
prove, to	probar
publish, to	publicar
pull, to	jalar, tirar
push, to	empujar
put, to	poner

Q

quit, to	renunciar

R

rain, to	llover
reach, to	alcanzar
read, to	leer
receive, to	recibir
recognize, to	reconocer
recommend, to	recomendar
reduce, to	reducir
refer, to	referir
remember, to	recordar
rent, to	alquilar
repair, to	reparar
repeat, to	repetir
require, to	requerir
resent, to	resentirse por
resolve, to	resolver
respect, to	respetar
respond, to	responder
rest, to	descansar
retire, to	retirar
return, to	regresar
ride, to	montar
run, to	correr

S

sail, to	navegar
save, to	ahorrar
say, to	decir
scratch, to	rascar
search, to	buscar
see, to	ver
seem, to	parecer
select, to	seleccionar
sell, to	vender
send, to	enviar, mandar
separate, to	separar
serve, to	servir
set, to	colocar
sew, to	cocer
shake, to	sacudir
share, to	compartir
shine, to	brillar
shoot, to	disparar
shout, to	gritar

show, to	mostrar	tire, to	cansar
sing, to	cantar	touch, to	tocar
skate, to	patinar	translate, to	traducir
sleep, to	dormir	transmit, to	transmitir
smoke, to	fumar	travel, to	viajar
snow, to	nevar	trim, to	podar
speak, to	hablar	try, to	tratar
spend, to	gastar	turn around, to	voltear
stay, to	quedar	turn off, to	apagar
stick, to	adherir	turn on, to	prender
stir, to	batir, revolver	twist, to	torcer
study, to	estudiar		
subtract, to	restar	**U**	
suffer, to	sufrir	uncover, to	destapar
suppose, to	suponer	understand, to	comprender
surprise, to	sorprender	use, to	usar
surrender, to	rendirse	utilize, to	utilizar
swallow, to	tragar		
sweat, to	sudar	**V**	
sweep, to	barrer	visit, to	visitar
swim, to	nadar	vote, to	votar

T

take care of, to	cuidar	**W**	
take out, to	sacar	walk, to	andar, caminar
take, to	tomar	want, to	querer
talk, to	hablar	wash, to	lavar
teach, to	enseñar	wear, to	llevar
tell, to	decir	win, to	ganar
thank, to	agradecer	wish, to	desear
think, to	pensar	work, to	trabajar
threaten, to	amenazar	worry, to	preocupar
throw, to	tirar	write, to	escribir

Reflexive Verbs

English	Spanish	English	Spanish
bathe, to	bañarse	*have a good time, to*	divertirse
become, to	hacerse	*hurry up, to*	darse prisa
behave, to	portarse	*leave, to*	irse
brush, to	cepillarse	*lie down, to*	acostarse
change address, to	mudarse	*make a mistake, to*	equivocarse
comb, to	peinarse	*make fun of, to*	burlarse
complain, to	quejarse	*put on, to*	ponerse
dive, to	zambullirse	*realize, to*	darse cuenta de
dress, to	vestirse	*get tired of, to*	cansarse
drown, to	ahogarse	*remember, to*	acordarse
fall asleep, to	dormirse	*remove, to*	quitarse
fall down, to	caerse	*shave, to*	afeitarse
forget about, to	olvidarse	*sit down, to*	sentarse
get angry, to	enojarse	*stand up, to*	pararse
get better, to	mejorarse	*stay, to*	quedarse
get ill, to	enfermarse	*wake up, to*	despertarse
get married, to	casarse	*wash, to*	lavarse
get ready, to	prepararse	*worry about, to*	preocuparse
get up, to	levantarse		

Answers to Exercises and Activities

CHAPTER 1

¿Cuánto sabe usted?

1. To distinguish it from the word si
2. The second to the last (for words ending in a vowel or in n or s, the next to the last part of the word is stressed)
3. Example: iai
4. 25
5. None of them

La práctica 1

Answers will vary

La práctica 2

Answers will vary

La práctica 3

1. mi-lla
2. ex-tra-ño
3. tí-o
4. es-cri-bir
5. con-struc-ción
6. en-viáis
7. U-ru-guay
8. ca-rro
9. mi-ér-co-les
10. pa-ga-réis
11. nues-tro
12. re-í-mos
13. die-ci-séis
14. ciu-dad
15. vie-ne
16. _____
17. averiguáis
18. violín
19. _____
20. _____
21. _____

22. túnel
23. _____
24. francés
25. murciélago
26. carácter
27. búho
28. capítulo
29. _____
30. viví

CHAPTER 2

¿Cuánto sabe usted?

1. Subject: Mi tío Jaime / Predicate: nunca se casó
2. A command
3. Both are conjunctions
4. An indirect object
5. A relative pronoun

La práctica 1

1. I
2. F
3. E
4. G
5. H
6. J
7. A
8. B
9. C
10. D

La práctica 2

1. No había allí una hermosa porcelana china.
2. Mi primo no vivía en una casa de las afueras.
3. Los médicos y las enfermeras no son peruanos.
4. No se despierta temprano.
5. Al ver la policía, el muchacho no se marchó.
6. Las tiendas no cerrarán a las once.
7. ¿Por qué no estás en el jardín?
8. No se abrazaron los novios.
9. Toda la noche no llovía.
10. Cuando entramos a la oficina, no sonó la alarma.

La práctica 3

1. No baila mucho.   ¿Baila mucho?
2. No van a bajar la ventana.   ¿Van a bajar la ventana?
3. No tiene una familia grande.   ¿Tiene una familia grande?
4. No fumaron.   ¿Fumaron?
5. No son argentinos.   ¿Son argentinos?
6. No se escapó.   ¿Se escapó?

7. No trabaja hasta tarde.   ¿Trabaja hasta tarde?
8. No es muy difícil.   ¿Es muy difícil?
9. No entiendes español.   ¿Entiendes español?
10. No han comprado la ropa.   ¿Han comprado la ropa?

La práctica 4
1. Juana vendía ropa.
2. el vendedor barrió la entrada.
3. Hablamos con la policía
4. Marta y Samuel viven juntos
5. me compraría una casa.
6. él llamó por teléfono.
7. Ella ha viajado
8. Quitó la olla del fuego
9. escuchamos la música clásica.
10. Vamos a repasar el capítulo

Crossword 1

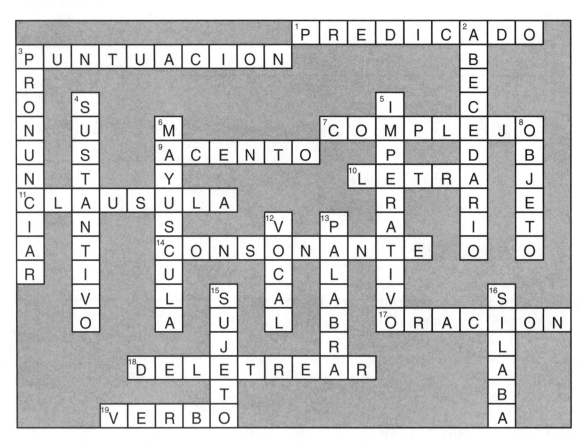

CHAPTER 3

¿Cuánto sabe usted?

1. Mi esposa duerme
2. conozco   conocemos
   conoces   conocéis
   conoce   conocen
3. protejo y contribuyo
4. voy   vamos
   vas   vais
   va   van
5. Hablamos mañana

La práctica 1

1. Jaime come mucho.
2. Nosotros apagamos las luces.
3. ¿Fuma usted?
4. Ellos no beben café.
5. Yo compro la comida hoy.
6. ¿Dónde vives tú?
7. El señor Lara vende carros.
8. Nosotros recibimos mucho correo.
9. ¿Cuándo viajan ustedes?
10. El gato corre en el jardín.
11. Trabajo los sábados.
12. Nosotros salimos del colegio a las tres.
13. Ellos están estudiando sus tareas.
14. Yo leo el libro hoy.
15. ¿Tú manejas ese carro?
16. Ella limpia su casa cada domingo.
17. No asisto a las clases.
18. ¿Usted baila mucho?
19. La tienda abre a las nueve.
20. ¿Qué repasamos nosotros?
21. Sí, ella lee las noticias, también.
22. Sí, yo vivo en Los Angeles, también.
23. Sí, Roberto vende zapatos, también.
24. Sí, él recibe el correo.
25. Sí, usamos el martillo.
26. Sí, ellos asisten a la escuela.
27. Sí, yo dibujo bien.
28. Sí, Paulo come vegetales.
29. Sí, nosotros llegamos temprano.
30. Sí, ella aprende rápido.

La práctica 2

1. Yo hago la comida.
2. Yo traigo la pelota.
3. Yo voy a la tienda.
4. Yo digo la verdad.

5. Yo obedezco la ley.
6. Yo salgo temprano.
7. Yo tengo una sonrisa.
8. Yo sé hablar español.
9. Yo merezco un regalo.
10. Yo pongo la música.
11. Jaime va a Chicago.
12. Yo veo las películas nuevas.
13. Sara y Daniel dicen muchos chistes.
14. Nosotros hacemos la tarea.
15. Tú vienes conmigo al supermercado.
16. Yo doy una fiesta en mi casa.
17. Ellos conocen al alcalde.
18. La Dra. Laura conduce un Mercedes.
19. Uds. no oyen el ruido afuera.
20. El metro sale a las cinco y media.

La práctica 3
1. Paulo es médico.
2. El agua en la tina no está caliente.
3. Ellas son las hijas de la señora.
4. Nosotros somos de Cuba.
5. ¿Dónde está la policía?
6. Yo soy un buen estudiante.
7. ¿Cómo estás tú hoy día?
8. Los hombres están en la cocina.
9. Yo estoy listo para salir.
10. ¿Qué hora/horas es/son?
11. I
12. C
13. I
14. C
15. I
16. I
17. I
18. C
19. C
20. I

La práctica 4
1. recomiendo
2. apuesto
3. recuerdo
4. sonrío
5. despido
6. demuestro
7. sirvo
8. niego

9. cuento
10. tropiezo

La práctica 5
1. C
2. C
3. C
4. C
5. C
6. I
7. I
8. C
9. C
10. I

La práctica 6
1. destruyen
2. recojo
3. envías
4. seguimos
5. protejo
6. convence
7. se gradúan
8. contribuyes
9. confío
10. escogemos

La práctica 7
1. pongo
2. venimos
3. conozco
4. tienen
5. oyes
6. cae
7. vence
8. sé
9. pueden
10. repetimos
11. sigues
12. recojo
13. continúa
14. incluyen
15. nos reímos
16. ¿Qué buscas?
17. Hace un mes que no veo a Ana María.
18. No lo conozco.
19. Ellos vienen mañana.
20. Siempre llueve mucho.
21. ¿Ella dice la verdad?

22. A veces hacen el trabajo.
23. ¿Terminamos más tarde?
24. Quiere trabajar esta noche.
25. Yo recojo el correo.

Crossword 2

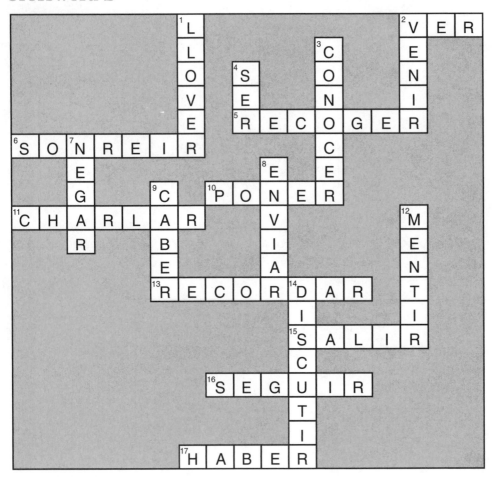

CHAPTER 4

¿Cuánto sabe usted?

1. vi
2. they went, they were
3. Comió means *he ate*, whereas comía implies *he was eating/he would eat/he used to eat*
4. Yo leía revistas.
5. bebía   bebíamos
    bebías   bebíais
    bebía   bebían

La práctica 1

1. Carlos tomó café.
2. Nosotros vendimos el carro.
3. ¿Qué estudiaste?
4. No vivieron aquí.

5. Entendí el ejercicio.
6. Conversaron en español.
7. Ella pidió comida.
8. No encontré las llaves.
9. ¿Cuándo viajaste?
10. El bebé durmió mucho.
11. Me llamó dos veces.
12. Yo compré el vestido ayer.
13. Ella vivió allí por dos años.
14. Nuestro vecino murió anoche.
15. Pidieron más plata.
16. ¿Cerraste la puerta?
17. No manejé ayer.
18. Repitió la lección.
19. No visitamos a España.
20. ¿Qué sirvieron?

La práctica 2
1. sequé
2. alcancé
3. coloqué
4. pegué
5. averigüé
6. freí
7. vi
8. gruñí
9. masqué
10. crucé

La práctica 3
1. Organicé la oficina ayer.
2. Tocó el piano.
3. Llegaron tarde.
4. Distribuiste los periódicos.
5. Construyó el mueble.
6. Empecé a estudiar.
7. Leímos la historia.
8. Vio una película.
9. Pagaron la cuenta.
10. Pescaron en el río.

La práctica 4
1. Anteayer usted fue al cine.
2. Hicimos la tarea.
3. Anduvieron al supermercado.
4. Puso las plantas en el jardín.
5. Viniste conmigo a la escuela.
6. No quise ir al trabajo.
7. Tuvo problemas con su carro.

8. Trajimos libros a la clase.
9. Tradujeron los ejercicios.
10. Me dio un chocolate.

La práctica 5

1. investigábamos
2. encontrábamos
3. elegíamos
4. agarrábamos
5. sentíamos
6. mordíamos
7. comenzábamos
8. golpeábamos
9. hacíamos
10. partíamos

La práctica 6

1. Samuel comía en el hotel con frecuencia.
2. A veces los estudiantes iban a la biblioteca.
3. Yo jugaba con el perro todos los días.
4. Ella vivía cerca de un lago en las montañas.
5. ¿Cantaba mucho cuando era más joven?
6. En aquella época tú te dormías a las doce.
7. Nosotros siempre veíamos películas con la familia.
8. En esa esquina habían dos gasolineras.
9. Cuando llegamos ellos hablaban inglés.
10. De vez en cuando Lupe era muy traviesa.

La práctica 7

1. Anoche ellos comieron el pastel.
2. Ella lavaba los platos.
3. Limpiábamos el baño.
4. ¿Te despertaste a las seis?
5. Todo el día yo estudiaba.
6. Ustedes no quisieron ir.
7. La fiesta duró seis horas.
8. ¿Quién vivió aquí el año pasado?
9. Le gustaba bañarse en el río.
10. Hubo un accidente el viernes.
11. Mientras que practicábamos, él llegó con la pizza.
12. Ella tocaba la guitarra y tú cantabas.
13. Fui a mi casa después del trabajo y me bañé.
14. Se paró y comenzó a leer.
15. Ellos dijeron que tú ibas a la tienda.

Crossword 3

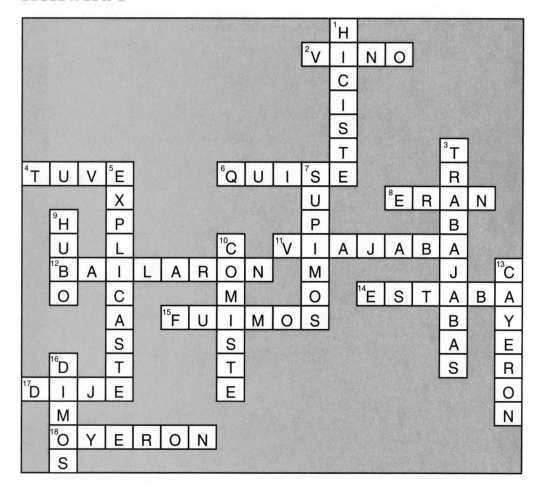

CHAPTER 5

¿Cuánto sabe usted?

1. podré ir
2. haría   haríamos
   harías   haríais
   haría   harían
3. We would leave
4. aprenderé / voy a aprender
5. It was probably one A.M.

La práctica 1

1. guardarán
2. se juntarán
3. mostrarán
4. se vestirán
5. barrerán
6. persistirán
7. se sentarán
8. perdonarán
9. esconderán
10. abandonarán

La práctica 2

1. tendrá
2. harán
3. vendrás
4. pondré
5. volveremos
6. saldrán
7. dirá
8. habrá
9. podrán
10. estaremos

La práctica 3

1. pondrá
2. dormirán
3. podré
4. tomarás
5. empezará
6. habrá
7. seremos
8. estarán
9. valdrá
10. haré
11. Diré
12. Saldremos
13. Tendrán
14. Cabrá
15. Vendrás
16. Sabremos
17. Harán
18. Querrá
19. Podrán
20. Pondré
21. ¿Llegará pasado mañana?
22. ¿Habrá contaminación?
23. ¿Comenzará un poco tarde?
24. ¿No comeremos con ella?
25. ¿Mirará televisión ahora?
26. ¿Traerá algo de España?
27. ¿Pasaremos por su casa?
28. ¿Haré el trabajo?
29. ¿Sabrás la dirección?
30. ¿Saldrán con Ronaldo?

La práctica 4

1. ordenaría
2. crecería
3. jugarían
4. iríamos
5. verías
6. tocarían
7. oiría
8. sería
9. estarían
10. aplicarías

La práctica 5

1. C
2. I
3. C
4. I
5. I
6. C
7. C
8. I
9. C
10. C

La práctica 6

1. saldrían
2. tendría
3. se casarían
4. podrías
5. volvería
6. diría
7. estarían
8. llamaría
9. deberías
10. habrían
11. Sabía que él querría manejar.
12. Dijimos que saldríamos a la medianoche.
13. ¿Podría Ud. venir a la oficina?
14 Estaba preguntando si trabajarían.
15. Nosotros lavaríamos la ropa.
16. ¿Dónde estaría Cristina?
17. Él prometió que cantaría.
18. Dijeron que estarían en el cine.
19. En ese caso, yo compraría el carro.
20. Sería las seis de la mañana.

CHAPTER 6

¿Cuánto sabe usted?
1. No te cepilles los dientes
2. Perder is *to lose* and perderse is *to get lost*
3. Nos casaremos.
4. Beber means *to drink* and beberse means *to drink up*
5. hacerse, ponerse, volverse

La práctica 1
1. se despiertan
2. se estiran
3. se bañan
4. se secan
5. se lavan los dientes
6. se afeitan
7. se cepillan
8. se peinan
9. se maquillan
10. se visten

La práctica 2
1. C
2. I
3. I
4. C
5. C
6. I
7. C
8. I
9. C
10. I

La práctica 3
1. despertarse
2. bañarse
3. levantarse
4. irse
5. vestirse
6. sentarse
7. lavarse
8. peinarse
9. arreglarse
10. secarse

Crossword 4

Across / Down answers in grid:

- ¹CE²PILLARSE ³D ⁴S
- ⁵MOJARSE ⁶DUCHARSE
- ⁷AFEITARSE
- ⁸ACOSTARSE ⁹C
- ¹⁰I ¹¹PEINARSE ¹²L ¹³A
- ¹⁴L
- ¹⁵ENFERMARSE ¹⁶ENOJARSE
- ¹⁷VESTIRSE
- ¹⁸CAERSE
- ¹⁹EQUIVOCARSE

La práctica 4

1. se quita, se pone
2. te cepillas
3. se lavan
4. me mareo
5. nos perdemos
6. se viste
7. se maquilla
8. me aburre
9. te emborrachas
10. nos acostamos
11. *Felipe got tired quickly.*
12. *Tobacco isn't sold in schools.*
13. *Don't file your nails in front of the teacher.*
14. *The girlfriends called each other on their cell phones.*
15. *Sit with me, please.*
16. *I would need to leave soon.*
17. *Leaves fall from the tree in October.*
18. *We helped one another.*

19 *I want to shave in the other bathroom.*
20. *A message will be sent by e-mail.*

La práctica 5
1. cortarme
2. se dieron
3. amárrate
4. se dice
5. nos equivocamos
6. se rebelan
7. te despediste
8. se vayan
9. me olvidó
10. aprovecharse
11. mudarse   *to change residence*
12. inclinarse   *to bend over*
13. alabarse   *to praise oneself*
14. engañarse   *to deceive oneself*
15. matarse   *to commit suicide*
16. enfriarse   *to catch cold*
17. asustarse   *to become afraid*
18. quejarse   *to complain*
19. caerse   *to fall down*
20. callarse   *to become quiet*
21. enfermarse   *to get sick*
22. cortarse   *to cut oneself*
23. reírse   *to laugh*
24. pelearse   *to get into a fight*
25. abrazarse   *to hug*
26. El agua se convertirá en hielo.
27. Yo me volveré loco.
28. Ella se pondrá nerviosa.
29. Uds. se quedarán callados.
30. Nosotros nos haremos abogados.

CHAPTER 7
¿Cuánto sabe usted?
1. he ido
2. has escrito
3. Habríamos comido más tarde.
4. roto
5. The endings change as follows: AR > ado / ER, IR > ido

La práctica 1
1. Ver   Visto
2. Poner   Puesto
3. Ir   Ido
4. Tener   Tenido
5. Devolver   Devuelto
6. Ser   Sido
7. Escribir   Escrito
8. Hacer   Hecho
9. Estar   Estado
10. Oír   Oído

La práctica 2
1. hemos visto
2. he puesto
3. has tenido
4. han podido
5. han estado
6. he abierto
7. han dicho
8. has escrito
9. han roto
10. hemos vivido

La práctica 3
1. ¿Qué han hecho?
2. ¿Has salido tú?
3. ¿Ha llamado él?
4. ¿Dónde han estado ellos?
5. ¿Qué ha roto ella?
6. ¿Cuánto hemos leído?
7. ¿Cuántos han visto ustedes?
8. ¿Por qué ha muerto?
9. ¿Quién ha escrito?
10. ¿Qué han dicho?

La práctica 4
1. había comido
2. había devuelto
3. habían dicho
4. habíamos escrito
5. había sido
6. había puesto
7. habías hecho
8. habían descubierto
9. habíamos venido
10. había visto

La práctica 5
1. No, habían estudiado antes.
2. No, había escrito antes.
3. No, habían estacionado antes.
4. No, había comido antes.
5. No, habían vuelto antes.
6. No, había salido antes.
7. No, habían llamado antes.
8. No, se había despertado antes.
9. No, habían trabajado antes.
10. No, se había ido antes.

La práctica 6
1. habré tenido
2. habremos ido
3. habrá contado
4. habrán escrito
5. habrás visto
6. habré dicho
7. habremos abierto
8. habrán puesto
9. habrás podido
10. habrá muerto

La práctica 7
1. se habrá ido
2. habremos comprado
3. se habrán quedado
4. habrá vuelto
5. habrán terminado
6. me habré graduado
7. habrá llegado
8. habremos hecho
9. habrás ganado
10. habremos puesto

La práctica 8
1. habríamos puesto
2. habría vendido
3. habrías roto
4. habrían dicho
5. habríamos dicho
6. habrías visto
7. habría abierto
8. habrían cubierto
9. habría podido
10. habrías escrito

La práctica 9
1. Habría visitado a mis amigos.
2. Habríamos vuelto a la casa.
3. Habría vivido muchos años más.
4. Habrías hecho el trabajo.
5 Habrían creído la historia.
6. Habríamos visitado el museo.
7. Habría conocido a mucha gente.
8. Habría jugado al golf.
9. Habrían bebido la leche.
10. Habrías puesto la música.
11. habría estudiado
12. habría hablado con mi familia.
13. habría llegado más temprano.
14. habría salido a las ocho.
15. habría visto un DVD.
16. habría tomado una cerveza.
17. habría comprado la computadora.
18. me habría puesto el abrigo.
19. habría leído el capítulo dos.
20. habría preparado el almuerzo.
21. **Past perfect**
They had given the money to the salesman before.
22. **Present Perfect**
We have always been friends.
23. **Conditional Perfect**
They wouldn't have eaten the meat.
24. **Future Perfect**
When the class starts, I will have studied.
25. **Present Perfect**
When did you see the girls?
26. **Past Perfect**
They told me she had already opened the windows.
27. **Future Perfect**
They probably will have gone to Colorado.
28. **Conditional Perfect**
Without medical help, he would have died sooner.
29. **Future Perfect**
What might have become of my friends in California?
30. **Past Perfect**
She hadn't had breakfast when she left her house this morning.

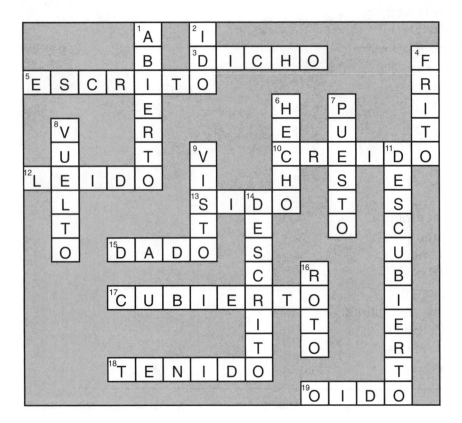

CHAPTER 8

¿Cuánto sabe usted?

1. I would be running.
2. Estoy viendo la película
3. By placing the future tense of haber before the past participle of the main verb
4. estaba lloviendo, llovía
5. leyendo, sirviendo, durmiendo

La práctica 1

1. cayendo
2. sirviendo
3. leyendo
4. diciendo
5. pudiendo
6. sintiendo
7. creyendo
8. muriendo
9. trayendo
10. oyendo
11. corrigiendo
12. leyendo
13. midiendo
14. durmiendo
15. repitiendo

La práctica 2
1. teniendo
2. viendo
3. haciendo
4. abriendo
5. yendo
6. diciendo
7. leyendo
8. durmiendo
9. poniendo
10. volviendo

La práctica 3
1. estaba trabajando
2. estaré bebiendo
3. estuvimos viendo
4. estarían pagando
5. estaba saliendo
6. estarán poniendo
7. estaba tomando
8. estuviste haciendo
9. estarán dibujando
10. estaríamos yendo

La práctica 4
1. Lo estamos permitiendo.
2. ¿Te estarás lavando las manos?
3. Estaban jugando con los niños.
4. ¿Está nevando?
5. Estaré cenando a las siete.
6. ¿Qué te estaban haciendo?
7. Estarían oyendo música.
8. Me estaban mirando cuando entré.
9. Estarán sacando los boletos.
10. No me estoy sintiendo bien.
11. Estaba corriendo en el parque.
12. Estoy haciendo el trabajo.
13. Estarán llegando a las cuatro.
14. Ella no estaría caminando a la escuela.
15. ¿Te estás bañando?
16. ¿Quién estará llamando?
17. Estaríamos tomando el bus.
18. ¡La lámpara se está cayendo!
19. ¿Qué estaba diciendo?
20. Me estoy acostando.

The crossword contains the following filled entries:

- 1. (down) CREYENDO
- 2. MURIENDO
- 3. (down) USANDO
- 4. PIDIENDO
- 5. (down) DICIENDO
- 6. JUGANDO
- 7. (down) PREGUNTANDO
- 8. SIRVIENDO
- 9. OYENDO
- 10. (down) LEYENDO
- 11. (down) REPITIENDO
- 12. ABRIENDO
- 13. (down) VIENDO
- 14. CANTANDO
- 14. (down) CAYENDOSE
- 15. DURMIENDO
- 16. SINTIENDO
- 17. YENDO
- 18. CORRIENDO

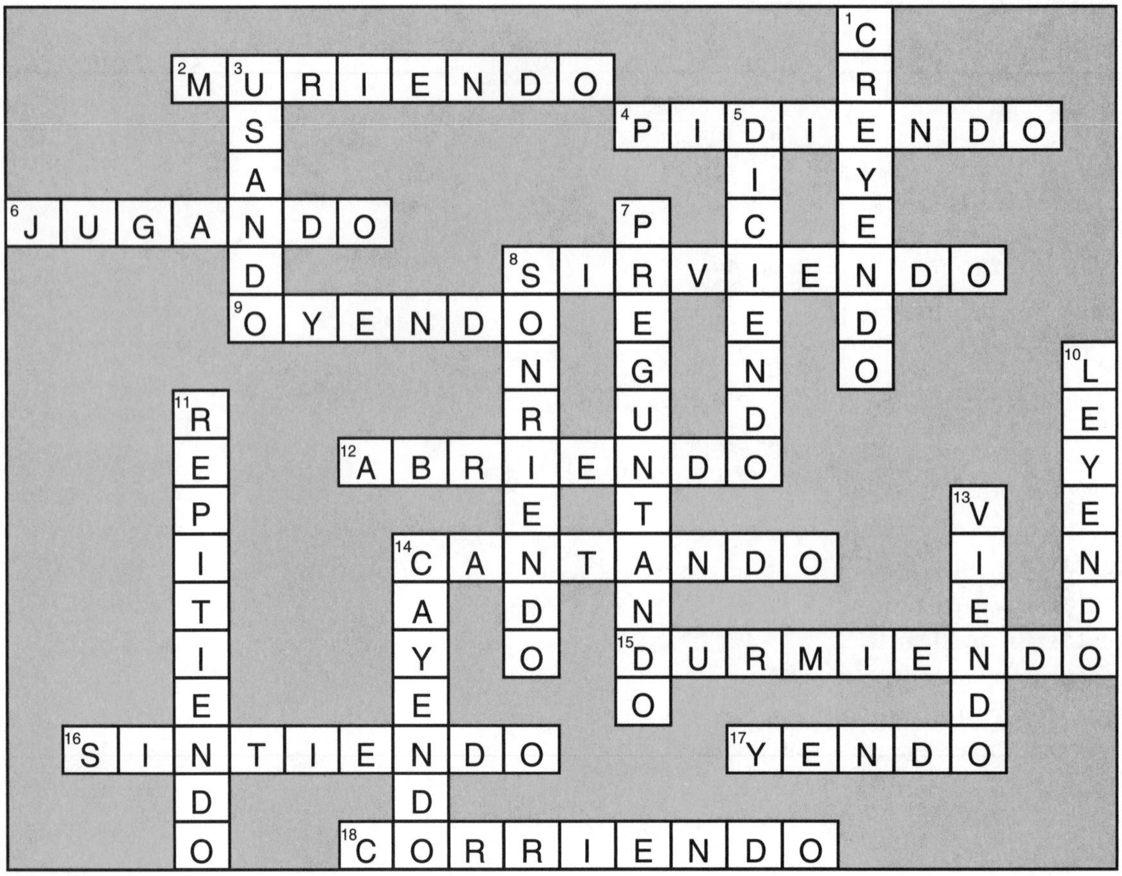

CHAPTER 9

¿Cuánto sabe usted?

1. Una carta fue escrita por ella
2. Example: Si se vende la casa, nos mudamos
3. Los libros fueron perdidos por ellos.
4. fue apagado (por), estuvo apagado
5. One lives to dance.

La práctica 1

1. El libro fue escrito por el autor.
2. El número fue cambiado por nosotros.
3. El gato será atacado por el perro.
4. La carta ha sido perdida por el cartero.
5. La comida es preparada por ellas.
6. Raymundo es amado por Delia.
7. Los soldados son admirados por todos.
8. Las ventanas fueron cerradas por la vecina.
9. Los instrumentos serán tocados por los niños.
10. La basura es recogida por el camión.

La práctica 2

1. Se calentará el cuarto.
2. Se construyeron dos casas.
3. Se habla inglés aquí.
4. Se servirá el almuerzo a las doce.
5. Nunca se sabe.
6. Se publicó el libro en México.
7. Se mandará un mensaje.
8. Se sale por aquí.
9. Se ha pagado la cuenta.
10. Se venden casas por todas partes.

CHAPTER 10

¿Cuánto sabe usted?

1. pida   pidamos
   pidas   pidáis
   pida   pidan
2. Si ella estudiara, pasaría el examen.
3. dijera   dijéramos
   dijeras   dijerais
   dijera   dijeran
4. By combining the present subjunctive of haber with the past participle
5. Necesito a alguien que pueda trabajar en la noche.

La práctica 1

1. estudies
2. piense
3. cierren
4. viva
5. envíe
6. se queden
7. vuelva
8. entiendan
9. duermas
10. sigan

La práctica 2

1. vaya
2. parezcan
3. salgas
4. oiga
5. estén
6. diga
7. conduzcamos
8. venga
9. caiga
10. sea

La práctica 3

	Singular	Plural
1.	rece, reces, rece	recemos, recéis, recen
2.	proteja, protejas, proteja	protejamos, protejáis, protejan
3.	saque, saques, saque	saquemos, saquéis, saquen
4.	persiga, persigas, persiga	persigamos, persigáis, persigan
5.	pague, pagues, pague	paguemos, paguéis, paguen
6.	convenza, convenzas, convenza	convenzamos, convenzáis, convenzan
7.	escoja, escojas, escoja	escojamos, escojáis, escojan
8.	mastique, mastiques, mastique	mastiquemos, mastiquéis, mastiquen
9.	consiga, consigas, consiga	consigamos, consigáis, consigan
10.	empuje, empujes, empuje	empujemos, empujéis, empujen

La práctica 4

1. sea
2. venga
3. vaya
4. vuelva
5. hagan
6. llegue
7. estés
8. merezca
9. tenga
10. abran
11. quiera   *She doesn't believe he loves her.*
12. entiendas   *I'm surprised you don't understand.*
13. griten   *I don't like it when you yell at me.*
14. duerma   *I recommend that she sleeps more.*
15. se vayan   *We demand that they leave.*
16. salgamos   *They insist that we leave now.*
17. conozcas   *I don't think you know him.*
18. pague   *They're thrilled that you are paying the check.*
19. sirva   *Would you like me to serve you something to eat?*
20. leamos   *He/She tells us to read more books in Spanish.*

La práctica 5

1. mienta
2. vuelva
3. entienda
4. caiga
5. escoja
6. construya
7. saque
8. haya
9. oiga

10. conozca
11. sea
12. tenga
13. recoja
14. pegue
15. rece
16. masque
17. persiga
18. pueda

La práctica 6
1. Prefiero que no se lo haya dicho.
2. ¿Crees que hayas tenido razón?
3. Dudamos que haya llovido mucho.
4. Teme que no le hayan escrito.
5. Me alegro que Ud. haya venido.
6. Ella quiere que hayamos esperado aquí.
7. Nos sorprende que no lo hayas sabido.
8. Les pido que me hayan llamado.
9. Mandan que no lo hayan hecho.
10. ¿Piensas que él haya sido honesto?

La práctica 7
1. Es malo que los gatos corran en el jardín.
2. Es triste que mis abuelos se enfermen mucho.
3. Es raro que no haga calor en el garaje.
4. Es importante que aprendan mucho español.
5. Es probable que ellos vengan al mediodía.
6. No es cierto que pueda conducir el autobús.
7. Es preciso que mandemos las cartas por correo.
8. Es una lástima que él siempre traiga amigos traviesos.
9. Es dudoso que su madre sea la nueva profesora.
10. Ojalá que tengamos todo listo para mañana.

La práctica 8
1. que yo estudiara
2. que él quisiera
3. que ustedes dieran
4. que tú reconocieras
5. que nosotros saliéramos
6. que ellas tuvieran
7. que Ud. fuera
8. que yo hiciera
9. que ellos pensaran
10. que él dijera

11. Sugirieron que practicara.
12. Espero que Ud. tenga buena suerte.
13. Me suplicó que bailara con él.
14. Preferimos que tú hagas el trabajo.
15. Yo no creía que ellos salieran.
16. Le pedieron que él sirviera la comida.
17. Insistimos que ellos pagaran.
18. Él teme que no lleguemos el martes.
19. Ellos negaron que fuera cierto.
20. Ella se alegró que ustedes vinieran.

La práctica 9
1. haya
2. hubiera
3. haya
4. había
5. hubiera
6. ha
7. haya
8. hubiera
9. haya
10. hubiera

La práctica 10
1. supiera
2. prestaría
3. me quedaría
4. hubieran ganado
5. veo
6. habríamos acabado
7. viene
8. habrías llegado
9. hubiera estado
10. hubiera tenido

La práctica 11
1. llegara
2. tengamos
3. llame
4. llueva
5. sepan
6. despidan
7. salga
8. mientas
9. surja

10. vayan
11. *They cleaned everything before my girlfriend arrived.*
12. *She does it so that we won't have to.*
13. *The cat will come when the lady calls for it.*
14. *They're going to the desert even though it's raining.*
15. *Practice the song until you know it.*
16. *I left without you saying good-bye.*
17. *He brought a hat in case the sun came out.*
18. *As long as you lie, I won't listen to you.*
19. *I'll do it unless a problem arises.*
20. *Although the others are going, we're not.*

La práctica 12
1. Mercedes busca un carro que tenga cuatro puertas.
2. Ellas querían un apartamento que esté cerca del mercado.
3. Hablaré con una persona que entienda inglés.
4. No conocemos a nadie que viva en San Antonio.
5. ¿Prefieres comprar algo que no cueste tanto?
6. No había ninguna persona que supiera usar la máquina.
7. Santiago quiere tomar las clases que sean más divertidas.
8. Siempre he deseado amigos que toquen un instrumento.
9. Escoge las galletas que nos gusten.
10. Le encanta cualquier ropa que venga de Italia.

CHAPTER 11
¿Cuánto sabe usted?
1. No traigan nada
2. Estudiemos / Vamos a estudiar
3. escoja
4. No se vayan Uds.
5. No te las pongas

La práctica 1
1. *Don't bring anything.*
2. *Think about it.*
3. *Let's buy them.*
4. *Don't smoke.*
5. *Let's go out.*
6. *Turn on the light.*
7. *Don't tell me.*
8. *Let's be quiet.*
9. *Sing.*
10. *Don't sign it.*

Crossword 7

```
    ¹C  ²L          ³E  S  ⁴C  R  I  B  A
     I   L                   O
⁵M  U  E  V  A          ⁶V  E  N  G  A
     R      M                 T
     R      ⁷E  S  ⁸C  U  C  H  E      ⁹P
     E          A              S       O
            M      ¹⁰V      ¹¹T  E  N  G ¹²A
         ¹³D  I  G  A      E        G      B
      ¹⁴C      N      Y          A         R
   ¹⁵C  O  M  P ¹⁶R  E      A               A
      M         E              ¹⁷H
      A       ¹⁸P  I  D  A      A
              I                 G
            ¹⁹T  R  A  I  G  A
   ²⁰C  O  R  R  A
```

La práctica 2

1. Ten fiesta hoy
2. Siéntate
3. Entra
4. Ciérrala
5. Sal
6. Ponte la gorra
7. Contesta
8. Dile todo
9. Levántate
10. Ve a tu cuarto

La práctica 3

1. Que coman la carne.
2. Que la preparen.
3. Que la pague ella.
4. Que no se lo dé a ellos.
5. Que regresen el domingo.
6. Que no se queden allí.
7. Que Camacho lo haga.
8. Que me llamen mañana.
9. Que no espere en el carro ella.
10. Que se casen.

La práctica 4

1. Favor de traerme el pastel.
2. Favor de no subir por la escalera.

3. Favor de poner la carta en el sobre.
4. Favor de ir a la tienda con Laura.
5. Favor de no comer la fruta seca.
6. Favor de decirnos la verdad.
7. Favor de hacer el trabajo Uds.
8. Favor de no escuchar la radio.
9. Favor de poner los cubiertos en la mesa.
10. Favor de venir acá.

CHAPTER 12

¿Cuánto sabe usted?

1. Quiero escuchar.
2. Example: Pensaron en casarse.
3. Debe ir means *should go*, and debe de ir means *must go*.
4. Los vi llegar.
5. Example: Descansaron en lugar de jugar.

La práctica 1

1. Le ayudaron a caminar.
2. Acaban de llegar.
3. Pensamos en hacerlo más tarde.
4. Quisiera _____ invitar a Susana.
5. Me cansé de manejar solo.
6. Llegará a ser un policía.
7. Insistían en no comprar un nuevo estéreo.
8. ¡Fíjate en tus estudios!
9. Se olvidó de enviarle el regalo.
10. Podemos terminar de pintar mañana.

La práctica 2

1. Busco algo bonito para comprar.
2. Estábamos listos para comer el desayuno.
3. Trabajaba toda la noche sin dormir.
4. Correré al parque en lugar de caminar.
5. Te llamé antes de acostarme.
6. No hay nada que decirle.
7. Se bañaron después de jugar béisbol.
8. Estoy para tocar música.
9. Ella tenía mucho que hacer.
10. Iría a pesar de no tener carro.

La práctica 3

1. para
2. después de
3. en vez de
4. de
5. sin
6. antes de
7. al

8. a pesar de
9. con tal de
10. hasta
11. Es posible nadar en el lago.
12. El cuarto es fácil de pintar.
13. Tenemos que escribir estas palabras.
14. Usted debe jugar tennis.
15. Dime qué hacer.
16. Tienen muchas cosas para comprar.
17. ¡A trabajar!
18. ¿Sabe como pronunciarlo ella?
19. Es importante traer los libros.
20. Estaba buscando algo para comer.

CHAPTER 13

¿Cuánto sabe usted?

1. Un agua is a serving of water; el agua is water in general
2. Los lápices son verdes
3. los paraguas
4. It is both
5. Es lo mejor

La práctica 1

1. el disfraz
2. el mapa
3. la edad
4. el cometa
5. el lodo
6. el pasaporte
7. la especie
8. la pared
9. el tema
10. el rubí
11. la faringitis
12. el pez
13. el valor
14. la cumbre
15. el jarabe

La práctica 2

1. idioma
2. clima
3. fantasma
4. problema
5. programa
6. mapa
7. drama
8. poeta
9. planeta

10. sistema
11. dilema
12. diagrama

La práctica 3
1. el
2. ____
3. el/la
4. la
5. el
6. el
7. el
8. el
9. el/la
10. el
11. el francés, la francesa
12. la manzana
13. el/la víctima
14. el jueves
15. la papa
16. la frente
17. el/la artista
18. el diez y ocho
19. el olivo
20. el campeón/la campeona

La práctica 4
1. los reyes
2. los ingleses
3. los relojes
4. los ganadores
5. los trombones
6. los jabalíes
7. los sábados
8. las cruces
9. los abrelatas
10. los tés
11. No
12. No
13. No
14. Yes
15. Yes
16. No
17. Yes
18. No
19. Yes
20. No

La práctica 5

1. La oficina abre a las siete.
2. El amor está por todas partes.
3. Cuesta un dólar el pie.
4. No han trabajado de noche.
5. El hombre y la mujer están aquí.
6. Ponte tu suéter, mi amor.
7. Mi amiga va a venir el jueves.
8. Fuimos a la iglesia.
9. Lima está en el Perú.
10. La Sra. Toledo ha llegado.
11. Vivían en la España romántica.
12. He hablado con el Sr. Hugo.
13. No puede decirlo en ____ inglés.
14. Tomaban ____ cerveza toda la noche.
15. La primavera es la estación más hermosa.
16. Venga a Quito, ____ capital del Ecuador.
17. Mañana no es ____ martes.
18. Lo escuchamos en la radio.
19. El Uruguay está en América del Sur.
20. Cruzaría el océano Atlántico.
21. Hay ____ niños en el jardín.
22. Los choferes manejan los camiones.
23. Hola, ____ Dra. Roberts.
24. El montar caballo es divertido.
25. Hablo ____ alemán.

La práctica 6

1. un
2. un
3. unas
4. un
5. un
6. una
7. un
8. unas
9. un
10. un
11. ¿Dónde está el arma que compraste?
12. Creo que tiene _____ problemas personales.
13. Trajo el agua y la leche?
14. Soy _____ japonés.
15. ¡Qué _____ lástima!
16. No me lavé las manos.
17. Me costó _____ cien dólares.
18. La música clásica me interesa mucho.
19. Me dijo que el clima había cambiado.
20. ¿Sabes tocar el arpa?

La práctica 7

1. Es lo bueno, lo malo, y lo feo.
2. Escuché lo del médico.
3. Ella corrió lo menos posible.
4. Vimos lo alto que es.
5. Ellos harían lo mismo.
6. Lo que se ha hecho es lo más importante.
7. ¿Han leído lo que está escrito?
8. Yo sé lo necesario que es.
9. Merecemos lo mejor.
10. Me sorprende lo bien que canta él.

La práctica 8

1. el gato de mi hermana
2. las páginas del libro
3. el dueño de estos zapatos
4. los libros de la Dra. Ortega
5. el restaurante del hotel
6. las herramientas de los obreros
7. la recetas de Silvia
8. el negocio de tu familia
9. las sonrisas de Carla y Lidia
10. el trono del rey David

CHAPTER 14

¿Cuánto sabe usted?

1. I dance as much as you do.
2. No necesito tanto dinero. Adjectives that express number or quantity (tanto) precede the noun in Spanish
3. very smooth
4. berlinenses
5. costarricenses

La práctica 1

1. Hay sopa caliente.
2. Hay plumas negras.
3. Hay niños preguntones.
4. Hay amigas cosmopolitas.
5. Hay ingleses alegres.
6. Hay aire fresco.
7. Hay fruta podrida.
8. Hay compañeros comunistas.
9. Hay agua sucia.
10. Hay estudiantes canadienses.
11. alemanas
12. griegas
13. italianas
14. españolas
15. vietnamitas

16. brasileñas
17. portuguesas
18. salvadoreñas
19. chinas
20. puertorriqueñas

Crossword 8

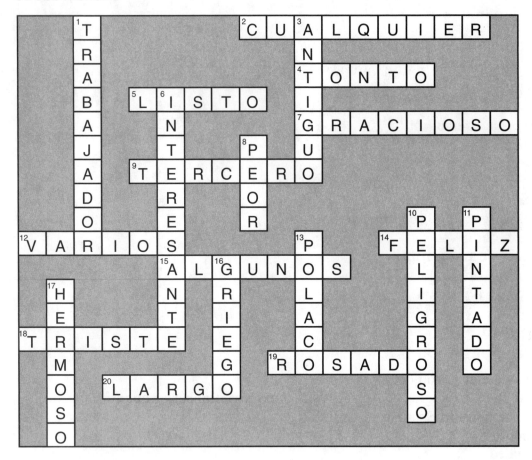

La práctica 2

1. la única pluma
2. mala suerte
3. una pera muy deliciosa
4. la nieve blanca
5. las sillas verdes
6. cierta profesora
7. el mismo papel
8. un hombre pobre
9. las flores nuevas
10. ¡Qué grandes ojos!

La práctica 3

1.	tercer	*third*
2.	cualquier	*any*
3.	cien	*hundred*
4.	gran	*great*
5.	primer	*first*
6.	algún	*some*
7.	mal	*poorly*
8.	San	*Saint*
9.	ningún	*none*
10.	buen	*good*

La práctica 4

1.	mesas y sillas	mesas y sillas feas
2.	apartamentos y casas	modernos
3.	conejos	gordos y pequeños
4.	calles y caminos	anchos
5.	el único libro	rojo y azul
6.	plátanos y duraznos	dulces
7.	vendedores y clientes	españoles
8.	pantalones	nuevos y bonitos
9.	muchachas y muchachos	felices
10.	el otro problema	difícil
11.	cuatro casas pintadas	
12.	un ojo cerrado	
13.	cinco chicas confundidas	
14.	dos juguetes perdidos	
15.	nueve cartas escritas	
16.	seis platos preparados	
17.	ocho huevos fritos	
18.	tres cheques firmados	
19.	siete papas peladas	
20.	diez ollas cubiertas	
21.	Me dió el sucio.	
22.	¿Dónde están las negras?	
23.	Tráigame la grande.	
24.	Llevaron las nuevas.	
25.	No me gusta la azul.	
26.	¿Has visto el italiano?	
27.	Solamente sirva la fría.	
28.	¿Prefieres leer la romántica?	
29.	Invitamos a los ingleses.	
30.	A mí me interesa la religiosa.	

La práctica 5

1. más alto que
2. más pesado que
3. más divertido que
4. menos fuertes que
5. menos importante que
6. más duro que
7. menos profundos que
8. más famoso que
9. menos peligrosos que
10. más seco que

La práctica 6

1. Él es mayor que su hermana.
2. Ella cocina más que yo.
3. Las revistas son más interesantes que los periódicos.
4. Esa pelota es mejor que la otra.
5. Yo corro más lento que Juan.
6. La situación era más difícil de lo que había dicho.
7. Tienen tantos libros como la biblioteca.
8. Ud. estudia menos que nosotros.
9. Sara baila mejor que nadie.
10. Tomará menos de dos horas.
11. Ella es tan bonita como una rosa.
12. La cocina es peor que el baño.
13. Usamos más plumas de las que compraste.
14. Las niñas trabajaron más cuidadosamente que los niños.
15. Mi abuelo es más joven que mi abuela.

La práctica 7

1. el cuchillo más útil
   the most useful knife
2. los soldados más valientes
   the bravest soldiers
3. la doctora más capaz
   the most capable doctor
4. las oficinas más elegantes
   the most elegant offices
5. la avenida más ancha
   the widest street
6. los policías más simpáticos
   the nicest policemen
7. el programa más terrible
   the worst program
8. el divorcio más rápido
   the quickest divorce
9. los árboles más verdes
   the greenest trees

10. la mesera más cortés
    the most courteous waitress
11. la tela finísima
12. el poema famosísimo
13. la cara palidísima
14. las tareas facilísimas
15. la comida riquísima
16. la falda hermosísima
17. el perro ferocísimo
18. los retratos feísimos
19. el pelo larguísimo
20. el hombre felicísimo

CHAPTER 15

¿Cuánto sabe usted?

1. Este: *this*, ese: *that* (near the person spoken to)
   Aquel: *that* (away from the speaker and the person spoken to)
2. esto, eso, aquello
3. Ese refers to an item or a person that is closer to the speaker than aquel
4. tu/tuyo
5. Estas son mis llaves.

La práctica 1

1. ¿Dónde viven estos chicos?
2. Estas sillas están rotas.
3. Creo que aquellos pájaros son cuervos.
4. ¿Quién compró esas galletas?
5. Estos aviones tienen problemas.
6. Subieron aquellas montañas.
7. Apagaré estas luces.
8. ¿Cuánto cuestan estos maletines?
9. Aquellos discos compactos no funcionan.
10. Tráigame esas salchichas.

La práctica 2

1. éste
2. ése o aquél
3. esto o éste
4. ésta
5. eso o aquello
6. esos
7. ésa
8. eso
9. esto
10. éstas

La práctica 3

	Short-form	Long-form
1.	su camisa	la camisa suya
2.	tus zapatos	los tuyos
3.	nuestras faldas	las nuestras
4.	sus medias	las suyas
5.	su suéter	el suyo
6.	mis pantalones	los míos
7.	sus guantes	los suyos
8.	sus botas	las suyas
9.	su cinturón	el suyo
10.	nuestras gorras	las nuestras

La práctica 4

1. Ese país es más grande que el nuestro.
2. Tu computadora tiene más memoria que la mía.
3. Mi hijo es más alto que el suyo.
4. Ella respeta mis opiniones más que las suyas.
5. Sus amigas parecen ser más fieles que las nuestras.
6. Tengo el número de él pero no tengo el suyo.
7. Aquella bicicleta cuesta mucho más que la tuya.
8. ¿Quieres ver mis formularios o los suyos?
9. Mis hermanos son tan valientes como los tuyos.
10. Tus gatos duermen menos que los míos.

CHAPTER 16

¿Cuánto sabe usted?

1. Yo and me
2. Él nos los dio.
3. le
4. Me gusta: *I like it.* Le gusta: *he, she, likes it, you like it.*
5. They act like they are rich.

La práctica 1

1. Nosotros
2. Ella
3. Ustedes
4. Ellas
5. Él
6. Nosotros
7. Ellos
8. Ella
9. Nosotros
10. Ellos
11. Yo (*I am*)
12. Tú (*You are*)
13. Él (*He is*) Ella (*She is*) Usted (*You are*)
14. Nosotros / nosotras (*We are*)

15. Vosotros /vosotras (*You are*)
16. Ellos (*They are*) Ellas (*They are*) Ustedes (*You are*)

La práctica 2
1. ella
2. mí
3. nosotros
4. conmigo
5. tú
6. él
7. contigo
8. yo
9. vosotros
10. yo

La práctica 3
1. Ayudo a mis amigos.
2. Ella busca al gato.
3. Llamamos al doctor.
4. ¿Cuántas primas tienes?
5. No puedo ver nada.
6. No conozco a nadie.
7. Compraron la casa del Sr. Romo.
8. Ella juega con muchos niños.
9. Nosotros no vimos a Rogelio.
10. ¿Busca él a alguien?
11. *Who do you teach?*
12. *We listen to both.*
13. *Martín went out with anyone.*
14. *Did you find the other one?*
15. *I want to know the fat one.*
16. *We did not invite any teacher.*
17. *How many will they take in the car?*
18. *I hugged the same one.*
19. *We will visit the first one.*
20. *Which client do I call?*

La práctica 4
1. Lo tengo.
2. No los puedo ver.
3. La está estudiando.
4. Lo compró.
5. ¿Las enviaste?
6. Los visitamos.
7. Las tiraron.
8. La buscaban.
9. ¿Las has visto?
10. No los encontramos.

11. Tráigalo.
12. Enséñeme.
13. Tóquelos.
14. Apáguela.
15. Invítenos.
16. La reconocí.
17. Te reconocí.
18. Las reconocí.
19. Lo reconocí.
20. Los reconocí.
21. Su casa la vendió.
22. A Lidia la he invitado.
23. Los cuadernos los necesitarán.
24. A tus compañeros los vimos.
25. Su uniforme no lo trae.

La práctica 5
1. le
   You should give her the address.
2. les
   What did they ask you for?
3. me
   He showed me all the money.
4. le
   I asked the owner for a job.
5. nos
   He has given the two of us music books.
6. te
   Did he/she tell you the secret?
7. Escríbeles
   Write a letter to your cousins.
8. nos
   He was speaking to us in Spanish.
9. me
   Why did you remove my hat?
10. le
    They have sent something to Juanita.
11. Ella les daba muchas flores.
12. ¿A mí me manda los datos?
13. A él le quitaban la pelota
14. A ti te dijo todos los números.
15. A Ud. le está enseñando arte.
16. Tráiganos la fruta fresca.
17. Les mostraron el apartamento.
18. Les contaba mentiras.
19. Quiere regalarnos diamantes.
20. ¿Le devolvió el martillo?

La práctica 6
1. *She's missing a notebook.*
2. *Whose turn is it?*
3. *We have twenty minutes left.*
4. *Do you have a lot of work left?*
5. *They love New York.*
6. *It would be better for you to drive.*
7. *I'm interested in seeing the movie.*
8. *Don't you care about the result?*
9. *The conversation motivated us.*
10. *He likes to skate alone.*

La práctica 7
1. Quiere prestársela.
2. Estoy explicándoselo.
3. Él te los vendía.
4. Se los di.
5. René lo trajo.
6. Nos los está mandando.
7. A Uds. se las llevé.
8. Ya se las bajaron.
9. Siempre se los hacía.
10. Ella te las ha devuelto.
11. No me los preste.
12. No nos la muestre.
13. No se lo entregue.
14. No se la traiga.
15. No me los compre.

CHAPTER 17

¿Cuánto sabe usted?
1. El dos mil fue el año en que me casé.
2. que
3. When the relative pronoun is the object of the verb and the antecedent is a person
4. lo que, lo cual
5. Ana es la maestra que habla alemán.

La práctica 1
1. Me gusta el postre que es muy dulce.
2. Acabo de leer el libro que me regalaste.
3. La señora que murió vivía en la esquina.
4. La niña que usted vio es mi hija.
5. Ella es la cajera que trabaja conmigo.
6. Uso los guantes que ellos me compraron.
7. Esta es la clase de español que necesito.
8. Llame a los estudiantes que estudian mucho.
9. Tengo algo que quiero decirte.
10. Las botellas que están en el piso están vacías.

La práctica 2

1. Ya salieron los niños a quienes encontraste en el parque ayer.
2. El chofer, a quien llamamos a las ocho, llegó temprano.
3. Ella es mi sobrina, a quien vi en el banco con su novio.
4. Las maestras, a quienes queremos mucho, se han ido.
5. La chica, a quien conocí el año pasado, siempre está enferma.
6. La doctora, quien abrió una clínica, trabaja en el hospital.
7. Alfredo, quien es un estudiante excelente, no vino hoy.
8. Algunos jugadores, quienes practican aquí, son atletas profesionales.
9. La Sra. Arenas, quien ha sido la directora, escribe libros de gramática.
10. Mis hermanas, quienes no quieren mudarse, viven conmigo.

La práctica 3

1. el que
2. lo que
3. lo que
4. la que
5. lo que
6. los que
7. las que
8. lo que
9. el que
10. la que

La práctica 4

1. Ella es la dueña cuyo apartamento está debajo de nosotros.
2. Quisiéramos ver el artista cuyas pinturas están en exhibición.
3. No he encontrado la persona cuyo perro mordió al cartero.
4. Hablé con el profesor cuyos estudiantes no pasaron el examen final.
5. Acaba de llamar a la señora cuyo bebito llora toda la noche.
6. Este es el pueblo cuyos edificios son tan antiguos.
7. Hablaremos con los clientes cuyas cuentas no están pagadas.
8. Presénteme al chico cuya hermana tiene el pelo largo.
9. Ellos son los autores cuyas novelas son tan famosas.
10. Se casó con la señorita cuyo padre es el alcalde.

La práctica 5

1. *This is the place where I prefer to eat Chinese food.*
2. *The woman with whom I work is Russian.*
3. *The chair on which I sat down was broken.*
4. *The company that you work for is Chilean.*
5. *I met the man who lives next to you.*
6. *I don't know the person who Alicia is going to marry.*
7. *The lady who arrived with you is my cousin.*
8. *The school to which I go is new.*
9. *This is the window through which the dog escaped.*
10. *Give me the box in which I keep my jewels.*
11. Los clientes para los que trabajo son muy ricos.
12. No me gusta el mundo en que vive.
13. Fui a su casa, detrás de la cual vi el árbol grande.

14. Conocimos a los estudiantes con quienes ella habló.
15. Vendieron el bolígrafo con el que Washington escribió sus cartas.

CHAPTER 18
¿Cuánto sabe usted?
1.
2.
3.
4.
5.

La práctica 1
1. verbalmente
2. inteligentemente
3. justamente
4. tanto
5. históricamente
6. naturalmente
7. ciertamente
8. simplemente
9. bien
10. peor
11. sucesivamente
12. científicamente
13. verdaderamente
14. tristemente
15. útilmente
16. abiertamente
17. desafortunadamente
18. alegremente
19. profundamente
20. demasiado

La práctica 2
1. Ella baila elegantemente.
2. Ellos mueven tímidamente.
3. Yo pronuncio distinto.
4. Ud. traduce cuidadosamente.
5. Nosotros no viajamos tranquilamente.
6. Tú trabajas diplomáticamente.
7. Él viene rápidamente.
8. Los tigres atacan violentamente.
9. Uds. salen tristemente.
10. Ellas duermen tranquilamente.
11. *You didn't do anything well.*
12. *He changed the program systematically.*
13. *He cleaned his room completely.*
14. *He spoke to me very firmly.*
15. *We cried desperately.*

La práctica 3

1. Ya no tiene el bote.
2. Ella siempre explica las respuestas.
3. Regreso en seguida.
4. Casi nunca comemos pescado.
5. Ellos comieron allí anoche.
6. He manejado antes a Las Vegas.
7. ¿Ya salieron?
8. Nuestros vecinos son recién casados.
9. ¿Adónde va ella después de la escuela?
10. Ya lo hicieron.

La práctica 4

1. detrás
2. cerca
3. más acá
4. debajo
5. afuera
6. a la derecha
7. abajo
8. por algún sitio
9. adelante
10. en lo bajo

Crossword 9

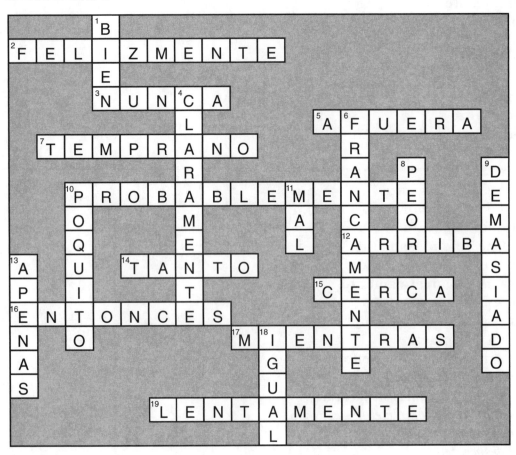

CHAPTER 19

¿Cuánto sabe usted?

1. *Fui al banco para sacar dinero.*
2. They all mean *except*
3. Both translate as *for*, but **por** generally focuses on a cause, whereas **para** looks forward to a result
4. *Ella vive conmigo.*
5. They left on foot.

La práctica 1

1. *I'm looking for the gold earrings.*
2. *They trembled with fear.*
3. *I want to use her coat.*
4. *I'm dying of hunger.*
5. *Where were they from?*
6. *Bring me the bottle of wine.*
7. *I'm returning from the bank.*
8. *They do not go out at night.*
9. *It's a girl of wealth.*
10. *The room was painted red.*

La práctica 2

1. *Conozco al Sr. Goya.*
2. *A él le gusta bailar.*
3. *Es la una y media.*
4. *La pareja montó a caballo.*
5. *¿A qué hora llegaste a tu casa?*
6. *Le dio el agua a ella.*
7. *No han salido todavía.*
8. *Te volvió a llamar.*
9. *No subimos al tren.*
10. *¿Cuánto cuesta la bicicleta?*

La práctica 3

1. *Can I speak with you?*
2. *He dried it with a towel.*
3. *Paulo will marry his girlfriend.*
4. *We are going to celebrate with happiness.*
5. *She remained with the white house.*
6. *I used to work with this hammer.*
7. *With all of his problems, he keeps studying.*
8. *Who is the girl with the large eyes?*
9. *They met with their friends.*
10. *They answered with timidity.*

La práctica 4

1. Salimos en diez minutos.
2. Fui en coche y en avión.
3. La comida está en la nevera.
4. El precio subió en diez por ciento.
5. Limpiaron la casa en un día.
6. ¿Te fijaste en él?
7. En realidad, él no tiene la menor idea.
8. Ella insiste en conducir.
9. Durmieron en el piso.
10. Se parecen en el habla.

La práctica 5

1. Para estudiante tan inteligente, no fue una pregunta muy difícil.
2. Son producidos por máquinas.
3. Vino para ayudarnos.
4. ¿Para qué es el martillo?
5. Todo lo hizo por su madre.
6. Trabajan para la misma señora.
7. No puedes salir por esa puerta.
8. Dejaremos todo para mañana.
9. Se venden por libra.
10. Para un bebito, es muy fuerte.
11. Ha vivido aquí por dos días.
12. Para ella, es muy caro.
13. Pagaré cien por el boleto.
14. ¿Para dónde van Uds.?
15. Fue un honor para mí.
16. por
17. por/para
18. para
19. por
20. por
21. para
22. para
23. por
24. por
25. por

La práctica 6

1. Yo te vi desde la ventana.
2. Se quedó sin conocimiento en la cama.
3. Hacía veinte grados bajo cero.
4. Ante todo, hay que respetar a la gente mayor.
5. Según Noé, la profesora es muy simpática.
6. Me dijo que Victoria se durmió durante la ópera.

7. **Hasta** mi padre lloraba cuando se casaron.
8. Se puso la bufanda **sobre** la cabeza.
9. Tenía que caminar **hacia** adelante.
10. Todos hablaban en español **menos** Sandra.
11. según
12. sobre
13. en
14. acerca
15. hacia
16. contra
17. ante
18. excepto
19. tras
20. contra

CHAPTER 20

¿Cuánto sabe usted?

1. ¿Por qué se van?
2. ¿Has ido a Chicago?
3. Cuántas
4. ¿Quiénes son esos hombres?
5. ¿No leyó ella el libro?

La práctica 1

1. ¿Adónde?
2. ¿Cuál?
3. ¿Dónde?
4. ¿Cuántos?
5. ¿Por qué?
6. ¿Qué?
7. ¿Cuánto?
8. ¿A qué?
9. ¿Quién?
10. ¿Cómo?
11. ¿**Cuáles** son tus mejores cursos?
12. ¿**Cuál** es su fecha de nacimiento?
13. ¿**Quién** es el dueño de ese carro?
14. ¿**Cuántos** hijos tiene Ud.?
15. ¿**Adónde** fueron los chicos ayer?
16. ¿De **qué** nacionalidad son Uds.?
17. ¿**Cómo** te sientes?
18. ¿**Cuánto** tiempo falta para la boda?
19. ¿**Cuándo** tiene que regresar a su casa?
20. ¿**Dónde** está ubicado el teatro?

La práctica 2

1. ¿Está trabajando los martes Perla?
   ¿Perla está trabajando los martes?
2. ¿Se venden periódicos allí?
   ¿Allí se venden periódicos?
3. ¿Salió Jesús con Olivia anoche?
   ¿Anoche salió Jesús con Olivia?
4. ¿Se van a mudar ellos en julio?
   ¿Ellos se van a mudar en julio?
5. ¿Tenía la computadora problemas?
   ¿La computadora tenía problemas?
6. ¿Trabajaba Paco en el banco?
   ¿Paco trabajaba en el banco?
7. ¿Siempre se queda ella en casa?
   ¿Ella siempre se queda en casa?
8. ¿A Mari le gusta comer pollo?
   ¿Le gusta comer pollo a Mari?
9. ¿Mi hijo perdió la pelota?
   ¿Perdió la pelota mi hijo?
10. ¿Se va mañana el Sr. Ortiz?
    ¿El Sr. Ortiz se va mañana?

La práctica 3

1. Me preguntó dónde vivía Astrid.
2. Le preguntó si Valeria fumaba.
3. Te pregunté dónde lo comprarían.
4. Nos preguntan cómo se deletrean las palabras.
5. Te preguntaron cuántos años tenía la profesora.
6. Le pregunté si entendía alemán.
7. Me preguntó cuándo trabajaron / habían trabajado.
8. Les pregunté que pasó / había pasado ayer.
9. Me preguntarán por qué Eva siempre llega tarde.
10. Te pregunté quién sería el alcalde.

CHAPTER 21

¿Cuánto sabe usted?

1. Él no lee nada.
2. No hemos terminado.
3. *I don't play football anymore.*
4. Más vale tarde que nunca.
5. No vi nada en la caja.

La práctica 1

1. todavía — ya no
2. algo — nada
3. por algún lado — por ningún lado
4. o — ni
5. también — tampoco
6. de algún modo — de ningún modo
7. siempre — nunca
8. alguien — nadie
9. sí — no
10. alguno — ninguno
11. *He has no interest in doing it.*
12. *She doesn't want the jacket either.*
13. *I will never do it.*
14. *And if neither she nor he arrive?*
15. *We saw no one.*
16. *The cat is nowhere to be found.*
17. *They didn't tell me anything.*
18. *They no longer play as before.*
19. *I did not eat a single chocolate.*
20. *There's no way I will let you leave.*
21. *He does not dance, but she does.*
22. *No one explains anything ever.*
23. *Not to us either.*
24. *He doesn't practice at all.*
25. *None of them called me.*
26. *The clock is of no use at all.*
27. *You do not have any idea.*
28. *We only ate.*
29. *I do not drink any alcohol.*
30. *The argument came to nothing.*

La práctica 2

1. Vimos algunos bailando en la fiesta.
2. Cualquiera puede hacer eso.
3. Toda Toledo es hermosa.
4. Por algo será que no vino.
5. Alguien me llamó anoche.
6. Yo podría vivir aquí para siempre.
7. Tienen cualquier tipo de medicina.
8. Ella quiere besar a alguien.
9. Terminaremos la tarea de alguna manera.
10. Es lo de siempre.

Crossword 10

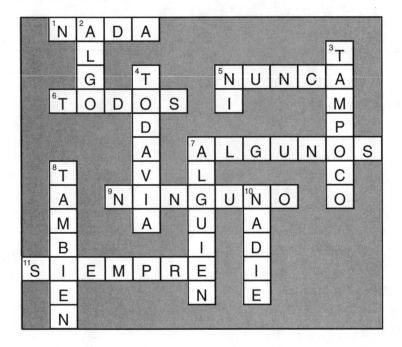

CHAPTER 22

¿Cuánto sabe usted?

1. A third-rate actor (the –zuelo suffix is sarcastic)
2. From taza to tacita
3. entristecer
4. el gasto
5. envasar

La práctica 1

1. prontito
2. pobrecito
3. bolsillito
4. abuelita
5. jardincito
6. Carlitos
7. dueñito
8. cuerpito
9. tempranito
10. doctorcito
11. cachorrito
12. fiestita
13. vocecita
14. rojito
15. lucecita

La práctica 2

1.	oreja	*big-eared female*
2.	zapato	*giant shoe*
3.	pregunta	*one who asks too many questions*
4.	malo	*very bad*
5.	cuarto	*cheap, run-down room*
6.	contestación	*one who always talks back*
7.	grande	*very big*
8.	tarjeta	*large card*
9.	flaco	*very thin, ugly person*
10.	gorda	*very fat or huge*

La práctica 3

1. el amo
2. la alineación
3. la cuenta o la factura
4. el rezo
5. la anulación
6. la coincidencia
7. el crecimiento
8. la competencia
9. la asistencia
10. el abrazo

11.	el pago	*payment*
12.	la carga	*freight*
13.	el abrazo	*hug*
14.	el aumento	*raise*
15.	la entrega	*delivery*
16.	el trago	*swallow*
17.	la práctica	*practice*
18.	el regreso	*return*
19.	el espanto	*fright*
20.	el fracaso	*defeat*

La práctica 4

1. Al pastelero le gusta el pastel.
2. El té está en la tetera.
3. Le dió una cuchillada con el cuchillo.
4. El carcelero trabaja en una cárcel.
5. Te dí un codazo con el codo.
6. No hay sal en el salero.
7. El payaso hizo una payasada.
8. Me tiró la piedra y me cayó una pedrada en la cabeza.
9. El cocinero trabajará en la cocina.
10. La sopa está en la sopera.
11. Tiró una palada con la pala.
12. El libro está en el librero.

13. La **muebleria** no tenía ese **mueble**.
14. Me dió una **palmada** con la **palma**.
15. Él es mi **padre** y él es mi **padrazo**.

La práctica 5
1. teclear
2. endurecer
3. enrojecer
4. batallar
5. empapelar
6. enganchar
7. endulzar
8. encapuchar
9. agrandar
10. parpadear

CHAPTER 23
¿Cuánto sabe usted?
1. ciento cincuenta y seis mil, uno
2. ninth floor
3. tres cuartos
4. décimo
5. 2,2 (dos coma dos) libras

La práctica 1
1. seiscientas setenta y una niñas
2. ocho millones de niños
3. ocho dólares cincuenta centavos
4. un billón
5. ciento cincuenta hogares / casas
6. cincuenta y un sombreros
7. un problema
8. noventa y nueve, cien, y ciento uno
9. once mil ciento diez
10. veintiún águilas

La práctica 2
1. El primer mes del año es enero.
2. La sexta palabra es *en*.
3. Estoy leyendo el capítulo veintitrés.
4. Es el miércoles.
5. Era Alfonso XII.
6. Estamos en el siglo veintiuno.
7. Era Luis XIII.
8. Fue el primero.
9. El segundo.
10. La octava.

La práctica 3

1. Trece más doce son veinticinco.
2. Un medio menos un cuarto es un cuarto.
3. Tres libras y un tercio.
4. Diez por ciento de la población.
5. Quinientos dividido entre veinticinco son veinte.
6. Un quinceavo de todo.
7. Doce por diez son ciento veinte.
8. El largo, el ancho y el alto.
9. Tengo que sumar los porcentajes
10. Seis por cinco dividido entre tres más seis menos diez dividido entre seis es uno.
11. Hay treinta y dos onzas.
12. Hay mil gramos.
13. Es mil.
14. Hay veinticuatro.
15. Es cero.

CHAPTER 24

¿Cuánto sabe usted?

1. El primero de enero, mil novecientos y nueve
2. The 24-hour clock
3. Ocho cuarenta y cinco, un cuarto para las nueve
4. Tu reloj está adelantado.
5. *It's very cold and windy*

La práctica 1

1. Son las dos de la mañana.
2. A la una de la tarde.
3. A eso de las once.
4. Nueve de la mañana.
5. Es medianoche.
6. A las diez en punto.
7. Son las ocho de la noche.
8. Son las cuatro de la tarde.
9. Al mediodía.
10. Tú reloj es lento.

La práctica 2

1. 11:55
2. 4:00
3. 4:15
4. 7:40
5. 7:08
6. 3:45
7. 1:14
8. 2:45
9. 4:30
10. 5:12

La práctica 3

1. Comenzaron en mayo.
2. Salgo los viernes.
3. Como pollo los sábados.
4. Viajo el primero de junio.
5. Estudio inglés los fines de semana.
6. Hablo con mi mamá los domingos.
7. Nací el primero de enero de mil novecientos setenta y dos.
8. Me casé el cinco de diciembre de dos mil dos.
9. Tengo vacaciones en agosto.
10. Trabajo la próxima semana.
11. el once de febrero, dos mil cuatro
12. el primero de diciembre de mil novecientos setenta y cinco
13. el nueve de julio de dos mil
14. el veinticinco de octubre de mil novecientos sesenta y seis
15. el treinta y uno de enero de dos mil siete

La práctica 4

1. *It's very cold in April.*
2. *There was a lot of thunder during the storm.*
3. *Last night it was raining and hailing.*
4. *It's hot and very sunny in the summer.*
5. *I do not like the cold and the wind.*
6. *There was nice weather in the spring.*
7. *It will be drizzling all the day.*
8. *Fall is my favorite season.*
9. *It is cloudy but not windy.*
10. *The bad weather began with lightning.*

CHAPTER 25

¿Cuánto sabe usted?

1. Quiero presentarle a...
2. *You're welcome*
3. *No wonder*
4. Gracias and Muy amable
5. last name

La práctica 1

1. Hasta luego
2. Feliz cumpleaños
3. Muchas gracias
4. Buenas noches
5. Buena suerte
6. Feliz Navidad
7. Buen viaje
8. Bienvenido
9. Que se mejore
10. Próspero año nuevo

La práctica 2
1. *It can't be.*
2. *I have grief.*
3. *Really?*
4. *It does not matter.*
5. *I am sorry.*
6. *What a pity!*
7. *I think so.*
8. *No wonder.*
9. *Of course.*
10. *Why not?*

CHAPTER 26
¿Cuánto sabe usted?
1. elegir, escoger
2. *pregnant, bookstore, to stir*
3. *to begin*
4. oso(s), osa(s)
5. aceptar

La práctica 1
1. caminar
2. señora
3. mandar
4. bonita
5. lograr
6. trabajador
7. nunca
8. contento
9. seguir
10. lento
11. Se fueron
12. rezando
13. serio
14. comienza
15. las caras
16. lengua
17. pájaros
18. perezozo
19. Tira
20. ha regresado

La práctica 2

1. rechazar
2. largo
3. silencio
4. ir
5. nada
6. amar
7. salida
8. moderno
9. presente
10. perder
11. dar
12. reír
13. el este
14. separar
15. perder
16. la paz
17. vacío
18. apagar
19. recordar
20. el día

Crossword 11

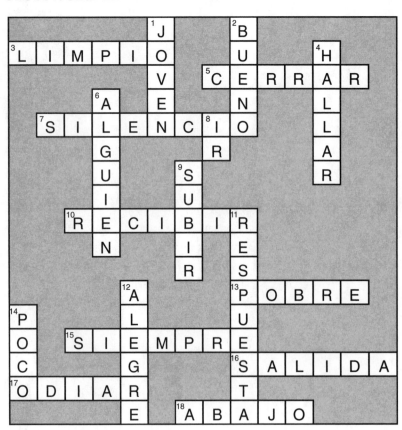

La práctica 3

1. *to remember*
2. *to answer*
3. *to sweep*
4. *to insert*
5. *to faint*
6. *to introduce, present*
7. *to investigate*
8. *to assist*
9. *to adore*
10. *to get pregnant*
11. general   a. absolute   b. <u>general</u>   c. leader
12. vencer   a. <u>to conquer</u>   b. to surrender   c. to arrive
13. collar   a. collar   b. to gather   c. <u>necklace</u>
14. delito   a. removal   b. <u>crime</u>   c. cancellation
15. hallar   a. to lose   b. hallway   c. <u>to find</u>
16. trampa   a. vagabond   b. thief   c. <u>trick</u>
17. éxito   a. <u>success</u>   b. exit   c. departure
18. asistir   a. to join   b. to help   c. <u>to attend</u>
19. actual   a. <u>actual</u>   b. current   c. eventful
20. vulgar   a. primitive   b. criminal   c. <u>vulgar</u>

CHAPTER 27

¿Cuánto sabe usted?

1. *to be lucky*
2. Dios lo ayuda
3. ponerse colorado
4. *to be of little value*
5. No todo lo que brilla es oro.

La práctica 1

1. Matar dos **pájaros** de un tiro.   *to kill two birds with one stone*
2. Hablé hasta por los **codos.**   *I didn't stop talking.*
3. Mandar a freír **espárragos, monos.**   *to go jump in a lake*
4. No tener pelos en la **lengua.**   *to be very outspoken*
5. Nuestro negocio iba sobre **ruedas.**   *Our business was running smoothly.*
6. Meterse en un **callejón** sin salida.   *to get into a jam.*
7. Poner los puntos sobre las **íes**   *to dot the I's and cross the T's*
8. Hacer de tripas **corazón.**   *to cause great emotional pain*
9. Estar con el **pie** en el aire.   *to be unsettled*
10. Dar entre ceja y **ceja**   *to tell it like it is*
11. V
12. F
13. F
14. F
15. F

16. **F**
17. **F**
18. **F**
19. **V**
20. **F**
21. *I lost my temper.*
22. *I didn't say anything.*
23. *I blushed.*
24. *I didn't notice.*
25. *I was surprised.*

CHAPTER 28

¿Cuánto sabe usted?

1. **¡Ven acá, Lupita!**
2. **A comma:**
   separates words, phrases, or clauses that interrupt a sentence
   separates three or more words in a series
   is used after a long subordinate clause
3. **el pasado progresivo**
4. at the closing
5. **la arroba**

La práctica 1

1. **La vecina, me explicaba tu madre, ya no tiene marido.**
2. **No, no vamos al desierto hoy.**
3. **Favor de traer el tenedor, el plato y el vaso**
4. **El capitán me dijo en voz baja—¡Siéntate y cállate!—y yo me senté.**
5. **Es decir, hay tanto sufrimiento en el mundo.**
6. **¿Cuándo va a llover?**
7. **Es cierto lo que dices; sin embargo, todos no están de acuerdo.**
8. **No sé, Emilio, qué vas a hacer con tu vida.**
9. **Nos dió una lista: las medias, los zapatos, los pantalones y la camisa.**
10. **Sí, ya hemos comido.**

La práctica 2

1. *Cordially,*
2. *Respected Madame:*
3. *Affectionately,*
4. *Distinguished Sir,*
5. *You are attentively greeted by*
6. *Here's a hug from your pal,*
7. *Respectfully,*
8. *Bidding farewell with love and admiration,*
9. *Thank you for your attention,*
10. *With my utmost respect and concern,*

La práctica 3
1. arroba
2. la contaseña
3. el nombre del usario
4. pulsar
5. el correo electrónico
6. punto
7. el sitio web
8. el mensaje
9. el proveedor
10. eliminar

Crossword 12

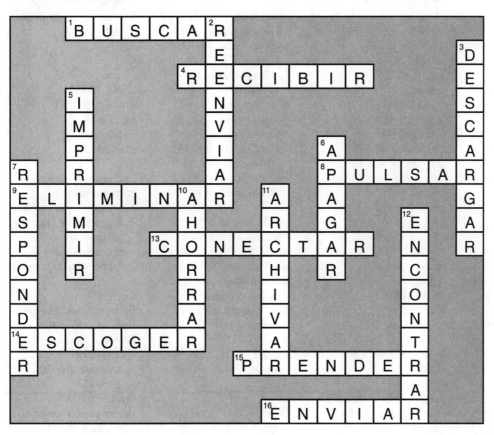

Index